AF836801

Copper King in Central Africa

Africa: Past, Present & Prospects

Series Editors: Toyin Falola (University of Texas at Austin) and Olajumoke Yacob-Haliso (Babcock University)

This series collates and curates studies of Africa in its multivalent local, regional, and global contexts. It aims fundamentally to capture in one series historical, contemporary and multidisciplinary studies which analyze the dynamics of the African predicament from deeply theoretical perspectives while marshalling empirical data to describe, explain, and predict trends in continuities and change in Africa and in African studies.

The books published in this series represent the multiplicity of voices, local and global in relation to African futures. It not only represents diversity, but also provides a platform for convergence of outstanding research that will enliven debates about the future of Africa, while also advancing theory and informing policy making. Preference is given to studies that deliberately link the past with the present and advances knowledge about various African nations by extending the range, breadth, depth, types and sources of data and information existing and emerging about these countries.

The platform created proceeds from the assumption that there is no singular "African experience", nor is it possible to, in any way, homogenize the identities, histories, spaces and lives of African people.

Titles in the Series

A Tight Embrace: Narratives and Dynamics of Euro-African Relations
Edited by Marco Zoppi

Promoting Gender Equality in Political Participation: New Perspectives on Nigeria
Damilola Taiye Agbalajobi

Rethinking Institutions, Processes and Development in Africa
Edited by Ernest Toochi Aniche and Toyin Falola

Religious Beliefs and Knowledge Systems in Africa
Toyin Falola and Nicole Griffin

Civil and Political Rights in Cameroon: A Theoretical and Contextual Appraisal
Avitus Agbor

Copper King in Central Africa: Corporate Organization, Labor Relations, and Profitability of Zambia's Rhokana Corporation
Hyden Munene

Copper King in Central Africa

Corporate Organization, Labor Relations, and Profitability of Zambia's Rhokana Corporation

Hyden Munene

ROWMAN & LITTLEFIELD
Lanham • Boulder • New York • London

Published by Rowman & Littlefield
An imprint of The Rowman & Littlefield Publishing Group, Inc.
4501 Forbes Boulevard, Suite 200, Lanham, Maryland 20706
www.rowman.com

86-90 Paul Street, London EC2A 4NE

Copyright © 2022 by Hyden Munene

All rights reserved. No part of this book may be reproduced in any form or by any electronic or mechanical means, including information storage and retrieval systems, without written permission from the publisher, except by a reviewer who may quote passages in a review.

British Library Cataloguing in Publication Information Available

Library of Congress Cataloging-in-Publication Data

Names: Munene, Hyden, author.
Title: Copper King in central Africa : corporate organization, labor relations, and profitability of Zambia's Rhokana Corporation / Hyden Munene.
Other titles: Africa: past, present & prospects.
Description: Lanham : Rowman & Littlefield Publishers, 2021. |
Series: Africa: past, present & prospects | Includes bibliographical references and index.
Identifiers: LCCN 2021040414 (print) | LCCN 2021040415 (ebook) | ISBN 9781538146422 (cloth) | ISBN 9781538146439 (ebook)
Subjects: LCSH: Rhokana Corporation—History. | Mining corporations—Zambia—History—20th century. | Copper mines and mining—Zambia—History—20th century. | Mineral industries—Zambia—History—20th century. | Labor unions—Zambia—History—20th century. | Zambia—Economic conditions—20th century. | Zambia—Politics and government—20th century.
Classification: LCC HD9506.Z334 M75 2021 (print) | LCC HD9506.Z334 (ebook) | DDC 338.2/7430968940904—dc23
LC record available at https://lccn.loc.gov/2021040414
LC ebook record available at https://lccn.loc.gov/2021040415

Contents

Acknowledgments

I express my heartfelt appreciation and gratitude to the effort and influence of the following institutions, individuals, and groups of people for their invaluable support in these uncertain times of COVID-19 we find ourselves in. This research work would not have been possible without the financial support from the International Studies Group (ISG) during my sixth-year stay at the University of the Free State, and extra funding from the African Humanities Program of the American Council of Learned Societies. I owe a great debt to Professor I.R. Phimister, whose supervision during my PhD and postdoctoral studies was crucial for this research to be completed. A special thank you is also due to my co-supervisors, Dr. D. Van Zyl-Hermann and Dr. D. Money, for their encouragement and guidance during my PhD research. I am also grateful to Mrs. Ilse Le Roux, the office manager, and Ms. Tarisai Gwena, the assistant manager of the ISG, for their administrative support. I am also grateful to my colleagues in the ISG for their motivation and support. Here I wish to single out Dr. V. Gwande and Dr. C. Fevre for reading through all the draft chapters of this book even when they had their own studies to focus on.

I am also indebted to the various institutions and individuals who assisted me during my fieldwork. I am thankful to the interviewees for their cooperation and information. The following institutions deserve a special mention for their cooperation and support: Mineworkers' Union of Zambia Headquarters, National Archives of Zambia, Secretariat of the first Zambian president, United National Independence Party Archives, and the Zambia Consolidated Copper Mines Archives. It is from these sources that this monograph was crafted.

Most important, I owe a great debt of gratitude to my wife, Machendu Mufinda; my children, Chipego Munene and Lutangalo Munene; Dominic Munene and all my other siblings; and my sisters-in-law, Buzandi Mufinda and Lorraine Mufinda, for their unwavering support, understanding, and tolerance in many ways during the study period. Even in times of despondency and discouragement, they strengthened me to work hard.

Above all, glory is to the enabling power of the Almighty God whose hand worked through many ways in seeing me through this book.

Tables

Figures

Chapter 1

Introduction and Background

The book examines the history of Rhokana/Rokana Corporation and its Nkana mine between 1928 and 1991. It analyzes three themes, namely, corporate structure, labor organization, and profitability in Rhokana/Rokana's history, which have previously been considered separately. In order to conceptualize these themes in Rhokana/Rokana's corporate history, the book relates them to the political economy of several successive periods: the Great Depression, 1929–1939; the Second World War and its aftermath, 1939–1949; Korean Crisis, 1950–1953; Central African Federation (CAF), 1953–1963; first years of Zambian independence, 1964–1969; and nationalization, 1970–1991.

As observed by Richard Sklar, "The first care of a commercial company is the security of its investment; the second is the realisation of profits for the owners."[1] Effective corporate organization and sound labor relations are important for the security of any business venture. Corporate structure refers to the organization system of a business firm. There are two major issues related to the corporate organization of the Rhokana/Rokana Corporation. These are the corporate system and "whether the firm organised itself in a way that enhanced its effectiveness and profitability."[2]

When discussing the corporate structure of Rhokana/Rokana, this book considers the Corporation's relationship with its parent companies Anglo American Corporation (AAC) of South Africa and Rhodesian/Zambian Anglo American (RAA/ZAMANGLO), as well as its cooperation with Rhodesian Selection Trust/Roan Consolidated Mines (RST/RCM), Nchanga Consolidated Copper Mines (NCCM), and Zambia Consolidated Copper Mines Limited (ZCCM). It further examines Rhokana/Rokana's corporate strategy and business interactions with other internal and external companies and International Financial Institutions (IFIs), notably the World Bank and International Monetary Fund (IMF), as well as its response to shifts in government policy. The book demonstrates that cooperation with key stakeholders in the national, regional, and global copper mining industry was vital for the Corporation's security and profitability.

Labor and racial relations on the Northern Rhodesian/Zambian Copperbelt were changed by not only the introduction of the dual (European and African) labor structure, comprising a segregated workforce and separate trade unions, but also the impact of the color bar, Labor Stabilization, African Advancement, indigenization, and Zambianization policies.[3] The Labor Stabilization Policy of the mines, which was introduced in the 1930s on the Copperbelt, created a group of workers who increasingly understood that collective labor action was their most potent weapon in the struggle against capitalism and exploitation.[4] Labor Stabilization was a practice by the mining companies whereby African miners were "accommodated [or allowed to stay] in [mine] compounds, often segregated by ethnic group, and contracted for" a number of months or years.[5] Charles Perrings notes that the daily experiences at work and in the compounds where most African workers on the Copperbelt were accommodated led to a rapid understanding among miners of both their common interests and their exploitation by management.[6] This marked the beginning of worker consciousness. Worker consciousness refers to a "sense of economic self-interest and an awareness of their colonized status . . . through the immediate experiences of labour conditions" on the mines.[7] This created an uprising of the proletariat against capitalism and a racial or class struggle among black and white miners in Northern Rhodesia.

The Copperbelt mines tried to promote the idea of partnership between black and white workers in the industry by introducing the African Advancement Policy in the mid-1950s, which opposed the job color bar embraced in the gold and diamond mines in South Africa and Southern Rhodesia.[8] African Advancement was a policy of advancing African workers into certain jobs and positions previously reserved for Europeans.[9] After Zambia's independence in 1964, the new policy of Zambianization, designed to speed up the advancement of Africans in both private and public institutions, was introduced to the industry.[10]

Management at Nkana and the other Copperbelt mines was concerned with not only industrial politics but also matters of infrastructural development and the provision of basic services for the community.[11] The Copperbelt companies developed roads and provided services such as education, housing, and health in their compounds. This partly affected their profitability.

As demonstrated later in this chapter, a number of social science researchers and labor historians have studied social relations, experience, and the political role of the African labor force on the Copperbelt.[12] One hotly contested question in the debate on the importance of African Advancement and Zambianization policies in the industry has been whether these policies were introduced based on moral, political, and/or economic factors.

To answer this question in full, one would need to focus on the role played by management and workers of individual mines on the Copperbelt in promoting these policies. Thus, this book is concerned with the role of management at Nkana and its African and European workers in the labor movement on the Copperbelt, as well as the impact of labor relations in general on the production and profitability of the Corporation.

Profitability in the mining industry depends largely on the production cost and the price level.[13] Sklar said that profit is simply the difference between value of sales and cost of sales.[14] In the case of Nkana and the other Copperbelt companies, cost of sales comprised mining, labor, treatment, and overhead costs at the mine, together with transport and other charges for exporting copper to buyers in Europe, the United States of America (USA), and Asia.[15] In the global copper industry, social and technical conditions of mining determine variations and changes in the cost of production.[16] By contrast, the copper price "is extremely sensitive to fluctuations in demand and supply."[17] The cost of sales and price level are both sensitive to trends in the national, regional, and global political economy. Other factors, which affect production and profitability, are entrepreneurship and managerial tendencies, the nexus between technology and overall corporate goals, and growth strategies (horizontal and vertical).[18]

In the case of Rhokana/Rokana, which was both a mining firm and an investment company on the Copperbelt, major factors directly related to its profitability included the extent of horizontal and vertical integration; growth and diversification; quantity and quality of ore reserves and ore mills; utilization of machinery and technology; sources of fuel and power; modes of transport; cost of sales; price of metals on the market, which affect value of sales; and economic downturn and inflation.[19] Taxes and surcharges, which have significant effects on gross and net profits, as well as dividends, are also analyzed.

These factors are discussed appropriately, that is, highlighted within the period in which their influence mattered most in Rhokana/Rokana's history. In this book, production, value of sales, cost of sales, royalty and export tax, and operating profit represent figures for Nkana mine.[20] Value and cost of sales indicate total amounts for both copper and cobalt. The amounts for royalty and export tax are combined because they were both charged against the price of copper on the London Metal Exchange (LME) and, as indicated in the proceeding chapters, were part of the cost of sales or production. This also includes royalties paid on cobalt exports.

The operating profit is the difference between the value of sales and the cost of sales. Gross profits, income tax, net profits, and dividends represent amounts for the Corporation.[21] Gross profits are divided into two parts: that which came from the Nkana mine and profits from Rhokana's investments in other mines and properties on the Copperbelt. The difference is added to unappropriated profits brought forward from the previous year to come up with the total net profit for the Corporation in the particular financial year. Net dividends are calculated from net profits.

As discussed in the proceeding section, much light has been shed on the Copperbelt with regard to mine ownership and mineral rights, investment, labor strategies, production, technology, taxation, profits, and the relationship between copper mining and economic growth in Northern Rhodesia/Zambia. Yet, there has been less attempt to synthesize these themes in a single narrative covering a long period, providing a more detailed perspective than those so far adopted. Besides, and as stated elsewhere later, even less research has been done on the economic performance of individual companies on the Copperbelt. Thus, these factors are intertwined and examined as such, thematically and chronologically, in Rhokana/Rokana's corporate history between 1928 and 1991. The book covers a broad geographical area, touching on political and economic relations among actors on five continents: Africa, Asia, North America, Latin/South America, and Europe.

HISTORIOGRAPHICAL APPROACHES TO THE ZAMBIAN MINING INDUSTRY

Despite its historical significance and contemporary importance, the copper mining industry in Northern Rhodesia, now Zambia, has never been analyzed in the round. Writing in 1982, Andrew Roberts recognized the need for a "sustained attempt" to synthesize the disparate themes of corporate organization, labor relations, and profitability.[22] These themes, he suggested, "could usefully be seen in a perspective both wider and deeper than those so far adopted."[23] Roberts's call has not yet been answered, until now. Most of what has been written about the Copperbelt since 1982 has remained within the same self-contained thematic boundaries he identified a generation ago.

It is within this context of a still-fragmented literature that this book is situated. Its underlying hypothesis is that the Copperbelt's history was shaped by the complex interaction of local, regional, and international dynamics. When the Copperbelt is reviewed as a whole, it is clear that aspects and periods of the industry's past have been studied in detail, as elaborated next.

Industrialization, Urbanization, and Social Transformation

Between the 1930s and the mid-1960s, an anthropological literature covered African experiences of living and working on the Copperbelt. Owen Letcher explored Nkana and Roan Antelope's role in the development of the Copperbelt's infrastructure, while the region's mines received considerable coverage in Merle Davis's interdisciplinary study of the impact of Western society on Central Africa's indigenous peoples.[24]

Davis examined the problems that the development of the Copperbelt mines posed for the future of Africans. He observed that, from their first boom in 1930, the Copperbelt mines were dependent on abundant supplies of unskilled African labor recruited from all over Southern Africa. He also observed some differences in the labor policies of Nkana and Roan Antelope. Between 1928 and 1932, Roan Antelope and Mufulira mines encouraged the growth of a stable resident workforce, while management at Nkana mine feared that the stabilization of African labor for more than two years would lead to detribalization. The government and the mining companies feared that detribalization would lead to greater worker consciousness and militancy. Thus, Nkana decided to employ more single men than married ones—a practice already common in South African mining. Single men worked for a short period of time and returned to their villages. Davis's insights are utilized in chapter 2, when assessing the emergence of the dual labor structure at Nkana and in the other Copperbelt mines between 1928 and 1931.

Anthropologists affiliated to the Rhodes-Livingstone Institute (RLI) followed these authors.[25] The RLI was established in 1937 following the 1935 strike by African miners on the Copperbelt.[26] The commission of inquiry into the 1935 labor unrest observed that one of the major causes of the strike was the lack of connection or contact between the government and the African workers.[27] The RLI worked in collaboration with tribal chiefs, district commissioners, labor officials, and compound managers in investigating and advising government about the welfare of Africans in the territory. The Institute's anthropologists focused on questions of industrialization, urbanization, and social transformation on the Copperbelt. Like Davis, they noted that the investment capital on Nkana and the other Copperbelt mines by the multinationals had a social and economic impact on African miners, who were paid low wages in relation to the huge profits made by the mine owners. But even so, participation in the industrial process had changed the attitudes and behaviors of African workers who, as discussed later in this book, fought for better conditions of service through wildcat strikes.

Writing about the broad history of Northern Rhodesia, Lewis Gann, also affiliated to the RLI, devoted considerable space to the development of the Copperbelt.[28] Gann offered a concise description of the role played by explorers, financed by Edmund Davis and Robert Williams, in prospecting ventures on the Copperbelt between 1895 and 1918.[29] In a later publication, he focused exclusively on the corporate history of the Copperbelt mines between 1923 and 1952.[30] He linked the Copperbelt mines to the global mining industry and concluded that they emerged as a competitive force during the Great Depression and the Second World War vis-à-vis their established counterparts in the

USA and Latin America—the reason being that the Copperbelt mines were low-cost producers.

Prospecting, Technological Innovations, and Entrepreneurship Skills

In addition to RLI anthropologists, geologists, Tarrant Guernsey and Austen Bancroft, and an economic historian, Francis Coleman, are among the earliest scholars who have surveyed the mining history of the Copperbelt from a technical perspective. Guernsey provided a concise introduction to early prospecting on the Copperbelt,[31] while Bancroft contributed to an understanding of the development of the Copperbelt mines by noting the importance of technological innovations.[32] Bancroft not only "had the intimate knowledge of his subject consistent with being an explorer by nature and an omnivorous reader of historical accounts" but was also actively involved in "mineral exploration in the Rhodesias, Nyasaland and Bechuanaland" between 1927 and 1940.[33] His study showed that scientific methods adopted during and after the second phase (1922–1928) of mineral prospecting and exploration in Northern Rhodesia accelerated the development of the Copperbelt mines.

Coleman examined underground production processes and technology on the Copperbelt mines in the period between 1899 and 1962. For Coleman, the period from 1950 to 1960 witnessed significant technological advances, particularly the use of front-end loaders and trackless loaders to remove overburden and ore in opencast/open-pit and underground operations.[34] According to Coleman, mechanization improved production of the mines. His study gives valuable insights into the effect of mechanization on labor productivity at Nkana and Nchanga mines.

By contrast, Theodore Gregory's study emphasized the entrepreneurship skills of Ernest Oppenheimer, the founder and chairman of AAC, and the business activities of the Corporation in the Southern Africa region.[35] Gregory further noted that AAC, through the shrewdness of Oppenheimer, became the biggest investor in the Northern Rhodesia mining industry.[36]

John Phillips criticized Bancroft, Coleman, and Gregory for concentrating their discussion on mines owned by the AAC and largely ignoring RST holdings.[37] With the exception of the works of Bancroft, Coleman, Gregory, and Guernsey, all the anthropological studies discussed previously are general histories of the copper industry in Northern Rhodesia.

Government, Mining Corporations, and the Labor Movement

The political relationships among mining corporations, organized African labor, and the government have received considerable coverage in a number of studies of the Copperbelt conducted by social scientists and political historians. However, few studies link business and politics in Central Africa. The work of Larry Butler and Andrew Cohen, which assessed the corporate policies adopted by AAC and RST in response to political change in the CAF, is one exception.[38] Butler and Cohen demonstrated that big businesses had initially supported the Federation of Rhodesia and Nyasaland (which included Northern Rhodesia and Southern Rhodesia). Butler's main argument was that, in order to safeguard its investment in the Northern Rhodesian mining sector, RST latterly supported decolonization by collaborating with nationalists to bring about the demise of the Federation.[39] In contrast, Cohen contended that big businesses delayed decolonization of the Federation as they continued to fund the Federal political economy despite the rise of African nationalism after 1959.[40]

Butler's and Cohen's studies are useful in contextualizing the role of the Rhokana Corporation in the political economy of the Federation of Rhodesia and Nyasaland. However, they are not conventional economic or business studies of the Northern Rhodesian Copperbelt and focus instead on the triangular relationship between the imperial state, the colonial state, and the mining sector. They constitute a major contribution to both African political history and the burgeoning literature on the economics of late colonialism in Central Africa.

It has been well established that the postwar period of decolonization was fraught with problems for business, but less understood is that this period was also one of unprecedented opportunities as the old colonial order disintegrated and the new nationalist movement established itself. Nowhere was this more clearly exhibited than on the Copperbelt. Thus, *Copper King in Central Africa* examines the evolving relationship between the government and the mining companies before and after Zambian independence in order to explore the major political, economic, and social transformations in the region and how they shaped Rhokana/Rokana's corporate strategy.

Numerous studies have focused on labor when examining the growth, expansion, and profitability of the Copperbelt mines. Proletarianization of African labor, especially in the 1930s and 1940s; the politics of African Advancement in the 1950s; and Zambianization after independence in 1964 are prominent topics on labor and profitability studies of the Copperbelt. Henry Meebelo provided a detailed study on primary resistance to colonialism in Northern Rhodesia between 1893 and 1939.[41] Meebelo argued that some educated African miners and religious movements such as the Watch Tower Movement and the Mbeni Dance Society played a vital role in influencing workers at Nkana, Mufulira, and Roan Antelope to strike in 1935.[42] Ian Henderson has also examined the articulation of African grievances in the Copperbelt strikes of 1935 and 1940, as well as the pressures, which resulted in the formation of the African Mineworkers' Union (AMU) in 1949.[43] Henderson's study is particularly useful when analyzing the role of African workers at Nkana in the formation of the AMU.

Charles Perrings's works are seminal in applying the theory of proletarianization to the development of the Copperbelt mines.[44] He argued that the emergence and subsequent history of African mine labor, protests, and organization on the Copperbelt between 1935 and 1966 were the results of the proletarianization of black labor, itself one of the major factors underpinning the productivity and profitability of the Copperbelt mines.

The term "proletarianization" originates from Karl Marx's theory of capitalism and initially referred to the process of creating a class of workers (the proletariat) who sold their labor to factory and business owners (the bourgeoisie) or the owners of the means of production.[45] Proletarianization is often characterized by downward social mobility, a shrinking market for skilled individuals, and the pushing of the middle class into the working class and low-wage employment.

Using a Marxist perspective, Guy Mhone analyzed the evolution of the dual labor structure in the Copperbelt mines between 1929 and 1969.[46] He argued that proletarianization and discrimination based on race and class were introduced by the mining companies to maximize profits. Africans performed the difficult and hardest work despite their labor being cheaper than that of European workers. European workers, however, provided needed expertise in technical, managerial, and supervisory jobs, mainly because of being more skilled in these jobs than Africans. According to Perrings and Mhone, proletarianization of African labor was the driving force behind African Advancement (1955–1963) and Zambianization (1964–1991) in the copper industry. However, this was not unique to the Copperbelt.[47]

Elena Berger, Michael Burawoy, Phillip Daniel, and Robert Bates have also contributed to the debate regarding African Advancement and Zambianization on the Copperbelt, focusing on the problems of these policies and how they impacted the evolution of relations between the government, mining companies, and trade unions. Berger analyzed the nexus of capital, labor, and profitability of the Copperbelt mines during and after colonial rule (1929–1974).[48] She noted that the advancement of Africans into semiskilled and other comparable jobs, which had been done by some European workers, enhanced the profitability of the mines, since the wages of the former were by far lower than those of the latter. Berger suggested that the Copperbelt mines could have made further profits had they advanced Africans into skilled jobs performed by the majority of European workers.[49]

Bates, Burawoy, and Daniel focused on the interplay between the government, trade unions, and the copper industry in Zambian development during the first years of independence and nationalization (1964–1975).[50] Their studies show that the new government had three major tasks with regard to labor in the copper industry, and the results were less than satisfactory. First, the government failed to eliminate the monopoly status of Europeans while securing adequate African skilled labor. The second task, which proved particularly difficult, was expanding mineral output while Zambianizing the labor force with average wage increases. African workers had become agitated that political independence did not bring about a significant improvement in wages and conditions of service. This partly explains the failure of government's third task, namely, to mobilize or influence mineworkers to support national development.

James Ferguson discussed the personal and social problems of workers on the Copperbelt and noted that their social life was undermined by the effects of the global recession after the mid-1970s: a decline in revenue from copper sales and the resultant low wages against rising inflation.[51]

Beyond this literature, George Chauncey and Jane Parpart employed a gendered approach in each of their analysis of the role played by women in the copper industry during the colonial era in Zambia.[52] Both of them argued that African women, though not employed on the mines, were allowed to stay in the compounds in order to stabilize labor and to relocate the social reproduction of labor to the Copperbelt. Stabilization of labor improved the productivity of African workers, as they learnt from their experience over the years.

Following Chauncey's and Parpart's studies was Bbole Dandule's work on the role of African women in the labor movement on the Rhodesian Copperbelt between 1935 and 1964.[53] Dandule criticized Parpart for suggesting that women on the Copperbelt were invisible, especially in the 1935 African mineworkers' strike, and produced evidence indicating that women at Nkana, Mufulira, and Roan were actively involved in these labor protests. In addition to chanting slogans against mine management and the colonial government, African women were also involved in organizing many protests in solidarity with men, as Dandule observed. She further argued that married men were forced to fight for better conditions of service on account of pressure from their wives.

Ian Phimister criticized the work of Berger, Parpart, Butler, and Cohen, to mention but a few, for mistakenly emphasizing the RST management's self-glorifying role in fighting white racism and promoting African Advancement in the mining industry.[54] He examined issues of corporate profitability and observed that "the Companies had declared themselves in favour of abolishing the colour bar but had taken that position explicitly on economic and not on ethical grounds."[55] Phimister's argument is that the African Advancement agreement was not born out of a moral obligation of the mining companies but due to the abrupt increase in African and European wages and other operating costs, coupled with the fall in copper prices in the late 1950s. According to Phimister, Rhokana and the other Copperbelt companies believed they could reduce costs by advancing Africans into comparable jobs previously performed by Europeans and pay less wages.

Duncan Money and Miles Larmer's recent studies have criticized the existing historical literature for concentrating on the stabilization of labor, African Advancement, and Zambianization, excluding negotiations over wages, bonus allowances, and general conditions of service.[56] According to Larmer, the wages paid to African miners, which were low compared with those paid to their European colleagues, compensated for recurring costs for the industry, in the form of recruitment and transportation expenses and the provisioning of a wide range of basic services such as health, housing, and food. In addition to Money and Larmer's observations, the existing historical literature does not discuss the crucial role played by Rhokana and the other RAA-operated mines in promoting stabilization of African labor and pursuing African Advancement and Zambianization policies in the industry—an omission this book will rectify.

Larmer also investigated the role of mineworkers in industrial action and politics after independence and during nationalization of the mining sector in Zambia between 1964 and 1991.[57] Larmer disagrees with the historical literature depicting Zambia's mineworkers as apolitical and without a progressive political role. Instead, he contends that mineworkers played a variety of political roles, which had a significant impact on postcolonial political development in Zambia. He further demonstrates that Zambia's mineworkers were the precursor to African nationalism in the colonial era and formed the opposition base to the postcolonial state.

While engaging Ferguson's study, Patience Mususa's thesis looked at social life on the Copperbelt after privatization of the ZCCM in 1991.[58] Like Ferguson, she argues that the removal of subsidies in line with Structural Adjustment Policies worsened the life of mineworkers on the Copperbelt.

In general, these studies analyzed unionized conflict and cooperation, as well as labor productivity, without systematically relating the quality of copper ores, capital, production costs, fluctuating price of copper, and taxes to the industry's overall trajectory or profitability. By contrast, *Copper King in Central Africa* considers the proportion of labor costs to overall expenses on mining and production. It also analyzes the impact of capital expenditure, mechanization, and labor efficiency on the overall productivity of Nkana and the other Copperbelt mines.

Mining Policy and Economic Growth

A substantial number of scholars have traced the ownership of the state's mineral rights, as well as the disputed relationship between copper mining and economic growth in Northern Rhodesia/Zambia. These studies have separately explored a wide range of topics with regard to mine ownership, mineral rights, capital, profits, and taxation in the Northern Rhodesian/Zambian copper industry. Robert Baldwin was among the first of a set of post-independence scholars to analyze the role of the copper industry in the economic development of Northern Rhodesia.[59] The central tenet of his study was that the export of copper formed the core of the Northern Rhodesian economy between the mid-1930s and 1964.

On the same subject, Klas Ronnback and Oskar Broberg engaged in the long-standing debate over the relationship between capitalism and imperialism by examining the return on British investments in Africa over a century, from 1869 to 1969.[60] They observed that, during this period, mining was the most important business for investment in African ventures, and this sector contributed significantly to the political economy of Britain.[61] This book engages Ronnback and Broberg in chapter 3 when investigating the contribution of Rhokana/Nkana to the war economy of Britain during the Second World War.

There is another body of literature focusing on the relationship between the mining companies and the post-independence Zambian government. A book edited by Mark Bostock and Charles Harvey provides a detailed analysis of the development of the Zambian copper mining industry since 1895 and nationalization of this sector in 1969.[62] The development of the copper industry and the end of private control in the sector in 1969 form part of the current investigation.

Anthony Martin wrote on the early years of the Zambian government's struggle to control the economy.[63] Martin examined the formulation and implementation of policies laid down in the Mulungushi and Matero Reforms of 1968 and 1969, when the government nationalized the manufacturing and mining sectors, respectively. He praised policies prior to the Mulungushi Reforms as both liberal and necessary for economic development. In contrast, Martin condemned the reforms thereafter as politically driven, predicting economic doom for Zambia. According to Martin, nationalization in Zambia was a product of political and philosophical thinking of the governing elite in response to a wave of change in Africa and Latin America.[64]

President Kenneth Kaunda associated himself with other national leaders spearheading socialist policies.[65] In February 1967, Julius Nyerere of Tanzania introduced Ujamaa, a version of socialism, and Kaunda followed suit by introducing humanism in August the same year.[66] Humanism placed human beings at the center of development, with a desire to change their environment and improve their economic and social conditions.[67] The Zambian government knew that it would not be an easy task to improve the quality of people's lives in a harsh and competitive world. It required "a continued reassessment and reorganisation of the development or productive machinery in the economy" and changes in the distribution of goods and services to "ensure the fair and effective flow of wealth into every Zambian home."[68] Therefore, humanism "as a way of life" logically implied "in its practical implementation that . . . Zambians must control their own economy" through nationalization.[69] For these reasons, Martin argued, Zambia brought forward the decision to nationalize the mining sector following Chile's example in June 1969.[70] On August 11 the same year, Kaunda announced the new mining strategy in a speech, which was named the Matero Reforms.[71]

Stuart Barton's study examined the past 50 years of Zambia's economic history by showing how institutional exclusivity has hindered economic growth. He observed that Kaunda's increasingly exclusive control of Zambia's policy machinery intensified both formal and informal expectations of him, resulting in a shortening of Zambia's policy horizon and, thus, an increase in investor perceptions of policy volatility.[72] He further demonstrated that this rise in perceived policy volatility restricted foreign investment in the local economy so much so that undercapitalization had lowered productivity levels to below consumption, triggering a balance-of-payments crisis in Zambia during the 1970s.[73] Barton's study attributed Zambia's economic troubles to factors within the government's control. However, as discussed in chapters 5–7, there were more important economic factors, which influenced the government's decision to nationalize the mining industry than the political and philosophical concerns advanced by Barton and Martin.

Similar studies to the work of Bostock and Harvey, Martin, and Barton have discussed the impact of partial nationalization on the corporate structure of the copper industry in Zambia. For example, Richard Sklar's work concentrated on the impact of multinationals on the domestic policies and foreign relations of Zambia.[74] He focused on three broad objectives of Zambian policy: economic independence, social equality, and Southern Africa liberation. With regard to the nationalization policy, Sklar argued that multinationals cooperated fully with the government, despite many unfavorable external and internal conditions. In Sklar's view, the private companies were loyal to the Zambian authorities and cooperative with respect to contingency planning following the Unilateral Declaration of Independence (UDI) in 1965 and the resultant isolation of Southern Rhodesia and rerouting of raw materials and supplies. He further argued that, in spite of high operating and transport costs, the companies agreed to promote Zambianization and introduce a single-wage structure in 1966, by which both locals and expatriates would receive equal wages. Sklar also claimed that, when the government decided to establish a local fabricating industry and develop the Maamba Colliery in 1968, the companies acquiesced and invested capital. Whereas Sklar suggested that there was complete cooperation between the government and the mining companies, chapters 5–7 of this book observe that there was a limit to this cooperation. These chapters suggest that the companies were merely window-dressing government policies in order to protect their investment.

Simon Cunningham investigated the Zambian copper industry's financial performance and its position in the world of copper production during the so-called dynamic decade of 1964 to 1974.[75] He analyzed the various techniques employed by the American Metal Climax/Selection Trust and the AAC in capitalizing their operations and placing their financing decisions within the international financial markets. Building on Cunningham's study, *Copper King in Central Africa* pays particular attention to the technical and financial aspects of production. John Phillips praised Cunningham's assessment of the appropriateness of nationalization and argued that it was "thorough and adept at portraying the various techniques employed by the Selection Trust and Anglo American in capitalising their operations, and [placing their financing decisions] within the global financial market."[76] In line with Martin's prophecy, Cunningham observed that the post-nationalization period did not see the dynamic development that was hoped for, partly due to overreliance on foreign capital and investment.

Fergus McPherson offered a direct critique of nationalization in Zambia.[77] He contended that, between 1976 and 1991, economic reforms were often abandoned due to not only the effects of the global recession but also mismanagement and the adoption of off-beam policies by the government.[78] For example, the devaluation of currency without a real increase in domestic production and heavy borrowing from the World Bank and IMF reduced the value of the Zambian currency, the kwacha.[79] Nevertheless, he was noncommittal on whether nationalization was wrong or not, though he blamed the government for taking too long to introduce effective reform.

Patricio Meller and Anthony Simpasa compared the nationalization of mining in Zambia and Chile.[80] They found that the driving force behind nationalization in both nations was a belief that foreign companies undertook investment and production decisions, which served their interests and not those of the host nations. They noted substantial differences in the paths taken by both copper industries after change of government, for instance, in Chile, where after the coup in September 1973, the military government privatized the mines, removed tariff protections for local industries, and banned trade unions. McPherson's and Meller and Simpasa's observations are crucial in understanding the response of Rhokana/Rokana and the Copperbelt companies toward nationalization and Zambianization policies in the industry.

The impact of privatization of the mining sector in Zambia after 1991 has also been well documented by scholars.[81] John Lungu compared nationalization and privatization and concluded that the revenues that flowed into the government's coffers were not much different under either state or private ownership.[82] John Craig looked at the changing role of state enterprise during nationalization and the first years of privatization in Zambia (1968–1998).[83] He noted that nationalization proved commercially and financially unstable, resulting in the "adoption of a strategy of comprehensive privatisation."[84]

A book edited by Alastair Fraser and Miles Lamer addressed the extent to which Zambia's valuable deposits of copper have spawned a complex range of political, social, and economic institutions and relations following the reprivatization of the mining sector.[85] Fraser and Lamer were concerned with the challenges and opportunities of the current privatized mining investments. Thus, they paid little attention to the historical perspectives of boom and bust on the Zambian Copperbelt, which the present book seeks to shed light on.

ADDRESSING THE MISSING LINK IN THE HISTORIOGRAPHY

Historiographical coverage of the Northern Rhodesian/Zambian Copperbelt's history has been uneven. Without exception, studies of Zambia's copper mining industry have been segmented by period, by theme, and by discipline. Many studies effectively begin in the 1930s with the Great Depression and end in 1964 when Northern Rhodesia became the independent state of Zambia. Even where disciplinary boundaries have been crossed, for example, Gregory and Ferguson, such excursions have been confined by theme and era.[86] Crucial subjects and entire periods have scarcely been analyzed, and primary archival research is completely lacking in key respects.

These points can best be made by two major examples. The first is that literature dealing with the hitherto disparate themes of corporate structure and labor organization dwindles between 1964 and 1991. Second, a dimension largely absent from studies of the Northern Rhodesian/Zambian copper mining industry has been any sustained account of the economics of production. While touched on by Gann, Gregory, and Ronnback and Broberg, the fundamental task identified by Roberts, that of "the formation, accumulation and circulation of capital" in its "fiscal and social environment," has not been systematically undertaken.[87] On the same subject, very few scholars have linked these themes to individual mines on the Copperbelt. Bernard Alford and Charles Harvey analyzed Rhokana's financial strategies, but their analysis is very narrow in scope, as it covers a short period (1930–1932), and no mention is made of labor.[88] Phillips's dissertation is the only major study focusing on an individual mine on the Copperbelt, although his analysis stops at 1953.[89]

By disaggregating both capital and labor, and by closely periodizing the profitability of the copper mining industry, the possibility exists of recasting accounts of the Copperbelt's volatile development. Overall, this book seeks to produce an integrated political, economic, and social history of the kind envisaged by Roberts. By taking the whole period between 1928 and 1991, the book investigates the copper industry's developments, while tracing over 63 years its changing corporate structure, capital mobilization, patterns of profitability, commodity market movements, and contested labor relations, both black and white. In this regard, the book addresses in a single narrative the three intertwined major themes—corporate structure, labor organization, and profitability—in Rhokana/Rokana's history, reaching over an extended time period. This creates a wider perspective than those so far adopted in order to give detailed insights into the totality of mining in Zambia.

Between 1928 and 1969, Rhokana was privately owned, and from 1970 to 1991, it was state owned. The corporate history of Rhokana/Rokana is viewed through these developments, and these developments are reflected through the case study of Nkana mine. The year 1928 is a natural starting point for the book because the first shaft was sunk at the Nkana mine in this year. Instead of ending abruptly in 1964 with the coming of independence—a date that makes little sense in terms of the copper mining industry's economic imperatives—the book takes 1991 as its stopping point. By then, not only had nationalization been replaced by privatization but the government also stopped subsidizing the ZCCM. Politically, the one-party system was replaced by multiparty democracy followed by fresh economic politics.

Rhokana/Rokana Corporation and its Nkana mine is a suitable case study for a number of reasons. The Nkana mine has been in continuous operation since 1928, and from 1931 to 1969, the Rhokana/Rokana Corporation was both a mining firm and an investment company on the Copperbelt, generating more profit for its owners, AAC of South Africa, and tax revenue for the government.[90] Rhokana/Rokana Corporation did not only control the Nkana mine but also owned shares in the other mines, on behalf of the AAC, who were consulting engineers to the British South Africa (BSA) Company, Nchanga/Chingola mine, and later on Bancroft/Konkola mine. It also invested in RST-owned mines, notably Mufulira, Chibuluma, Chambeshi, and Baluba.

As explained in chapter 6, after the nationalization of the mining sector in 1969, Rhokana Corporation changed its name to Rokana/Nkana Mine Division, dropping the *h* in order to lose or end any Rhodesian connotations. The names are used interchangeably throughout this book, depending on context and time.[91]

During nationalization (1970–1991), Rokana/Nkana Mine Division operated three underground and three open-pit sources.[92] Although Rokana lost its interests in the other mines during nationalization, the Division owned the largest mining and metallurgical facilities on the Copperbelt, which proved vital to the mining, smelting, and refining operations of other mines owned by the NCCM (1970–1981), Roan Consolidated Mines (RCM) Limited

(1970–1981), and ZCCM (1982–1991).[93] In addition, Nkana was the center of organized labor on the Copperbelt. A close examination of operations at Nkana has the potential to cast light on wider mining developments over much of the twentieth century in Zambia.

The book aims to answer one major question as it endeavors to explore the origins and development of Rhokana/Rokana: How did local, regional, and global forces between 1928 and 1991 influence the corporate profitability of Rhokana/Rokana? To answer this question, the book examines the impact of the Great Depression, Second World War, Korean Crisis, and the development and disintegration of the CAF on the corporate and labor history of Rhokana/Rokana between 1928 and 1969. It also analyzes how the first and second phases of nationalization, Zambianization, and the indigenization of labor, as well as the oil-shock and world recession, coupled with the burst in the copper market, interconnected to affect Rokana/Nkana's development under the NCCM, from 1970 to 1981.

The book further investigates the extent to which deteriorating geological mining conditions, the third and final phase of state participation in the industry and the introduction of Structural Adjustment Policies, coupled with the acceleration of the world recession and volatile copper prices, interconnected to affect Rokana/Nkana's corporate strategy, labor relations, and financial performance under ZCCM between 1982 and 1991.

By addressing these factors in Rhokana/Rokana's corporate history through a single narrative over a long period, the book delves deeper and reaches more refined conclusions about the economic performance of the Corporation and its mine than previous studies have done. In this way, the book provides the reader with fresh insights into the operations of the mining industry on the Copperbelt, in particular, and Zambia, more broadly. *Copper King in Central Africa* reveals to the reader the contribution of Rhokana/Rokana to the national, regional, and global political economy. It also helps the reader to understand not only the major political, economic, and social transformations in Zambia before and after independence bound by the privatization—nationalization—of the economic sector but also the influence of colonialism, decolonization, and one-party-state rule in the country.

This book engages with existing scholarship and develops it in several ways. For example, drawing from the experience of Rhokana Corporation, this monograph challenges claims by Dumett, Phillips, Butler, and Ronnback and Broberg that financial measures introduced by the Northern Rhodesian and British governments during the Second World War eroded the profits of the Copperbelt companies. Instead, it posits that Rhokana made a substantial amount of profit despite heavy taxes and price controls during the war.

The book further rejects the arguments of Berger, Parpart, Mhone, Butler, and Phimister that RST spearheaded the African Advancement Policy on the

Copperbelt. It provides evidence indicating that Rhokana and the other RAA-owned companies were the first to endorse the African Advancement Policy before RST signed a similar agreement to the one endorsed between the former and the Northern Rhodesia European Mineworkers' Union (NRMWU).

Similarly, the monograph questions Martin's, Cunningham's, and Barton's arguments that the nationalization of the mining sector in Zambia in 1969 was the result of the new government's political and philosophical thinking in response to ideological change in Africa and Latin America. By contrast, it suggests that the government's decision to nationalize the industry was largely driven by the huge profits realized by the mining companies and the record dividends distributed to shareholders abroad.

Overall, the book demonstrates that most of the current political and economic challenges affecting the Zambian mining industry are not new but historical. These challenges include the volatile relationship between the government and mining companies, disputes over labor relations and unsustainable mining tax regimes, deteriorating mining conditions and rising operating costs, volatile copper prices, unbalanced payments and reduced revenue from copper sales, and a heavy reliance on foreign debt for capital.

METHODOLOGY AND SOURCES

I utilized both qualitative and quantitative analyses to uncover trends in Rhokana/Rokana's corporate strategies, labor policies, and financial performance between 1928 and 1991. The book draws from and corroborates various sources to address any limitations these sources might have. The narrative derives from archival documents, interviews, and questionnaires. The significance of interviews and questionnaires is manifest in the discussion in chapters 6 and 7 of the impact of the nationalization of mining from 1970 to 1991.[94] I rely on the narratives and recollections of 43 respondents whom I interviewed in 2017. These include former management- and ordinary-level employees in the copper industry and Nkana mine. I also draw from archival documents accessed from the National Archives of Zambia (NAZ) in Lusaka, the ZCCM Archive in Ndola, Mineworkers' Union of Zambia Headquarters (MUZ HQ) in Kitwe, and the United National Independence Party (UNIP) Archive in Lusaka.[95] Equally important are contemporaneous British and South African mining magazines. These magazines carried important information on mining developments in the Southern Africa region between the 1920s and the 1950s.

While Zambia's mining industry can be investigated using international and overseas archives, this book finds scholarly reliance on these archives alone problematic and limited in terms of its scope. There are two major criticisms. First, archives in Britain and the USA have much more detailed information on the RST's group of companies than they do on the RAA's subsidiaries. In the case of RAA, however, its parent company, AAC, has historical records and information in their library in Johannesburg, South Africa. Researchers have been unable to access its documents freely because AAC is still active and, like the majority of active corporations, AAC determines who can access their records.

By contrast, Selection Trust archives in London are easy to access because RST has ceased to exist and the personal papers of key figures of the Company, such as Sir Chester Beatty and Sir Ronald Prain, are available. In addition, the American Heritage Center at the University of Wyoming contains Ronald Prain papers, comprising his speeches, reports, and correspondence with British, Rhodesian, and Zambian government officials, especially between 1950 and 1972 when he was the chairman of RST.

Even so, the records in Britain and the USA are less useful for studies focusing on AAC's subsidiaries; they contain RST and American Metal Climax's (AMAX) papers. Besides, the primary sources held in the National Archives of Britain at Kew and the Bodleian Library at Oxford are suitable for studies entirely focused on the relationship between the mining companies and the colonial government.

The second major criticism is that, although archives in Zimbabwe, Britain, and the USA contain detailed information about the Zambian mining industry during the colonial era, their holdings dwindle rapidly as far as the period after independence is concerned. By contrast, archival data on both groups of companies is available in Lusaka and on the Copperbelt, for the period before and after independence, allowing for a comprehensive analysis of the copper industry trends in particular, as well as general political, social, and economic transformations in Zambia.

Yet, very few studies on the Zambian mining industry have benefited from the primary material held in the MUZ HQ and the UNIP Archive. Even the latest studies have used only a few of the records held in these local archives.[96] Their records are important for researching the major political, economic, and social transformations in Zambia especially in the period between the 1890s and early 2000s. The ZCCM Archive and MUZ HQ, though, have some records that cover the information gap to the present and help to fill the absences, silences, and gaps in the NAZ and UNIP Archive, whose sources go up to 1972 and 1991, respectively.

The major weakness of the material from these four archives is that their information on individual mines dwindles after 1970.[97] For example, data on finished production at Nkana and other NCCM-controlled mines between 1970 and 1981 is not recorded in the company's reports. Similarly, overall profitability of individual mines between 1970 and 1991 could only be related to their parent companies: NCCM, RCM, and ZCCM. Limitations of sources make it hard to probe the profitability of individual mines on the Copperbelt during nationalization. These limitations could probably be ascribed to a focus on the performance of these parent companies after nationalization as opposed to their subsidiaries. Thus, this book tries to bridge the gaps in archival sources by engaging some information from interviews and questionnaire. As indicated earlier, the interviews and questionnaire explored the impact of mining nationalization from 1970 to 1991.

STRUCTURE OF THE BOOK

I draw from these sources important statistical data about capital expenditure, labor strength and emoluments, quantity and quality of ores, production, power consumption, transport costs, the price of metals on the world market, the value of metal sales, taxes, and net profits and dividends in the period under consideration. I interpret this data in a wider context to make sense of the many factors—geological mining conditions, colonialism, decolonisation, economic downturn, wars, corporate structure and labor organization—which affected the political economy of Northern Rhodesia/Zambia, in general, and the corporate profitability of Rhokana/Rokana, in particular.

As mentioned, these factors are intertwined, and I examine them thematically and chronologically in Rhokana/Rokana's corporate history between 1928 and 1991 in six substantive chapters. Each chapter addresses the three main themes of the book: corporate structure, labor relations, and profitability. As indicated earlier, the three themes are related to major political, economic, and social developments in local, regional, and global contexts to provide a broader perspective on trends in Rhokana/Rokana's fortunes over a longer period. Arranging the book in this manner enables the reader to appreciate the changes over time in Rhokana/Rokana's corporate history, while the careful attention paid to the three themes in each chapter ensures that the reader does not lose sight of the book's argument.

This chapter is followed by chapter 2, which traces the formation of the Rhokana Corporation and development of the Nkana mine between 1928 and 1939. The chapter begins by tracing the financial origins of Rhokana Corporation and the development of the corporate organization, the management system, and the dual labor structure between 1928 and 1931. It proceeds by looking into Rhokana's productivity and financial performance during the Great Depression, from 1929 to 1939. It concludes by analyzing the events leading to the formation of the NRMWU in 1937.

Chapter 2 makes three major arguments. First, it demonstrates that the rapid development of large-scale mining at Nkana between 1928 and 1931 resulted from the discovery of rich copper sulfide ores, which were easier and cheaper to treat, while the formation of the Rhokana Corporation resulted from the convergence of multinational interest and capital from South Africa, Britain, and the USA. Second, the chapter shows that, for Nkana and the Copperbelt mines, the Great Depression was not a setback at all because the Northern Rhodesian mines were low-cost producers due to cheap mining, processing/treatment, labor, and transport expenses compared to their North American counterparts, which were high-cost producers. In addition, rising demand for mineral resources from European electrical and automotive industries, coupled with the rearmament after 1934, increased the price of copper on the international market, moving the world out of recession. Third, the chapter posits that Nkana was the center of the labor movement on the Copperbelt, and its white workers played a leading role in the formation of the NRMWU, the first trade union to be established in the Northern Rhodesian mining sector.

While booming industrial activity in Europe and the USA revamped the copper business and ended the Great Depression, the demands of the Second World War (1939–1945) and the Korean Crisis (1950–1953) "called forth the extraction of raw materials . . . from all [producing] continents on an unprecedented scale."[98] Thus, chapter 3 addresses the financial incentives of war between 1939 and 1953. Corporate profitability and its contribution to the war economies of Britain and the USA are both examined. The chapter analyzes British and American foreign aid and economic relations with less developed countries during the Second World War and the Cold War. It casts light on how their policies on foreign aid and economic relations with developing countries intersected and diverged as they sought to strike a balance between their domestic or national interests and their role as two of the super powers in a bipolar world. The chapter observes that the financial measures introduced by the British and US governments during and after the Second World War and Korean Crisis brought their imperial relations with developing countries under the spotlight.

Chapter 3 contends that Nkana was the most important mine in the Northern Rhodesian mining industry in terms of production; hence, it was strategic to the war economy of Britain and the USA. This period also witnessed an increase in black labor activism on the Copperbelt, which culminated in the formation of the AMU. The chapter suggests that African workers at Nkana played a leading role in the formation of the AMU.

Between 1953 and 1963, Rhokana was transformed by new developments in the regional political economy. On September 1, 1953, the CAF was formed, encompassing Southern Rhodesia (Zimbabwe), Northern Rhodesia (Zambia), and Nyasaland (Malawi). The Federation lasted up to 1963, and in the following year, Northern Rhodesia and Nyasaland became independent, while Southern Rhodesia remained a settler colony. Chapter 4 relates the corporate strategy and profitability of Rhokana to the political economy of the Federation of Rhodesia and Nyasaland. The chapter begins by discussing political, economic, and social reasons advanced by the Copperbelt mining companies in support of the idea of a federation in Central Africa. It then analyzes the importance of the Northern Rhodesian mining sector, in general, and Rhokana/Nkana, in particular, to the Federal economy. It also examines the part played by Rhokana's management in the politics of African Advancement on the Copperbelt and demonstrates that Nkana and the other RAA-owned mines played a leading role in fighting white racism in the industry ahead of their counterparts operated by RST. The chapter further scrutinizes the economic reasons for the end of colonial rule in the CAF and Rhokana's response to the decolonization of this region.

Chapter 4 argues that labor and racial inequalities embedded in the public and private sectors in the region, coupled with economic imbalances among the federated states, fueled African nationalist sentiments across the region from 1959 onward. As a result, the Federation of Rhodesia and Nyasaland collapsed after 1963.

Chapter 5 traces the trajectory followed by the Corporation and its mine during the first five years of Zambian independence, from 1964 to 1969. During this period, the complex interaction of local, regional, and international dynamics shaped Rhokana/Nkana's productivity and profitability. These dynamics include Zambianization, the official embracing of socialism through humanism, Southern Africa's intensifying liberation struggle, taxation regimes, deteriorating underground mining conditions, the falling grade of ore, and the marked rise in the price of copper on the world market.[99] The chapter starts by identifying economic problems in the Zambian mining sector at independence in 1964 and proceeds by discussing the issue of mineral rights and the new threefold mining tax regimes. The transition from African Advancement to Zambianization and its impact on labor organization at Nkana are both contextualized.[100] The chapter further addresses the effect of these factors on operating costs for Nkana vis-à-vis the price of copper on the world market and overall profitability. The chapter concludes by discussing the part played by economic issues in the nationalization of Nkana and the other Copperbelt mines in 1969.

Chapter 5 challenges arguments that mining nationalization in Zambia was a product of political and philosophical thinking of the governing elite in response to a wave of change in Latin America and Africa and President Kenneth Kaunda's associating himself with other national leaders spearheading socialist policies. It contends that the government's decision to nationalize the industry was largely driven by the marked increase in the price of copper, the huge profits realized by Rhokana and the other Copperbelt mining companies, and the record dividends distributed to shareholders abroad.

Chapter 6 continues the focus on the evolving relationship between the mining companies and the new government. It analyzes the impact of nationalization and Zambianization on Rokana's corporate strategy, now under NCCM, from 1970 to 1981. Gavin Keeton and Mike Beer define nationalization as "the acquisition of privately owned enterprises by a Government, with or without compensation."[101] The Zambian government took the path of partial nationalization with compensation. Nationalization was not unique to Zambia. Several countries in Africa and Latin America nationalized their mining sector after independence.[102] The discussion in this chapter is divided into four main sections. The first section analyzes the government takeover and reorganization of the industry in 1970. The second traces the events leading to the redeeming of bonds in NCCM and its counterpart RCM in 1973. Third, the progress of indigenization and Zambianization of labor in the copper industry is addressed. The last section examines the impact of deep level mining, nationalization, Zambianization, the liberation wars in Southern Africa, and the global recession on operating costs vis-à-vis the fluctuating price of copper on the world market and overall profitability of Rokana/Nkana and NCCM.

In this manner, the chapter shows the extent to which the mining companies and the government cooperated in implementing the new corporate structure and labor policies in the industry. As stated elsewhere earlier, scholars have glorified the Copperbelt companies' wisdom of accommodation and cooperation with interest groups that were important to the industry's efficient operation, such as government, African workers, expatriate employees, and trade unions.[103] This chapter, however, accentuates the point that there was a limit to their cooperation due to a combination of internal and external forces, most of which were beyond the government's control. Thus, the chapter argues that nationalization in Zambia was severely undermined by economic woes emanating from the impact of the world recession that began in the mid-1970s.

After 1981, NCCM, RCM, and their mines were merged into a single company, ZCCM. With the formation of a large single company, the government attempted to consolidate nationalization and Zambianization between 1982 and 1991. Thus, chapter 7 focuses on Rokana's corporate profitability under the ZCCM. It discusses perceived benefits of the merger, which, in effect, made ZCCM a mining giant, the world's second-largest copper-producing company, after Corporation Nacional del Cobre de Chile (CODELCO-Chile).[104] The chapter also looks at the impact of the global economic downturn, inflation, and austerity measures dictated to the ZCCM by the IFIs on Rokana/Nkana's corporate policy, productivity, and financial performance.

Chapter 7 indicates that Rokana/Nkana was central to the productivity capacity of the ZCCM, as this Division owned the largest metallurgical processing facilities in the Zambian mining sector. It argues that the government's effort to consolidate nationalization and Zambianization in the industry was largely undermined by declining revenue from the mines. The decline came as a result of copper prices continuing to plummet relative to the price of imports due to the world recession that began in the mid-1970s. This was coupled with political pressure from IFIs on President Kenneth Kaunda to adopt Structural Adjustment Policies in the 1980s. Zambianization at Nkana and in the other Copperbelt mines was also stymied by the companies' reliance on expatriate labor in managerial positions. There were few trained Zambians to replace expatriate workers in technical and supervisory jobs. The book concludes on the eve of the reprivatization of the mining industry under the new government of the Movement for Multiparty Democracy (MMD).

Chapter 8 provides a synopsis of the main points from the six substantive chapters of the book. It ties together the various aspects written about corporate structure, labor organization, and profitability of Rhokana/Rokana Corporation and its Nkana Mine Division between 1928 and 1991. The book locates Rhokana/Rokana Division as a strategic mining entity on the Northern Rhodesian/Zambian Copperbelt, which contributed hugely to the mining, smelting, and refining operations of the copper mines, as well as overall viability of this industry in national, regional, and global contexts. A broad array of factors including internal and external forces in the local, regional, and global political economy affected Rhokana/Rokana's operations and the profitability of the Zambian mining industry over much of the twentieth century.

IMPORTANT BACKGROUND TO NKANA MINE: FROM HUMBLE BEGINNINGS TO A GIANT, 1895–1927

> New comers and visitors are usually amazed at the technical and social development at Nkana and it is perhaps time we let the rest of the world know that we have, in just over twenty years, carved out a piece of civilization—and a very pleasant piece of civilization—in the middle of what used to be known as "darkest Africa." We are an important community, turning out an important product, [copper] . . .
>
> —Oliver B. Bennett, October 1951[105]

The Rhokana Corporation and its Nkana mine were among several companies in the Northern Rhodesian/Zambian mining industry controlled by the AAC.[106] Situated 378 km from the capital, Lusaka, the Nkana mine was the largest copper producer on the Northern Rhodesian/Zambian Copperbelt as early as 1932.[107] Before 1957, Nkana was also the only mine on the Copperbelt producing cobalt.[108]

The Copperbelt (see the maps on pages 195 and 196) was not only among the richest copper fields in the world but also one of the most powerful agents of social change in Africa.[109] Whereas in the late 1920s, the sprawling Copperbelt areas supported just over 1,000 Africans in scattered villages, 30 years later, in 1960, the Copperbelt was home to 260,000 Africans and some 40,000 Europeans.[110] Nkana-Kitwe, the geographical center of the great Copperbelt mining complex, now accommodated 87,000 of the Copperbelt's 300,000 population.[111] The history of Rhokana and its Nkana mine, thus, is closely linked to the development of the Copperbelt as a whole.

Nkana is one of the oldest copper mines discovered on the Copperbelt.[112] In 1890, the Litunga, king of the Lozi people of Barotseland, granted mineral rights to the BSA Company, which eagerly sought to find a Second Rand similar to the gold mines of South Africa. At this time, the Copperbelt was:

> a sparsely inhabited, narrow strip of country, about 80 miles long, in the north-central section of the country [Northern Rhodesia]. About 4,000 feet above sea level and approximately 13° south of the equator. The rocky, infertile soil discouraged productive farming. The infertility, however, was compensated for by the rich mineral deposits, particularly copper ore, which had been worked by the local Lamba people since the seventeenth century.[113]

The BSA Company was quick to grant prospecting rights to any interested company soon after securing the mineral rights from the Litunga.[114] Prospecting on the Rhodesian Copperbelt evolved in two phases.[115] The first phase was from 1895 to 1919, and the second was from 1920 to 1928. Two groups financed prospectors: Edmund Davis's Bechuanaland Exploration Company and Robert Williams's Tanganyika Concessions Limited dominated the first phase.[116] Prospectors found low-grade copper oxide ores on the Hook of the Kafue River (a huge bend) and Kansanshi in 1899 and at Bwana Mkubwa and Roan Antelope in 1902.[117] It is, however, not clear who pegged the Nkana prospect. In an article published in *Horizon* magazine in April 1962, Orlando Baragwanath, one of the first prospectors on the Copperbelt, claimed that he, alongside Frank Lewis, pegged what became known as Nkana mine in 1901.[118] He further stated that the discovery of Nkana triggered wider explorations, which induced Lewis and himself "to send William Collier and J.J. Donohoe up there. . . [where they] . . . pegged Roan Antelope and Bwana Mkubwa."[119] J.A. Austen and W.E.A. Fowler, who were also pioneers on the Copperbelt, claimed to have been the first to discover the copper outcrops on the south bank of the Wusikili stream in the Nkana area in 1905.[120]

Undisputed is the fact that the Nkana copper deposits were pegged in 1910 by Moffat Thomson, "a Government District Commissioner based at Ndola, whose Government duties entailed a certain amount of travelling throughout the territory."[121] He named the deposits "The Nkana Claim," after Chief Nkana of the Lamba people.[122]

Low-grade oxide ores, coupled with inadequate technology to treat them profitably, prevented the large-scale development of Nkana and the other Copperbelt mines until after the First World War (1914–1918).[123] This, together with the BSA Company policy of granting prospecting rights to small companies and individuals, resulted in Nkana changing many hands.[124] Among the original holders of the Nkana Claim were the Susman Brothers of Livingstone, pioneers in Northern Rhodesia, who disposed the Claim in 1913 for £900.[125]

The Nkana Claim was largely ignored until the 1920s when the Bwana Mkubwa Company, Copper Ventures/Rhodesia Congo Border Company (CV/RCBC), and AAC undertook serious development and intensive drilling.[126] By then, the BSA Company had changed its policy of granting concessions to small companies. The Chartered Company issued prospecting rights over much larger concessions to multinational companies with greater capacity in terms of financial and technical resources, which ended the speculative nature of mining in the previous years. In return, the Chartered Company would not only receive royalties on any minerals extracted but also have some "fully-paid shares in any production companies formed in return for a concession."[127]

The result was further discovery of high-grade copper sulfide ores, averaging 4%, running into millions of tons at Nkana in 1927.[128] The discovery of rich copper deposits at Nkana led to the merger of the Rhokana Corporation and closer association of the operations of the Bwana Mkubwa Company (1910), RCBC (1923), and NCCM (1926).[129] The rapid development of the Nkana mine and the merger involving these companies after 1928 form part of this book's investigation.

Chapter 2

Rhokana/Nkana during the Great Depression

Problems and Challenges, 1928–1939

FINANCIAL ORIGINS OF RHOKANA CORPORATION AND DEVELOPMENT OF CORPORATE STRUCTURE, 1928–1931

The discovery of sulfide ores averaging 4% in the 1920s prompted the development of Nkana mine.[1] The Nkana North Shaft was sunk early in 1928, while shaft sinking began at the Central Orebody and Mindola underground the following year.[2] Similarly, development work began to accelerate at Roan Antelope, Mufulira, and Nchanga.[3] These four Copperbelt mines attracted capital from South Africa, Britain, and the United States of America (USA). A consortium of eight companies from Britain and South Africa funded the development of Nchanga mine, including the Anglo American Corporation (AAC) of South Africa, Johannesburg Consolidated Investment Corporation, British South Africa (BSA) Company, Minerals Separation, and Rio Tinto.[4]

Further integration occurred when the Selection Trust (ST) and American Metal Company (AMC) formed the Rhodesian Selection Trust (RST) in May 1928. The AAC followed suit by floating Rhodesian Anglo American (RAA) in December the same year.[5] RST controlled Roan Antelope and two-thirds of Mufulira. RAA was a holding company for AAC shares in the Rhodesia Congo Border Company/Concession (RCBC), Nchanga, and Bwana Mkubwa, the majority shareholder in Nkana. This is how Nkana came under AAC and, latterly, Rhokana. With the AAC exercising control over all three companies, it moved toward merging them into a single firm, Rhokana Corporation.

Through RAA and the Rhokana Corporation, Ernest Oppenheimer, chairman of Anglo American, wanted to consolidate AAC's presence on the Copperbelt in order to fend off large North American mining companies from dominating the Northern Rhodesian industry.[6] Oppenheimer wished to "attract the financial support of other large British and South African companies" so as to avoid what he perceived to be the dangers of US control.[7] Between 1928 and 1929, Oppenheimer vetoed an attempt by the American Smelting and Refining Company (ASARCO) to purchase shares in Nchanga mine. According to one historian,

> Oppenheimer who, though willing to use American capital in a minority role, was not amenable to the idea of it becoming further entrenched on the Copperbelt. He argued that American control would irreparably harm the empire's ability to manage its resources by surrendering suzerainty to an outside power. Oppenheimer, with tacit support from the British Government, was able to pressure ASARCO into withdrawing its offer. He then put together a British-based scheme to replace ASARCO's bid, in cooperation with Lord Auckland Geddes and the Rio Tinto Zinc Corporation.[8]

An all-British scheme meant that the dangers of US control were averted.

Also, there was a serious problem of finding additional capital for infrastructural development, which worsened with the onset of the Great Depression.[9] One large company, it seemed, would be better placed to raise fresh capital, loans, and debentures from abroad. Besides, stakeholders in all three companies anticipated that the Great Depression would last for several years and undermine the price of copper.[10] They stressed "the strong position that one large company, as compared with three companies, would have when it came to negotiating output restrictions with the other large copper producers."[11] A large firm would also be able to negotiate more effectively with the government and the BSA Company, the owner of the mineral rights in the territory.

In 1931, the RCBC and Nchanga were amalgamated with Bwana Mkubwa and formed the Rhokana Corporation.[12] The establishment of the Rhokana Corporation "essentially achieved the corporate structure that remained until [1969 in the Northern Rhodesian/Zambian mining industry]."[13] The name "Rhokana" was itself an amalgamation of "Rhodesia" and "Nkana".[14] AAC, Newmont Corporation, Kennecott, BSA Company, Rand Selection, Consolidated Mines Selection, New Era Corporation, and Johannesburg Consolidated jointly owned RAA.[15] RAA also owned shares in the BSA Company.[16] In the Rhokana Corporation, RAA owned about 52% shares, with the remainder distributed among Rio Tinto, Johannesburg Consolidated, and Minerals Separation.[17] In addition, Rhokana owned 47% of Nchanga and 32% of Mufulira.[18] Rhokana Corporation retained a "one-third interest in any property found" in these concessions, "which was a wise decision as . . . after the Second World War, Chibuluma, Chambishi, Baluba [and Bancroft] were developed in [these areas]."[19] Rhokana Corporation had become both a mining company and an investment firm on the Copperbelt.

The Corporation raised "£4,500,000 7 percent debentures, at par, which were convertible to ordinary shares, pro rata, at rising prices up to the year 1940."[20] The capital was intended to both open Nkana mine and construct a copper refinery. Nkana began large-scale mining operations in 1932. As discussed later, Rhokana Corporation discontinued development of Nchanga and active prospecting in the RCBC, "throwing all its effort and weight into the rapid development and equipping of the Nkana mine, and its interests in the Mufulira."[21] It was considered reasonable to concentrate on Nkana and Mufulira as "they were all showing up large tonnages of sulphide ore, whereas Nchanga, further from the railway, had two problems to solve: water, and mixed sulphide ore."[22]

Management Structure

As a result of these mergers, the management structure of the AAC-controlled companies was streamlined. For Rhokana Corporation, Auckland Geddes (Rio Tinto) became chairman; Ernest Oppenheimer, Edmund Davis, and Francis Gibbs became deputy chairmen.[23] Leslie Pollak (brother-in-law to Oppenheimer) and S.S. Taylor became managing directors in South Africa and London, respectively.[24] Moreover, Oppenheimer and Pollak became part of the African committee with the former as chairman and the latter with Drummond Chaplin as ordinary members; Carl Davis and J. Buchanan sat on the board.[25] The board members of Rhokana also sat on the RAA Board of Directors, consisting of nine executive committee members, of whom Oppenheimer, Edmund Davis, Carl Davis, and Taylor were the leading lights. Britons and white South Africans dominated the composition of the board of Rhokana Corporation.[26] Even so, the board included not only AAC but also Barnato Brothers, the BSA Company, Newmont Mining Corporation, Kennecott, and Morgan Grenfell.[27] What Oppenheimer did not like was that two-thirds of the board of RST was composed of American nationals.[28] As stated earlier, he viewed this dominance as inimical to British imperial interests.

North America had pioneered the mining of low-grade copper deposits, and the Copperbelt too benefited from the continent's experienced mining engineers. Chester Beatty used AMC and his network of friends to secure key personnel from America, which included Roan's first general manager, D.D. Irwin; mine superintendent, R.M. Peterson; and managing director, Arthur Storke.[29] Similarly, AAC used Newmont Corporation to utilize American experience in the Northern Rhodesian copper industry, and therefore, Nkana and the other Copperbelt mines benefited from an international mining network with a North American flavor.[30] Both groups (RAA and RST) organized their mines around two corporate administrative structures, one in Northern Rhodesia and the other in Britain. AAC Head Office, though, was in South Africa.

The existence of two main administrative departments enhanced cooperation between the parent and subsidiary companies. Despite RST being largely American funded, its administrative headquarters were in London where ST was located. Similarly, despite RAA being principally funded by AAC of South Africa, its head office was also in London.[31] London had long been the center of the international copper trade, which largely explains why the Rhokana Corporation and the other Copperbelt companies preferred their headquarters to be established there.[32] Both mining groups, however, also had partner consulting departments in New York—Newmont, Kennecott, Morgan Grenfell for RAA, and AMC for RST—as well as in Johannesburg for AAC. Accordingly, strategic decision-making for RST remained with the directors in London, while for RAA, strategic decision-making remained in Johannesburg.[33] Phillips observed that the management structure of AAC compared to ST was different:

> Micro-management of the facility [Roan's] layout caused some irritation, but in most aspects London proved [more] receptive to junior management's input and gave mine staff wide [liberal] latitude in the carrying out of policy. As a result, the decision making process within Roan occurred at a lower level within the organisation than was typically found in the American copper industry. This was also true in comparison to the authoritarian and [conservative] structure of the Anglo American mines, where the field managers were closely monitored and supervised by consulting engineers residing in Johannesburg.[34]

Figure 2.1 Rhokana/Nkana management in 1932. *Source:* Picture taken from Raymond Brooks, "How the Northern Rhodesia Coppers Were Found (III)," *Rhokana Review* 8, no. 4 (1959): 30.

Figure 2.1 shows Rhokana/Nkana's management after the formation of the Corporation in 1932. Leslie Pollak, Rhokana's managing director who was based in Johannesburg, is at the center of the front row.

Labor Structure

Alongside the corporate organization described earlier, the Copperbelt mines, like their counterparts in Southern Africa and North and South America, introduced a dual (skilled and unskilled) labor structure, which was designed to maximize profits.[35] There was need for both skilled and unskilled labor in mine production, mine development, and construction at Nkana and in the other Copperbelt mines. Consequently, a dual-wage labor structure emerged between late 1920s and early 1930s. The large number of Africans, without a formal education, could only sell unskilled labor, while skilled employment was reserved for Europeans. By 1931, when all four copper-producing mines on the Copperbelt began large-scale operations, they employed a total of 2,221 Europeans and 13,948 Africans.[36] The majority of European workers came from as near as Southern Rhodesia and South Africa and as far as Britain, America, and Australia.[37] The majority of African workers originated from within Northern Rhodesia; a substantial number from Nyasaland, Tanganyika, and Portuguese East and West Africa; and a few from the Belgian Congo, Southern Rhodesia, and South Africa.[38]

African workers were "obtained in two ways: by contracting villagers (sometimes with the use of coercion) through recruitment agencies (contract labor) and by directly hiring workers who came to the mines on their own (voluntary labor)."[39] Voluntary labor was cheaper than contracted or recruited labor; hence, the Copperbelt companies depended on the former. This was because voluntary labor cost nothing up front, while recruited labor was expensive as each laborer purchased from the Native Labour Association cost £10.[40] It is interesting to observe that some Africans, despite being unskilled, came to work in the Copperbelt mines with work experience from other mines in the Southern African region. Through labor migration, Nkana and the Copperbelt mines were linked to the national, regional, and global industrial politics, as workers of similar and different racial and ethnic backgrounds mingled.[41]

For efficient operation of the mines, the labor force needed to be accommodated. To this end, Rhokana constructed residential quarters, offices, recreation halls, schools, and hospitals, "all of which at first were of Kimberly bricks and had thatched roofs."[42] Some of the early infrastructure developed at Nkana by 1931 included the erection of 166 huts to accommodate 828 European employees and 850 dwellings for 4,565 single and married African workers.[43] Accommodation, especially for African labor, was inadequate; there were not enough dwellings for everyone. Informal settlements mushroomed, accommodating those who could not be sheltered in mine compounds.[44]

The compound system (see Figure 2.2A and 2.2B), which was imported from the gold mines in South Africa and adopted elsewhere in the Southern Africa region, was one of the most important strategies employed by the companies to not only create a controlled environment in the mine areas but also reduce desertions and recruitment, thus labor costs, and maintain profitability.[45] One unintended consequence of this for the mining companies was that black workers lumped together in the workplace and mine compounds developed, what Mhone, Parpart, and Perrings, following Van Onselen, called "worker consciousness," coupled with new ideas about labor organization

Figure 2.2A African mine compound at Nkana, 1929.

Figure 2.2B Part of European compound at Nkana, 1929. *Source:* Both images taken from Austen J. Bancroft, *Mining in Northern Rhodesia: A Chronicle of Mineral Exploration and Mining Development* (Bedford, England: The Sidney Press Limited, 1961), 154, 158.

and industrial politics, on the Rhodesian Copperbelt.[46] As discussed in the subsequent sections, the Great Depression caused Rhokana and the other Copperbelt companies to improve their corporate strategies, managerial tendencies, and industrial relations.

PROFITABILITY OF RHOKANA/NKANA DURING THE GREAT DEPRESSION, 1929–1939

The Great Depression was a global phenomenon of economic downturn, which began in the USA and spread to Europe, Africa, Asia, Latin America, and Australasia. The October 1929 New York Stock Exchange crash was followed by a major slowdown in business activity coupled with bank failures.[47] This led to a reduction in the amount of money that was available for domestic and foreign investments, causing unemployment to increase, as companies tried to cut back on their workforce in order to reduce costs. Between 1929 and 1932, the USA's economy halved in size and shed 14 million jobs.[48]

By comparison, Britain escaped relatively unscathed, with employment rising to 20%, and recovered from the effects of the Depression faster than the USA.[49] But even so, the economic meltdown in the metropole spread to the periphery through market ties, investments, and trades. The immediate impact on the global copper industry was that prices halved between 1929 and 1931, as world consumption fell from 2,084,560 to 1,406,535 short tons.[50]

Management, Production, and Profitability

Rationalization of production among producers in Africa, North America, and Latin America, in line with the demand on the international market, was one of the initial measures devised to stabilize the copper price. Six leading US copper companies devised two key measures, which were implemented around the world.[51] The first method was to focus on selective mine production. This involved concentrating on high-grade ore mines and closing lower-grade ones. This policy was followed in Northern Rhodesia, the Belgian Congo, Chile, and Canada. Other companies followed suit. The RAA group closed its mining operations at Bwana Mkubwa and Kansanshi and halted operations at Nchanga until 1938, leaving only Nkana in operation. Mine development was halted at Nchanga because the entire underground workings were flooded in 1931 and remained underwater until 1937.[52] Similarly, the RST group operated the Roan Antelope mine but reduced production at Mufulira until 1933. On the other side of the border, Union Miniere du Haunt Katanga (UMHK) closed two high-cost producing mines, Luishia and Lukuni, and operated three low-cost producing mines, Kambove, Shangulowe, and

Shituru.[53] Rhokana and the other Copperbelt companies lowered production costs by operating low-cost mines.

The second method was an attempt to control the export market, by stabilizing prices through a cartel called Copper Exporters Inc., which comprised the major producers, including the Copperbelt mines. In the USA, Copper Exporters sought protection against foreign competition by demanding that Washington impose a tariff of 4 cents per pound on imported copper; externally, the cartel sought to support prices by restricting production to 25% of capacity.[54]

On the Northern Rhodesian Copperbelt, Rhokana scaled down production to 31,000 long tons per year, while Roan Antelope and Mufulira each reduced annual production to 29,000 long tons.[55] In Katanga, the UMHK's production fell to 10,000 short tons per month.[56] For the Copperbelt mines, this meant that it kept their copper out of the US market and directed exports toward Europe where there were fewer restrictions.[57] Meanwhile, the enforcement of this restriction, together with the tariff on imported copper, caused the collapse of Copper Exporters Inc., as non-US producers who felt disadvantaged pulled out of the cartel.

In March 1935, there was further effort at bringing production in line with international demand.[58] The chief executive of Chile's Anaconda mine invited the world's leading copper producers to a meeting in New York to secure an agreement to cut back output. However, the meeting produced scant results. It saw Chile, Katanga, and Northern Rhodesia agree only to a meager reduction of 10%. Canada did not even attend, and the two Northern Rhodesian groups refused to stop development of new mines.[59] Rhokana and the Copperbelt producers felt that, in view of the magnitude of their investments, they were entitled to a reasonable proportion of the world's markets.[60]

However, when a second cartel, the Production Control Committee, was formed to control the production of copper from sources and its sale in markets outside the USA, the Northern Rhodesian mines joined and kept their production within the limits agreed on for the rest of the 1930s. Between May 1, 1935, and November 1, 1936, the basic production quota was placed at 77%, and, in line with this restriction, Rhokana maintained production at an average of 4,416 long tons of copper per month.[61] From December 1, 1937, to October 4, 1939, when world copper production was fixed at 100%, Rhokana scaled its production to an average of 6,247 long tons per month.[62] These restrictions partially helped to reduce production and supply, thereby easing world stocks, which contributed to an increase in the price of copper (see table 2.1).

Despite the negative economic climate, the Great Depression actually saw the competitiveness of Nkana and the Copperbelt mines enhanced vis-à-vis that of its more established counterparts in the Belgian Congo, USA, and Canada. A number of factors enhanced the competitiveness of the Northern Rhodesian copper industry. One of the first initiatives taken by the Copperbelt mines to maintain profitability was to reduce production costs by negotiating with key Southern Rhodesian companies, Rhodesia Railways and Wankie Colliery, for cheaper railway rates and coal supplies.[63] The three producing mining companies, Rhokana, Roan Antelope, and Mufulira, entered into a 13-year contract with Rhodesia Railways to send all their exports and imports along the Rhodesian system at reduced rates from October 1931.[64] Similarly, the mining companies secured a 13-year contract with Wankie Colliery, to run from 1931 to 1944, for the supply of all their coal requirements at a reduced price. On the Rhodesia Railways, export rates for copper fell from £5.10 to £4 a ton; for coal from 22 shillings to 20 shillings a ton; and on general goods, plant, and machinery, from £9 to £8 a ton.[65]

But the Rhodesia Railways would not have reduced their rates without being cushioned by Wankie. As such, Wankie offered the Railways coal at a special rate of 7.6 shillings per ton for a 10-year period.[66] For the Northern Rhodesian mines, the price of coal per ton was reduced from 10.6 shillings to 8.0 shillings.[67] This agreement would have been difficult to negotiate without the concerted efforts of Sir Edmund Davis and Sir Ernest Oppenheimer who were "powerful figure[s] in the interlocking world of [the] Central African Mining Company boards and directorships."[68] They sat on the BSA Company Board of Directors, which owned 86.56% shares in the Rhodesia Railways and a substantial interest stake in Wankie Colliery.[69] Davis was also chairman for the Wankie Colliery Company until his death in 1939. Following this agreement, the Colliery's supply to the Copperbelt mines increased from 423,392 tons in 1934 to nearly 1 million tons in 1937.[70]

Presence of High-Grade Copper Ores

The profitability of the Copperbelt mines during the Great Depression was also enhanced by the presence of high-grade copper ores compared with their counterparts in the USA with low-grade ores. For instance, in 1931, the Copperbelt and Katanga mines contained huge ore reserves averaging 4% and 8% copper, respectively, while those owned by the USA contained an average of 1.6% copper.[71] By comparison, the quality of ore reserves in Canadian mines averaging 2.9 per cent copper was 1.1 per cent lower than the copper reserves on the Copperbelt.[72] Similarly, in 1931, copper ores on the Copperbelt totaled 540,780,000 tons in reserves; ore reserves in the USA were 26,263,000 tons; and total copper reserves in Canada at 11,355,000 tons were almost 48 times smaller than the quantity of copper sulfide ores in the former.[73] Given the high quantity and quality of copper ores in the mines of the Katanga and the Copperbelt, the two regions produced at a cost below the selling price on the market. The US and Canadian mines with low quantity and quality of copper ore remained high-cost producers.

Specifically, the quantity and quality of the Nkana sulfides were not higher than those of Nchanga, Mufulira, and Roan Antelope. For example, in the 1930s, the Nchanga sulfides averaged 143,780,000 short tons carrying 5.4% copper, sulfide ores of the RST mines averaged 4.11% to 4.41% copper, and the sulfide ores of Nkana mine averaged 127,000,000 short tons with about 4% copper.[74] But the mineral veins of Nkana existed in continuous series on the surface layer and hence could easily be extracted using stopping and pillar mining compared to the copper veins of the other three mines, which were detached. Despite having the highest quality of copper deposits, as mentioned earlier, Nchanga was not operational because its underground workings were submerged and the company lacked advanced machinery to pump out the water.[75]

As stated elsewhere earlier, sulfide ores, compared to oxide ores, were cheap to treat because they could be fed direct into the furnace without passing through the flotation process.[76] Additionally, the quantity and quality of the copper ore were largely responsible for the overall improvement in both labor productivity and metal output.

Labor Costs, Capital, and Price Level

Another major factor behind the enhanced profitability of Nkana, Roan Antelope, Mufulira, and the UMHK during the Great Depression was that, compared with the copper mines of North and South America, they were more labor-intensive than capital-intensive. For example, capital invested in mine development, plant, equipment, and day-to-day operations in the copper mines of the USA totaled £131,589,119 in 1929.[77] That year, capital expended on major projects and operations totaled £98,557,213, £15,566,298, and £8,106,238 in the copper industries of Chile, Canada, and Katanga, respectively.[78] By comparison, working capital and expenditure on mine development and metallurgical facilities when all the Copperbelt mines began large-scale operations in 1931 amounted to £8,439,495.[79]

In terms of labor force, employment at 14 major producing mines in the USA averaged 22,176 per year from 1930 to 1935.[80] In this period, the number of workers employed in the three producing mines on the Copperbelt averaged 12,360 per year and 9,483 in the three operating mines of its neighbor, Katanga.[81] The disparities in labor force and capital expenditure in the copper industry in Africa and North America were mainly due to differences in the nature of ore deposits and mining methods utilized. The low-grade porphyry copper deposits of North America occurred in huge mineralized rock formations, which were easily worked using large-scale mechanization. Additionally, in the 1930s, majority of North American companies—49 out 71, to be specific—utilized open stoping, square-set, and shrinkage mining methods, which were extremely expensive compared with block and sublevel caving methods utilized elsewhere in the industry.[82]

More skilled labor was required to operate machines in these underground mines. Thus, North American copper mines utilized more skilled labor than unskilled labor.[83] Skilled labor was more expensive than unskilled labor, making labor costs in the mines of USA and Canada more expensive compared to anywhere else in the industry, despite their mines being low labor-intensive.[84] The ore bodies of the Katanga and Copperbelt mines were predominantly flat stopes, which were more accessible and required greater use of unskilled labor (hoist men), semiskilled labor (hoist drivers and blasting license holders), and less advanced machinery.[85]

In the late 1920s, when the Copperbelt mines were developing, they devoured capital, but between 1931 and 1934, production techniques and labor policies were recalibrated to underpin the mines' profitability. Capital expenditure on major projects at Nkana increased from £14,113 in 1932 to a peak of £693,693 in 1935 (see table 2.2). The increase in capital expenditure was due to development activities at Nkana, such as construction of the concentrator, smelter, and refinery.[86] As explained earlier, the capital invested by Nkana would still not be more than the amount expended by its counterparts in America. Between 1932 and 1938, the labor force at Nkana grew from 5,393 to 7,678.[87]

When the Great Depression struck, the closure of the majority of the mines led to a drastic reduction in the labor force of all the mining groups. The UMHK scaled down its black labor from 11,621 in 1931 to 5,065 by the end of 1932 and its white labor from 1,388 to 664. Rhokana, Roan, and Mufulira followed suit, with their total African labor force falling from 13,948 in 1931 to 5,831 in 1932, while white labor dropped from 2,221 to 959.[88] The reduction in labor enabled the mines to save funds for other developmental projects. It is not clear how much Nkana saved in this manner, but between 1932 and 1934, Roan Antelope managed to save £1,151,962.[89]

As the mines began production after 1933, however, there was a demand for African labor, due to greatly increased production and construction activities.[90] On the UMHK mines, the number of African employees increased tremendously from 10,564 in 1935 to 15,727 by 1939, while European workers increased steadily from 596 to 870 in the same period.[91] At Nkana, the African labor force was 5,853 against 844 Europeans in 1935; both categories of workers increased to about 6,190 compared to 1,231 in 1939, respectively.[92]

Similarly, the African labor force on RST mines rose from 7,156 to 12,808, while the number of European workers increased from 946 to 1,422 over the same period.[93] By comparison, the UMHK relied more on African workers compared to its Copperbelt counterparts. The reason being that the UMHK, unlike the Copperbelt mines, employed more semiskilled African workers from Nyasaland, who had gained experience working in the mines of South Africa and Southern Rhodesia.[94] However, the Copperbelt mines, especially Nkana, relied more on white and colored semiskilled labor from South Africa.[95] Colored labor at Nkana was placed in jobs where it was not economical to employ Europeans, yet such jobs were beyond those occupied by Africans.[96] It was economical to employ experienced Nyasas and semiskilled Coloreds from South Africa because they were cheaper compared to their European counterparts. Skilled or semiskilled labor enabled the mines to increase production more rapidly and efficiently especially when the copper market improved.

In 1937, the annual turnover rate of African labor was 41.9% at Roan, 73.1% at Mufulira, and 70.2% at Nkana, coupled with a service record of between one and four years, especially among married men.[97] The low turnover rate for Roan compared to Nkana and Mufulira resulted from the stabilization of labor, practiced by the former since its incorporation in 1928. Perrings observed a similar increase in the stabilization of African labor on the UMHK due to the fact that an increasing number of voluntary workers had longer service records. For example, in 1932, there was less than 1% of voluntary workers with under three years' service, but by 1934, the figure was more than 50% and in 1935 more than 70%, the majority of them married.[98]

Throughout the 1930s, however, Rhokana relied more on migrant labor than stabilized labor because the former was cheaper than the latter. This can be seen from the high percentage of single men compared with married ones working at Nkana. Between 1932 and 1939, married men averaged 33.6%, and the remainder was single men.[99] In the same period, married workers at Roan averaged 53.3%.[100]

By comparison, Roan relied more on stabilized labor than Nkana. As mentioned earlier, the majority of the mining companies relied more on migrant African laborers recruited from the rural areas in the region. These laborers performed unskilled tasks and were "cajoled into selling their labo[u]r power by expropriation of land [and] imposition of taxation" and "became attracted to wage employment as a way of making up or supplementing their means of subsistence, [farming]."[101] Migrant laborers worked for a period of 6 to 12 months and returned to the villages. As explained in chapter 1, Labour Stabilisation was meant to settle parts of "the African mining workforce with their families on the properties of the mining companies . . . to diminish the dependence on (foreign) migrant labour, lower the costs of recruitment and create an environment for long-term investments in workers' health, skills and offspring."[102] By comparison, migrant African workers were still cheaper because their wages, working conditions, and standards of living were lower than those of stabilized laborers on the mines.

Nonetheless, stabilization enhanced the productivity of Africans as they gained from experience and became more efficient. Thus, as these workers became familiar with their work, fewer workers were required to produce the same amount of copper ore. In 1932, it took 198 Africans and 35 Europeans to produce 1,000 tons of copper at Nkana; by 1938, however, the mine only required 88 Africans and 14 Europeans to produce the same quantity.[103] At Roan, about 112 Africans and 19 Europeans produced 1,000 tons of copper in 1932, but in 1938, the number of employees involved was 100 Africans and 11 Europeans.[104] In addition to experience and efficiency, the quantity and quality of ore discussed earlier partly determined the productivity of African workers.

Table 2.1 compares average African wages in shillings per shift for all workers in semiskilled, surface, and underground employment on the Copperbelt. It also compares the average price of copper and cost per long ton.

Table 2.1 indicates that African wages began to increase on the Copperbelt mines after 1935. Three factors were responsible for this state of affairs. First,

Table 2.1 Trends in Prices on the London Metal Exchange, Operating Costs, and African Labor Costs for the Copperbelt Mines, 1931–1939.

	Average Price per Long Ton	*Average Cost per Long Ton Delivered to Buyers and Average African Wages in Shillings per Shift*			
		RST (Roan/Mufulira)		*RAA (Rhokana/Nkana)*	
Year	*London Metal Exchange (LME)*	*Average Cost per Long Ton*	*Average African Wages in Shillings*	*Average Cost per Long Ton*	*Average African Wages in Shillings*
1931	£42.66	–	0.87s	–	0.93s
1932	£36.39	£28.85	0.92s	£31.47	0.98s
1933	£36.71	£22.36	0.99s	£21.58	0.85s
1934	£33.78	£26.00	0.84s	£23.47	0.84s
1935	£35.70	£25.15	0.90s	£22.20	0.90s
1936	£42.88	£25.10	0.96s	£23.86	0.96s
1937	£60.08	£26.35	0.95s	£22.59	0.98s
1938	£45.84	£25.55	0.96s	£23.06	1.00s
1939	£49.84	£23.75	0.99s	£23.67	1.04s

Source: Compiled from Secretary of the Northern Rhodesia Chamber of Mines, Kitwe, to General Managers of Mufulira, Nchanga, Rhokana, Roan Antelope, and Chibuluma, May 21, 1953, ZCCM 3.7.2B; RC Limited, *Annual Reports and Accounts*, 1931–1939, ZCCM 3.8.2F; RST Limited, *Annual Reports and Accounts*, 1931–1939, ZCCM 12.6.1E; RST Limited, *Annual Report and Accounts*, 1948 (London: RST Head Office, 1948), 17, ZCCM 12.6.1E; Gregory, *Ernest Oppenheimer and the Economic Development of Southern Africa*, 419; Perrings, *Black Mineworkers in Central Africa*, 243, 258; Phillips, "Roan Antelope," 222, 366.

Note: RST figures on production costs between 1932 and 1934 represent amounts for Roan Antelope only. As explained elsewhere earlier, operations at the Mufulira mine were halted when the Great Depression struck. Despite reopening after 1933, Mufulira failed to produce at a profit compared to Roan and Nkana because, like Nchanga, it lacked advanced equipment for extracting the ore until after 1935 when the Selkirk Haulage Shaft was completed. For further details, see: RST Limited, Annual Report and Accounts, *1935 (London: RST Head Office, 1935), 9, ZCCM 12.6.1E.*

as the Great Depression eased and the mines stepped up production, expanding construction work on the Copperbelt mines caused African wages to rise. For the RST group, the reopening of the Mufulira mine raised African wages from an average of 0.87s per shift in 1931 to 0.99s in 1933, partly to attract more labor. For the RAA group, the construction of the Rhokana Refinery raised African wages from an average of 0.84s per shift in 1933 to 0.90s in 1935. It should be added that the international demand for copper, following rearmament in Europe, also increased wages and bonus allowances as the mines stepped up production and increased working hours over the normal duration of eight hours per day.[105]

The second factor behind the increase in African wages on the Copperbelt mines was the strike in 1935 by African workers against low wages and falling living standards. The government sparked the strike when it increased the poll tax in urban areas by 50% but reduced it by 25% in rural areas, provoking workers at Roan, Nkana, and Mufulira to take strike action.[106] "The realisation that mobilisation and resistance had been organised in compounds and settlements" led the mining companies and the government to "reintroduce pass-laws along with other measures to restrict and reverse labour stabilisation" in the aftermath of the 1935 strike.[107] Third, the reopening of Nchanga mine after 1937 also increased wages at Nkana. Despite Rhokana's reliance on migrant labor, which was cheaper than stabilized labor, the Corporation still paid more for African labor than Roan and Mufulira did because of the three factors noted earlier. Increased wages for African mineworkers added to unit labor costs but were offset through reduced turnover or desertions and increased efficiency.

European workers were expensive at this time because they had the skills not yet acquired by African laborers. Despite the high wages paid to attract skilled European workers, Nkana and the other Copperbelt mines were low-cost producers largely because of low African wages.[108] The difference in wages between European and African workmen per shift at Nkana, in particular, and in the Copperbelt mines, in general, was in the ratio of about 25:1. The average monthly wage of a European miner was £40 and that of an African was 22.6s, plus rations and housing in each case.[109] The disparity in European and African monthly wages was greater than elsewhere in the Southern African mining industry.

This disparity was not borne out by comparable disparities in the cost of living on the Copperbelt. When Nkana and the Copperbelt mines were opened in the late 1920s, housing and health conditions were bad, general amenities were lacking, and the cost of living was high.[110] An unusually generous scale of pay was, therefore, necessary to attract skilled labor from Europe, the USA, South Africa, and Southern Rhodesia.

Overall, labor on the Copperbelt was still cheaper than in North America and Europe. For example, basic wages for both skilled and unskilled labor at three USA mines (Butte, Arizona, and Michigan) averaged £1.03 per shift and a maximum of £31 per month.[111] On the Copperbelt, monthly wages for both unskilled and skilled labor averaged £20.[112] As indicated in the earlier paragraph, skilled (European) miners were expensive than unskilled (African) workers on the Copperbelt. But the cheapness of unskilled labor compensated for the high cost of skilled labor. Due to cheap African labor, the Copperbelt mines constructed a copper refinery at Nkana instead of in Britain.[113] Butler supports this proposition, observing that it cost £415,000 to construct the Rhokana Copper Refinery, £291,800 less than it would have cost to build it in Britain, "the difference largely being due to the relative cheapness of African labour."[114] The cheapness of African labor in the Northern Rhodesian mining industry kept operating costs low, despite the high cost of European labor. The construction of the Refinery enabled Rhokana and the Copperbelt mines to reduce processing costs as they minimized exporting blister copper to the USA for refining.[115]

It is true that the cheapness of African labor in the Northern Rhodesian mining industry kept total labor costs low, despite the high cost of European labor. However, after 1935, African wages also increased substantially relative to operating costs (see table 2.1). Despite an enormous increase in African wages after 1935, the average cost of producing a long ton of copper in the Copperbelt mines was generally maintained primarily due to inexpensive transport, mining, and processing costs. Throughout the Great Depression, the cost of producing a long ton of copper at the Nkana mine was below the selling price. At the same time, concerted efforts by the major producers to align production with demand paid off as prices began to improve. In 1934, a better copper market and price was reached due to the reduction in copper stocks in the USA of 200,000 short tons and 77,000 short tons in Europe.[116] This improving economic situation was boosted by the booming automotive and electrical industries and rearmament by Germany and Britain.[117] There was a high demand for minerals, especially copper. Germany alone purchased about 22,000 short tons of copper per month and became the second-largest buyer of Katangese and Northern Rhodesian copper. Between 1937 and 1939, Britain purchased about half of Northern Rhodesia's copper output, with Germany buying one-third.[118] As a result, the average monthly copper consumption in Europe increased from 85,600 short tons in 1936 to 111,600 short tons in 1937, pushing the price of the metal up to £60.08.[119]

The result of all these factors taken together was that the cost of production remained very low compared with copper's selling price, making copper mining at Nkana and other Copperbelt mines increasingly profitable after 1932 (see table 2.1). Between 1932 and 1934, when the Depression was at its most severe, the average cost of producing a long ton of copper at Nkana was approximately £25.5, and £25.7 for the RST group, when the metal was selling at an average price of £36 on the London Metal Exchange (LME).

Among many other factors, which influenced operating costs in the USA (North America), the most important were the mining method utilized, ore grade, scale of operations, natural underground conditions, labor expenses, climate, topography, government regulations, and prices of supplies and power.[120] The most influential factors were mining and labor costs, and these "accounted for over half the cost per ton of mining copper ore [which averaged £40 in the early and mid-1930s]."[121] The majority of American mines could only produce at a profit after 1935 when the price per long ton of copper increased.[122]

By comparison, operating costs on the Copperbelt were largely influenced by the quality of copper ore, labor costs, transport expenses, and the price of supplies/coal. Following expansion and improved efficiency of the Copperbelt mines, driven by reduced transport expenses and price of coal, as well as mechanization and better labor productivity, production costs fell. By expense class, mining and labour costs averaged £11.67, processing or treatment expenses amounted to £6.72, transport charges totaled £5.06, and other expenses accounted for £5.08 of the total annual average cost of £28.53 per ton of salable copper produced at Mufulira mine between 1934 and 1939.[123] Mining and labor costs on the Copperbelt accounted for 41% of the total cost of producing a ton of copper.

It is clear that mining and labor costs were cheaper on the Copperbelt than in the USA. It can be seen that the Copperbelt mines were in control of four important components of production costs: rich ore reserves, mill-feed quality, mine operations' labor productivity, and transport networks. These four elements comprised approximately 82.2% of the total cost of sales per long ton of copper in the period from 1935 to 1939.[124] Northern Rhodesian copper was produced and landed in Europe for an average of £25.2 per long ton for the RST group and £23.1 for Rhokana, at a time when the metal was selling for an average price of £47 between 1935 and 1939 (see table 2.1).

The benefits accruing from the low cost of producing copper on the Copperbelt can be seen from table 2.2 indicating capital expenditure, production, cost and value of sales, and operating profits secured by Nkana during the 1930s.

Between 1932 and 1939, total copper output in Northern Rhodesia was about 1,141,962 long tons or 9.2% of world production; the UMHK's total production was 818,156 long tons or 6.6% of the world output.[125] The Northern Rhodesian Copperbelt mines produced and contributed more toward world production than the UMHK in this period. According to Butler, Northern Rhodesia ranked fourth in terms of world copper production during the Great Depression.[126] Despite its low-grade ores, the USA was still the largest

Table 2.2 Capital, Copper Production, Value and Cost of Sales, and Operating Profit for Nkana, 1932–1939.

Year	*Capital Expenditure £*	*Production Long Tons*	*Value of Sales £*	*Cost of Sales £*	*Royalty/ Export Tax and Others (£)*	*Operating Profit (£)*
1932	14,113	17,318	450,188	424,466	339,069	25,720
1933	74,788	53,224	1,792,275	1,631,221	1,276,674	515,601
1934	556,302	60,164	2,339,374	1,489,182	918,169	614,412
1935	693,693	64,059	2,549,662	1,539,810	1,054,682	575,869
1936	465,466	56,231	2,635,059	1,306,500	871,303	826,744
1937	512,025	83,586	4,417,512	1,748,893	1,147,924	2,166,910
1938	607,415	82,877	4,647,857	1,978,258	1,366,299	2,158,486
1939	474,848	91,110	5,777,606	2,201,432	1,559,946	2,900,196

Source: Compiled from RC Limited, *Annual Reports and Accounts*, 1932–1939; *Times*, October 31, 1935; *Daily Telegraph and Morning Post*, October 28, 1937; *Financial Times*, November 16, 1939.

Note: Capital refers to expenditure on prospecting, properties (plants), machinery, mine development, building, administrative, and overhead expenses. Total copper sold was more or less than what was produced in a financial year depending on the demand. Similarly, Value of Sales more or less depended on the demand and price of the metal. Cost of Sales included operating costs incurred on mining, concentrating, smelting, and royalty/export tax, plus realization charges expended on rail-age, handling, freight, outside refining expenses, and selling costs. Thus, royalty and export taxes were part of Cost of Sales. The Operating Profit was the difference between the Value of Sales and the Cost of Sales.

producer in the world because porphyry copper deposits tend to have large mineral resources.[127] Between 1932 and 1934, Rhokana produced more copper than the RST-operated mines, with 130,706 long tons (see table 2.2) compared to 124,631 long tons, respectively.[128] Between 1935 and 1939, the latter, with a total output of 508,762 long tons, outstripped the dominance of the former, whose total production was 377,863 long tons.[129]

The major reason for the decrease in production at Nkana was adherence to world copper production restrictions. Gregory notes that these restrictions affected Nkana and Nchanga more than Roan and Mufulira because of different opinions among the affiliated offices of AAC in Northern Rhodesia, South Africa, Britain, and the USA. With the latter at the center of global production strategies, its decisions determined market prices.[130] In a letter dated August 5, 1938, Pollak lamented to Taylor about the loss of Rhokana's bargaining power compared with that of RST between 1935 and 1939.[131] Pollak regretted the advice from their American counterparts that had led to major reductions in production at Nkana and neglect of the Nchanga mine, while RST had minimally reduced output in line with international regulations. As discussed earlier, the management structure of AAC-controlled companies embraced a top-down approach in decision-making compared with RST, whose bottom-up approach "gave mine staff wide latitude in the carrying out of policy."[132] "Rhokana lost its preferential position and the Roan was put on equality. Mufulira was recognised as a second producer, while Nchanga was treated as a joke."[133]

Table 2.3 shows Rhokana's issued capital per annum with fully paid shares of £1 each on Preference, Ordinary, and "A" stock. It also disaggregates data into gross profits, net profits, and dividends for the Corporation between 1932 and 1939. Dividend amounts include those paid on Preference shares as well as interim and final dividends declared on Ordinary and "A" shares. Between 1931 and 1934, Rhokana failed to declare dividends because it was undercapitalized in relation to the rapid expansion and magnitude of its undertakings on the Copperbelt, which compelled it to use all its profits as working capital.

Rhokana posted a total net profit of £6,152,225 between 1935 and 1939. During the same period, the Copperbelt mining companies realized after-tax profits totaling £13,155,073.[134] Beyond net profits, Rhokana, Roan, and Mufulira paid their first after-tax dividends in 1935.[135] Between 1935 and 1939, their total dividends amounted to £7 million.[136] Rhokana paid the highest after-tax dividends, averaging 41% per annum, amounting to a total of £5,184,250 during this period.[137] The total gross profit of the Copperbelt

Table 2.3 Rhokana Corporation's Issued Share Capital, Gross Profits, Net Profits, and Dividends, 1932–1939.

	Rhokana's Share Capital, Profits, and Dividends							
		Nkana Mine			*Other Mines*	*Rhokana Corporation*		
Year	*Issued Share Capital (£)*	*Operating Surplus (£)*	*Income Tax and Others (£)*	*Net Profits (£)*	*Received Profits (£)*	*Gross Profits (£)*	*Net Profits (£)*	*Net Dividends (£)*
1932	1,428,267	28,236	–	–	–	–	–	–
1933	2,442,291	515,915	475,053	40,862	–	40,862	40,862	–
1934	2,442,291	614,656	225,612	389,044	–	389,044	389,044	–
1935	3,942,291	576,018	94,734	481,284	–	911,192	634,732	331,848
1936	3,942,291	831,221	230,927	600,294	–	1,002,194	737,912	509,900
1937	4,000,002	2,175,057	300,015	1,875,042	144,826	2,226,510	1,790,413	1,645,001
1938	4,000,002	2,171,254	669,505	1,501,749	217,149	1,950,405	1,761,031	1,645,001
1939	4,000,002	2,913,990	1,878,108	1,035,882	144,664	1,435,950	1,228,137	1,052,500

Source: Compiled from RC Limited, *Annual Reports and Accounts*, 1932–1939; *Times*, October 31, 1935; *Daily Telegraph and Morning Post*, October 28, 1937; *Financial Times*, November 16, 1939.

Note: Gross Profits are divided into two parts: those from the Nkana mine and those from Rhokana's investments in other mines and properties on the Copperbelt. The Operating Surplus indicated for Nkana mine was arrived at after adding the Operating Profit, discount on transfer fees, interest receivable, and revenue on sundry items. Income tax, general maintenance, administrative expenses, depreciation, exchange rate and development amounts, and debenture and loan interests were deducted from Nkana's Operating Surplus. The Net Profit for Nkana was added to Rhokana's returns on investment in other properties and unappropriated profits brought forward from the previous year to come up with Gross Profits for the Corporation in that particular financial year. Net Profits for the Corporation were arrived at after deducting reserve amounts for depreciation, development, and general accounts from Gross Profits. Dividends were calculated from Net Profits.

mines was about £25 million.[138] But their gross profit was less than a third of the total value invested in the mines.

The prosperity of Nkana and the Copperbelt mines can also be seen from their tax contributions. For example, in 1934, the mining companies paid an income tax of £43,000, of which Nkana contributed £2,892.[139] Between 1935 and 1937, taxes generated by mining contributed 45% of total government revenue.[140] The mining companies also paid over £300,000 to the BSA Company in royalties. From the remaining profits of about £4 million, the British and Northern Rhodesian governments received £500,000 each and also taxed the BSA Company's royalty receipts, each getting £40,000.[141] However, in terms of retained earnings, although 25% of the companies' profit was taxed, only half went to the Northern Rhodesian government. Even so, the low royalty tax rates levied by the BSA Company on the companies—compared with the relatively high income tax paid in Britain, where their headquarters were domiciled, and in Northern Rhodesia, their host nation—cushioned the effects of double taxation on the mines. The BSA Company's revenue in the form of royalty was on the following sliding scale per long ton of standard or blister copper, "2% when the price was less than £55; 2.25% on £55 or more, but less than £60; 2.5% on £60 or more, but less than £80; 5% on £80, plus 10% on such portion of the price as exceeds £80."[142]

RHOKANA/NKANA AND THE FORMATION OF THE EUROPEAN MINEWORKERS' UNION, 1937

If 1937 marked a breakthrough in the corporate profitability of Nkana and the other Copperbelt mines, it was also a breakthrough in the history of industrial labor. That year, Rhokana and the other Copperbelt companies recognized the Northern Rhodesian (European) Mineworkers' Union (NRMWU). As noted earlier, the Copperbelt mines were able to produce more cheaply than their counterparts in America and Europe, partly because of the relative cheapness of African labor. But what was effectively a dual labor structure eventually gave birth to separate trade unions.

The Nkana mine was central to the formation of a trade union for white miners on the Copperbelt. The idea of forming a European trade union in the Copperbelt mines was initiated by Richard Olds, employed on Nkana mine.[143] Little is known about Olds, apart from his being born in 1881 in Cumberland, England.[144] He trained as a machine operator and worked as a machine agent. In the 1920s, he migrated to South Africa to seek employment in the mines, where he learnt about the boom conditions developing on the Copperbelt mines. He then moved to the Copperbelt and worked at Nkana mine as a painter.[145] In September 1934, Olds relinquished his job to organize a trade union for European miners. Because of its importance in this discussion, an excerpt from the *Copperbelt Times* is provided:

> Mr. R. Olds has relinquished his position on the Nkana mine to organise an Industrial Workers' Federation. In the course of an interview reference was made to words uttered some 12 years ago by the late Sir Evelyn Wallers, sometime President of the Transvaal Chamber of Mines, the substance of which was that no industry could be considered on a sound footing until both employers and employees were well organised. Mr. Olds said that the 2,000 odd workers on the copper mines had felt for some time that an organisation was needed which could provide the men with a medium of expression, and negotiate and mediate between them and the managements. . . . The desire for something of the sort had led to him being asked to organise a Federation whose scope would not be confined to the miners, but be capable of extension to other spheres of industrial enterprise if needed. Mr Olds is establishing his office in Ndola.[146]

However, Olds wanted to extend the influence of the Industrial Workers' Federation (IWF) to industries beyond the copper mines.[147] This ambitious agenda brought him into conflict with his colleagues, especially from Roan Antelope.[148] It is also clear that African workers did not feature in his vision. But Olds soon realized that many European workers did not share his ideas. Earning more than their counterparts in Southern Africa, they were slow to become involved. In October 1934, Olds published an article in which he argued vehemently that:

> the white worker in Northern Rhodesia is faced with two alternatives viz. [as follows]. To either organise against the encroachment of the Native in their skilled trades or get ready to leave the country. To my mind a great many still considers themselves Birds of Passage, they have no interest in the affairs of the country further than trying to evade the Income Tax. . . . Who have we today who will champion the cause of the white population [?] Where are the Men who can think WHITE and will stand out and fight the cause of the white worker and his children? Are we going to maintain our WHITE STANDARD or allow ourselves to descend to the level of the blacks by always thinking BLACK[?] . . . Let us visualise and see what is going to happen if we do not organise.[149]

Olds feared that, as Africans settled down to an industrial way of life and learnt new skills, they would threaten future European employment.[150] Africans at Nkana, Roan, and Mufulira were already doing certain jobs previously reserved for Europeans, such as surveying, mail-posting, locomotive driving, bricklaying, fitting, tailoring, and carpentry, and held blasting certificates.[151] With a counter message to African Advancement, some European workers supported Olds's idea of a European trade union in the three copper-producing mines. Within two months of his initial campaign, he managed to convince about 417 (50%) of the daily-paid European workers at Nkana, 100 at Mufulira, and 50 at Roan.[152] These figures suggest that, initially, Olds was successful at Nkana, much more so than he was at Roan and Mufulira.

Money attributes the relative lack of success of Olds's agenda in the early months of his campaign at Roan and Mufulira to management opposition.[153] These mining companies were worried by Olds's activities and, in most instances, stopped him from holding meetings with their employees. The companies opposed the color bar proposed by Olds, as it would limit "skilled work to people of European descent. . . [and] raise costs."[154] When he realized that the mining companies would not easily be budged, Olds decided to affiliate the IWF to the South African Mineworkers' Union (SAMU) in order to bring in more support. Support from SAMU might force the Copperbelt companies to accept a European workers' trade union. In 1935, he visited the Rand frequently and, early in 1936, invited the SAMU organizing secretary, Charles Harris, to campaign for the formation of a branch of the union on the Copperbelt.[155] By the end of their campaign on the three Copper mines, Olds and Harris claimed no less than 80% support among the European miners, had representatives at each mine elected, and affiliated them to the SAMU, though not officially.[156] Olds was elected overseer and organizing secretary of the IWF on the Copperbelt.

The mining companies, especially Roan Antelope, opposed the setting up of branches of SAMU. They argued that "gold and copper producers' interests seldom coincided, and that laws affecting the settlement of trade disputes in South Africa did not apply in Northern Rhodesia."[157] In this particular instance, the companies were correct, as the SAMU Constitution could not be applied beyond South African borders. This explains why Harris failed to formally identify his Union with the IWF. Indeed, the position of the copper companies concurred with that of colonial officials. Lusaka and London repeatedly argued that "no colour bar legislation would be allowed in Northern Rhodesia" and that Africans with skills or qualifications must be allowed to advance in industry.[158]

The fall of Olds came later, after an altercation with the Roan branch chairman, Ben Rount, over organization and administrative policies. At a meeting held in September 1936, Rount accused Olds of appropriating union funds and diverting part of it to Harris in South Africa. Consequently, branch officials dismissed Olds through a vote of no confidence.[159] The mining companies welcomed this, because, as stated earlier, they did not like Olds's color bar ideology.

However, his dismissal did not prevent the formation of a recognized European union, as trade unions in Northern Rhodesia could be registered under Company Laws. Section 16(i)(e) of the Workmen's Compensation Ordinance provided that a workman who was a party to an application to the court under the ordinance could be represented by an officer of a trade union to which he belonged.[160] In addition, the "English statute law had been applied to Northern Rhodesia in 1911, and protection for trade unions was, therefore, provided by the British Trade Unions Acts of 1871, 1876 and 1906."[161] As a result, in April 1937, the copper mines, based on the British model of trade unionism, recognized the NRMWU.[162]

British labor law recognized trade unions as lawful voluntary bodies but without particular and entrenched legal practices such as a color bar or increased wages after a certain period of time. By contrast, registered trade unions in Southern Rhodesia and South Africa were entrenched through conciliation boards with a color bar. The government accepted the constitution of the NRMWU, because it did not contain any color bar provision, though Clause 39 of the 1937 Agreement between the companies and the Union "enforced a standstill on the advancement of native labour."[163]

Total membership of the NRMWU was 834, of which 374 came from Nkana, 240 from Roan, and 220 from Mufulira.[164] A significant number of general secretaries and presidents of the NRMWU worked at Nkana.[165] For example, the presidents, T.S. Ross (1938–1940), B. Goodwin (1943–1947), J.T. Moll (1952–1953), and E.L. Williams (1958), all worked at Nkana mine.[166]

Through the NRMWU, the privileged position of white workers was entrenched on the Copperbelt. The Union led the successful 1940 strike, which resulted in substantive wage increases and allowances. However, the major achievement of the NRMWU was when the Closed Shop was formalized in 1941.[167] The Closed Shop blocked African Advancement and maintained the privileged status of white miners up to 1955.[168] The Closed Shop, however, led to the fragmentation of the Union, with salaried officials organizing themselves into the Mines Officials Salaried Staff Association (MOSSA).[169] Monthly paid officials saw the NRMWU as only representing daily-paid white miners who performed quite different tasks from themselves.

CONCLUSION

This chapter has demonstrated that European miners at Nkana were central to the formation of the NRMWU on the Copperbelt, the first trade union to be established in the Northern Rhodesian mining industry. The dual labor structure gave birth to worker consciousness, collective labor action, and trade unionism. Nevertheless, Rhokana and the other Copperbelt companies were relieved that Africans were not included in the NRMWU, as they feared that a joint black and white union would be more powerful and militant in its activities.[170]

What has become clear, too, is that Nkana and the Copperbelt mines emerged during the Great Depression as strong and profitable competitors in world copper production. In the region, the economic importance of Northern Rhodesia became second to that of South Africa, outstripping Southern Rhodesia.[171] At the same time, Nkana and the Copperbelt mines established copper mining as the dominant sector of the Northern Rhodesian economy, far surpassing the importance of peasant and settler agriculture. Furthermore, copper production added an element of diversification of the Northern Rhodesian economy, now embracing mining, cattle rearing, growing of maize and cotton, and rubber plantations.[172]

It can be seen that the period between 1929 and 1939 was such an important decade for the Copperbelt mines' future. As demonstrated in this chapter, the Great Depression was not a setback at all for the Northern Rhodesian mines. In fact, the economic crisis generated by the Great Depression enhanced the development of the Copperbelt mines in several ways. First, the Copperbelt mines were able to attract foreign capital from South Africa, Britain, and the USA because of being low-cost producers. Foreign capital was necessary for infrastructural and mine developments in this region. Second, the low-cost of production enabled continued economic and productive growth on the Copperbelt despite the worldwide depression. Third, volatility in the price of copper on the international market encouraged cooperation between the Copperbelt mining companies and other major producers in the world in devising and implementing measures, which helped to avoid wider price fluctuations. Fourth, and most important, the Great Depression caused the Copperbelt mining companies to improve their corporate and growth strategies, managerial tendencies, and industrial relations, which proved vital in the near future. As the clouds of the Second World War darkened, Nkana's strategic importance for Britain was to become obvious.

Chapter 3

Financial Incentives of War

Rhokana/Nkana during the Second World War and Korean Crisis, 1939–1953

RHOKANA/NKANA DURING AND IMMEDIATELY AFTER THE SECOND WORLD WAR, 1939–1949

The outbreak of the Second World War in September 1939 boosted the economies of a number of colonies.[1] African and Asian colonies became strategic sources of minerals for war efforts. As alluded to in chapter 2, rearmament by Germany and Britain helped to pull the world out of recession, but it was the demands of the Second World War that saw the extraction of raw materials on an unprecedented scale.[2] The copper mining industry of Northern Rhodesia, in particular, benefited from this increased demand. Copper played a key role in the execution of the war between the Allied and Axis powers. Before 1939, copper was mainly used in domestic and industrial appliances, but during the war, demand more than doubled due to copper's importance in the manufacture of munitions, aircraft, and naval equipment.[3]

Prior to the war, about 90% of the British wire-drawing industry depended on imported dies principally from France, Belgium, the Netherlands, and Portugal.[4] However, the outbreak of war and the subsequent German attacks on Belgium and France forced Britain to purchase half of its supplies from the United States of America (USA). But as the war intensified, insufficient supplies compelled the USA to reduce its deliveries to the United Kingdom. Britain was forced to look elsewhere in the colonies for cheap supplies of minerals, including copper, for manufacturing diamond dies.[5] A diamond die was an important "tool for making fine wire of any sort—and fine wire [was] essential in the production of a tremendous range of articles," utilized in the wiring of aircraft, submarines, motor cars, electrical appliances, telephone systems, and radio communications used during the war.[6]

The USA obtained part of its copper supplies from Canada, Chile, Mexico, and the Belgian Congo, while the deposits of Northern Rhodesia and South Africa were utilized by Britain. In the early stages of the war, Germany and Japan controlled access to minerals in Central and Western Europe, Scandinavia, and Southeast Asia.[7] But even so, at the height of the war, Britain and the USA commanded about 57% by value of the world's mineral production, whereas Germany and her partners were short of supplies in many strategic items.[8]

Operations, Production, and Costs during the War

During the Second World War, government and the private sector worked closely together, as did metropolitan and colonial economies. The Ministry of Supply in London required Nkana and the other Copperbelt mines to supply a certain amount of the red metal, but the Copperbelt mines failed to meet the required quantity.[9] Specifically, the Ministry of Supply wanted Nkana to supply 9,500 short tons of copper per month, but initially, the mine only managed to produce a maximum average of 6,852 short tons a month, obliging Britain to purchase the balance from the Union Miniere du Haunt Katanga.[10]

A number of problems were responsible for this undercapacity, for instance, shortages of European labor, plant materials, new equipment, and fuel; shipping delays; and closed capital markets.[11] Because of these problems, production costs at Nkana during the war increased compared to the prewar period from an average of £24 during the Great Depression to £31 per long ton of copper delivered to England between 1940 and 1945 (see table 3.1). For the Rhodesian Anglo American (RAA) group, Nkana was still cheaper to operate than Nchanga, the latter being a high-cost producer due to difficult underground conditions, especially flooding.[12]

Table 3.1 demonstrates that, between 1940 and 1945, Nkana was the largest Copperbelt supplier of copper to the Ministry of Supply, totaling 493,321 long tons. The Northern Rhodesian mines sold 68% of their copper to Britain and contributed 9.12% to global output.[13] Over this period, Northern Rhodesia moved up from fourth to third in terms of world production, behind USA and Chile, but ahead of Canada, the Belgian Congo, and the Soviet Union.[14]

In addition to copper, Nkana produced cobalt, supplying a total of 15,219 short tons of cobalt alloy, yielding 6,154 short tons of cobalt metal treated in Canada and England. Of particular wartime importance, cobalt metal was utilized in the manufacture of cutting tools and drills, welding rods, stock for tipping tools, dies, valve steel, magnets, and electroplating.[15] Even more valuable was its use in the production of essential military equipment and consumption in high-speed steel, stellate and carbide-type alloys, magnets, and jet-propulsion gas turbines.[16]

Table 3.1 Copper Production, Costs, and London Metal Exchange Price for Copperbelt Mines, 1940–1945.

Name of Mine	*Production of Copper in Long Tons*	*Average Cost of Production per Long Ton*	*London Price per Long Ton*
Nkana	493,321	£30.77	£62
Mufulira	457,982	£26.09	£62
Roan Antelope	396,877	£31.02	£62
Nchanga	76,584	£50.75	£62

Source: Constructed from Bancroft, Mining in Northern Rhodesia, 144, 162–3; RACM Limited, *Summary of Operations for the Six Years Ended 30 June 1945* (London: RACM/RST Head Office, 1945), 3, ZCCM 19.2.6D; RC Limited, *Annual Report and Accounts for the Year Ended 30 June 1945* (London: RC Head Office, 1945), 16–7, ZCCM 19.2.4F.

Moreover, Nkana's mine workshop was used to manufacture and repair ordnance. Between 1941 and 1944, certain parts of R.A.F practice bombs and brass tank parts were made, as well as urgent repairs were done, at Nkana for the military transport units.[17] Both black and white women were employed in the manufacturing of bomb parts and fuse bodies.[18] Women were also employed to do certain surface jobs previously done by men in order to alleviate the critical shortage of white and black male labor as the mines stepped up production.[19]

The Impact of Wartime Financial Measures on Profitability

Three major financial measures were introduced by the British and Northern Rhodesian governments for the purpose of supporting the war effort: the fixed price of copper (see table 3.1), double taxation in the form of income tax in Britain and Northern Rhodesia, and surcharges or excess profits tax (EPT) and the national defense contribution.[20] Excess profits tax "was a wartime instrument designed by the state to capture above-normal profits by industrialists [businesses] as a way of curbing wartime profiteering."[21] These measures had a significant impact on Rhokana's profitability. The price of copper, originally fixed at £43.10 per long ton in London, was substantially lower than the price in New York of £80 per ton.[22] Even when it stabilized at £62 in Britain, it was still lower than in the USA. As a result, Nkana and the Copperbelt mines together lost £500,000 per month.[23]

The burden of double taxation, EPT, and the national defense contribution became even more onerous when, in 1941, the Northern Rhodesian government requested the mines to pay part of the estimated tax in advance.[24] In 1938, Nkana and the other Copperbelt mines paid out on average a manageable 17% of operating surplus in taxes. However, in 1941, this figure increased tremendously to 67%, largely because of double taxation, national defense contribution, and EPT.[25]

Table 3.2 compares the capital expenditure, labor strengths, and operating profits of Nkana mine during and immediately after the Second World War. Between 1940 and 1944, capital expenditure fell, while the African labor force increased. Capital expenditure declined owing to inadequate supplies of equipment and machinery, coupled with transport bottlenecks and disruption to international trade because of the war. Furthermore, Rhokana halted major construction projects and development activities at Nkana, concentrated on production for the war.[26] Declining profits obliged Nkana to rely on a labor-intensive mode of production in order to maintain production.

Table 3.2 shows that, between 1940 and 1945, the cost of producing a ton of copper at Nkana was half the selling price in London. Production costs during the war were successfully contained for two reasons. Table 3.2 indicates that African labor costs marginally increased between 1940 and 1945. High-grade ores averaging 3.58% copper in reserves and yielding 3.29% of this metal meant that it was economical to produce copper at Nkana.[27] Therefore, the increase in transport costs was largely offset by low labor and mining costs during the war. The average operating cost per long ton of copper delivered to buyers in the period under review was about £31 for Nkana, and the selling price stabilized at £62 in London. As a result, the total value of sales at £33,685,643 was more than double the total cost of sales at £15,721,490 between 1940 and 1945 (see table 3.2).

Table 3.2 Capital Expenditure, African Labor Strength, and Operating Profits for Nkana Mine, 1940–1949.

Year	*Capital Expenditure (£)*	*No. of African Workers*	*Wages per Shift (Shillings)*	*Value of Sales (£)*	*Cost of Sales (£)*	*Royalty/ Export Tax and Others (£)*	*Operating Profit (£)*
1940	126,028	7,784	1.04	5,777,606	2,231,653	1,585,263	2,869,978
1941	93,106	8,885	1.30	4,927,403	2,232,322	1,704,016	2,172,198
1942	85,746	9,318	1.39	4,788,221	2,377,401	1,852,656	1,791,125
1943	85,422	10,430	1.46	6,124,553	2,831,222	2,348,103	2,503,016
1944	84,538	9,490	1.45	5,938,198	2,995,812	2,365,595	1,972,496
1945	295,361	9,655	1.47	6,129,662	3,053,080	2,444,924	2,098,464
1946	217,989	9,565	1.69	6,513,232	3,498,068	2,445,641	2,118,112
1947	241,747	9,187	1.83	7,555,325	3,449,233	2,614,564	2,887,507
1948	225,963	9,670	2.15	9,623,205	4,264,612	3,547,363	4,390,987
1949	423,562	10,463	2.31	10,832,455	5,031,161	4,224,343	4,743,280

Source: Compiled from Secretary of Northern Rhodesia Chamber of Mines to Divisional General Managers, May 21, 1953; RC Limited, *Annual Reports and Accounts*, 1940–1944, ZCCM 3.8.2F; RC Limited, *Annual Reports*, 1946–1949, ZCCM 12.7.2F; RC Limited, *Annual Report and Accounts for the Year Ended 30 June 1945*, 2–20.

Note: Wages are in shillings per shift per African. As indicated elsewhere earlier, Royalty/Export Tax was part of operating costs or Cost of Sales. The sources consulted do not indicate the actual amount of these taxes, but they are included in the cost of mining and processing.

Table 3.3 indicates Nkana's operating surplus, profits from Rhokana's investments in other mines and properties on the Copperbelt, and the Corporation's issued share capital, gross profits, income tax, and dividends between 1940 and 1949.

Between June 1940 and June 1945, Rhokana's gross profit, before subtracting income tax, double taxation, national defense contribution, and preference shares redemption fund, was approximately £13,955,996 (see table 3.3). Income tax, provision for double taxation, and national defense contribution amounted to £5,460,751, and within this amount, the EPT aggregate was £170,000.[28] The total dividends on Preference, Ordinary, and "A" shares in this period amounted to £4,495,002 (see table 3.3), whereas the additional expenses on directors' remuneration and allocation to the general reserve account and preference share redemption fund totaled roughly £1,855,380, leaving an unappropriated (net) profit of about £2,144,863.[29]

Table 3.3 Rhokana's Issued Share Capital, Gross Profits, Net Profits, and Dividends, 1940–1949.

	Corporation's Share Capital and Gross Profits				*Income Tax, Net Profits, and Dividends*		
		Nkana Mine	*Other Mines*				
Year	*Issued Share Capital (£)*	*Operating Surplus (£)*	*Received Profits (£)*	*Gross Profits (£)*	*Income Tax (£)*	*Net Profits (£)*	*Total Dividends (£)*
1940	4,000,002	2,883,772	177,668	3,005,602	1,650,000	1,348,102	1,082,501
1941	4,000,002	2,188,785	–	2,098,404	1,006,044	1,084,860	832,500
1942	4,000,002	1,802,789	177,668	1,882,948	744,570	730,878	457,500
1943	4,000,002	2,517,458	–	2,441,880	753,833	1,180,547	707,500
1944	4,000,002	1,997,833	97,500	2,190,041	517,159	1,242,502	707,500
1945	4,000,002	2,132,952	97,500	2,337,121	789,145	1,240,476	707,501
1946	4,000,002	2,139,735	97,500	2,708,376	1,008,984	1,391,892	876,408
1947	4,000,002	2,907,302	227,500	3,221,880	1,563,642	2,336,531	1,212,705
1948	4,000,002	4,411,675	325,000	4,668,094	2,573,084	2,586,336	1,418,759
1949	4,000,002	4,769,742	715,000	5,425,175	2,805,324	3,111,440	1,418,670

Source: Compiled from Secretary of Northern Rhodesia Chamber of Mines to Divisional General Managers, May 21, 1953; RC Limited, *Annual Reports and Accounts*, 1940–1944; RC Limited, *Annual Reports and Accounts*, 1946–1949; RC Limited, *Annual Report and Accounts for the Year Ended 30 June 1945*, 2–20.

Note: Nkana's Operating Surplus was arrived at after adding interest and sundry small items of revenue and deducting London Administrative charges and other expenses. Rhokana's investment profits from other mines in the region, and the balance brought forward from the Profit and Loss Account for the previous year, were added to the Operating Surplus from Nkana mine to determine the Corporation's Gross Profits either before or after deducting reserve amounts. Income Tax, Double Taxation, National Defense Contribution, and Preference Shares Redemption Funds were deducted from Gross Profits, while Dividends were calculated from Net Profits. In 1941 and 1943, Mufulira and Nchanga could not pay dividend profits to Rhokana owing to heavy taxation.

As Butler, Dumett, Phillips, and recently, Ronnback and Broberg, claimed, price controls, double taxation, EPT, and the national defense contribution had a negative impact on the Northern Rhodesian mining industry. For some scholars, "wartime financial measures, especially price controls and tax increases, severely cut into the industry's ability to finance expansion of mining operations and stifled reinvestments and improvements," as they reduced profit.[30] True, income tax, provision for double taxation, royalty, and EPT reduced the net profits and dividends. Between June 1940 and June 1945, Rhokana surrendered approximately £91,012.52 per month or £1,092,150.2 per year through heavy taxes.[31] By comparison, Britain was able to save almost £41.67 million per year and a gross of £250 million by the end of the war in terms of foreign exchange because of purchasing its copper within her empire.[32]

Because of heavy taxes, dividends paid to shareholders by Rhokana were reduced from 40% in 1940 to 25% per year throughout the war.[33] As indicated earlier, however, dividends totaled £4,495,002, which shows that Rhokana made a substantial amount of profit despite heavy taxes and price controls during the war. Therefore, the assertion by Butler, Dumett, Phillips, and Ronnback and Broberg that wartime financial measures corroded profits of the Copperbelt companies has been challenged previously, and the experience of Rhokana Corporation has been qualified.[34]

Operations and Profitability in the Immediate Postwar Period

Capital expenditure and African labor strength increased after 1944 but then stagnated until 1949, while labor costs increased throughout the postwar period (see table 3.2). Capital expenditure, labor force, and labor costs generally increased because of rehabilitation, construction, and developmental projects at Nkana after the war.[35] Even more, Rhokana and the Copperbelt companies continued to face a series of challenges, which impacted their productivity. The two major challenges for Rhokana were inadequate coal supplies from Wankie Colliery in Southern Rhodesia and railroad problems due to labor unrest and general wear and tear.[36] Thus, fuel and transport difficulties caused annual production costs per long ton of copper at Nkana to rise from an average of £31 during the war to £33 between 1946 and 1949.[37]

By contrast, international developments were much more positive, ushering Nkana and the other Copperbelt mines into a period of expansion. Unlike the aftermath of the First World War, a short-lived recession after 1945 did not result in the collapse of the copper market. The end of price controls in November 1946 saw the price of copper rise to an annual average of

£118.67 between 1946 and 1949, which was above the cost of production and transport.[38]

A number of factors drove the continued demand for copper. Postwar reconstruction increased demand in Europe, while in the USA, demand was spurred by booming electrical and automotive industries.[39] In addition, there was pent-up demand for copper immediately after the war, further compounded by the disruption of world production by strikes and high levels of consumption, especially in the USA.[40] Due to high levels of consumption, the USA suspended the copper tariff that was implemented from 1947 to 1949 to stimulate copper imports. The 44% devaluation of the British pound to curtail US dollar expenditure in 1949 also gave Nkana and the Copperbelt mines an added advantage, as copper prices rose by the same percentage.[41]

Another advantage of the devaluation of the pound was that the sales, which were quoted in American dollars but paid in British pounds, gained commensurately. The result was a double benefit, since prices on the New York market kept on increasing especially during the Korean War. At much the same time, Nkana and the Copperbelt mines were relieved from the burden of heavy taxes. National defense contribution and EPT ended in 1946, and from roughly this point, the financial position of the mines began to improve dramatically. Following the termination of the national defense contribution and EPT, coupled with the increase in copper prices, Rhokana announced net profits of £9,426,199 (see table 2.3) and paid total (interim and final) dividends averaging 86.25% per annum between 1946 and 1949.[42]

This section has demonstrated that, during the Second World War, the colonial government and the mining companies worked closely together in supporting the war effort. The Northern Rhodesian and British governments fixed the price of copper in London and introduced double taxation in the form of income tax in Britain, where the head offices of the companies were based, and in Northern Rhodesia, the host nation.[43] In addition, surcharges or EPT and the national defense contribution were introduced "as a way of curbing wartime profiteering," which had a significant impact on the profitability of Nkana and the Copperbelt mines. After the war, Nkana and the other Copperbelt mines were exhausted by wear and tear, as well as inadequate supplies of consumables, and this increased production costs.[44] Nonetheless, international developments were much more positive following the end of financial controls in the copper business and the devaluation of the pound sterling in September 1949, which indirectly increased the value of metals.[45]

The year 1949 also witnessed the birth of the African Mineworkers' Union (AMU), which had serious implications on industrial relations and labor costs on the Copperbelt.[46] Again, workers at Nkana mine played a vital role in the formation of the AMU.

RHOKANA/NKANA AND THE FORMATION OF THE AFRICAN MINEWORKERS' UNION, 1949

It took almost 12 years after the formation of the Northern Rhodesia Mineworkers' Union (NRMWU) for African mineworkers to form their recognized union. The formation of an African union was preceded by the African mineworkers' strikes in 1935 and 1940, through which black miners demonstrated signs of worker consciousness and organization. Workers from Nkana spearheaded the 1935 strike on the Copperbelt. For instance, false news about the success of the strikes at Mufulira and Nkana reached Roan through a letter delivered by an emissary. The emissary was believed to have been sent by Blackmore Musuku, Isaac Ngumbo, and Herbert Kamanga who worked as clerks at Nkana.[47]

Part of the evidence submitted before the commission of inquiry indicated that these gentlemen also connived with some leaders of the Mbeni Dance Society to boost morale during the strike action. During the 1940 strike, African workers demanded a wage increase of about 5s to 10s per shift. When the mine management refused, successive strikes occurred in the Copperbelt mines involving a total of 15,000 workers between March 24 and April 7.[48] Serious disturbances occurred at Nkana, involving about 3,000 strikers who fought running battles with the police. The police was almost defeated before firing live bullets, killing 13 and injuring 71 of the strikers.[49] The resultant Forster Commission of Inquiry stated, inter alia, in their report:

> For trades [*sic*] unionism, as trades [*sic*] unionism is generally understood by the British worker, the African worker in Northern Rhodesia is clearly not ready. The reason for this un-readiness is not far to seek. In no case has his education gone very far; in most instances, it has not even begun. Further, his introduction to industrialisation and industrial conditions is of a very recent date, too recent to admit of his intelligent participation in the more elaborate trades [*sic*] union system existing in Great Britain. It is nonetheless necessary that some scheme should be devised to make articulate mass grievances and to ensure that such mass grievances are properly brought to the notice of the managements. It is also desirable to devise a method whereby the African can be educated up to that point where his participation in his trades union will seem not only desirable but a natural and, indeed, an inevitable development.[50]

Because of the recommendations by the Forster Commission, the system of consultation between the mine managements and African tribal elders was developed into a general system of Tribal Representatives (TR).[51] The TR system was first established at Roan during the early years of stabilization and extended to Nkana, Mufulira, and Nchanga in 1942.[52] But the TR system became increasingly irrelevant for African miners since it was essentially designed to handle domestic conflicts in compounds, not industrial disputes. As a result, in 1943, daily-paid African workers rejected the TR system and formed Boss Boys' Committees (BBCs). BBCs evolved into Works Committees (WCs) in 1947, which represented African workers in all departments of the individual mines.[53] By then, there was anxiety in government and company circles concerning the growing power and influence of the African miners. Each protagonist tried to find the best method to control the African workers.[54]

In 1946, the NRMWU proposed deleting the word "European" from the Closed Shop Agreement in order to bring all African employees within its terms. This was because the European union "was sceptical as to the usefulness of a separate African Union in the mining industry."[55] However, the proposal was rejected by the Chamber of Mines as not being in the interests of African miners. In any case, neither government nor mining companies welcomed the prospect of a giant African and European trade union. Colonial officials in London and Lusaka were the most worried. Government officials and mine managers feared "that if workers [miners] in the colonies [mines] were left to themselves some might form communist [and South African] type unions."[56]

Colonial officials feared that communist trade unions would organize African workers to fight against colonial rule. South African type unionism, on the other hand, would not only entrench the job color bar for European miners but also antagonize African workers. These were the major reasons why, in March 1947, William Comrie, a British labor unionist, was appointed by the Colonial Office to promote moderate reformist trade unions for Africans in Northern Rhodesia.[57]

Within a month of his arrival, Comrie was successful in spreading, what Berger calls, the "gospel of trade-unionism" among Africans in the construction, retail, and mining industries.[58] As a result, shop assistants formed the first recognized African trade union in Northern Rhodesia. On the Copperbelt mines, Comrie aligned himself with core African groups composed of educated, foremen, clerks, orderlies, and interpreters.[59]

Out of each group, he chose a few disciples whom he entrusted with the mission. The first union for African miners on the Copperbelt was launched at Nkana in 1948 as the Nkana African Mineworkers' Union. Two major factors can help explain why the African trade union was launched at Nkana. The first was that Nkana-Kitwe is geographically located at the center of the Copperbelt mines, so it was convenient to operate from there. The second and possibly more important reason was that Nkana was home to African and European mineworkers who had taken a lead in industrial affairs on the Copperbelt.[60] Nkana African workers were the first to send a memorandum to Comrie and the Northern Rhodesian labor secretary advising them of the formation of an African miners' union (see figure 3.1).

Following the example by Africans at Nkana, African miners at Nchanga, Mufulira, and Roan formed their own unions. In May 1949, the four African mineworkers' unions were merged to form the Northern Rhodesia African Trade Union, commonly referred to as the AMU, with its head office at Nkana-Kitwe.[61] Lawrence Katilungu, from Nkana, became the first president of the Union. In August the same year, the Chamber of Mines signed, on behalf of RAA and Rhodesian Selection Trust (RST), an agreement recognizing the AMU as representing the interests of both companies' workers.

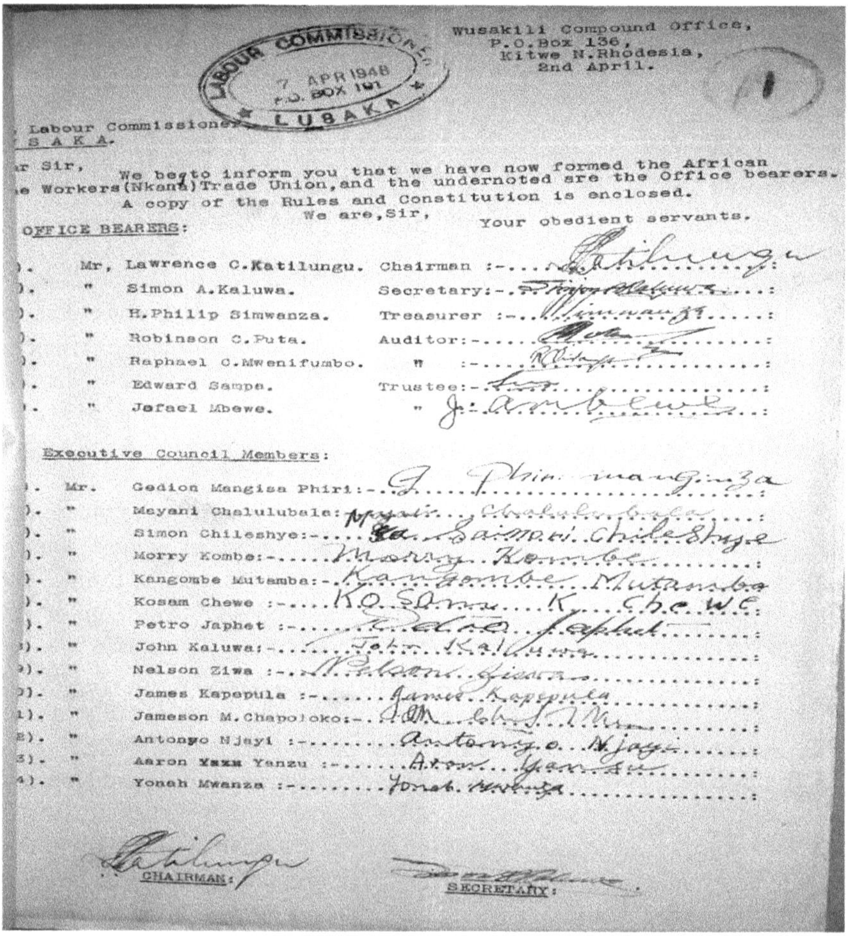

LABOUR COMMISSIONER 7 APR 1948 P.O. BOX 191 LUSAKA

Wusakili Compound Office,
P.O.Box 136,
Kitwe N.Rhodesia,
2nd April.

Labour Commissioner,
SAKA.

r Sir,
We beg to inform you that we have now formed the African e Workers(Nkana)Trade Union,and the undernoted are the Office bearers.
A copy of the Rules and Constitution is enclosed.
We are,Sir,
Your obedient servants.

OFFICE BEARERS:

Mr, Lawrence C.Katilungu. Chairman :-
" Simon A.Kaluwa. Secretary:-
" H.Philip Simwanza. Treasurer :-
" Robinson C.Puta. Auditor:-
" Raphael C.Mwenifumbo. " :-
" Edward Sampa. Trustee:-
" Jafael Mbewe. "

Executive Council Members:

Mr. Gedion Mangisa Phiri:-
" Meyani Chalulubale:
" Simon Chileshye:-
" Morry Kombe:-
" Kangombe Mutamba:-
" Kosam Chewe :-
" Petro Japhet :-
" John Kaluwa:-
" Nelson Ziwa :-
" James Kapepula :-
" Jameson M.Chapoloko:-
" Antonyo Njayi :-
" Aaron Yazu Yanzu :-
" Yonah Mwanza :-

CHAIRMAN:
SECRETARY:

Figure 3.1 Office bearers of the newly formed African Mineworkers' (Nkana) Trade Union, April 2, 1948. *Source:* Attachment to letter from Labour Commissioner, Lusaka, to the Chief Secretary of Labour Department, Lusaka, April 8, 1948, NAZ MLSS 1/26/18.

By then, the AMU had a membership of about 19,000 out of 33,656 black miners in the Copperbelt mines.[62] Nkana was the largest branch of the AMU with 7,068 members.

Between 1950 and 1953, the AMU made two major gains. To begin with, the AMU managed to gain an average wage increase of 70% for daily-paid African workers through a series of negotiations and arbitrations.[63] In 1953, African workers in the Copperbelt mines overwhelmingly voted for the abolishment of the TR system in the copper mines.[64] The mining companies wanted to maintain the TR system parallel to the AMU in order to weaken the union.[65] But through the power of the ballot, the AMU managed to get rid of the TR system.

Despite the foregoing semblance of unity, the AMU, like the NRMWU, experienced intra-union wrangles, leading to the formation of the Mines African Staff Association (MASA).[66] The idea of forming MASA was spearheaded by clerks and interpreters at Nkana shortly after the AMU was established. The key individual behind the formation of MASA and its first secretary general was Godwin Mbikusita Lewanika from Nkana mine.[67] The clerks and interpreters argued that, since they occupied senior posts, they should not belong to the same union as daily-paid workers. In May 1953, the mining companies and government were notified of the formation of the Rhokana African Staff Association, and similar branches were extended to the other copper mines. Despite welcoming the industrial politics of MASA, the mining companies only officially recognized MASA on December 3, 1955, after the African Advancement memorandum.[68] The Copperbelt mines delayed recognizing MASA "because of its small membership" and the original agreement between the mining companies and the AMU, which recognized the latter as the sole representative of African mineworkers.[69]

RHOKANA/NKANA AND THE KOREAN CRISIS, 1950–1953

The Korean War significantly affected all investment, production, marketing, sales, and taxation in the copper industry.[70] Washington and London passed legislation for appropriation on the basis of immediate need for copper to conduct the war in Asia.[71] Soaring demand for copper led to a shift in policy strategies, giving birth to a new era of modernization and expansion in the copper mining industry. This new era was characterized by, among other things, an emphasis on fostering new techniques for the discovery of mineral deposits, as the USA felt that, for security reasons such as combating the spread of communism, she should be prepared to invest in copper ventures abroad during the Cold War. This led to long-term trade agreements with producers at high prices that would assure them (producers) of better profit margins compared with the Second World War, when the price of copper in London was fixed.

Copper fitted into this general framework in several ways. First, the red metal is less indispensable in peacetime than it is in war. Copper along with other metals such as zinc and lead are basic raw materials of the electrical, building, motor car, shipbuilding, and general engineering industries. These industries, especially in America, forged rapidly ahead after the Second World War and increased production above prewar peaks.[72]

Second, copper was on the list of critical materials that the US government started to stockpile in earnest from mid-1948 onward.[73] Third, and most important, consumers' demand reacted quickly to the outbreak of the Korean War in 1950 and to the resulting prospect of substantial rearmament and accelerated stockpiling.[74] As stated earlier, copper is needed in great quantity in wartime for cartridge cases, shell bands, and fuses and is wanted extensively for electrical cables and wires utilized in batteries for armored vehicles, submarines, and aircrafts.[75]

United States' and Britain's Defense Mobilization Policies

The USA's defense mobilization policy was a purely strategic conception utilized for political purposes with the aim to combat the spread of communism in Asia and elsewhere in the world. For example, between 1950 and 1951, the US government agreed to buy 125,000 long tons of surplus Chilean copper, 50,000 tons from Northern Rhodesia, and another 50,000 tons from Canada for its stockpile to not only help these countries' economy but also check a possible growth of communism there.[76] This increased copper production and consumption due to expanded defense, civilian and industrial requirements, and competing with each other for scarce supplies. However, the Defense Production Act, which became law early in September 1950, gave the US president the power to regulate the economy to ensure adequate supplies of copper for expanded defense requirements.[77]

Pursuant to the Act, the Defense Minerals Administration (DMA) was established in the Department of the Interior to render government assistance to industry in expanding supplies of copper and other critical minerals and to act as claimant agency for the mining industry.[78] In the last quarter of 1950, the Defense Procurement Agency (DPA), a subsidiary of the DMA, entered into a number of negotiations with private companies locally and internationally for new copper production projects. In addition, the Office of Defense Mobilization requested for an expansion of mine output of over 300,000 long tons from major producers in the world.[79] Accordingly, three government departments, the Reconstruction Finance Corporation, Economic Corporation Administration

(ECA), and Export-Import Bank were established with over US$170 million, in direct loans "that would increase the nation's copper-mining capabilities by about 25%" and encourage investment abroad.[80] At the same time, the price of copper was increased from about 17 cents to 24.5 cents per pound in New York, while the 2 cents tariff on copper was removed to encourage imports.[81] Meanwhile, the consumption of copper in the USA more than tripled with demand surpassing supply despite production being maintained at 55%. As a result of its strategic stockpile, the USA was believed to hold upward of a million tons of copper by the end of the Korean War.[82]

The British government also started stockpiling copper for strategic purposes though not on the same scale as the American government. This was done by transferring its surplus trading stocks to the stockpile. The British government also allocated £140 million for purchasing strategic materials for stock.[83] Britain learnt that it was wise to lay in reserves of basic materials for "peace-time emergencies no less than those of war; and to do so when demand slackens [during the reconversion period] may be considered both helpful and a sound business move."[84] As a result, during the Korean Crisis, the British government disengaged itself from the control of supplies and prices for the United Kingdom market, which began in 1939 as a Second World War time measure.[85]

The British Ministry of Supply adopted US market prices after the devaluation of the pound sterling in 1949 and the continued closure of the London Metal Exchange (LME) during the Korean War. In the pre–Second World War days, the highly organized LME was an integral part of the pound sterling system. The pound sterling was directly convertible into almost any commodity of importance. The LME brought great benefit from earnings from financial, insurance, shipping, warehousing, and other services, not only in respect of metals sent to Britain but also from trade in metals all over the world.[86]

As mentioned earlier, during the Second World War, free trading on the LME was terminated because of government controls over production, labor, shipping, inland transport, consumption, and the war effort, in general.[87] After the war, much of the indecision over reopening the LME was linked with the argument that the pound sterling was no longer convertible and that the restored markets would not function effectively as a result of the devaluation of this currency.[88] Thus, Nkana and the other Copperbelt mines sold their copper and cobalt on the world market based on the US dollar quotation, which increased the value of these metals when converted into pounds.[89]

Investments in the Northern Rhodesian Copper Industry

US and British defense mobilization policies gave the mining companies a powerful impetus for the pursuit of their long-range objectives. Among

American companies abroad, the American Metal Company (AMC), later American Metal Climax (AMAX), in Northern Rhodesia benefited considerably from a US government loan of about US$12 million, with a contract to supply 50 million pounds of copper per year from 1951 to 1953.[90] One of the major benefits to Rhokana during this period was a loan worth £8 million to complete its power interconnection scheme to address fuel and power shortages.[91] The loan was partly repaid in supplies of copper and cobalt to the DPA/DMA of the US government.

While the Second World War and postwar demand for copper enabled the Copperbelt to develop, it was the huge demand for copper generated by the Korean War including huge strategic stockpiling purchases by the US government that stimulated a further search for, and development of, new mines and expansion of existing ones. For example, an extension program was launched at Nchanga to increase production to 64,000 long (72,000 short) tons of copper per year.[92] New companies were formed or planned to further exploit Northern Rhodesian mineral deposits, the first of which was the Chibuluma mine, a subsidiary of Mufulira. The ECA granted a loan, the equivalent of about £8 million to this company for developing the mine.[93] The firm would repay the agency in shipments of copper and cobalt to the US stockpile.[94] Active prospecting was being carried out by a new company, RST Services, on behalf of four other new companies formed in 1951 (Chisangwa, Mwinilunga, Kadola, and Luapula).[95] Several thousands of square miles west of existing copper mines were covered by the exclusive prospecting licenses granted to these companies by the British South Africa Company.

In addition to these investments, the US and British governments funded other projects in the entire region meant to meet the anticipated increased demand for mineral resources. In 1950, for example, the USA's ECA approved a technical assistance project to help the British government make a railway link between Rhodesia and East Africa in order to increase transportation of raw materials in the region.[96] The ECA and the British government financed the project jointly; ECA paid the dollar costs, estimated at US$40,000.[97] To alleviate continuing shortages of coal, owing in large part to inadequate transportation facilities, Rhodesia Railways received a £5 million ECA loan with provision that 21% "of Southern Rhodesia's output, when production of saleable coal and coke [at Wankie Colliery] equals 200,000 tons a month, was to be made available to Northern Rhodesian copper miners."[98]

As discussed elsewhere later, the Copperbelt companies assigned some of their own labor to the Wankie Colliery to alleviate its labor shortage and obtained additional coal as a result. The International Hydroelectric Power Commission recommended a gigantic hydroelectric power project to provide an eventual capacity of 1,000 megawatts.[99] The project would involve the creation of a lake 200 miles long at Kariba Gorge on the Zambezi River at an estimated cost of £174.5 million to supplement power deficits in the Copperbelt mines.[100]

Employment Opportunities, Wages, and Bonus Allowances in the Industry

The opening of new mines and expansion of existing ones, coupled with the international demand for copper following rearmament in the USA, created employment opportunities and also increased wages and bonus allowances as the mines stepped up production and increased working hours over the normal duration of eight hours per day. Table 3.4 shows the average number of African and European workers employed in the four producing mines on the Copperbelt between 1948 and 1952. Table 3.4 also indicates the percentage of married African workers, in particular, and the turnover rate of Africans, in general, in the mines. The African labor force in the Copperbelt mines increased significantly from 32,515 in 1948 to 35,736 in 1952. By comparison, the average number of European workers employed per annum increased substantially from 3,975 in 1948 to 5,427 by 1952.

The turnover rate of black labor in the four mines declined from 72.23% in 1949 to 56.60% in 1952, while the percentage of married men increased because of a drive toward the stabilization of black labor. But even as the

Table 3.4 African and European Labor Force and Percentage of Married African Employees at Nkana and in the Other Copperbelt Mines, 1948–1952.

Mine	*1948*		*1949*		*1950*		*1951*		*1952*	
Roan (RST)	A	E	A	E	A	E	A	E	A	E
No. Employed	10,782	1,249	11,136	1,370	11,275	1,424	10,359	1,479	10,074	1,510
% Married	54.40	–	49.40	–	53.75	–	58.50	–	63.65	–
Mufulira (RST)	A	E	A	E	A	E	A	E	A	E
No. Employed	7,526	966	7,734	1,017	8,769	1,113	8,548	1,231	8,893	1,276
% Married	56.40	–	58.30	–	61.42	–	62.13	–	62.84	–
Nchanga (RAA)	A	E	A	E	A	E	A	E	A	E
No. Employed	4,155	502	4,559	581	5,449	672	5,826	819	5,907	894
% Married	44.32	–	45.78	–	52.89	–	58.27	–	55.27	–
Nkana (RAA)	A	E	A	E	A	E	A	E	A	E
No. Employed	10,052	1,258	10,227	1,334	10,837	1,440	11,295	1,560	10,862	1,747
% Married	51.13	–	44.56	–	45.50	–	45.47	–	51.33	–
Turnover (%)	65.22	–	72.23	–	56.31	–	57.90	–	56.60	–

Source: Compiled from NRMD, *Annual Report for the Year 1952* (Lusaka: NRMD, 1952), 25, NAZ ML 8/4/18; RC Limited, *Utilisation of African Labour Report*, January 8, 1957, 28, ZCCM 3.8.1C; RAA Limited, *Reports of the Directors and Statement of Accounts*, 1948–1953, ZCCM 12.6.1E; RST Limited, *Reports and Accounts*, 1948–1953, ZCCM 12.6.1E; Phillips, "Roan Antelope," Table 31, 368.

Note: "A" stands for African and "E" for European workers.

mechanization and the stabilization of labor improved the efficiency reliability of black workers, some labor was discharged to reduce costs.

Nkana, though, continued to rely on both stabilized labor and migrant labor compared with Roan and Mufulira, which relied more on the former. This can be seen from the percentage of married men, which is more or less stable at Nkana, but growing in the other three mines, if less so at Nchanga, between 1948 and 1952. By comparison, married men tended to work longer periods than single men, not only because of the former's wider responsibilities to their families but also their being accompanied by their wives.[101] But single men were cheaper to maintain than married men. Stabilized labor consisted of married men, while migrant labor consisted of more single men.[102] Therefore, Nkana relied on both stabilized labor and migrant labor to offset the higher cost of the former.

However, the formation of the AMU in 1949 had increased the bargaining power of the African workers who fought for better wages and conditions of service. In 1950, a deadlock between the AMU and the mining companies over the need for an increase in wages resulted in a series of commissions of inquiry. The most important of these was the Guillebaud Commission, which recommended a wage increase of 77% for surface and 63% for underground African workmen across the Copperbelt mines.[103] Thus, the ratio of European to African wages per employee in the Copperbelt mines fell from approximately 18:1 in 1950 to 14:1 by 1953.[104] Table 3.5 shows the total and average earnings of European and African employees of the Northern Rhodesian copper mining industry between 1950 and 1953.

European workers were also expensive at this time because they had the skills not yet acquired by African laborers. Despite the high wages paid to attract skilled European workers, the Copperbelt mines were low-cost producers largely because of low African wages.[105] By one calculation, a 50% increase in African emoluments only contributed 5% of the total production costs.[106] Overall, labor on the Copperbelt was still cheaper than in America (Canada, Chile, and the USA) and Europe.[107]

Still, it can be seen that the wage bill on the Copperbelt mines more than doubled during the Korean War from £6,866,526 in 1950 to £14,526,268 in 1953 (see table 3.5). In 1950, basic wages accounted for 52.39%, while bonus allowances, overtime payments, and other earnings amounted to 47.61% of total cash earnings on the Copperbelt mines. But, in 1953, basic wages amounted to 48.53% of total labor costs, while overtime payments, bonus allowances, and other related expenses accounted for the remainder, which was the highest. In addition to Mhone's assertion that labor costs on the Copperbelt increased because of significant improvements in basic wages after the Second World War, bonus allowances, overtime expenses, and other

Table 3.5 Earnings of European and African Workers in the Copperbelt Mines in Pounds, 1950–1953.

Year	*1950*		*1951*		*1952*		*1953*	
Description	*Eur.*	*African*	*Eur.*	*African*	*Eur.*	*African*	*Eur.*	*African*
Basic Wages	2,414,248	1,182,964	2,863,389	1,436,225	3,669,431	1,568,812	4,450,881	2,598,959
Leave Pay	243,245	–	288,068	–	432,338	–	578,223	–
Half Basic Shift Payments	41,516	–	51,448	–	50,632	–	38,372	–
Contract Earnings	200,136	–	223,036	–	215,462	–	219,727	–
Copper Bonus	861,928	–	1,543,075	188,329	2,485,553	205,487	3,730,018	252,831
Cost of Living/Food Provided	758,824	734,131	1,006,452	891,481	646,818	1,130,513	563,630	1,262,292
Holiday Bonus	14,236	32,834	16,142	67,717	34,427	73,233	37,873	94,156
Overtime Payments	183,695	160,142	280,941	181,153	379,140	184,029	377,305	238,326
Other Payments	32,447	6,180	42,630	2,556	59,813	2,629	59,952	23,723
Total Earnings	4,750,275	2,116,251	6,315,181	2,767,461	7,973,614	3,164,703	10,055,981	4,470,287
Earnings per Employee	1,068	61	1,275	78	1,500	86	1,782	124
No. of Workers	4,448	34,814	4,955	35,432	5,317	36,668	5,700	36,147

Source: Taken from NRCM, *Northern Rhodesia Chamber of Mines Yearbook 1956* (Kitwe: NRCM, 1957), 69, 76, ZCCM 12.1.9C.

Note: The Copper Bonus was based on the price of copper. After 1950, Africans were paid Prosperity Bonuses, which were similar to Copper Bonuses awarded to European workers. Overtime Payments for African workers comprised overtime allowances, task bonuses, and efficiency awards. Other Payments for Africans included amounts paid on Safety Bonuses.

related payments contributed almost half of the total wage bill per year, especially during the Korean War.[108]

In order to compensate wage increases, the Copperbelt mines substituted machinery for labor.[109] Thus, investment in machinery and other capital projects at Nkana increased capital expenditure for Rhokana Corporation from £891,202 in 1950 to £2,968,000 in 1953, while after 1951, the African labor force reduced (see tables 3.4, 3.5, and 3.8).[110]

Operating Costs vis-à-vis the Price of Copper

Nkana and the other Copperbelt mines were ready to produce copper to meet the demands of the Korean Crisis. Even so, the Copperbelt mines could not escape labor, power, and transport problems. For many years, these mines relied on power stations and smelters, which mainly depended on coal supplies from Wankie Colliery in Southern Rhodesia. After the Second World War, however, coal supplies from Wankie were irregular, not because of any lack in reserves but due to strikes and equipment problems, coupled with a shortage of rolling stock on the Rhodesia Railways.[111] The shortfalls were severe, at times forcing the mines to burn firewood. The situation worsened between 1950 and 1951, when coal deliveries from the Wankie Colliery to the Copperbelt mines dropped from a monthly average of 40,700 tons to 37,000 tons.[112]

As mentioned elsewhere earlier, Nkana and the Copperbelt mines, with the help of financial assistance from the US and British governments, undertook short- and long-term measures to ease fuel and transport problems. Wood burning enabled Nkana to save about 55,886 tons of coal per annum between 1950 and 1953. To facilitate Wankie Colliery's recovery, Nkana, Roan, Mufulira, and Nchanga agreed to an increase in the price of coal from 14.3s per short ton to 19s.[113] The Copperbelt mines made a further contribution to the Colliery by training and sending workers there to alleviate labor shortages. In 1951, the mines constructed a hydroelectric power station on the Lualaba River in the Belgian Congo to help meet their energy requirements.[114] Rhokana also acquired 25% shares in the Rhodesia Congo Border Power Corporation.[115] Finally, in March 1953, the Anglo American Corporation (AAC) acquired a majority shareholding in the Wankie Colliery Company and took over its management.[116] Following the acquisition of the Wankie by the AAC, coal output increased to over 50,000 tons per month and, in the third quarter of 1953, supplied the Copperbelt mines with 74% of their requirements.[117]

In addition to fuel and transport challenges, Nkana, Nchanga, Roan, and Mufulira were now mining at a greater depth, as top-layer deposits on the Copperbelt were worked out. In the mid-1950s, the RST and RAA mines had produced almost 239,285,714.29 long tons of ore and driven close to

3,000 miles of underground workings.[118] One shaft at Nkana was 1,100 miles deep, making this mine the deepest on the Copperbelt.[119] Similarly, Roan was over 1,000 miles deep; Mufulira, over 590 miles; and, Nchanga, nearly 290 miles.[120] With increased depth, conditions deteriorated, aggravated by flooding and lower ore grades. The grade of ore hoisted at Nkana dropped from an average of 3.6% copper in 1936 to 2.8% in 1953.[121]

Because of all these problems, production costs at Nkana per long ton of copper increased from an average of £33 between 1946 and 1949 to £57.1 between 1950 and 1953.[122] By comparison, operating costs per long ton of copper on the Copperbelt increased from an average of £59.2 in 1950 to £101.1 in 1953.[123] Table 3.6 compares operating costs in the Copperbelt mines and the price of copper on the world market.

As production and transport costs increased, the Copperbelt mines' profitability would have declined between 1950 and 1953. However, the Korean Crisis turned the situation around and brought about greater demand and higher copper prices. It is necessary to take account of the factors that pushed the price of copper prior to the Korean Crisis.

As mentioned in the preceding subsection, after the Second World War (1946–1949), countries sought to rebuild and re-equip their houses, factories, and industries, which increased both the demand and the price of copper.[124] The United Nations Relief and Rehabilitation (1943–1947), the devaluation of the pound (1949), the Marshall Aid (1948–1952), and inflationary and full employment policies in most countries in general had supplied the economic lubricants.[125] As a result, general industrial activity in the world had by 1950 risen to a level about 50% above the pre–Second World War basis.[126] Thus, high demand was already showing signs of outstripping raw material resources.

While it is worth noting that most of the post–Second World War rise in copper prices took place before the Korean War started, it must be remembered

Table 3.6 Operating Costs in the Copperbelt Mines and Average Price of Copper in London, 1950–1953.

Years	*1950*	*1951*	*1952*	*1953*
Price per long ton in London (£)	179.0	220.7	259.5	256.3
Nkana's Operating Cost per ton (£)	40.5	47.5	63.0	77.4
Roan's Operating Cost per ton (£)	73.1	81.4	90.9	112.7
Mufulira's Operating Cost per ton (£)	64.0	82.0	89.0	113.2
Average Cost all Three Mines (£)	59.2	70.3	81.0	101.1

Source: Compiled from RC Limited, *Utilisation of African Labour Report,* Table 7; NRCM, *Northern Rhodesia Chamber of Mines Yearbook 1956,* 60; RST Limited, *Reports and Accounts,* 1950–1953; Phillips, "Roan Antelope," Table 21, 298.

Note: The Operating Costs for Nchanga are not available in the sources utilized. However, the trend can still be seen from the figures provided.

that it was only after the beginning of hostilities around mid-1950 that the high free prices of copper developed. The Korean War and accelerated rearmament not only foreshadowed further direct increases of demand for copper but also, at the same time, "stimulated fear of shortages and frantic buying by industry and by governments all over the world."[127]

The USA emerged as an importer of the red metal on the grand scale, with net imports (i.e., imports less exports) of 440,000 long tons in 1950.[128] The high demand for raw materials and upsurge of prices polarized the market with many different prices: "black market" prices, "grey market" prices, "controlled" prices, "official" prices, and "maximum" prices.[129] High demand improved the price of copper on the Commodity Metal Exchange (COMEX) in New York, averaging 19.1 cents a pound/£153 a long ton in January 1950, before increasing substantially to a record of 25.25 cents per pound/£202 per ton in September the same year.[130]

The increase in the price of copper in New York had knock-on effects on the price of the red metal elsewhere. Copper prices soared in London from an annual average of £118.7 per long ton between 1946 and 1949 to almost double at an annual average of £228.9 between 1950 and 1953 (see table 3.6).[131] The price of copper per ton in London tripled, far exceeding any increase in operating costs for the Copperbelt mines (see table 3.6). The fall of prices in 1953 (see table 3.6) was not due to the reopening of the LME; rather, it was the aftermath of the feverish Korean buying spree of 1951 and 1952.[132]

Copper Production and Sales

Because of these combined factors, the period between 1950 and 1953 saw greater copper output and sales for the Copperbelt mines than ever before. Up to 1950, the mine output of world copper producers had barely exceeded pre–Second World War levels. The highest pre–Second World War mine output in the world excluding Soviet Russia was 2,140,000 long tons in 1937.[133]

It was not until 1950 that output at 2,240,000 long tons rose above the 1937 rate.[134] Of this figure, the USA produced 810,000 long tons of copper, followed by Chile at 365,000 tons, Northern Rhodesia ranked in third place at 260,000 long tons, Canada in fourth position at 236,000 tons, Belgian Congo at 175,000 tons ranked fifth, and the rest of the world produced the remainder (394,000 tons).[135] Table 3.7 indicates copper produced and sold by the four major mines on the Copperbelt.

Total copper production was 1,186,749 long tons, of which 26.26% came from Nkana, 26.10% from Mufulira, 25.82% from Roan, and 21.82% from Nchanga (see table 3.7). By this time, the other three big mines were catching up with Nkana in terms of copper production. Mufulira surpassed Roan and was closing in on Nkana. Similarly, Nchanga was closing in on Roan.

Table 3.7 Copper Production and Sales for the Copperbelt Mines in Long Tons, 1950–1953.

	Rhodesian Anglo American				*Rhodesian Selection Trust*			
	Nkana/Rhokana		*Nchanga*		*Roan Antelope*		*Mufulira*	
Year	*Produced*	*Sold*	*Produced*	*Sold*	*Produced*	*Sold*	*Produced*	*Sold*
1950	80,540	76,667	38,761	38,761	63,557	62,059	77,048	87,875
1951	74,179	81,296	58,052	58,052	74,520	74,520	86,681	105,193
1952	82,764	83,025	68,816	68,816	81,027	81,027	76,369	76,369
1953	74,216	72,165	93,317	93,317	87,307	87,307	69,559	72,981
Total	311,699	313,153	258,946	258,946	306,693	304,913	309,693	342,418

Source: Compiled from NRMD, *Annual Reports,* 1951–1953; RC Limited, *Annual Reports and Accounts together with Statements by the Chairman,* 1950–1953, ZCCM 12.7.2F; RAA Limited, *Reports of the Directors and Statements of Accounts,* 1950–1953, ZCCM 19.2.4F; RST Limited, *Reports and Accounts,* 1950–1953, ZCCM 12.6.1E; Phillips, "Roan Antelope," Table 29, 366.

Note: Copper "Produced" refers to output of salable or finished metal (blister cakes and electrolytic cathodes) and not molten blister copper or primary production.

As indicated elsewhere earlier, investment in mine development on the Copperbelt following the outbreak of the Korean War improved production at Nchanga and Mufulira. Nchanga, in particular, was transformed from an underground mine to an open-pit mine, and its production improved significantly from a meager 38,761 long tons of the red metal at the start of the Korean War to a staggering 93,317 tons by the end of the war (see table 3.7).

Nchanga became the largest producer on the Copperbelt from 1953 onward. By world standards, Nchanga became the second-largest opencast mine after Chuquicamata in Chile, while Mufulira became the second-largest underground mine after El Teniente, also in Chile.[136] Nkana, however, made more profit than the three Copperbelt producers. In addition to copper production, Nkana produced and sold 6,889 short tons of cobalt alloy containing 2,803 short tons of cobalt metal whose price increased from an annual average of 15.6s per pound in 1949 to 20s between 1950 and 1953.[137]

In this period, the Copperbelt mines supplied 1,219,430 long tons of copper, which was 32,681 above what was produced (see table 3.7). It is evident that high demand fueled by the Korean War gave the mining companies, especially Nkana and Mufulira, an opportunity to sell previously accumulated stockpiles. As stated elsewhere earlier, this surge of demand broadly accounted for metal users' dissatisfaction with meager stocks, rationed supplies, and very high marginal prices.

Gross Profits, Income Taxes, and Net Profits

Table 3.8 indicates capital expenditure, value of sales, cost of sales, royalty/export tax, and operating profit of Nkana during the Korean War. Its operating

Table 3.8 Capital Expenditure, Value/Cost of Sales, Royalty/Export Tax, and Operating Profits for Nkana Mine between 1950 and 1953.

Year	*Capital Expenditure (£)*	*Value of Sales (£)*	*Cost of Sales (£)*	*Royalty/Export Tax and Others (£)*	*Operating Profit (£)*
1950	891,202	12,768,647	5,723,225	4,787,364	5,702,620
1951	–	18,172,913	7,266,867	6,177,847	9,047,908
1952	–	21,135,626	9,012,189	7,764,474	10,074,080
1953	2,968,000	22,026,344	9,943,179	8,729,678	9,885,159

Source: Compiled from NRMD, *Annual Report for the Year 1952*, 25; Secretary of the Northern Rhodesia Chamber of Mines to Divisional General Managers, May 21, 1953; RC Limited, *Utilisation of African Labour Report*, 4; RC Limited, *Annual Reports*, 1950–1953; Rhodesian Anglo America (RAA) Limited, *Annual Reports and Accounts*, 1950–1953, ZCCM 19.2.4F; *Northern News*, April 10, 1952; C. Turner et al., "Rhokana Corporation, Very Satisfactory Year: Increased Distribution," *Joint Stock Companies' Journal*, December 3, 1952; Daniel, *Africanisation, Nationalisation and Inequality*, 71.

Note: Figures on new capital expenditure for the financial years 1951 to 1952 are unavailable from the sources utilized.

profit almost doubled from £5,702,620 during the 1950 financial year to a record peak of £10,074,080 in 1952.

As indicated earlier, the first major reason behind Nkana's profitability was that this mine sold both copper and cobalt on the world market. The second major contributing factor to its overall profitability was the fact that the mother company, Rhokana, owned substantial shares in other mines and properties on the Copperbelt. In this period, combined retained profits from other mines and properties amounted to £6,952,968 or 16.5% of the total gross profit and one-third of the total net profit (see table 3.9).[138] The third contributing factor was double taxation relief due to Rhokana's emigration from Britain, where part of its management and control was based, to Northern Rhodesia in January 1951.[139] Because of this emigration, the Revenue Authorities regarded half of the dividends as free-of-tax payments, which increased distributable profits from 1951 onward (see table 3.9).[140]

Rhokana's income increased throughout the Korean Crisis. According to table 3.9, net profits from copper and cobalt after taxation rose from about £3.7 million in 1950 to a staggering £8.8 million in 1953. The corresponding declared dividend rates improved significantly from 120% to 225%, respectively.[141] Similarly, the holding company, RAA, reported a £6.5 million record gross profit increase to £21.3 million, while its final declared dividend rose from 55% in 1951 to 62.5% in 1952.[142]

These good returns were not only experienced by these multinational mining companies. Roberts notes that, between 1947 and 1953, the value of copper sales for the Copperbelt mines more than tripled from £31 million to £116 million, while mining taxes accounted for 57.5% of Northern Rhodesia's total revenue.[143] Indirect and direct benefits from the mining industry in the form of local expenditure and taxation increased from £21,164,448 in 1951 to a record £38,141,134 in 1953.[144]

Table 3.9 Rhokana's Issued Share Capital, Gross Profits, Net Profits, and Dividends, 1950–1953.

	Corporation's Share Capital and Gross Profits				*Income Tax, Net Profits, and Dividends*		
		Nkana Mine	*Other Mines*				
Year	*Issued Share Capital (£)*	*Operating Profit (£)*	*Profits Received (£)*	*Gross Profits (£)*	*Income Tax (£)*	*Net Profits (£)*	*Net Dividends (£)*
1950	3,929,820	5,702,620	1,021,718	6,687,165	3,590,223	3,657,212	1,693,463
1951	3,929,820	9,047,908	1,200,000	10,483,687	3,718,292	8,130,616	5,060,950
1952	3,342,327	10,074,080	2,071,250	12,241,357	4,255,535	7,860,922	5,687,488
1953	3,334,841	9,885,159	2,660,000	12,751,084	4,219,784	8,845,376	5,671,126

Source: Compiled from NRMD, *Annual Report for the Year 1952,* 25; Secretary of the Northern Rhodesia Chamber of Mines to Divisional General Managers, May 21, 1953; RC Limited, *Annual Reports,* 1950–1953; RAA Limited, *Annual Reports and Accounts,* 1950–1953; *Investors' Guardian,* October 25, 1952; *East Africa and Rhodesia,* November 27, 1952; *Northern News,* April 10, 1952; Ernest Oppenheimer, "Rhokana Corporation Limited," *South African Mining and Engineering Journal* 65, no. 3225 (1954): 599.

Note: Between 1950 and 1953, Rhokana received a total of £6,952,968 profits from its investments in other properties on the Copperbelt. Of this figure, Nchanga and Mufulira copper mines contributed a combined total of £5,000,000.

CONCLUSION

The corporate structure and profitability of Rhokana, in particular, and the copper industry of Northern Rhodesia, in general, were transformed by the effects of the Second World War, Korean Crisis, and the formation of the AMU between 1939 and 1953. In the period under review, Nkana continued to be the center of the labor movement in the Copperbelt mines. Looking at the causes and course of the 1935 and 1940 African strikes, black workers at Nkana proved the most militant of all the Copperbelt mines. The events leading to the formation of the NRMWU (see chapter 2) and the AMU suggest that the Nkana's white and black workers were prominent leaders in the industrial politics of the Copperbelt mines. Not surprisingly, then, "all eyes were set on Nkana/Rhokana" and its role in the mining sector in the Central African Federation. This is discussed in the next chapter.

Chapter 4

Rhokana/Nkana and the Political Economy of the Central African Federation, 1953–1963

RHOKANA/NKANA AND THE FORMATION OF THE CENTRAL AFRICAN FEDERATION

> Rhokana Corporation is one of the most important commercial units in the new Federation of Rhodesia and Nyasaland, and the future of one is inextricably bound up with the future of the other . . . In differing degrees, they will both be confronted with difficult practical problems and the political issues, and it is in the interest of both that wise European leadership and imaginative planning should be applied to ensuring the wellbeing of industry and individuals alike in the Federal territories. I am confident that the right men and the right methods are, and will continue to be, available to deal with the tasks that lie ahead.
>
> —Sir Ernest Oppenheimer, June 1954[1]

The birth of the Federation of Rhodesia and Nyasaland in 1953 had a long gestation period dating back to the 1930s. At that time, the Copperbelt mining companies opposed the idea of closer cooperation among the three Central African territories because they did not favor the color bar policies promoted in industrial relations in Southern Rhodesia. Rhokana, Roan, and Mufulira argued that labor policies in Southern Rhodesia were:

> completely opposed to the policy of the [Northern Rhodesian] mining companies and to the native policy of the colonial office [which] allowed and encouraged [the native] to do such work as he is capable of doing and no colour bar industrial legislation exist[ed].[2]

The mining companies further emphasized that the principle of closed shop was not in operation in Northern Rhodesia since they refused to countenance it in spite of persistent demands by the Northern Rhodesia Mineworkers' Union (NRMWU).[3] They favored the principle of open shop, which they enshrined in their agreement with the NRMWU to "prevail at all mines in the Copperbelt for a period of two years from the 20th [of] September 1937."[4] In a letter dated March 17, 1938, to the Secretary of the Bledisloe Commission, Rhokana's Management stated that it favored "a continuance of the separate administration of Northern Rhodesia."[5] Partly because of these objections, the idea of amalgamation of Rhodesia and Nyasaland failed.

In the late 1940s and early 1950s, the colonial government and settlers revived the idea of closer association of the three Central African territories. This time, the idea of a federation coincided with the change in leadership and management styles in the Copperbelt mines, and the Copperbelt mining companies now supported the vision. In this regard, Navin noted that "the old guard, most of them the surrogate heirs of the founders, was passing and was being replaced mostly by engineers promoted from within."[6]

By then, Ernest Oppenheimer, chairman of Rhokana's parent company, Anglo American Corporation (AAC), was close to retirement. His son, Harry Frederick Oppenheimer, was becoming instrumental in the affairs of AAC in Central Africa. H.F. Oppenheimer sat on the Board of Directors of the AAC and Rhokana from 1947 onward.[7] In addition, he was elected member of parliament for Kimberley on the ticket of the opposition, the white-dominated United Party in South Africa in 1948.[8] In 1951, Oliver B. Bennett, who had worked as an engineer for Rhokana since 1936, was appointed general manager of the Corporation.[9] Meanwhile, Chester A. Beatty retired as Rhodesian Selection Trust (RST) managing director and was succeeded by Ronald Prain, who was also associated with the operations of RST's mines "for virtually his entire working life."[10]

Compared with the old guard, who were generally conservative in their style of management and policy, the new leaders were liberal thinkers with new ideas in line with current trends in the political and economic environment. Harry Oppenheimer "believed apartheid was an impractical solution to the problem of achieving a successful multi-racial society."[11] Consequently, he supported the idea of partnership among the races in the Federation, hoping it would provide a model for South Africa. Like Oppenheimer, Bennett was a liberal of sorts, politically close to Roy Welensky, who later became Federal prime minister. In 1962, Bennett resigned as general manager of Rhokana upon being appointed minister for Central African Federation Affairs in the United States of America (USA).[12]

The managers of the Copperbelt mines felt that their mines could benefit from the idea of partnership among races.[13] Their liberal ideology fitted squarely with the British government's idea of partnership among races in Central Africa. To the British government, federation was viewed "as a middle way between the extremes of Black nationalism to the north and Afrikaner racial ideas to the South."[14] In this vein, federation would promote a multiracial partnership in the three Central African territories. Through a limited franchise, "the Federation would, in theory, allow for gradually increasing African political participation, while preserving effective white hegemony for the foreseeable future."[15]

In particular, the RST management felt that close association, especially between the two Rhodesias, would be a means of curbing the "growing power [and demands] of settler politicians, many of whom were sponsored by, or linked to, the [NR]MWU."[16] Under these conditions, federation would "create a more balanced political climate, embracing a broader range of local opinion."[17] Besides, federation would be a way of not only strengthening minority control through closer association but also ensuring stability in the three Central African territories.[18]

White settlers in Central Africa had their own notion of racial partnership between Africans and Europeans. It is worth noting that the concept of racial partnership was at that time under scrutiny due to the changes in global racial ideology resulting from the fall of Nazi Germany and Fascist Italy after the Second World War, as well as the formation of the United Nations Organisation (UNO) and the rise of Apartheid South Africa.[19] According to the UNO, "Africans had become equals to Europeans in their humanity. Europeans and their institutions were everywhere under scrutiny for the possibility that they were racist."[20]

It was in this context that white politicians in Central Africa established the Federation of Rhodesia and Nyasaland based on "a racial partnership that was only a smoke screen for continued racial domination."[21] Godfrey Huggins, prime minister of Southern Rhodesia and later first Federal prime minister, notoriously referred to this policy as one of "[black] horse and [white] rider in which African beasts of burden would be ridden toward economic development and prosperity by Europeans."[22] Thus, Africans "ruefully noted the accuracy of the saying," and Harry M. Nkumbula of the Northern Rhodesia African National Congress (NRANC) and other black politicians rejected it from the start.[23] Indeed, the idea of racial partnership in Central Africa was extremely limited in practice.

There were also compelling economic factors for Rhokana and the Copperbelt mines to accept the idea of a federation. First, they were attracted by coal and transport networks in Southern Rhodesia.[24] Nyasaland was to remain one of the main sources of cheap but productive African labor, given that Nyasas were among the most experienced Africans in the Southern African mining industry.[25] By joining the Federation, Northern Rhodesia's Copperbelt mines would have unfettered and preferential access to Nyasa labor and thus would be able to elbow out South Africa, which had so long been their biggest threat and competitor in this regard. Second, the Copperbelt companies felt that white control of the three territories would assure foreign investors that Central Africa was a safe place in which to invest.[26] The AAC and RST believed that in this way the region would attract overseas capital, which was crucial for boosting the economic profile of the territory, in general, and the mines, in particular.[27]

For these reasons, the mining companies offered financial support toward the formation of the Central African Federation (CAF). Between 1950 and 1953, the AAC and RST contributed a shared total of £10,000 to the United Central Africa Association for Central African Federation (UCAA), led by Godfrey Huggins and Roy Welensky as president and vice president, respectively, to campaign for the Federation in the territories.[28] Meanwhile, by 1952, the two mining houses shifted their offices from London to Lusaka because of two major reasons: first, the fear of double taxation, and second, to fully identify with the host nation.[29]

Rhokana followed in the footsteps of its parent company, AAC, and became incorporated in Northern Rhodesia on May 11, 1954, thus ceasing to be incorporated in Britain.[30] In 1956, the AAC and RST shifted their corporate offices to Salisbury, then the Federal capital. Rhokana also transferred its head office to Salisbury on August 5, 1957, where the AAC had an established office at Charter House.[31]

RHOKANA AND THE FEDERAL POLITICAL ECONOMY

Federal corporate tax came from seven industries, namely, mining, agriculture, manufacturing, construction, transport, communications, and service. Nkana and the Copperbelt mines were the major sources of Federal and territorial revenues in the form of income tax and heavy customs duties on imported supplies. The capital raised in this manner funded Federal projects, infrastructure development, and the provisioning of services in member states.[32] Nkana and the Copperbelt mines paid taxes to the Federal government, as well as a surcharge in the form of additional tax to the Northern Rhodesian government.[33]

In 1954, the initial tax rate imposed by the Federal government on copper profits was 7.6s in the pound and remained identical to the previous Northern Rhodesian Income Tax Ordinance.[34] The Copperbelt mines also indirectly provided much of the tax paid by Wankie Colliery, the Rhodesia Railways, and the British South African (BSA) Company in the territory.[35] In 1955, the Copperbelt mines used over 28% of the coal and coke from Wankie, provided 58.5% of tonnage by Rhodesia Railways, and consumed 66% of the electricity produced.[36]

The BSA Company was also a big taxpayer. The Federal government guaranteed the terms of the 1950 Agreement, which the BSA Company entered into with the British and Northern Rhodesian governments. The agreement allowed the BSA Company to enjoy its royalties until 1986.[37] In return, the Northern Rhodesia government was awarded 20% of the BSA Company royalties.[38] Under this new agreement, "royalties on the copper content of mined ore were payable according to a formula of 13.5% of the average London Metal Exchange [LME] quotation per long ton, less £8."[39] Income tax paid to the Federal government by the Copperbelt mines, BSA Company, and their employees averaged about 28% of total revenue per year.[40]

The CAF economy was also bound up with copper in terms of its contribution to the region's total exports and Net Domestic Product (NDP). In 1955, copper accounted for 94% of the exports of Northern Rhodesia and 63% of the total exports of the Federation.[41] In addition to being the largest copper producer in the Federation, Northern Rhodesia was the largest copper producer in the Commonwealth and the second largest in Africa after the Belgian Congo.[42] Apart from copper and cobalt, the biggest export in the Federation was unmanufactured tobacco, which, in 1955, accounted for nearly 15% of the region's total exports.[43]

In 1955, the NDP of Northern Rhodesia was £165 million and of the Federation as a whole £348 million.[44] The NDP of the mining industry represented 61% of the NDP of Northern Rhodesia and 34% of the NDP of the Federation. By comparison, agriculture accounted for 14%, secondary industry amounted to 19%, while service, transport, and other forms of trade accounted for 33% or a third of the Federation's NDP.[45]

By 1953, Rhokana was already a large and complex organization, bigger than any of the other Copperbelt mines.[46] Its overall operations were enormous by world standards. Nkana mine and mill handled over 360,000 tons of copper per month, while the smelter processed about 16,000 tons. Rhokana also smelted copper from Nchanga mine. By comparison, Mufulira had the second-largest smelter on the Copperbelt, capable of processing 10,000 tons of copper per month.[47] Rhokana had the largest copper refinery on the Copperbelt, capable of handling over 13,000 short tons of copper per month, while its cobalt plant produced 100 short tons per month.[48]

Among the mines in the Federation, Nkana was the largest employer, with about 10,000 workers.[49] The biggest corporation in the mining industry (see figure 4.1), Rhokana, generated more tax revenue than any other firm in the Federation. At the same time, Rhokana was the consulting engineer to all the Copperbelt mines. Nchanga and Mufulira were among the largest mines not only in the Federation but also in the world, and Rhokana owned about 33.6% and 26.6% shares in them, respectively. These shares provided about one-third of Rhokana's net profits between 1953 and 1963.

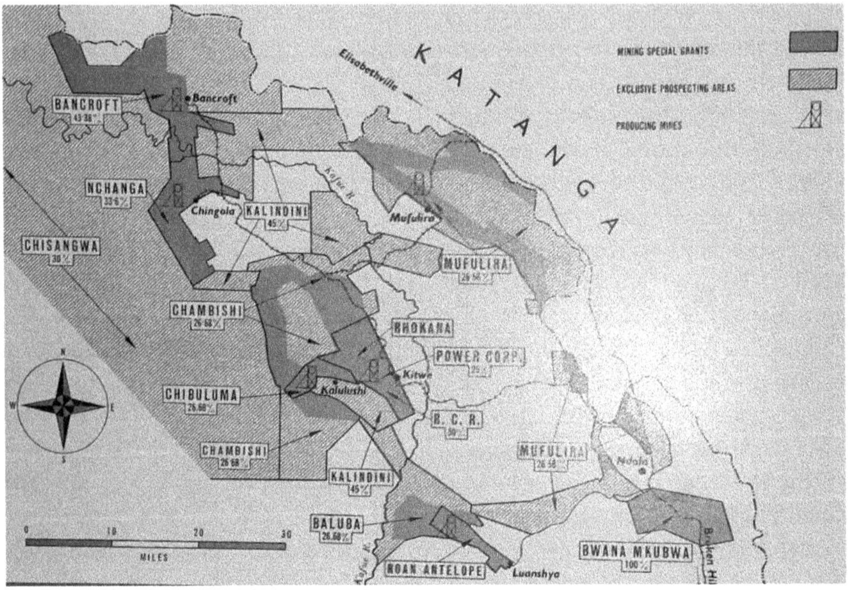

Figure 4.1 Rhokana Corporation interests in the Copperbelt, 1953. The shares were as follows: Nchanga mine 33.6%, Bancroft mine 43.38%, Kalengwa Exploration Limited 45%, Bwana Mkubwa mine 100%, Rhodesia Copper Refineries 50%, Rhodesia Congo Border Power Corporation 25%, Mufulira mine 26.56%, Chibuluma mine 26.68%, Chambishi mine 26.68%, Baluba mine 26.68%, and Chisangwa mine 30%. *Source:* Adapted from RC Limited, *Annual Report, 30 June 1960* (Salisbury, England: RC Head Office, 1960), 22, ZCCM 12.7.2F.

RHOKANA'S CORPORATE STRATEGY AND PROFITABILITY

Nkana's profits during the Federal period were affected by two major factors. These were the increase in the cost of sales and the fluctuating price of copper on the LME. Cost of sales constitutes two major elements, namely, production and transport costs. As discussed in chapters 2 and 3, during the Great Depression and the Second World War, Nkana and the Copperbelt mines were generally low-cost producers. But, in the 1950s, the cost of production at Nkana and in the other Copperbelt mines, together with transport to either Europe or the USA, had risen to the point where the mines were intermediate between low- and high-cost producers; that is, producing about £160 per long ton of copper.[50]

There were two major reasons for this increase in the cost of production. Labor had become more expensive, and technical conditions underground were deteriorating despite improved mechanization, which doubled expenditure on production. Table 4.1 compares the average price of copper on the LME and production cost per long ton at Nkana mine between 1952 and 1956.

Table 4.1 demonstrates that mining costs per ton of copper increased from 51% of the total production cost in 1952 to 60% in 1956. Production costs apart from African labor did not rise as much because power costs actually fell.[51] These other costs fell from 36.8% of total production costs per long

Table 4.1 Average Price of Copper on the London Metal Exchange and Production Costs per Long Ton at Nkana Mine, 1952–1956.

Years	*1952*	*1953*	*1954*	*1955*	*1956*
Average Price of Copper per Long Ton on the LME (£)	259.5	256.3	249.3	351.7	328.7
Total Production Costs per Long Ton at Mine (£)	54.1	63.3	62.8	76.4	83.4
Mining Costs:					
Total Mining Costs (£)	27.8	34.0	32.7	41.9	49.7
Mining Costs Excluding African Labor (£)	24.0	29.2	27.6	34.8	39.6
Mining African Labor Costs (£)	3.8	4.8	5.1	7.1	10.1
Other Production Costs:					
Total Other Costs (£)	26.3	29.3	30.1	34.5	33.7
Other Costs Excluding African Labor (£)	19.9	21.8	22.3	25.2	22.0
Other African Labor Costs (£)	6.4	7.5	7.8	9.3	11.7
Percentage Contribution of Certain Costs to the Total Production Costs:					
Total Mining Costs as Percentage of Total Production Costs	51%	54%	52%	55%	60%
Mining African Labor Costs as Percentage of Total Mining Costs	14%	14%	16%	17%	20%
Total African Labor Costs as Percentage of Total Production Costs	18.7%	19.4%	20.4%	21.5%	26.1%
Other Costs excluding African Labor as Percentage of Total Production Costs	36.8%	34.4%	35.5%	33.0%	26.4%
Average Monthly European Basic Wages per Employee (£)	57.5	65.1	68.1	71.2	73.8

Source: Compiled from RC Limited, *Utilisation of African Labour Report*, Tables 7 and 9; NRCM, *Northern Rhodesia Chamber of Mines Yearbook 1956* (Kitwe: NRCM, 1957), 69, ZCCM 12.1.9C.

Note: Total Production Costs per long ton of salable copper, excluding copper bonus. Total Mining Costs comprised costs of mineral extraction including underground African labor, costs of mineral processing, and costs of surface African labor (concentrator, smelter, refinery, and cobalt department). Other Production Costs include expenditure on services (townships, administration, and hospital), plant materials (stores), fuel and transport up to and within the mine, and royalty/export tax. Average Monthly Europeans' Basic Wages refers to average basic wage salaries for white workers in all Copperbelt mines.

ton of copper in 1952 to 26.4% in 1956. Accordingly, Rhokana assumed that production costs excluding African labor per ton of copper would remain constant, at least up to 1961.[52]

As a single unit, total African labor costs formed the highest proportion of total production costs. Labor costs at Nkana and in the other Copperbelt mines were relatively high for a number of reasons. Between 1952 and 1956, 40% of the total African labor force was employed in mining, meaning that increases in African labor costs had a big impact on overall mining costs.[53] Total African labor costs as a percentage of total production costs per long ton of copper increased from 18.7% in 1952 to 26.1% in 1956. In addition to improved rates of basic wages and copper bonuses, African wages increased substantially because of the tendency by arbitrators to increase them to reduce disparities in the dual-wage structure.[54] For instance, the cost of African labor per employee per annum at Nkana increased from about £160 in 1951 to £240 by 1956.[55]

European wages were also a large proportion of total production costs. Salaries paid to European workers were high compared with those received by US miners and higher than those paid in the Belgian Congo, South Africa, Chile, and Southern Rhodesia.[56] The annual average earnings per European at Nkana and in the other Copperbelt mines increased from £1,275 in 1951 to £2,295 by 1956.[57] This was attributed to improved rates of basic pay following consolidations of cost-of-living allowances and the higher rates of copper bonuses. From the figures provided earlier, it is clear that the ratio difference between European and African wages increased slightly from 8:1 in 1951 to 10:1 in 1955. European labor was 8 to 10 times more expensive than African labor. Phimister has noted that "an increase of 50% in African emoluments only raised production costs by about 5%."[58]

Nevertheless, table 4.1 indicates that the rising cost of production was more than offset by the substantial increase in the price of copper, from an annual average of about £259.50 in 1952 to £351.70 in 1955. Had the upward trend persisted, total African labor costs would have accounted for 43.3% of total production cost per long ton by 1961; however, the price of copper fell abruptly from the record high of £351.70 in 1955 to £328.70 in 1956.[59]

Determined to reduce labor costs in order to offset rising production costs, Rhokana and other Copperbelt mines pressed for the partial substitution of African labor for European labor. African Advancement, as this policy was known, claimed to be one of opportunity for better and relatively high-paying jobs for black miners, but, in practice, their wages were lower than those paid to white workers in comparable jobs.[60] This marked the beginning of what Perrings called the "proletarianization of the new [black] middle class" as a cost-saving measure.[61] The role of Rhokana in the politics of African Advancement is discussed next.

Rhokana and the African Advancement Policy

After a series of prolonged and inconclusive negotiations between the mining companies and the NRMWU, the African Advancement problem came to the boil from late 1953 onward.[62] Prain announced that RST would advance Africans to certain jobs occupied by Europeans.[63] A similar announcement was made by the AAC though in somewhat more guarded terms.[64] According to Butler, the AAC was hesitant in pursuing African Advancement with the NRMWU because it had to consider "the impact changes in the labour policy [on the Copperbelt] might have on industrial relations in South Africa."[65]

In March 1954, Sir William Lawther, former head of the British National Union of Mineworkers, arrived on the Copperbelt on a peacemaking mission.[66] During his stay, a joint statement by the NRMWU and the African Mineworkers' Union (AMU) was drawn up, welcoming African Advancement on the basis of equal pay for equal work and no fragmentation.[67] The NRMWU would only accept revision of the closed shop clause in their agreement with the companies and allow dilution of labor if the mining companies accepted this principle.[68] The companies, however, were not willing to advance Africans and pay them European wages, which, from their point of view, would defeat the whole object of the exercise: a lower overall wage bill.

On August 27, 1954, the Northern Rhodesian government set up the Forster Board of Inquiry to examine the African Advancement question.[69] In evidence to this Commission, the NRMWU reaffirmed its stance as "equal pay or nothing."[70] Rhokana and the other Rhodesian Anglo American (RAA) companies accepted the conclusions of the Commission and resumed negotiations with the NRMWU.

On November 3, 1954, Rhokana and the other members of the RAA group met with the NRMWU to discuss the African Advancement issue based on the findings of the Forster Commission.[71] At the meeting, Bennett, Rhokana's general manager, informed the NRMWU's representatives that he had contacted Sir Ernest Oppenheimer, who, in turn, had given a policy statement setting the tone of negotiations with the Union. The policy statement restated the key principles of the AAC's advancement proposal. The AAC believed that an enduring solution of the African Advancement problem could only be achieved with the cooperation and assistance of its European employees.[72] Another principle stated that the AAC would not quicken the rate of African Advancement at the expense of European workers but would rather implement the policy gradually to give the necessary time for the substantial human and economic adjustments.[73]

On November 4, 1954, in the face of the continued refusal by the NRMWU to relax its attitude, the RST management served six months' notice of its intention to end its agreement with the Union.[74] While this issue was being discussed within the RST group, the AAC-owned mines led by Rhokana decided to meet the NRMWU again to discuss their advancement proposal.[75] At a meeting held on December 22, 1954, Bennett encouraged the NRMWU and the RST to be reasonable in their outlook.[76] On January 21, 1955, the RST and the NRMWU met to discuss the former's advancement scheme.[77]

There were a number of differences and similarities between the proposed advancement schemes of RST and AAC. The fundamental difference was that the AAC-owned mines gave the NRMWU power to veto any proposal, which they felt would be against the interests of their members.[78] RST opposed this proposal as being against African Advancement. Another cardinal difference was that the RST group's scheme meant the relinquishment of five categories of work on a permanent basis, while the RAA group's proposal comprised two categories of jobs.[79] Categories of jobs in the RAA scheme were very similar to those jointly submitted by the Copperbelt companies to the Forster Commission.[80]

Because of these differences, Bennett accused the RST scheme of departing from the proposals put forward by both groups of companies jointly at the Forster Board of Inquiry.[81] The RST's scheme was accused of not only having more categories of jobs but also containing "the germ of continual dispute" by leaving an allowance for the unions to negotiate for wages.[82] A suggestion, which came from Rhokana and was included in the RAA's scheme, was that European workers in the lowest paying jobs would be given opportunities to advance in the industry. To this effect, the RAA companies set out to provide adequate facilities for the training of Europeans in lower posts, technical and skilled jobs that would make them fit for more advanced posts.[83] Other safeguards and guarantees promised to Europeans were that any member of the union in old age or poor health would not be displaced and that European workers on probation at the time of signing the agreement would be given permanent jobs.[84]

These differences did not escape the notice of the NRMWU members and the Mines Officials and Salaried Staff Association (MOSSA).[85] The MOSSA announced its acceptance of the RAA/AAC's scheme and rejected the RST one.[86] The major similarity was that both groups of companies promised that no European miner would lose his job because of African Advancement.

On January 30, 1955, the NRMWU decided to hold a ballot among its members to decide whether they wished their executive to adhere to their original mandate of "equal pay for equal work and no fragmentation as a guiding principle in their negotiations with the companies on the subject of African Advancement" or abandon this principle and permit the concessions being made.[87] In the poll, 59.7% of the NRMWU's membership voted in favor of amending the mandate and allowing for dilution of labor.[88]

A second ballot was held to see whether members recognized the implications of the first, and again, the majority remained in favor of conceding the jobs. Though the gap was narrow, the majority vote gave the negotiating parties power to push for African Advancement. The result of the ballot broke the deadlock between the companies and the NRMWU on the problem of African Advancement. Rhokana and the RAA group were the first to sign an agreement with the NRMWU on July 30, 1955 (see figure 4.2).

The RST group followed suit by signing an agreement with the NRMWU on August 10, 1955.[89] Bennett claimed that RST signed a similar agreement to the one endorsed between the RAA-owned mines and the NRMWU.[90] On September 27, 1955, all Copperbelt mines adopted both agreements.[91] The contents of the provisional agreement contained substantial information from Rhokana and the RAA's scheme. For instance, 24 jobs from the RAA's scheme were included under Schedule "B" jobs to be given to Africans.[92]

These developments indicate that Rhokana and the RAA-owned mines stepped up to endorse the African Advancement Policy, together with the NRMWU and ahead of RST. This evidence suggests that African

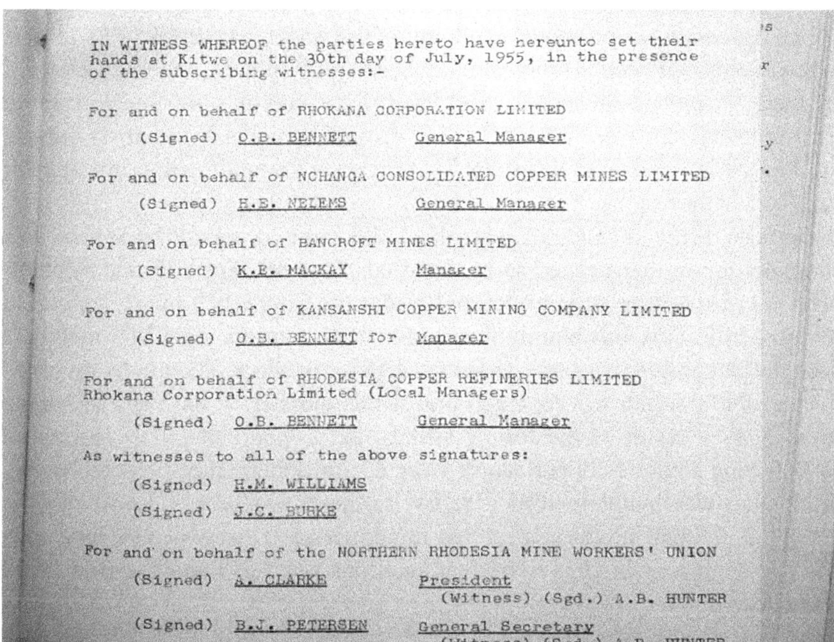

IN WITNESS WHEREOF the parties hereto have hereunto set their hands at Kitwe on the 30th day of July, 1955, in the presence of the subscribing witnesses:-

For and on behalf of RHOKANA CORPORATION LIMITED

(Signed) O.B. BENNETT General Manager

For and on behalf of NCHANGA CONSOLIDATED COPPER MINES LIMITED

(Signed) H.E. NELEMS General Manager

For and on behalf of BANCROFT MINES LIMITED

(Signed) K.E. MACKAY Manager

For and on behalf of KANSANSHI COPPER MINING COMPANY LIMITED

(Signed) O.B. BENNETT for Manager

For and on behalf of RHODESIA COPPER REFINERIES LIMITED
Rhokana Corporation Limited (Local Managers)

(Signed) O.B. BENNETT General Manager

As witnesses to all of the above signatures:

(Signed) H.M. WILLIAMS

(Signed) J.C. BURKE

For and on behalf of the NORTHERN RHODESIA MINE WORKERS' UNION

(Signed) A. CLARKE President
(Witness) (Sgd.) A.B. HUNTER

(Signed) B.J. PETERSEN General Secretary
(Witness) (Sgd.) A.B. HUNTER

Figure 4.2 Signatories to memorandum of an agreement made on African Advancement between the Northern Rhodesia Mineworkers' Union (NRMWU) and the Rhodesian Anglo American (RAA) Group of companies on July 30, 1955. *Source:* Adapted from RC Limited, Directors' Minutes of Meeting, July 30, 1955, ZCCM 3.8.2A.

Advancement could not have been realized in the mid-1950s; otherwise, it would have remained "a dream to be realised" if Rhokana's management had not stepped up to pursue this policy with the NRMWU because, to borrow Bennett's words, RST's advancement proposal contained "the germ of continual dispute [by leaving an allowance for] the European Union [to] be involved in discussions concerning pay or conditions [of service] for Africans."[93] Thus, this chapter questions the argument by Berger, Butler, Cohen, and Phimister that RST's management was instrumental in pursuing the African Advancement Policy with the NRMWU.[94]

In November 1955, jobs in the advancement agreement and those outside the European field but of an advanced type were fragmented into 75 jobs.[95] In order to reduce labor costs, Nkana and the other Copperbelt mines decided that most of these fragmented jobs would be awarded to Mines African Staff Association (MASA) members. Therefore, on December 3, 1955, the mining companies officially recognized MASA, with Godwin Mbikusita Lewanika, from Nkana mine and the founder of this union, as its leader.[96]

Early in 1956, the number of African workers who joined the MASA was 492 at Nkana, 453 at Nchanga, and 423 at Mufulira.[97] Of the 75 jobs for advancement, 62 fell within the MASA, 2 went to the Mines' African Police Association, and only 11 fell within the AMU.[98] In April 1956, almost 428 Africans had been promoted to advanced jobs on the Copperbelt mines.[99] By then, Nkana had advanced almost 95 Africans into jobs previously reserved for Europeans, 20 were put into newly created senior African posts outside the European fields, and a further 71 Africans were undergoing training for various advanced jobs.[100]

Because of this division of jobs, the AMU came to regard the MASA as a company union that needed to be defeated. Between April 26 and September 17, 1956, rolling strikes occurred across the Copperbelt mines supported by the AMU. This was mainly due to dissatisfaction among AMU members with the categories of jobs awarded to MASA members. The unrest involved over 25,000 African workers, and out of this number, 7,400 were at Nkana mine.[101] As a result of the rolling strikes, the Copperbelt mines lost about 12,000 long tons of copper worth over £3 million.[102] However, at Nkana, production was maintained at 75% by European workers.[103] Consequently, copper and cobalt production at this mine increased from 71,288 long tons and 871 short tons in 1955 to 81,566 long tons and 1,271 short tons in 1956, respectively.[104]

Power, Fuel, and Technical Problems

In addition to labor unrest, Rhokana and the other Copperbelt companies experienced power and fuel shortages and technical problems after 1956. As mentioned in chapter 2, the Copperbelt mines relied on Wankie Colliery for coal supplies, but these supplies remained inadequate. Following the AAC's purchase of Wankie in 1953, the Colliery's productive capacity increased from 2,500,000 tons to 5,000,000 tons a year.[105] But output was restricted by the railways' shortage of rolling stock. The AAC, through its newly formed subsidiary, the Anglo American Rhodesian Development Corporation, funded Rhodesia Railways in an attempt to overcome transport difficulties.[106] It offered 2,500 trucks for hire to the railways. But this proved to be only a temporary solution, as both power and transport challenges remained. Meanwhile, railway rates for transporting copper to Beira or Lourenco Marques increased from £7.1 in 1955 to almost £15 per long ton in 1957, compounding transport woes.[107]

With such problems, production costs could hardly be reduced. Nevertheless, the completion of the Le Marinel hydroelectric power station, ahead of schedule in 1956, briefly cushioned shortages of power. Le Marinel power station supplied about half of the Copperbelt's power, nearly 63 million kWh per month, at a favorable price and under a five-year contract to be renewed in 1961.[108]

Even so, the Copperbelt's demand for electricity increased significantly following the opening of new mines. Electricity was the life blood of the mining industry, and a lack thereof, even for a few hours, would be disastrous to Nkana and the Copperbelt mines. Without electricity to drive the pumps, for example, the mines would be flooded—an average of about 11.5 million gallons of water a day were pumped out of Nkana mine alone.[109] Le Marinel could not satisfy the power demands of the mines. Besides, the generating thermal plant at Nkana was nearly 30 years old and needed to be replaced with equipment that would cost about £70 per kW installed.[110] To satisfy the electricity needs of the mines and the Federal economy as a whole, it was decided that the Kariba Hydro-Electric Power (HEP) station be constructed.

The cost of constructing Kariba HEP was estimated at £114 million, while the cost of building thermal stations of equivalent capacity was estimated at £101 million.[111] It was projected that Kariba HEP would save Nkana and the Copperbelt mines £31 million in the first 10 years, and, thereafter, £10 million per year.[112] It was also envisaged that Kariba HEP's output would be more than double the output of all the combined existing stations in the Federation. Based on these calculations, the Copperbelt mines were persuaded by the Federal government to raise £20 million toward the construction of the Kariba HEP station, of which Rhokana contributed the largest share of £4.25 million.[113] Nkana was the largest consumer of power among the Copperbelt mines, with its peak electric loads increasing from 56,700 kW in 1957, through to 65,700 kW in 1960, to 68,600 kW in 1962.[114]

Thanks to the Kariba HEP station, which began supplying electricity in 1959, the power supply to the Copperbelt increased from 482,000 kWh that year, to nearly 762 million kWh in 1960, and about 1.4 billion kWh in 1963.[115] Furthermore, the opening of the Kariba HEP station was timely, because the supply of electricity from the Le Marinel power station was disrupted by the outbreak of the civil war in 1960 in the newly independent state of the Congo.

Capital Expenditure, Labor Productivity, and Quality of Ores

Adequate and efficient supplies of power did little to ease the problems associated with deeper-level mining at Nkana. By 1958, Nkana was the Copperbelt's deepest mine at 3,742 feet.[116] Mining at such great depth brings with it challenging underground conditions: Increased pressure makes pillar construction difficult, which may result in collapsing of the walls. Deep-level mining was also characterized by flooding and significantly diluted ore grades. At Nkana, there was a drop in the grade of the ore mined to an average of 2.6% copper in 1956, compared with an average of 3.2% in 1944.[117] This meant that, in order to produce the equal amount of copper in 1956, the company had to mine and hoist about 122 tons of ore as against 100 tons in 1944.[118]

With increased depth, more capital (see table 4.2) for mechanization was needed. This included the utilization of underground crushers, scrappers, automatic trip switches, and charging sets. Mechanization improved the productivity of African labor and the manning structure. In 1949, productivity per African per shift was 2.33 tons compared with 3.90 tons in 1956.[119] It took 5,215 African workers to hoist 316,500 tons in June 1949, compared with 4,184 African workers to hoist 408,005 tons in December 1956.[120] As mechanization improved the productivity of African labor, Nkana was spurred to reduce African labor in order to save costs. Hence, underground strength was decreased by 408 from 5,215 in June 1949 to 4,807 in December 1956, while surface strength was reduced by 623 in the same period.[121]

At Nkana, the number of workers declined relative to capital. The size of the African workforce increased annually by 0.5% between 1948 and 1955 but shrunk by −0.2% from 1956 to 1962.[122] In the same periods, the annual growth in the size of the European workforce slowed from 2.7% to 1.7%, while net total capital declined relatively from 5.7% to 3.7%.[123] Partly because of mechanization and the stabilization of labor, the number of African workers at Nkana declined relative to the number of European workers between 1953 and 1963. Although capital expenditure at Nkana increased tremendously after 1953, it fell away dramatically after 1957. This partly reflected the collapse of the copper price toward the end of 1956.

For capital expenditure and labor force between 1953 and 1963, see table 4.2. Compared to the marked decline in the turnover of African labor,

Table 4.2 Capital, Labor Strength, Turnover Percent, and Length of Service for Nkana Mine, 1953–1963.

		African Labor			*European Labor*		
Year	*Capital Expenditure £*	*Strength*	*Turnover %*	*Length of Service (Years)*	*Strength*	*Turnover %*	*Length of Service (Years)*
1953	2,968,000	10,574	52.0	–	1,747	17.6	–
1954	5,600,000	9,733	47.6	–	1,761	17.3	–
1955	5,123,294	8,610	125.8	–	1,805	13.8	–
1956	2,300,000	9,099	27.6	–	1,844	13.1	–
1957	3,300,000	8,583	33.4	–	1,835	24.9	–
1958	1,690,000	7,523	26.2	–	1,698	36.0	–
1959	1,180,000	7,553	28.3	–	1,716	16.2	–
1960	1,800,000	7,575	30.2	5.8	1,716	17.4	5.6
1961	960,000	7,626	22.8	5.6	1,737	20.6	5.5
1962	1,270,000	8,861	17.7	6.2	1,921	33.0	6.0
1963	1,400,000	8,928	9.3	6.7	1,991	25.1	5.6

Source: Compiled from Ministry of Labour and Social Services, Strikes and Disputes Lab Form 4: Kitwe-Nkana, November 1962–December 1963, NAZ MLSS 1/25/121; GRZ, *Report of the Commission of Inquiry into the Mining Industry 1966* (Lusaka: The Government Printer, 1966), 160, NAZ 11/57C; Bates, *Unions, Parties and Political Development*, 81, 250; Berger, *Labour, Race and Colonial Rule*, 208; Mhone, *The Political Economy of a Dual Labour Market in Africa*, 163.

Note: The figures for the years 1955 and 1958 are abnormally inflated since some Africans and Europeans were discharged and subsequently re-engaged due to strikes. Some of the Turnover Rates and Length of Service are average figures for Copperbelt mines.

European turnover was influenced by strike action in 1958 and by the advent of Northern Rhodesian independence.

Overall Production and Profitability

While all the aforementioned factors had an impact on the productive capacity of Nkana mine, the overall profitability of this mine was also affected by the fluctuating price of copper. The formation of the Federation of Rhodesia and Nyasaland coincided with an economic boom on the Copperbelt. In 1954, Nkana produced 79,755 long tons of copper and a record 1,264 short tons of cobalt. Rhokana made the Federation the second-largest producer of cobalt metal in the world after the Belgian Congo (9,414 tons), surpassing the USA (1,110 tons), Canada (1,091 tons), and French Morocco (811 tons).[124]

However, between January 3 and March 2, 1955, a strike by African workers across the Copperbelt mines demanding an increase of 10.6s per shift reduced production of copper and cobalt at Nkana by 8,467 long tons and 393 short tons, respectively.[125] The Copperbelt miners' strike, coupled with similar strikes in Chile and the USA, reduced world copper stocks and, consequently, increased both demand and the price of copper by about £150 per long ton on the LME.[126]

The increase in the price of copper, however, was not sustained. It fell by more than 40% between 1956 and 1958 and continued to fluctuate until 1961, due to a combination of factors including industrial unrest, international tension, political disturbances, and government measures.[127] During the Korean Crisis, financial loans by the US government encouraged the development of new copper mines in order to increase production for the war. Because of the time lag between the development of the sites and the start of large-scale production, these mines only came onstream in 1956. This resulted in a surplus.

The supply–demand situation was further unbalanced by the slackening of industrial activity in the USA and Britain following the end of the Korean Crisis. World stocks rose from 710,100 long tons to 920,000 long tons between 1956 and 1957, while consumption declined by 40% in the USA and Britain.[128] Consequently, the average monthly price of copper dropped from £400 a long ton on the LME in 1956, through £240 in 1957, to £160 in February 1958.[129]

Between 1955 and 1957, world cobalt production increased by 7.5% from 13,500 metric tons to 14,600 tons.[130] In this period, consumption of cobalt in the USA, which was the main buyer, reduced by almost 6%.[131] The price of cobalt metal per pound declined from US$2.35 in 1956 to US$1.75 by 1959.[132]

In order to address the surplus on the market, Rhokana and other major copper producers cut back on production by about 10% between 1956 and 1958, amounting to a total of 400,000 short tons or about 12% of the free world's annual production of new copper.[133] As a result of this reduction in world stocks between February 1958 and the first quarter of 1959, the demand for copper increased. This raised and stabilized the copper price on the LME at a monthly average of about £260 per long ton.[134]

Other factors also caused fluctuations in the price of copper. In April 1958, a 51-day strike by mineworkers in Chile "[deprived] the market of 40,000 tons of copper . . . causing the price to move a few pounds a ton."[135] Likewise, about six months later, the supply position was altered by the strikes in Northern Rhodesia and Canada, causing the price of copper to increase by £40 a ton on the LME.[136]

The price of copper was also indirectly influenced by local and international conflicts. In the same year (1958), trouble was brewing in the Middle East with a revolution in Iraq, civil war in Lebanon, and Jordan being threatened by Syria.[137] Elsewhere, mainland China threatened to invade Quemoy held by Taiwan, supported by the USA.[138]

Taken together, these events stimulated copper prices in two ways. First, the Middle East troubles coincided with the US government's decision to protect its industry by imposing an import duty of £14 per long ton of copper.[139] However, the conflict in the Middle East increased demand and restored and raised copper prices to over £200 per long ton.[140] Second, the Western world copper industry was given a shot in the arm when, on August 15, 1958, restrictions on sales of copper, other than copper of US origin, to the Soviet bloc were lifted.[141]

Political disturbances in the Federation of Rhodesia and Nyasaland also disrupted production and maintained the demand and price of copper per long ton on the market from an annual average of about £230 in 1961 to £234 in 1963.[142] In Northern Rhodesia, there was a tendency by nationalist leaders to woo mineworkers and their trade unions. They found a receptive audience, because the disparities created by the dual-wage structure caused many African mineworkers and their families to look to the nationalist movement led by the Northern Rhodesia African National Congress (NRANC) and the United National Independence Party (UNIP).[143] Despite Katilungu's attitude, the majority of the AMU leadership, especially those on Nkana mine, were closely associated with the NRANC.[144]

Cooperation between the labor and nationalist movements caused the government and mine companies to accuse union and nationalist leaders of instigating a wave of strikes by mineworkers between 1961 and 1963.[145] The strikes at Nkana reduced production to an average of 103,122 long tons per year.[146] But reduction in production and supply, as a result of strikes on the Copperbelt and elsewhere, did not cause the price of copper to increase in this period because of the stockpile in the world market.

The foregoing wide variety of factors combined to affect the profitability of Nkana. Table 4.3 summarizes finished production and overall operating profit of Nkana during the Federal period.

Table 4.3 shows that, between 1954 and 1963, Nkana mine produced 897,431 long tons of copper. In the same period, Nchanga produced 1,260,973 tons; Mufulira, 895,256 tons; and Roan, 849,915 tons.[147] Thus, Nkana was the second-largest producer of copper in the Federation of Rhodesia and Nyasaland.

After 1961, production at Nkana was declined for two major reasons. First, Nkana experienced several challenges associated with deeper-level mining, such as flooding, high underground temperature, falling walls and dilution of ore, and a resultant decline in the grade of ore reserves and ore milled. Second, Rhokana invested part of its capital in expanded production at Bancroft, Mufulira, and Nchanga; hence, Nchanga surpassed Nkana in terms of production.

While Nkana was the second-largest producer of copper in the Federation of Rhodesia and Nyasaland, it also produced 11,026 short tons of cobalt. Between 1954 and 1959, combined cobalt production from Nkana and

Table 4.3 Nkana Mine's Production and Operating Profits, 1954–1963.

	Production (Tons)		*Price of Copper*	*Value of Sales*	*Cost of Sales*	*Royalty Tax*	*Operating Profit*
Year	*Copper Long T.*	*Cobalt Short T.*	*LME £*	*£*	*£*	*£*	*£*
1954	79,755	1,264	249.3	23,995,987	11,953,251	–	9,326,698
1955	71,288	871	351.7	26,611,844	13,632,028	2,888,132	9,849,116
1956	81,566	1,271	328.7	36,422,691	16,582,479	3,033,162	16,578,288
1957	88,306	1,330	219.4	29,124,251	16,626,558	1,950,486	7,775,226
1958	86,216	1,269	197.7	22,054,391	14,686,867	1,413,505	2,406,967
1959	76,983	1,092	237.7	23,093,996	14,319,626	2,390,525	4,906,546
1960	103,981	1,307	245.8	31,899,608	16,521,400	2,726,467	10,227,468
1961	106,881	837	229.7	30,397,770	17,856,112	2,594,210	8,329,514
1962	104,476	951	234.0	31,339,683	16,866,283	2,344,890	8,411,314
1963	97,979	778	234.4	29,400,000	22,601,000	2,503,727	6,172,000
Total	897,431	11,026	–	284,340,221	161,645,604	21,845,104	83,983,137

Source: Compiled from NRCM, *Northern Rhodesia Chamber of Mines Yearbooks,* 1956–1963, ZCCM 12.1.9C; RC Limited, *Annual Reports and Accounts,* 1954–1963, ZCCM 12.7.2F.

Note: Cost of Sales includes total expenses on mining, labor, redemption fund, mine development, depression, and mineral processing. Tax represents amounts charged on royalty payable to the BSA Company on both the copper and cobalt metals produced each year and was part of the total operating costs or Cost of Sales. The amount of Royalty Tax paid to the BSA Company in 1954 is not represented in the sources utilized in this book.

Chibuluma mines totaled 8,798 short tons, making the Federation of Rhodesia and Nyasaland the third-largest world producer of cobalt after the Belgian Congo (54,281 tons) and Canada (9,232 tons).[148] Indeed, the Central African Federation surpassed the USA and French Morocco, whose respective production was 8,424 tons and 5,172 tons in this period.[149]

Table 4.4 indicates Rhokana's issued share capital per year worth a pound each on Preference, Ordinary, and "A" shares. It also shows the Corporation's gross and net profits, as well as total income tax paid to the Federal and the Northern Rhodesian governments. Furthermore, the table shows dividends distributed to shareholders between 1954 and 1963.

The prosperity of Rhokana is reflected in the tax it paid to the Federal and Northern Rhodesian governments, as well as to the BSA Company. During the Federal period, tax paid by the Copperbelt mines in the form of income tax, customs duties on imports, and mining and vehicle licenses amounted to about £163,969,000.[150] Of this figure, Rhokana contributed approximately £32,630,000 or nearly 20% to the Northern Rhodesian and Federal tax revenue. The total value of tax paid by the Copperbelt mines, BSA Company, and their employees into Federal coffers was almost £239,078,000.[151] Of this amount, 48.5% accrued to the Federal government, 37.2% to the Northern Rhodesian government, 9.9% to the Southern Rhodesian government, and 4.4% to the Nyasaland government.[152]

Table 4.4 Rhokana's Issued Share Capital, Gross Profits, Net Profits, and Dividends, 1954–1963.

	Corporation's Share Capital and Gross Profits				*Income Tax, Net Profits, and Dividends*		
		Nkana Mine	*Other Mines*				
Year	*Issued Share Capital (£)*	*Operating Profit (£)*	*Profit Received (£)*	*Gross Profit (£)*	*Income Tax (£)*	*Net Profit (£)*	*Net Dividends (£)*
1954	3,328,008	9,326,698	3,819,517	13,146,215	3,450,000	9,544,021	6,287,223
1955	3,321,004	9,849,116	4,128,058	13,977,174	3,660,000	10,022,463	6,590,847
1956	3,302,704	16,578,288	5,715,568	22,293,856	6,120,000	15,936,704	8,777,670
1957	3,292,622	7,775,226	4,026,511	13,055,366	2,900,000	9,872,331	5,652,297
1958	3,284,607	2,406,967	2,121,154	5,633,715	1,100,000	4,259,475	3,151,973
1959	3,276,307	4,906,546	2,042,457	7,990,130	2,090,000	5,625,326	5,026,689
1960	25,767,975	10,227,468	4,222,350	15,771,415	3,930,000	11,534,278	8,776,406
1961	25,759,275	8,329,514	6,394,647	14,724,161	3,420,000	10,955,993	8,776,107
1962	25,751,000	8,411,314	6,221,790	14,633,104	3,480,000	10,742,214	8,774,774
1963	25,742,000	6,172,000	4,659,000	12,237,000	2,480,000	9,338,000	8,774,000
Total	122,825,502	83,983,137	43,351,052	133,462,136	32,630,000	97,830,805	70,587,986

Source: Compiled from NRCM, *Northern Rhodesia Chamber of Mines Yearbooks*, 1956–1963; RC Limited, *Annual Reports and Accounts*, 1954–1963.

Note: Gross Profit for Rhokana was arrived at by adding Operating Profits from Nkana, the Corporation's investment income from other mines and properties on the Copperbelt, and interest receivable (in certain years). Year-in-year Net Profit was calculated from Gross Profit by subtracting administrative expenses, directors' fees, and Income Tax. Preference, Ordinary, and "A" share dividends were calculated from Net Profit, less tax.

In addition, between 1955 and 1963, the Copperbelt mines paid out a total of £108,221,903 BSA Company royalties, of which Rhokana contributed £21,845,104 or 20.2% (see table 4.3).[153] Total gross profits for Rhokana between 1954 and 1963, before provision for income tax, amounted to £83,983,137 from the mine, £43,351,052 from investments in other properties on the Copperbelt, and a further £6,127,947 from interest receivable and sundry income. From a grand net profit of £97,830,805, final dividends paid out to shareholders amounted to £70,587,986 during the entire Federal period. Accrued unappropriated profits amounted to £6,148,954.[154] Much of this sum was spent on expansion, renovation, and projects at Nkana mine.

POLITICAL AND ECONOMIC REASONS FOR THE COLLAPSE OF THE CENTRAL AFRICAN FEDERATION

Rhokana and the Copperbelt mining companies were central to the Federal economy. Yet, the Federal government spent far more in Southern Rhodesia than in Northern Rhodesia and Nyasaland. For instance, the Federal government was responsible for European education and agriculture, and most white children and farmers were in Southern Rhodesia.[155] In addition, the Federal capital was placed in Salisbury, as were all the other main Federal institutions: the University College, the Bank of Rhodesia and Nyasaland, the Supreme Court, and the head offices of the Northern Rhodesia mining companies, including Rhokana.[156]

Similarly, the bulk of the Federal investment also took place in Southern Rhodesia. The biggest single Federal project, the Kariba HEP, was chosen in preference to a scheme on the Kafue River in Northern Rhodesia, which would have been cheaper to build, as well as be nearer to the copper mines, the chief consumer of electricity.[157] Moreover, the first-stage generating stations were set up on the south bank of the Zambezi River, on the Southern Rhodesian side.

More than half of the total public and private investment in the Federation went to Southern Rhodesia. Consequently, Southern Rhodesia's income grew more rapidly between 1953 and 1963 than that of Northern Rhodesia and Nyasaland. Gross Domestic Product rose by 59% for Southern Rhodesia and only 42% for Northern Rhodesia.[158] These economic imbalances among the three states did not escape the notice of the members of the African nationalist movements, especially in Northern Rhodesia and Nyasaland. In Northern Rhodesia, the NRANC and UNIP argued that "federation [was] bad" and accused the Federal government of appropriating Northern Rhodesia's mineral resources at the expense of national development.[159]

Political uncertainty was the main deciding factor for the future of the Federation, especially from 1959 following the rise of mass African nationalism. In February and March that year, a state of emergency was introduced in Nyasaland and the two Rhodesias, following rumors of African nationalist plots.[160] The business community, including the two main mining companies, RST and AAC/RAA, interpreted this development differently to mean the end of white rule.[161] The rise of African nationalism in Northern Rhodesia and decolonization throughout Africa, starting with the independence of the Gold Coast (Ghana) in 1957 and the Belgian Congo (Congo-Kinshasa) in 1960, made the managers of the Copperbelt companies aware of the need to identify themselves with emerging nationalist leaders.[162] The AAC/RAA group remained conservative, but the RST group, led by its chairman, Ronald Prain, took the lead and ingratiated itself with Kenneth Kaunda of UNIP.[163] With the winds of change blowing increasingly stronger by 1962, Rhokana's parent company, AAC, and its chairman, Harry Oppenheimer, also met with Kaunda.[164]

In addition, the Copperbelt companies transferred their headquarters from Southern Rhodesia back to Northern Rhodesia.[165] The move of Rhokana's head offices to Lusaka, announced by the directors in May 1963, was effected on January 1, 1964.[166] Mr. P.H.A. Brownrigg, the AAC director in Southern Rhodesia, was transferred to Northern Rhodesia and put in charge of Rhokana Corporation and other head offices of the AAC's subsidiaries in Lusaka and Kitwe.[167] At the same time, the registered office was moved from Nkana to Lusaka. Anglo American Corporation (Central Africa) Limited appointed secretaries and administrative and technical advisers to Rhokana with effect from January 1, 1964.[168] By the time Northern Rhodesia became independent on October 24, 1964, with the new name of Zambia, Rhokana had already shifted its head office from Salisbury to Lusaka.[169]

CONCLUSION

The corporate structure, labor organization, and profitability of Rhokana Corporation and its Nkana mine changed during the Federal period. To safeguard its operations and profitability, like the other Copperbelt companies, Rhokana cooperated in implementing new policies in line with the unfolding political and economic environment. However, the Federation proved unsustainable after 1959 mainly due to the rise of African nationalism and economic imbalances among the states themselves. The Copperbelt mining companies tried to fund various developmental projects in the three territories, but since the headquarters of the Federation was based in Salisbury, Southern Rhodesia was much more developed than its partners, Nyasaland and Northern Rhodesia.

During the late 1950s and early 1960s, a "wind of change" was sweeping the African continent. African colonies were now demanding political independence from their colonial powers. As observed by Butler and Cohen, and seconded in this chapter, RST and Rhokana's Mother Company, RAA, the two mining giants in Northern Rhodesia, interpreted this differently to mean the collapse of the Federation in Central Africa, until after 1962 when "it was abundantly clear that the Federation's fading condition was terminal."[170] By the dissolution of the Federation in December 1963, Rhokana and all the Copperbelt companies had already migrated back to Northern Rhodesia.

Chapter 5

Zambianization and Nationalization

Rhokana/Nkana during the First Five Years of Zambian Independence, 1964–1969

ECONOMIC PROBLEMS IN THE ZAMBIAN MINING SECTOR AT INDEPENDENCE

At independence, there were three major problems facing the Zambian mining sector.[1] First, the mining sector was dominated by foreign capital, drawn from South Africa, Britain, and the United States of America (USA). Second, Nkana and the Copperbelt mines were largely dependent on South Africa and Southern Rhodesia for much of their skilled labor and transport of exports and imports.[2] Third, private companies such as the British South Africa (BSA) Company, Anglo American Corporation (AAC), and American Metals Climax/Selection Trust (AMAX/ST) controlled mining activities in Zambia (see chapters 1–4). The government only benefited from royalties and export and income taxes paid by these companies. Between 1964 and 1969, copper supplied over 90% of the state's exports and about 60% to 70% of government revenue.[3]

As far as the copper industry was concerned, the new government had two major tasks. The main task was to encourage investment in mining developments to improve on production and benefits from mining profits.[4] The United National Independence Party (UNIP) government also aimed at eliminating European labor through rapid Zambianization.[5] In addition, there was an effort to mobilize labor in the mines and other sectors to support national development as a whole.[6]

The government adopted two ways to implement these priorities, initially through liberal economic policies and latterly through nationalization of the private sector.[7] The former, at least up until 1968, was intended to mobilize foreign investment by assuring private investors that the new regime would not nationalize their assets.[8] Consequently, Kaunda's initial approach "accumulated a great fund of goodwill both inside the country and abroad."[9] Rhokana and its holding company, Zambian Anglo American Corporation (ZAMANGLO), were relieved that Kaunda did not nationalize the mines and welcomed the new government's mining policies.

In the copper industry, there were three controversial issues in the first years of independence. The first controversy concerned mineral rights and taxation.[10] The second problem had to do with labor relations in the industry.[11] The third controversy was the extent to which the government would participate in the mining sector.[12] It is to these issues that the following sections turn.

MINERAL RIGHTS AND THE NEW THREEFOLD MINING TAX REGIMES

It should be noted that the Zambian government was not the first to question the ownership of mineral rights by the BSA Company. In 1938, for instance, settler politicians objected to the Chartered Company's claims, but nothing changed. Later on, Roy Welensky, a representative in the legislature, argued that the BSA Company should surrender its mineral rights to the government, but the controversy ended with the signing of the 1950 Truce Agreement, which merely "provided for an extension of the company's ownership of its mineral rights, free from special taxation, until 1986."[13]

At independence, the Zambian government questioned the very validity of the BSA Company's mining and mineral rights, forcing it to relinquish them for only £4 million, half of which was paid by the British government.[14] In the past, the BSA Company had been handsomely rewarded through their mining rights. The Company's royalty earnings in 1925 were a paltry £12,781, but by 1937, it had risen to a substantial £311,000 per annum, and by 1964, it was estimated that the Company had received a total of £70 million after tax in royalty payments.[15]

Following the government acquisition of mineral rights, royalties continued to be increased and paid on the BSA Company standard, based on the price of copper, not profits. As such, Rhokana and the Copperbelt companies complained of remaining with meager retained profits for mining investment, because royalties "levied [at a rate of 13.5 percent] on the value of copper produced . . . added to production costs."[16]

Between 1964 and 1969, royalties and export taxes paid by Nkana to the Zambian government amounted to 28.5% of total operating costs or cost of sales (see table 5.5). Certainly, Rhokana had suggested that the mineral royalty be based on sales proceeds.[17] But in the colonial era, Rhokana never complained of paying high royalties to the BSA Company. This was because AAC was a major shareholder in the BSA Company, so Rhokana benefited from mining royalties paid to the BSA Company.[18]

Between May 1965 and April 1966, monthly copper prices fluctuated from £438 to £790 per long ton on the London Metal Exchange (LME), spurring the government to increase tax rates.[19] The new export tax regime on copper "was set at 40 percent of the amount by which the average LME price for the month [exceeded] £300 per long ton," while "income taxes, at a maximum rate of 45 percent, were levied on company profits after the payment of royalties and export taxes."[20] Consequently, the post-1964 mining tax had three components: royalty tax (13.5%), export tax (40%), and corporate or income tax (45%).[21]

Royalty and export taxes continued to be charged against the LME price of copper, while income tax was levied on profit. On average, the threefold mining tax regime produced a tax rate of about 74.4%.[22] Mineral taxes in Zambia, which had been relatively mild, totaling a tax rate of 40% during the Federation of Rhodesia and Nyasaland (1953–1963), now approximated levels elsewhere in the copper industry.[23] For instance, the tax on profits in the USA was 52%, while, in Chile, the basic profits tax on the big foreign companies was 50%, plus a surcharge of 25%.[24] High tax rates became part of the many problems facing private companies in Zambia at independence. Labor-related problems in the private sector added to this burden.

FROM AFRICAN ADVANCEMENT TO ZAMBIANIZATION POLICY

There were two problems facing the government concerning labor in the copper industry at independence. According to Bates, Burawoy, and Daniel, the major objective of the government policy was to eliminate reliance on white workers while securing an adequate supply of skilled African labor. Even so, the new government was not the first to address the issue of advancing African workers in the mines. The policy of African Advancement began in 1955, but the government felt that little had been done to implement it in the period up to 1964.[25] At Nkana, for example, only 211 Africans were employed in advanced jobs by the fourth quarter of 1959.[26] The mining companies attributed the slowness of advancement to the difficulties arising from the low educational standard among Africans.[27] For its part, Nkana spearheaded an advancement policy designed to maintain productivity but at low labor costs. However, white mineworkers remained entrenched in semiskilled and skilled jobs.

The identification of these obstacles underpinned the Zambianization of labor, which Nkana and the other mining companies were expected to implement in order to speed up African Advancement. Accordingly, the color bar and closed-shop policy were done away with in 1965, and a formula was devised for white workers to be displaced by trained Zambians.[28] White workers were given expatriate status. Expatriate status was reinforced by offering them fixed contracts of three years that could only be renewed twice.[29] The purpose of expatriates was to help in the training of Zambians for advancement in the industry.

Table 5.1 demonstrates the impact of the new labor policy at Nkana. Between 1964 and 1969, the African labor force increased, while the number of white workers fell; the annual turnover rate of African workers went down from 8.4% to 6.4%, while that of white workers increased. In the same period, the length of service of African workers increased from about seven to nine years, while that for white workers ranged between five and six years.

Table 5.1 shows that a substantial number of white workers continued to work at Nkana mine after independence. According to Burawoy, Zambianization in the Copperbelt mines was thwarted by the practice whereby:

> the succession [of European workers by African workers] was accompanied by the creation of new posts for some of the displaced expatriates. This not only provide[d] further employment for expatriates but also increase[d] the number of authority levels between the Zambian and the head of department.[30]

This chapter, however, observes that rapid Zambianization in the industry was mainly stymied by the fact that Africans could not easily replace European workers because the latter's skills were still needed in managerial, supervisory, and technical positions. For example, at Nkana in 1967, of the 176 Zambian section bosses, only 47 had a Standard VI and above qualification, with more than five years' underground experience.[31] Moreover, only 23 new Zambian shift bosses were promoted in 1967, and three Zambian mine

Table 5.1 Labor Strength, Turnover, and Length of Service at Nkana, 1964–1969.

	African Labor			*European Labor*		
Year	*Strength*	*Turnover %*	*Length of Service (Years)*	*Strength*	*Turnover %*	*Length of Service (Years)*
1964	9,413	8.4	7.0	1,991	22.5	5.8
1965	10,207	7.3	6.9	1,328	33.9	6.4
1966	10,891	5.2	7.5	1,705	28.6	6.3
1967	10,489	5.3	8.2	1,876	32.0	6.0
1968	11,072	5.6	8.9	1,293	34.5	5.6
1969	11,179	6.4	9.4	–	26.7	5.0

Source: Compiled from Ministry of Labour and Social Services, Strikes and Disputes, Kitwe General, February 1964–December 1967, NAZ MLSS 1/25/137; GRZ, *Report of the Commission of Inquiry into the Mining Industry 1966*, 160; Bates, *Unions, Parties, and Political Development*, 81, 250; Berger, *Labour, Race and Colonial Rule*, 208; Mhone, *The Political Economy of a Dual Labour Market in Africa*, 163.

captains were to be appointed by 1970.[32] The problem of the small number of trained African workers, however, was not unique to Nkana but a national issue. In Zambia in 1964, the total number of Africans with a secondary school certificate was just over 1,200, while the "number of Zambian graduates at the same time was scarcely 100."[33]

Meanwhile, government officials and leaders of the Mineworkers' Union of Zambia (MUZ) tried to drive government policy toward indigenization and not mere Africanization.[34] Indigenization meant creating employment opportunities for local Zambians rather than foreigners.[35] The government encouraged Nkana and the other Copperbelt mines to recruit more Zambians than foreign Africans and expatriates. Zambianization was intended to replace foreign Africans and expatriates in technical, supervisory, and managerial positions by locals.[36] As a circular from the Ministry of Labour stated in 1967:

> A number of inquiries have been made regarding the Government policy on the employment of alien Africans in the mining industry and this Circular Minute is being issued as a guide to Labour Officers on the problem. At the moment, there are thousands of alien Africans employed on the mines and therefore their employment positions calls for caution in dealing with it, particularly in the light of the fact that the matter itself has serious political implications. However, policy on the matter is that no new employment of alien Africans will be permitted, that is, any alien who is not already in employment may not be engaged on the mine in any category of work; no promotion of alien Africans will be made, or training with a view to promote will be offered to alien Africans.[37]

Indigenization and Zambianization were encouraged in the mining sector for two major reasons. Mining was the second-largest employer after public service.[38] Thus, it was anticipated that indigenization and Zambianization would promote a greater degree of local participation across the board.[39] The UNIP government also encouraged indigenization and Zambianization in order to garner political support among local workers.[40]

Table 5.2 disaggregates the number of local, foreign African, and expatriate workers at Nkana and in the other Copperbelt mines between December 1965 and December 1966. It shows that Nkana employed the largest number of foreign African workers, many of them from Malawi and Tanzania. As mentioned in chapter 4, Nyasas were not only "the most literate people of any British tropical dependency" but also among the most experienced African miners in Southern Africa, while Nyakusas from Tanzania were among the most hardworking underground miners in the region.[41] However, Rhokana Corporation operated within the government policy of limiting their advancement in the industry, specifically by confining employment and advancement at Nkana mine to local Zambians while

Table 5.2 Average Local, Foreign African, and Expatriate Labor at Nkana and in the Other Copperbelt Mines between December 1965 and December 1966.

Name of Mine	*Local*	*Foreign Africans*	*Expatriates*	*Local Section Bosses*	*Foreign African Section Bosses*
Nkana	8,371	2,503	1,705	176	9
Bancroft	2,872	1,510	568	150	6
Nchanga	7,359	975	1,237	137	–
Mufulira	7,250	1,337	1,223	223	10
Roan	6,667	1,138	1,055	214	5
Chibuluma	1,500	549	306	374	104
Total	34,019	8,012	6,094	1,274	134

Source: Compiled from Zambianisation Committee (Mines), attachment to Minutes of Meeting held in the Ministry of Labour's Office in Lusaka, March 1, 1967, NAZ MLSS 1/18/3; Zambianisation Committee, Minutes of Meeting of the Committee on Zambianisation in the Mining Industry held in Lusaka, April 19, 1967, NAZ MLSS 1/18/3; General Managers, RST and RAA, Lusaka, to Permanent Secretary, Ministry of Labour, Lusaka, May 29, 1967, NAZ MLSS 1/18/3; ZCCM Manpower Planning and Development, *Comparing Labour Strength as at 31 December 1965 and 31 December 1988*, ZCCM 1.3.1H.

ensuring that no new foreign Africans would be employed and that existing foreigners would not be given further training.

The second government objective was to expand mineral output, even as it tried to Zambianize labor by holding wages down.[42] But this objective was undermined following strikes, which lasted from April 2 to 14, 1966, involving both Europeans and Africans. They were dissatisfied with wages, housing, and general conditions of service. Africans, in particular, were protesting against the disparity between local and expatriate wages. At Nkana, the number of workers on strike or locked out were as follows: all 1,870 Europeans belonging to the Zambia Mineworkers' Society, formerly called Northern Rhodesia Mineworkers Union; all Africans belonging to the Zambia Mineworkers' Union, formerly called AMU, except 689 offering essential services; and 184 members of the Mines' Local Staff Association, previously known as Mines' African Staff Association.[43] Because of this strike, total copper production at Nkana mine fell by 3,408 long tons in 1966 compared with the output in 1965.[44]

The Brown Commission of Inquiry's report on the causes of the 1966 strike was published in October the same year. The principal recommendation of the Commission was that a single-wage structure should be introduced on the mines so that locals and expatriates should be on the same basic salaries. Most important, the Commission "proposed that the establishment of this new single structure should be preceded by increasing the local wage scale throughout by 22%" in order to bridge the gap between Europeans and Africans.[45] Since the government agreed to this proposal, Nkana and the other Copperbelt mines had no option but to implement the new wage increase. The 22% increase in African wages raised labor costs at Nkana by about £900,000 per year.[46] Despite the increase in African wages, the objective of a single-wage structure remained unrealized. Instead, in August 1968, the government introduced new expatriate conditions, which were well received.

In general, the decline in the length of service and the increase in annual turnover of Europeans, especially between 1965 and 1968, was "the result of changes in the political climate and the resulting reclassifications of European labour through Zambianisation."[47] Nonetheless, the privileged position of white workers was maintained. White employees at Nkana, as well as in other mines, continued to earn higher wages than Africans, even when they performed comparable jobs. For example, in 1966, the monthly salary of an underground expatriate shift boss was £181.16, while that of an underground local shift boss was £110.[48] The expatriate conditions granted to Europeans raised labor costs at Nkana by about £1 million per annum.[49] Since the government guaranteed better conditions of service to expatriate miners, it decided that they should not have a trade union. In April 1969, the Zambia Expatriate Mineworkers Association was banned.[50]

CAPITAL EXPENDITURE, LABOR PRODUCTIVITY, AND ORE QUALITY

Table 5.3 shows capital expenditure, productivity, and efficiency of African miners at Nkana. The patterns revealed by table 5.3 show that African labor at Nkana was more productive and efficient between 1957 and 1962, before declining between 1963 and 1966. In the latter period, footage lashed per

Table 5.3 Capital Expenditure, Productivity, and Efficiency of African Labor at Nkana Mine, 1957–1966.

Years	*Capital Expenditure (£)*	*Footage Lashed per Man-shift*	*Feet Advanced per Machine-shift*	*Tons Hoisted per Tramming Man-shift*
1957	–	–	6.88	940
1958	–	–	7.07	1,167
1959	–	–	7.13	1,193
1960	–	2.25	7.07	967
1961	960,000	2.33	7.51	1.007
1962	1,270,000	2.33	8.57	1,250
1963	1,400,000	2.33	9.82	880
1964	1,565,000	1.82	8.82	740
1965	2,685,000	1.82	6.25	873
1966	1,606,000	1.75	5.44	907

Source: Compiled from Brown Commission, *Report on Productivity and Efficiency of African Labour from 1956 to 1966*, May 26, 1966, Charts IV–VI, ZCCM 11.7.8A; RC Limited, *Annual Reports and Accounts*, 1961–1966, ZCCM 12.7.2F.

man-shift fell from about 2.3 to 1.8, feet advanced per machine-shift also fell from 8.6 to 5.4, and tons hoisted per African per shift declined from 1,250 to 907.

As mentioned previously, a substantial number of African miners, both underground and on the surface, were already experienced, trained, and advanced by 1962. In addition, labor was supplemented with machinery, and therefore, African workers should have been more productive than they were. The explanation to this issue is threefold. The first explanation relates African labor inefficiency to growing indiscipline, following African Advancement and independence. Cases of absenteeism, refusing to obey lawful instructions, bad timekeeping, and loafing at work on the Copperbelt mines increased after independence.[51] Between October and November 1966, at Nkana mine, absenteeism accounted for the largest number of offences (403) despite a noticeable stiffening of penalties awarded.[52] The number of cases of refusing to obey instructions increased from 45 in October 1966 to 109 in November the same year.[53] Cases of bad timekeeping dealt with fell by 38% from 115 cases in October to 71 in November. But there was an increase of 37.5% to 72 cases of loafing at work in this period.[54] Overall, 7.96% or 838 out of the labor force of 10,504 was disciplined. From its inception, Zambianization resulted in high levels of indiscipline.

The second reason for the lack of workplace motivation among African miners was disparities created by the continuation of the dual-wage structure. African workers were disappointed by the government's failure to abolish the dual-wage structure and the lack of meaningful improvements in their conditions of service. This partly explains why the government's attempt to mobilize or influence mineworkers to support national development failed. In addition, African miners were not well informed about the nexus between the Zambianization of labor and national development. These issues were exemplified by African workers at Nkana in their report to the members of the Zambianisation Committee who were touring the mines in 1969:

> Zambianisation, as understood by Government officials, is not understood by us in the same context. There is some frustration regarding the training program[mes], and apparently the Government is not aware of what is happening. . . . There is a general belief among the African workers that conditions of work are deteriorating every day, and nobody knows where we are heading. Unless the situation is arrested and preferably reversed, only chaos lies ahead for the mining industry.[55]

Productivity was also adversely affected by mining problems encountered at depth. By 1966, Nkana mine was almost 3,900 feet deep.[56] With increased depth, values declined, as ground conditions were deteriorating with a substantial degree of dilution—a mixture of ore with rock waste—and there was a consequential reduction in the average grade of ore mined and treated. The grade of ore mined and milled fell steadily from an average of 2.43% copper in 1960, through 2.27% in 1964, to 2.05% by 1969, making it impossible to reap the full benefits of mechanization and labor efficiency.[57] Moreover, greater volumes of water were encountered at depth, resulting in an increase from the average of 11.5 million gallons of water pumped out per day between 1957 and 1963 to 14.9 million gallons between 1964 and 1969.[58] By then, a need existed for more power to drive the water pumps. The water pumps contributed largely to the increase in the electricity load at Nkana from 68.2 million W in 1964, through 76.8 million W in 1966, to 86.1 million W in 1968.[59]

OPERATING COSTS FOR NKANA VIS-À-VIS THE PRICE OF COPPER

The factors discussed had a significant impact on operating costs at Nkana. Table 5.4 indicates the average cost of sales per ton for Nkana and the price of copper on the LME between 1964 and 1969. The table shows that the cost of sales for Nkana increased significantly between 1966 and 1968. By comparison, the price of copper increased from 1964 to 1966, before decreasing in 1967 and again improving markedly between 1968 and 1969.

The cost of sales increased because of several factors. However, as indicated earlier, the main contributing factors were the royalty and export taxes that were calculated by reference to the average price of copper on the LME.[60] During the 1966 financial year, royalty tax alone accounted for £18.6 per long ton of the total increase of £49.3 per long ton in cost of sales.[61] The following additional factors make up the balance of the increase: "labour costs

Table 5.4 Annual Cost of Sales per ton at Nkana and the Price of Copper on the London Metal Exchange, 1964–1969.

Description/Years	*1964*	*1965*	*1966*	*1967*	*1968*	*1969*
Price LME per Long Ton	£352	£469	£541	£418	£517	£617
Cost of Sales per Long Ton	£177.7	£194.5	£243.8	£349.1	£388.2	£391.8
Year-on-year Increase	£17.7	£16.8	£49.3	£105.3	£39.1	£3.6

Source: Compiled from RC Limited, *Annual Reports and Accounts*, 1964–1969.

Note: Before the Currency Act of 1967, the currency was the pound exchanged at par with the sterling pound. That year, the Zambian government introduced a new currency, the kwacha, which was one-half of the old unit, that is, the pound. Therefore, from that year, most financial calculations in the documents appear in kwacha instead of pound. Accordingly, some of the figures for 1967, and all amounts for 1968 and 1969 have been calculated using the annual average exchange rates of K1.5 = £1 old pound = £1.17 pound sterling; K1 = £0.59; and, K1 = £0.58, respectively. For further information, see: Daniel, Africanisation, Nationalisation and Inequality, xvii; Currency History—Bank of Zambia, www.boz.zm/currency-history.htm (accessed July 25, 2020).

£9.8, capital expenditure to maintain production £6.9, the effect on unit costs because of the lower output £4.4, stores £4.2, transport and realisation costs £1.6, strike expenditure £1.5 and sundry items totalling £2.3 per [long] ton."[62]

Further, the cost of sales peaked by £105.3 in 1967, primarily because of export tax, which averaged £63.2 per long ton.[63] Still more liability for taxation increased by £21 in 1968, following the promulgation of the Income Tax Amendment Act, which fixed the rate at 37.5% for all companies and consequently withdrew the differential tax rates previously enjoyed by Nkana.[64]

Cost of sales also included an increased charge in respect of capital expenditure, which, at £26 per long ton in 1967, was £19.1 higher than in 1966.[65] Between 1967 and 1969, general operating costs also increased on account of the higher prices for stores and materials, as well as the full impact of the 22% wage increase granted to local employees, increases in the African labor force, and the conversion of expatriate employees to full expatriate conditions of service.[66]

Meanwhile, Southern Rhodesia proclaimed its Unilateral Declaration of Independence (UDI) against Britain in November 1965. In retaliation, Britain and latterly the United Nations Organisation imposed sanctions on Rhodesia. Zambia followed suit. This had a huge impact on Zambia, which had a close economic association with its southern neighbor.[67] The major impact was felt in the transport sector and the supply of coal.[68] After two and half years of UDI, sanctions cost Zambia about £35 million, forcing her to find alternative ways, notably railway routes, to the coast through Mozambique (Beira) and Angola (Lobito), as well as airlifting products to and from the Tanzanian port of Dar-es-Salaam.[69] Although power supplies from the Kariba Hydro-Electric Power station were not disrupted, Zambia decided to develop new sources of coal at the Nkandabwe and Maamba fields.[70]

The increase in the cost of sales was compensated for by rising copper prices. As shown in table 5.4, the annual average price of copper per long ton on the LME increased beyond corresponding costs of sales from £352 in 1964 to £541 in 1966. Despite falling to £418 in 1967, the upward trend returned in 1968 and peaked at a record price of £617 in 1969. Between 1965 and 1966, there was a high demand for copper and cobalt in the USA particularly, following the intensification of the Vietnam War and fears of interruptions to world supplies.[71] As a result, the 1.7 cents tariff on copper sales to the USA was removed to encourage imports, and the major producers were asked "to set aside [10%] of their output for government use."[72] In line with this high demand, the monthly average price of copper on the LME increased from about £508 per long ton in October 1965 to a record £790 in April 1966.[73] In addition, the interruption of rail transport from the Copperbelt through Rhodesia between June and July 1966, arising from UDI and the political situation in Central Africa, brought a temporary surge in copper prices on the LME to a monthly average of £435 per long ton.[74] Nkana was boosted by sales surpassing production: 103,850 against 102,020 long tons of copper in 1966 and 1,711 against 1,106 short tons of cobalt in 1965, respectively.[75]

Nonetheless, the price of copper declined in 1967 because of the adoption of a new pricing system based on a three-month forward quotation for wirebars.[76] Nkana and the Copperbelt producers adopted the new system in line with the Zambian government's new tax regimes based on the price of copper on the LME. The previous pricing system was based on contractual arrangements exercised by customers. The new system led to fluctuations, with the annual average price falling from £541 to £418 in 1966 and 1967, respectively.[77]

Following the fluctuation of copper prices on the international market, the Intergovernmental Council of Copper Exporting Countries (CIPEC) was formed early in 1967 by Zambia, Zaire, Chile, and Peru to monitor the production of and the market for copper. The CIPEC administrative headquarters was based in Paris.[78] Consequently, Zambian copper exports previously absorbed by Britain and the USA found their way to France, Italy, Japan, China, and Yugoslavia.[79] Moreover, the prolonged strike in the US mining industry had a marked effect on copper prices between 1968 and 1969 with a new annual record figure (see table 5.4).[80]

FINISHED PRODUCTION AND OVERALL PROFITABILITY

Nkana produced 572,435 long tons of copper between 1964 and 1969 (see table 5.5). In the same period, Nchanga produced 1,303,834 tons; Mufulira, 919,772 tons; and Roan, 585,733 tons.[81] Nkana slipped from being the second-largest copper producer during the Federation of Rhodesia and Nyasaland to being fourth in the first five years of independence. Also in the first years of independence, Nkana's cobalt production declined from 11,026 short tons produced during the Federal era to 8,210 short tons of cobalt. As explained elsewhere, the major causes of this reduction in Nkana's production were technical difficulties associated with deep-level mining and a decline in the quality of ore. Despite reduced production, the total value of sales increased because of rising copper and cobalt prices. Consequently, Rhokana's operating profits increased in this period despite rising operating costs and royalty and export taxes (see table 5.5).

Tables 5.5 and 5.6 show that the total amount of tax paid by Nkana mine and Rhokana Corporation between 1964 and 1969 was £68,279,000, while total net profits from Nkana mine and investment income from other properties amounted to £73,814,000. Of this latter figure, £54,015,000 was paid as dividends to shareholders, while preference redemption funds

Table 5.5 Production, Value of Sales, Cost of Sales, Royalty/Export Tax, and Operating Profits for Nkana Mine, 1964–1969.

	Production					
Year	*Copper*	*Cobalt*	*Value of Sales*	*Cost of Sales*	*Royalty/ Export Tax*	*Operating Profits*
	Long Tons	*Short Tons*	*£*	*£*	*£*	*£*
1964	107,014	1,048	29,400,000	22,601,000	3,554,000	6,799,000
1965	99,995	1,106	27,697,000	21,856,000	5,080,000	5,841,000
1966	96,587	1,694	29,983,000	25,173,000	5,685,000	3,911,000
1967	81,929	1,717	32,055,000	28,144,000	6,225,000	4,810,000
1968	90,272	1,499	46,157,000	36,899,000	11,397,000	9,258,000
1969	96,638	1,146	50,699,000	38,039,000	17,307,000	12,660,000
Total	572,435	8,210	215,991,000	172,712,000	49,248,000	43,279,000

Source: Compiled from CISB Limited, *Copperbelt of Zambia Mining Industry Yearbooks*, 1965–1968, ZCCM 12.1.9C; CISB Limited, *Mining Industry Yearbook of Zambia 1969* (Kitwe: CISB, 1969), passim; RC Limited, *Annual Reports and Accounts*, 1964–1969.

Note: Value and Cost of Sales represent total amounts for both copper and cobalt. The amounts of Royalty and Export Tax were combined because they were both charged against the LME price of copper and, as mentioned elsewhere earlier, were part of Cost of Sales or Production. These also include royalties paid on cobalt exports-.

Table 5.6 Gross Profits from Nkana and Other Mines and Issued Share Capital, Income Tax, Net Profits, and Dividends for Rhokana Corporation, 1964–1969.

		Gross Profits				
Year	*Issued Share Capital (£)*	*Nkana Mine (£)*	*Other Mines (£)*	*Income Tax (£)*	*Net Profits (£)*	*Net Dividends (£)*
1964	25,731,000	6,799,000	4,717,000	4,020,000	8,682,000	8,462,000
1965	25,720,000	5,841,000	5,195,000	2,840,000	9,940,000	8,771,000
1966	25,709,000	3,911,000	4,949,000	2,420,000	9,675,000	8,773,000
1967	25,698,000	4,810,000	5,863,000	1,700,000	9,055,000	7,522,000
1968	30,311,000	9,258,000	6,263,000	3,369,000	13,856,000	8,138,000
1969	29,783,000	12,660,000	12,044,000	4,682,000	22,606,000	12,349,000
Total	162,952,000	43,279,000	39,031,000	19,031,000	73,814,000	54,015,000

Source: Compiled from CISB Limited, *Copperbelt of Zambia Mining Industry Yearbooks*, 1965–1968; CISB Limited, *Mining Industry Yearbook of Zambia 1969*, passim; RC Limited, *Annual Reports and Accounts*, 1964–1969.

Note: Gross Profits are divided into two parts: profits from Nkana mine and profits from Rhokana's investments in other mines and properties on the Copperbelt. Income Tax was charged on total Gross Profits. The difference was added to unappropriated profits brought forward from the previous year to come up with the total Net Profits for the Corporation in that financial year. Total Net Dividends were calculated from Net Profits.

and general reserve amounts totaled £11,580,280, leaving unappropriated net profits of £8,218,720.[82] Clearly, the retained or reinvested profits were much lower than the appropriated earnings of shareholders. Mhone noted this in his analysis of percentage distribution of gross profits for Roan, Mufulira, and Nkana.[83] The annual average initial declared dividends between 1964 and 1969 from Nkana were 60.7%, which was the highest in the Copperbelt mines, whereas retained earnings in this period averaged 18.6% per year.[84]

ECONOMIC REASONS FOR THE NATIONALIZATION OF NKANA AND THE COPPERBELT MINES

The large difference between appropriated and retained profits for the mines, as well as in other sectors such as manufacturing, construction, retail, and service, annoyed the government, and it decided to limit dividend transfers abroad. The government accused private companies of appropriating and externalizing huge amounts of profits at the expense of reinvestment and expansion in the local economy.[85] This was the major reason why the Zambian government decided to nationalize the private sector in 1968 despite having promised previously not to do so. The UNIP government abandoned its liberal policies for radical policies of nationalization. Accordingly, private control came to an end in the manufacturing, construction, retail, and service sectors on April 19, 1968, when, following President Kaunda's Mulungushi Reforms speech, the government partially nationalized 25 leading private companies by acquiring 51% shares.[86]

The mining companies were not yet nationalized, but shareholders in Rhokana and the other Copperbelt mining companies felt the pinch of the new legislation limiting dividend remittances. The president argued that "mining developments [are] virtually grinding to a halt because of the reluctance on the part of the mining companies to plough some of their profits back into the industry. They [prefer] to distribute the profits as dividends."[87] Thus, a 50% limitation on the distribution of profits to shareholders outside Zambia was introduced in 1968.[88] As indicated in table 5.6, dividends distributed to shareholders, which amounted to 89.8% of total net profits between 1964 and 1967, reduced drastically to 56.2% of the profits from 1968 to 1969.

Rhokana and the other Copperbelt mining companies thought that the government was acting unfairly in limiting dividend transfers. Speaking on behalf of ZAMANGLO, the chairman, Harry Oppenheimer, argued that the companies had paid 65% of their gross mining profits to the government, only distributing to shareholders 80% of what remained to them.[89] He further claimed that the ZAMANGLO group invested no less than K36.4 (£21.5) million, equivalent to 41% of the dividends paid since independence, while an additional K12.6 (£7.4) million retained out of net profits was used for capital expenditure purposes.[90] This amounted to a total of 55.3% invested of the amount paid out in dividends since 1964.[91]

Table 5.7 Capital Expenditure, Production, Value of Tax, Net Profits, and Dividends for Rhokana, 1964–1969.

		Production				
Year	Capital (£)	Copper Long Tons	Cobalt Short Tons	Value of Tax £	Net Profits (£)	Dividends (£)
1964	1,565,000	107,014	1,048	7,574,000	8,682,000	8,462,000
1965	2,685,000	99,995	1,106	7,920,000	9,940,000	8,771,000
1966	1,606,000	96,587	1,694	8,105,000	9,675,000	8,773,000
1967	2,649,000	81,929	1,717	7,925,000	9,055,000	7,522,000
1968	3,077,000	90,272	1,499	14,766,000	13,856,000	8,138,000
1969	4,350,000	96,638	1,146	21,989,000	22,606,000	12,349,000
Total	15,932,000	572,435	8,210	68,279,000	73,814,000	54,015,000

Source: Compiled from CISB Limited, *Copperbelt of Zambia Mining Industry Yearbooks*, 1965–68; CISB Limited, *Mining Industry Yearbook of Zambia 1969*, passim; RC Limited, *Annual Reports and Accounts*, 1964–1969.

Note: Capital Expenditure and Production represent figures for the Nkana mine only. Value of Tax covers total amounts for royalty, export, and income taxes (see tables 5.5 and 5.6).

Table 5.7 disaggregates capital expenditure and metal output at Nkana mine, as well as total amounts of tax, net profits, and dividends for Rhokana Corporation in the period under examination.

Table 5.7 suggests otherwise for the Rhokana Corporation; dividends accounted for 73.2% of total net profits, whereas unappropriated or retained earnings after subtracting dividends, preference share redemption, and general reserve amounts from total net profits accounted for only 11.1% between 1964 and 1969.[92] For this period, the table shows that total dividends paid to shareholders abroad were almost three-and-a-half times over the total amount of capital consumed: £54,015,000 compared to £15,932,000, respectively. A large amount of capital was needed to invest in mining developments and machinery/technology to cater for the deteriorating quantity and quality of ores and improve on metal output at Nkana. As explained earlier and as indicated in table 5.7, copper production declined from 107,014 tons in 1964 to 96,638 tons in 1969. Similarly, cobalt output reduced drastically from a peak of 1,717 tons in 1967 to 1,146 tons in 1969.

The Roan Selection Trust (RST) group—a holding company for ST/AMAX shares in the Zambian mining industry—raised similar views as ZAMANGLO. RST chairman, Ronald Prain, argued that there was no relationship between dividend rates and mining development.[93] He claimed that the "high dividends simply reflecte[d] the extremely high taxation in Zambia . . . So, because taxation [was] so high, it follows that dividends from remaining profits must have a fairly high ratio to those profits simply to attract overseas investment in the company."[94] Despite high taxes, the Rhokana Corporation paid out a record dividend amount in 1969 (see table 5.7).

Thus, the government remained resolute on this issue and further accused Rhokana and the other mining companies of transfer pricing by "buying goods from parent companies overseas at up to 33 percent above cost price in order to increase expatriation of capital."[95]

As a result, the mining companies and most private enterprises relied excessively on foreign bank credit for capital.[96] For instance, early in 1968, AAC/ZAMANGLO concluded a loan agreement worth K50 (£29.5) million with two major Japanese companies, Mitsui and Mitsubishi, for which the Rhokana Corporation stood as a guarantor.[97] This loan was meant to be repaid in the form of copper supplies totaling 100,000 tons annually for a period of 10 years.[98] Given that the price of copper averaged £617 per ton during the 1969 financial year, the first instalment would be valued at £61,700,000. Nevertheless, after the Mulungushi Reforms in April 1968, the terms of this loan agreement were revised, and the balance due on that loan had been reduced to K11.4 (£6.6) million as on June 5, 1969.[99] Therefore, the assertion by Barton that limitations of government policy undermined investment in the industry has been challenged, and the experience of Rhokana has also been qualified.[100]

When presenting the national budget to members of parliament on January 30, 1969, the vice president, Simon Mwansa Kapwepwe, reiterated President Kaunda's Mulungushi Reforms speech, accusing private firms of "making excessive profits [but retaining] only a small proportion of the profits . . . in Zambia for expansion."[101] This supports this chapter's contention that the externalization of dividends to shareholders abroad from the private sector, at the expense of investment in the local industries, was the major reason for the partial nationalization of the Zambian economy.

As discussed earlier, the most influential international factor upon Kaunda's decision to nationalize the mining sector was the marked rise in the price of copper on the LME. Between January and July 1969, the copper price reached a monthly average peak of £624 per ton, spurring the government to nationalize the industry in August the same year.[102] Contrary to Martin's suggestion that the Zambian government simply mimicked the Chilean government's reasons for nationalization, it was in fact the peak in the price of copper that had the most impact upon the former's decision to partially nationalize the industry.[103]

The principle of 51% that was already being applied in the manufacturing, construction, and service industries was extended to the mining sector, with the government acquiring 51% ownership and the two firms, RST and ZAMANGLO, sharing 49% between them.[104] Other reforms included a 51% mineral tax and a continuation of the 50% curb on dividend remittances.[105] The government announced that the new mineral tax would be based on profitability, instead of the royalty and export tax system, which were related to prices on the LME.[106]

To implement the new state–private venture, the government determined that there would be modifications of the corporate structure of the group companies. Even so, the two mining giants retained managerial, sales, and marketing responsibilities but had to work hand in hand with government officials.[107] Another consoling factor to the multinationals, AAC and AMAX, was an agreement that Zambia would compensate them to the extent of US$178 (K127.1, £73.7) million to be paid over 12 years.[108]

CONCLUSION

Both Nkana mine's labor organization and profitability changed during the first years of independence. In order to safeguard their operations, Rhokana and the other Copperbelt companies implemented new government policies only to a limited extent. Rhokana/ZAMANGLO, like RST, worked with the government in promoting Zambianization in the industry and developing alternative sources of coal and new transport routes during UDI. Over and beyond this cooperation, however, Rhokana also maximized its dividend repatriation to shareholders abroad. The Zambian government was angered by Rhokana and the Copperbelt companies' distribution of huge dividends to shareholders abroad, even as they retained only a small proportion of their profits for investment in the industry. The government used this factor to introduce partial nationalization in the mining sector. The new policies of Zambianization and nationalization continued to affect the operations of Rhokana/Nkana after 1969.

Chapter 6

Rokana/Nkana during the First and Second Phase of Nationalization, 1970–1981

FIRST PHASE OF NATIONALIZATION: THE GOVERNMENT TAKEOVER AND REORGANIZATION OF THE MINING INDUSTRY

After the Matero Declaration of 1969, the Zambian government and the mining companies prepared to negotiate the new state–private joint venture. The bargaining position of the companies was strengthened by the fact that Zambia still needed them to run the mines, while the government's position was strengthened by the fact that the "companies had only two alternatives: [either] to do business on Zambian terms . . . or to pull out of the country altogether and lose their whole investment and prospects of future income."[1]

The government had three major aims in negotiating the takeover. As stated in chapter 5, the United National Independence Party (UNIP) leadership wished to acquire substantial control over the activities of the mining companies, since it no longer trusted their transactions.[2] At the same time, the government wanted to partner with the companies in order to direct their operations toward increasing mineral production.[3] Thus, the government desired to retain the companies' managerial and technical expertise until such a time that more Zambians could be trained to take over these functions.[4]

Four issues dominated the negotiations. These were "the method of valuing the assets; the terms of repayment; the future management fee for the companies; and guarantees that the agreement would be honoured."[5] The assets of Anglo American Corporation (AAC) in the Zambian mining sector were valued at K240 million, while those of Roan Selection Trust (RST) were valued at K165 million. The Zambian government would pay 51% of these valuations plus interest, that is, K125 million and K84 million, respectively.[6] Compensation was to be made through government/Zambia Industrial and

Mining Corporation (ZIMCO) bonds with an interest rate of 6%, to be paid over a period of 12 years, beginning in 1970.[7] The bonds were listed on the London Stock Exchange in order to maintain their true value.

Management contracts, covering a range of services from higher-level to staff positions, to the marketing of copper, were left under the control of the mining companies. The management fee was set at 0.75% and 2% of sales revenue and profits after mineral tax, respectively, while the sales service provided by the two mining companies was set at 0.75% of the gross revenue.[8] This represented a lucrative total of 3.5% to be appropriated by each of the two mining companies free from exchange control. In fact, management fees, service charges, and bond repayments were not subjected to the Zambian exchange control. The bonds would be paid in US dollars and could be remitted anywhere in the world designated by the companies. In addition, the parties agreed that future disputes over partial nationalization would be settled with the help of the International Centre for the Settlement of Investment Disputes.[9]

In the Matero announcement on August 11, 1969, President Kenneth Kaunda also stated that mineral concessions would revert to the state. Consequently, the Mines and Minerals Act was passed soon after the Declaration was signed and became effective on January 1, 1970. This Act specified that mineral concessions "reverted to the state, and a system of licenses was introduced under which companies [would] prospect, explore or mine in specific areas and for specific periods."[10]

The Act had further restrictions in terms of the acquisition of mining rights and the exploration regulations, mining conditions, and duration of prospecting. It also allowed the state to take part in any mining venture. The latter regulation was similar to that introduced by the British South Africa (BSA) Company in 1922. The government realized that Rhokana and the other mining companies held exclusive mining and prospecting rights extending over vast areas "in perpetuity [to 64,000 square miles of land without enough development being undertaken]."[11] So, it was important for the government to terminate exclusive mining rights in order to "encourage accelerated expansion in prospecting, and exploration by parties other than those that had obtained concessions in earlier years." Furthermore, "large areas were opened under the new Act for prospecting by other parties."[12] The government hoped to stimulate mineral exploration and development and expand production. It was also the best way to change the structure of production and initiate the new state–private enterprise.

The government responded to the companies' discontent with the tax system by replacing two taxes (royalties and export tax) previously paid against production and the price of copper with a 51% mineral tax levied on profits.[13] In addition, a uniform income tax rate of 45% on the profit was introduced.[14] However, the twofold mining tax regime raised taxes charged on the Copperbelt companies from about 74.4% between 1964 and 1969 to above 80% after 1970.[15] Capital expenditure on mining operations was also to be deducted from profits before taxation. But there were some incentives for the companies. For instance, the Mineral Tax Act "provided a mineral tax refund for a new mining company incorporated in Zambia."[16] The purpose of these tax reforms was to encourage the companies to open new mines and develop low-grade and high-cost ones. The Mineral Tax Act also provided that Nchanga Consolidated Copper Mines (NCCM) and Roan Consolidated Mines (RCM) would not pay tax on unprofitable mines.

Reorganization of the mining company structure was settled quickly. The AAC mining assets were placed under a new company, NCCM Limited, while the companies operated by RST International, owned by the American Metal Climax (AMAX), were placed under RCM Limited. The shares in each of the two mining groups were divided into two parts. The Mining and Industrial Development Corporation (MINDECO) Limited, a new state corporation, held the "A" shares comprising 51% of the capital, while the mining companies and international public investors shared the "B" shares comprising the remaining 49% of the capital.[17] Because of this reorganization, minority shares were streamlined as follows: AAC held, through Zambia Copper Investment (ZCI) Limited, a 49% interest in NCCM; RST International held 20.43% in RCM, on behalf of AMAX; ZCI also owned 12.25% in RCM; and international public investors held 16.32% in RCM.[18]

The Zambian government was "satisfied that the capacity had been bought much cheaper than new capacity could have been created."[19] By comparison, "the Zambians paid K550 per ton for operating capacity," whereas "the Chileans at the same time paid K650 per ton and expansion schemes throughout the world were costing around K1,400 per ton at the end of the sixties."[20] Even so, as noted in the previous chapter, Rhokana and the other Copperbelt mines had arguably been more than adequately compensated for their investments in the form of the massive profits sent abroad. Besides, foreign companies were not only compensated for agreeing to the principle of partial nationalization but would also remain minority shareholders in the Zambian mining industry.

By contrast, Zambia's neighbor, the Congo, introduced a 100% nationalization in 1969.[21] Despite full nationalization of the mining sector in the Congo, its mines continued to rely on technical and marketing services of foreign companies.[22] Similarly, minority shareholders kept effective control of the mines in Zambia, enjoying a wide range of safeguards. NCCM and RCM retained a veto power over certain areas of the mining activities such as "winding-up of operations; disposal of assets; grants of any retained concessions or mining rights to others; new financial commitments; borrowing powers; appropriation for capital expenditure; and exploration and prospecting."[23] These negotiations were finalized on December 24, 1969, and the new corporate structure came into effect in January 1970.[24]

The Importance of Rokana/Nkana Mine Division for NCCM

NCCM consisted of Rokana/Nkana Mine Division and Central Services Divisions in Kitwe, Chingola Division in Chingola, Konkola Division in Chililabombwe, and Broken Hill Division in Kabwe, which produced zinc and lead.[25] As stated in chapter 5, these divisions were controlled by the Zambian Anglo American Corporation (ZAMANGLO) and produced about 53% of Zambia's copper output per year between 1964 and 1969.[26] Prior to nationalization, AAC held 45% shares in ZAMANGLO. ZAMANGLO held the "highest controlling share of 53.7% in Rhokana Corporation Limited."[27] As indicated in chapter 1, Rhokana was not only a copper and cobalt mining company but also an investment firm in other mines and metallurgical properties on the Copperbelt. Thus, prior to nationalization, Rhokana owned a share percentage of 100% in Bwana Mkubwa mine, 50% in Rhokana Copper Refineries, 34.73% in Nchanga mine, 34.51% in Bancroft mine, 30% in Chisangwa mine, 26.68% in Baluba mine, 26.61% in Mufulira mine, and 8.63% in Mwinilunga mine.[28] Investment income from these properties contributed to almost half of Rhokana's net profits. Moreover, the Company smelted and refined its own copper from the Nkana mine and the surplus from other mines, including Nchanga, Bancroft, Bwana Mkubwa, and Mufulira. Rhokana's book balance of issued capital in shares of K4 was valued at slightly above K112 million in 1969.[29] Overall, Rhokana had the widest and biggest operations in the Zambian mining industry prior to nationalization.

As a result of the new Mines and Minerals Act, Rhokana lost investments in the other mines, as well as mining rights over vast areas. For example, in 1969, the Company held special grants of mining rights over 36,800 acres in the Nkana area and over 37,000 acres in the Bwana Mkubwa area, a grant of exclusive prospecting rights over 51 square miles in the Bwana Mkubwa area, and freehold and leasehold surface rights in the Nkana area over 44,812 acres and 23,908 acres over Bwana Mkubwa.[30]

In line with the new law, Rhokana's special grants for mining licenses were reduced to just over 16,882 acres in the Nkana area and 9,701 acres in the Bwana Mkubwa area. On the other hand, freehold and leasehold surface rights remained almost the same over 44,600 acres in the Nkana area and approximately 23,700 acres in Bwana Mkubwa.[31] Rhokana also ceased to be the consulting engineer to the Copperbelt mines, except for Bwana Mkubwa.[32] The government created the Geological Survey Department to work in conjunction with the two mining firms (NCCM and RCM) in carrying out mineral exploration. Furthermore, government issued some 120 new prospecting and exploration licenses to various companies from countries such as the United States of America (USA), Britain, Japan, Yugoslavia, Italy, France, and Romania to prospect for copper, uranium, and other minerals.[33] Individual mines did their own prospecting and exploration, although the parent company to Rhokana, AAC, was hired at times. Because of the new mining structure, Rhokana Corporation was renamed Rokana/Nkana Mine Division to end any Rhodesian connotations.[34]

Despite the restructuring, Rokana/Nkana remained one of the most important divisions of the mining, smelting, and refining operations, of NCCM, in particular, and the Zambian mining industry, in general. Its major importance lay in the fact that the Division operated three underground mines (South, Central, and Mindola orebodies) and one open-pit mine, with estimated ore reserves averaging 124,600,000 metric tons, containing about 2.6% copper in 1970.[35] The orebody averaged 55 degrees in dip and about 8 meters in thickness.[36]

From these sources, the division was capable of producing almost 100,000 metric tons of copper and 1,900 tons of cobalt a year.[37] The Rokana concentrator operated differential flotation of copper and cobalt mineralization from underground sulfides, and an oxide concentrator was commissioned after 1970. Rokana also operated one of the world's largest copper smelters.[38] It treated about 80,000 metric tons of copper a month of sulfide and oxide concentrates for the three major producing NCCM mines (Nkana, Konkola, and Chingola).[39] The refinery produced about 17,000 metric tons of electro-refined copper a month and also casted about 20,000 tons of wirebars per month, while the cobalt plant produced up to 2,000 tons of electrolytic metal a year from its complex leaching and purification circuits.[40] The Nkana cobalt plant also continued to treat cobalt from mines owned by RCM.

In terms of offering employment opportunities in the Zambian mining industry, Nkana employed a labor force of about 11,000 Africans and over 1,000 expatriates each year between 1968 and 1970.[41]

SECOND PHASE OF NATIONALIZATION: THE REDEEMING OF BONDS IN NCCM AND RCM

While Nkana and the other Copperbelt mines were implementing the industry's new corporate structure, the Copperbelt was severely hit by political and economic problems in the national, regional, and international arena between 1971 and 1973. The increased government control of the mining industry in Zambia brought about concomitant changes in the country's system of government. During the period from 1964 to 1971, Zambia was a multiparty democracy. Internal wrangles in the UNIP led to the formation of a rival party, the United Progressive Party (UPP), by Simon M. Kapwepwe in 1971.[42] The UPP became a threat to UNIP's ruling elites, who responded vigorously. In December 1972, UNIP declared a one-party-state rule in Zambia, and opposition political parties were banned.[43] Thus, for 17 years, Zambia was ruled as a one-party state, by the UNIP, under the leadership of President Kenneth Kaunda.

While UNIP was grappling with intraparty wrangles, the government was severely hit by falling tax revenue from the mines. Revenue from mining fell from K234 million in 1969 to an average of K42 million in 1971 and 1972.[44] This reduction was partly due to the 1969 contract agreement with the companies, which put a strain on the government's effective tax rate. As mentioned earlier, in theory, the total tax take was above 80% of profits, but the 1969 Agreement reduced the government's effective tax rate in 1971 and 1972 to 28% of the profits.[45] The balance of payment was further strained by greater leakage of foreign exchange through dividend remittances and capital repayments. Depending on the price of copper and profits, the "net foreign exchange cost of the management fees ran between K2 million and K6 million a year."[46]

The major problem of the 1969 Agreement was that it did not provide for a reduction of capital repayments if the price of copper dropped.[47] The government did not anticipate that the price of copper would drop below K800 per metric ton over the repayment period.[48] The price of copper actually fell from K1,252 per long ton in 1970 to K750 in 1971, rising minimally to K796 in 1972.[49] As a result, the balance of payments deteriorated from a surplus of K77 million in 1970 to a deficit of K97.5 million in 1972. Despite the fall in revenue from mining, the government could neither increase mineral export income nor withhold taxes and royalty payments as long as the bonds remained outstanding.

These problems were compounded by rising production costs and Rhodesia's closure of the border with Zambia in January 1973. The cost of sales per metric ton of copper at Nkana and NCCM-owned mines increased from an average of K519 in 1971 to over K600 by the end of 1972.[50] Previously, 50% of Rokana and NCCM copper had been exported through Beira and Rhodesia.[51] Now copper had to be rerouted, though consumables such as coke, sulfuric acid, chlorine, and explosives were mainly in short supply. Materials including machinery had to be airlifted into the Copperbelt. Nkana and the Copperbelt mines complained of rising production costs, but the government accused them and their mother companies of "artificially inflating costs as a hidden way of exporting profits and reducing tax payments."[52] Furthermore, the government claimed that some consumables could be obtained cheaply in Zambia.

By mid-1973, however, the price of copper per metric ton increased from an average of K766 in 1972 to K817 on the international market.[53] The monthly price of copper had risen since mid-1971 because of two major reasons. First, it began to rise in July 1971 following the strike involving 30,000 workers in the four big US mines. This partly reduced world stocks and indirectly stimulated demand and price.[54] Second, three of the four major copper exporting countries, Zaire, previously the Congo, Peru, and Zambia, were trying through the Intergovernmental Council of Copper Exporting Countries (CIPEC) to ensure stability in the world copper market.[55] These countries cut back production by 10% and, in 1972, reduced world copper stocks to help stimulate its demand and price. They also used the London Metal Exchange (LME) cash settlement price for sales purposes, which partly helped to stabilize the copper price. The military coup in Chile and resultant production problems also helped to ease world stocks—therefore, restoring demand and a rise in the price of copper in 1973.[56]

The Zambian government sought to take advantage in August 1973 of the increase in copper prices to redeem the remaining bonds in NCCM and RCM. Several reasons were advanced for the government's dramatic decision to redeem the bonds. One of the major considerations was that the government was not comfortable with the fact that the companies "retained effective control of the industry through" their managerial control and power of veto and "their resistance to Zambianisation."[57] In fact, the issue of Zambianisation had not been included in the 1970 Agreement, leaving the companies with the right to hire and fire.[58]

The major complaint from the government was that, "despite the generous tax provisions, and the relaxation of foreign exchange controls, the companies were not concerned to invest in Zambia, as they had been before the Matero announcement."[59] The government argued that the two companies, NCCM and RCM, transferred levies charged for their sales, marketing, management, and consultancy services abroad instead of reinvesting it in the industry. As a result, "capital for the expansion programmes of both companies [was mainly] obtained from external borrowing and not from retained profits."[60] By then, the two companies were planning to borrow about K65 million from abroad.[61]

The government further accused the mining companies of double-dealing, as they entered into separate arrangements with other foreign companies for acquisitions of loans, as well as sales, marketing, management, and consultancy services.[62] According to the UNIP leadership, this was what made the services from these companies expensive. The companies entered into separate arrangements, with either their parent companies or others, for one major reason: to avoid paying high tax. When asked how NCCM and RCM practiced transfer pricing, Charles Muchimba explained that one of the methods was through:

> selling their copper to parent companies [AAC and AMAX] or their agents abroad at a reduced price. The parent companies would later on re-sell the copper on the international market at a high price. Moreover, NCCM and RCM would obtain loans from lending institutions abroad at a higher rate than what was obtained on the market. When they sold copper, the companies would start by paying overdue tax on contracts. Then what remained was low profit. The Copperbelt companies, therefore, paid less tax by reducing declared profit. Therefore, the financial structure of the companies was designed to syphon profits abroad and to make it easy to discharge themselves should conditions in Zambia become unfavourable for their business.[63]

Given these factors, the government decided to revise the 1970 Agreement. Accordingly, the outstanding ZIMCO bonds were redeemed, while management and sales contracts between MINDECO, AAC, and AMAX were terminated on August 31, 1973. The outstanding "bonds were redeemed partly out of buoyant foreign exchange reserves due to the temporary high price of copper, which reached K1,500 in November 1973," and with "the proceeds from a US$115 million Euro-dollar loan raised earlier that year."[64]

However, many observers felt that the government was not sincere about the 1973 rearrangement of the mining industry. The 1973 takeover was criticized on four grounds. According to Andrew Sardanis, the government's decision was associated with personal interests within Kaunda's government and businessmen such as Tiny Rowland of London Rhodesia (Lonrho) Limited.[65] Prior to President Kaunda's announcement of the cancellation of the 1970 Agreement, Lonrho had purchased a considerable number of ZIMCO bonds on the London Stock Exchange, which, by August 1973, were trading at half their original value following rumors that the government would default.[66] In addition, Rowland's friendship with Humphrey Mulemba, minister of Mines, spawned accusations that "the cohort to this imprudent transaction influenced Kaunda's decision to redeem the outstanding bonds."[67]

Second, the government was charged for abrogating the management and sales contracts. For abrogating these contracts, the government compensated the AAC with K33 million and AMAX with K22 million.[68] The third major criticism was that the bonds were redeemed by borrowed money on the Euro-dollar market.[69] The short loan was obtained at an "exorbitant interest rate of 13%" to pay bonds with an interest rate of 6%.[70] In total, the government paid about "US$231 million when it could have bought the bonds on the [London Stock] market [where they were floated in August 1973] for just US$110.88 million, thus saving the country $120.12 million [than benefiting AAC, AMAX, and Lonrho]."[71]

The bonds had four significant advantages: "the bonds only had eight and a half years to run; there was no direct government obligation; and were to be repaid out of dividends"; and could be renegotiated if the mines became unprofitable.[72] Fourth, Lanning and Mueller suggested that "the best and cheapest way for the government would have been to buy out ZAMANGLO [NCCM] and sell off its non-Zambian assets."[73]

Once the bonds were redeemed, the companies were subject to normal taxation and exchange control regulations. With effect from December 1973, the companies' dividends to shareholders abroad were subject to a 20% tax rate.[74] The tax rate to which NCCM was granted 100% allowance for capital expenditure was withdrawn.[75] A high tax rate was introduced at 74.5% consisting "of a 51% minerals tax on profits and a 48% tax on profits after minerals tax and credit for minerals tax payment."[76] There was also high effective taxation on cobalt, zinc, and lead revenues at 58.4% comprising a 20% minerals tax and 48% income tax. These tax regimes, coupled with surcharges on dividend remittances, maintained government's total share of profits above 80%.

The sales contracts were also terminated, and the Metal Marketing Company (MEMACO), wholly owned by the government and based in Zambia, was established to market copper from RCM and NCCM.[77] Copper from Nkana and NCCM-operated mines had been marketed by Anmercosa Sales Limited, created by AAC in 1966 and based in London.[78] Anmercosa Sales had established trade links with various companies in South Africa, Europe, the USA, and Japan.[79] When asked why MEMACO was formed and subsidiary offices opened in London, Francis Kaunda (not related to President Kenneth Kaunda), responded jokingly, "Young man, when the copper reached the shore [to world markets], you literally know nothing about what happens to it thereafter, and this problem has continued up till now."[80] It can be seen from his illustration that, following the military coup in Chile in 1973 and the resultant weakness of the CIPEC, it became difficult for the Zambian government to monitor the copper market and sales abroad; hence, the formation of MEMACO in 1974.[81]

Besides the aforementioned restructuring, the government Zambianized the position of managing director in the two companies. It was proposed that the "A" shareholders and not the "B" shareholders would appoint the managing directors of NCCM and RCM. In this connection, W.M. Chakulya, an "A" director, was appointed managing director of the NCCM in February 1974.[82] But to prevent MINDECO or the management of NCCM and RCM from becoming a rival center of power, the relationship between these companies was restructured.[83] MINDECO ceased to be the holding company for the two mining companies, while the government's shares in these companies were transferred to the Ministry of Finance and Ministry of Mines.[84]

While the new changes did not have a direct impact on Nkana, the new tax rates totaling above 80% meant that tax in the Zambian mining sector was among the highest in the world. It left Nkana and the other Copperbelt mines with little resources to invest in expanded production. It also ate into the companies' net profits, as shall be discussed later. Also, the termination of managerial contracts with the mining firms and the subsequent emphasis on rapid Zambianization in the mining industry had a significant impact on labor organization in the mines after 1973.

Indigenization and Zambianization of Labor in the Mining Sector

As discussed in chapter 5, the Zambian government distinguished Zambianization from Africanization. In this vein, the government reduced the number of both expatriate and foreign African workers in order to provide more employment opportunities for local people. The UNIP government also emphasized discipline, efficiency, and productivity of labor for the sake of the country's wider economic development.[85] In September 1970, a productivity agreement was signed between the mining companies and the Mineworkers' Union of Zambia (MUZ).[86] It incorporated an integrated pay structure and improvements in conditions of service in return for measures to improve efficiency.[87]

For Nkana and the other NCCM mines, however, indigenization and Zambianization of labor not only promoted government policy but also induced greater stability in the labor force, permitting savings on recruitment and other incidental costs.[88] Table 6.1 shows the number of local, expatriate, and foreign Africans at Nkana from 1966 through 1970 to 1976.

The patterns that emerge from table 6.1 provide insight into indigenization and Zambianization of labor at Nkana. It was obvious that indigenization increased the number of local workers from 8,371 in December 1966 to 11,284 by December 1976. The number of expatriate workers declined from 1,705 in 1966 to almost half that number in 1970, falling to 600 in 1976. By 1980, there were less than 468 expatriate workers at Nkana.[89] The number of foreign Africans went down from 2,503 in 1966 to 1,448 by 1976, in line with the 1967 government policy of freezing them in their positions and squeezing them out of the industry to increase opportunities for Zambians. The reduction in the number of expatriate workers between 1970 and 1971 was largely due to the nationalization in the mining sector. When asked why the number of expatriate workers reduced drastically in these years, Sardanis stated that most expatriates were worried about their future following nationalization of the sector and resigned.[90]

One day after the Matero speech, the government sent a consortium of paramilitary and police officers to the Copperbelt to guard the mines and

Table 6.1 Comparing Local, Expatriate, and Alien (Foreign) African Labor Strength at Nkana in December of Each Year from 1966 through 1970 to 1976.

	Local Employees			*Expatriate Workers*			*Foreign African Workers*		
Year	*Total*	*Male*	*Female*	*Total*	*Male*	*Female*	*Total*	*Male*	*Female*
1966	8,371*	–	–	1,705*	–	–	2,503*	–	–
1970	11,545	11,213	332	843	712	131	–	–	–
1971	11,444	11,082	362	808	693	115	–	–	–
1972	9,739	9,421	318	726	628	98	1,807	1,759	48
1973	10,300	9,933	367	678	589	89	1,726	1,682	44
1975	10,784	10,365	419	698	598	100	1,550	1,514	36
1976	11,284	10,822	462	600	523	77	1,448	1,414	34

Source: Drawn from Rokana Mine Division, Employment Returns, 1970–1976, ZCCM T8.2A.

Note: *These figures represent total numbers for male and female workers. The number of expatriate workers between 1972 and 1976 has been calculated by adding figures for Zambians and non-Zambians and deducting number of Africans. There are no categorized figures for male and female workers for 1966 and for local and alien African employees in 1970 and 1971. Also, there are no figures categorizing alien male and female workers for 1970 and 1971.*

other workshops.[91] The government feared that expatriate miners would riot and cause damage to the mining properties following government takeover. A delegate of 40 government workers was sent to ascertain the attitude of the white miners and convince them that they would not be retrenched from the mines. This delegate soon joined the police officers. Sardanis, then permanent secretary in the Ministry of State Participation, was one of the delegates.

The delegation held meetings in each mine including Nkana. Expatriate workers raised a number of concerns. Some feared that their future was at stake since Zambianization and nationalization would displace them. Others were worried about their safety after complaining of being racially abused in the mine compounds, shops, and other public places.[92] Sardanis recalled one worker expressing worries about the future value of his pension following nationalization of the sector.[93] The delegation explained to the miners that their pension fund would be externalized and that this automatically meant that the expatriates' wages would increase. Government, Nkana, and the other mines were also forced to retain the expatriate workers because there were very few skilled and trained Zambians to take up skilled jobs in administration, mining engineering, metallurgy, mineral technology, electrical engineering, mechanical engineering, geology, and chemical engineering.[94] Expatriate employees were also retained in order to train local workers for Zambianization.[95]

Table 6.1 also points up the employment of female employees at Nkana. In 1956, the majority of women were employed in the colony's agricultural sector where there were 75 female European workers and 4,000 female Africans.[96] The same year, there were 460 female European workers and only

100 female African workers in the mining industry.[97] Most white women were employed in administration as secretaries, while black women performed duties such as cleaning and cooking in the mines. According to the *Mining Mirror*, "Before independence, the highest ranking female in the mining industry was a shorthand typist regardless of colour or qualifications."[98] But now, the total number of African female employees at Nkana increased from 332 in 1970 to 496 in 1976, while the number of expatriate female workers fell from 131 to 77.

As was the situation in the colonial era, there was no official government policy encouraging women to seek employment in the mining industry in Zambia.[99] Even so, the government quietly encouraged private companies and the mines to employ women.[100] Nkana and the Copperbelt mines consequently found some space within the policy of Zambianization and tried to promote the employment of women in the industry. When given employment opportunities, women worked on the surface and not underground.[101] Most women at Nkana and in the other Copperbelt mines were employed in administrative and medical departments.[102] But in the field of engineering, Chibuluma Division of RCM championed the cause of equal opportunities for women by appointing Margaret Bunyard as acting clerk of works at Chambishi.[103]

The labor movement followed suit by appointing women in administrative positions. For example, Betty Nkalabanda was appointed MUZ shop steward for the personnel department at Nkana.[104] In January 1975, NCCM-owned companies sponsored 193 female school leavers to be trained in typing and nursing at divisional craft and trades' training institutions.[105] Fifteen candidates who became typists were enrolled at Nkana, while 20 recruits pursuing a career in nursing were enrolled at Chingola.[106] In October the same year, Nkana employed a total of 35 nurses and midwives.[107] For the first time in the history of Nkana, two Zambian nurses were promoted to the post of hospital matron.[108] These were Margaret Ngoma, at Nkana Hospital, and Judith Bungoni, at Wusikili Hospital.

In other fields, Angela Kawandami was the first female mining controller in the Zambian mining industry, appointed at NCCM's Rokana Division.[109] As controller in the surface manning office, she was in charge of the daily movements of an engineering and administrative staff establishment of over 2,000.[110]

At the same time, various managerial positions at Nkana were Zambianized. Table 6.2 compares Zambianization of managerial positions at Nkana, Chingola, and NCCM Limited between 1974 and 1976.

Apart from administration, the positions where most Zambianization occurred were those of shift boss and mine captain. Expatriate workers remained entrenched in management and technical fields. Though the position of managing director was Zambianized at Nkana, an expatriate occupied

Table 6.2 Comparing Zambianization of Managerial, Supervisory, and Technical Positions at Nkana, Chingola, and NCCM between 1974 and 1976.

	Nkana Division				*Chingola Division*				*NCCM Limited: Total*			
	1974		*1976*		*1974*		*1976*		*1974*		*1976*	
Category	*E*	*L*	*E*	*L*	*E*	*L*	*E*	*L*	*E*	*L*	*E*	*L*
Management:												
General Manager	1		1		1		1		4		4	
Manager Mining	1		1		1		1		2		2	
Manager Metallurgical	1		1		1		1		2		2	
Manager Engineering			1								1	
Manager Administration		1		1		1		1		4		4
Mining Underground:												
Underground Superintendent	1		1		1		1		3		3	
Underground Manager	5		5		2		2		11		11	
Underground Assistant	11		11	2	6		6		23		21	4
Mine Captain Tech/Spec	13		8		6		8		25		22	
Mine Captain RBS	17	6	14	10	11	2	8	3	38	13	29	18
Mine Captain Other	1	7		10		2	2	3	1	14	2	20
Mining Engineer (Snr/Ass)	9		7	2	6		7	1	16	1	17	4
Shift Boss Tech/Spec	11	5	3	13	5	3	4	3	26	8	14	16
Shift Boss RBS	3	61	4	50	2	41		44	8	135	4	129
Mining Open Pits:												
Open-pit Superintendent	1		1		1		1		2		2	
Open-pit Manager	1		1		1		1		2		2	
Open-pit Assistant	1		1		4		4	1	5		5	1
Mine Captain Tech/Spec	1		1		3		4		5		5	
Mine Captain Open Pit	2		1	1	4	4	2	4	6	4	3	5
Shift Boss Tech/Spec	2		2		2		3		4		3	
Shift Boss Open Pit		6		1	1	32	1	33	1	38	1	37

Source: Compiled from Zambianization Committee, *Comparison of 1974, 1975 and 1976 Records of Actual Achievement*, April 29, 1977, Charts 1–3, ZCCM 11.7.9C.

Note: "E" stands for number of expatriate workers, while "L" stands for number of local workers.

the post of general manager until 1987.[111] Expatriates also held mining, metallurgical, and engineering management positions. Moreover, expatriate employees dominated underground and open-pit technical positions. This scenario was attributed to a number of factors. The government did not want to meddle with its main source of revenue and was also "quite content to have expatriates control the mines. Expatriates, on three-year renewable contracts, could be easily removed if they created trouble; if Zambians ran the mines, however, they could pose a political threat."[112]

There was also a marked contrast in the pace and direction of Zambianization in the government and the mining industry. In the government and the public sector, Zambianization proceeded both from the top down and bottom up. At Nkana and in the other Copperbelt mines, it was introduced from the bottom up.[113] Hence, there was little change in the management structure of individual mines since colonial times, with the lines of authority still running from white to black. Second, Rokana and the other mining companies controlled the extent of Zambianization:

> By controlling both the intake of Zambians and their advancement, [thereby restricting] the privilege of gaining more experience to expatriates or those Zambians who share[d] the values of the existing management. Where Zambians had been promoted, the mines created new supervisory or advisory posts, which were filled by the expatriates, and authority remained with the expatriate whatever nominal authority had been conferred on his Zambian superiors.[114]

This caused many frustrated Zambian graduates to leave the industry in the 1970s. But these were not the only major contributing factors to the slowness of Zambianizing managerial positions at Nkana and the other Copperbelt mines. Zambianization was also slowed by the low output of qualified personnel from various training institutions. There was generally few trained and skilled Zambians in technical fields. This was mainly due to the fact that the education/training system did not adhere to the basic education standards required for certain skills in fields such as engineering, metallurgy, chemistry, physics, and electricity.[115] For instance, only two graduates were allocated for Rokana from the University of Zambia in 1976, and five were expected in the following five years.[116]

In the technical services department, all positions in the ventilation section were Zambianized but not in the geology and survey sections. In these two sections, there was not any progress due to the lack of qualified geologists and surveyors.[117] Even so, Rokana sponsored a total of 13 students to the Zambia Institute of Technology (ZIT), now known as the Copperbelt University, to study surveying. Steady progress was made in the engineering department. There were three Zambian sectional engineers and six senior assistant engineers. At the artisan and technician levels, there were 135 Zambian artisans, 33 assistant foremen, and 4 foremen.[118] A further 72 were being trained, including technician improvers, craft improvers, and mechanics. With the larger numbers of students graduating from ZIT and Trades Training Institutions, it appeared that there was no need for recruiting abroad. But Nkana still lacked trained draftsmen, power plant operators, and shift engineers. Besides, Zambian-trained metallurgists at technician, foreman, and assaying levels were lacking.

Despite the challenges posed by Zambianization, Nkana continued to stabilize its labor force. Therefore, the turnover rate of African workers declined from an average of 9.17% in 1971 to 5.17% in 1980, while the average length of service remained high at almost 10 years in this period.[119] For expatriate employees, the turnover rate increased from 24.96% in 1970 to 32.33% in 1979, whereas the average length of service ranged between five and six years.[120] The turnover rate of Africans fell, while that of the expatriates remained high, partly due to the stabilization of local labor and the fact that rapid Zambianization of managerial positions was not attained. In fact, job fragmentation and training responsibilities led to an increased demand for skilled expatriate labor.

Indigenization and Zambianization increased labor costs at Nkana. Table 6.3 shows that total wages for both African and expatriate workers at Nkana mine increased from about K2,249,029.47 in December 1970 to about K3,965,420.47 in December 1976.

Late in 1969, a wage freeze was introduced after the government realized that workers in Zambia were the highest paid in the Southern African region. The government advised the mining companies not to increase wages in the industry. However, table 6.3 indicates that one of the major reasons for increased wages at Nkana was the introduction of special payments and overtime bonuses meant to motivate workers to work hard. The other reason was the impact of new expatriate conditions of service. Expatriate employees were put on contracts for three years. As noted previously, their salaries were externalized with remittance of earnings limited to one-third of annual salaries up to K600 per month and a gratuity payment of 25% of after-tax salary in foreign exchange.[121]

African wages increased for a number of reasons. First, following the 1970 Productivity Agreement signed between the MUZ, government, and mine

Table 6.3 Wages for Local and Non-Zambian Workers at Nkana in December of Each Year between 1970 and 1976.

	Local Employees			*Non-Zambian Employees*		
		Total Wages (K)			*Total Wages (K)*	
Year	*No. of Workers*	*Basic Pay*	*Special/ Overtime*	*No. of Workers*	*Basic Pay*	*Special/ Overtime*
1970	11,545	1,257,236.41	456,750.28	843	488,778.35	46,264.43
1971	11,444	1,213,070.13	141,937.72	808	371,867.60	96,957.86
1972	9,739	1,075,502.43	750,809.92	2,533	574,586.77	225,149.41
1973	10,300	1,192,099.56	183,141.43	2,404	577,235.79	173,131.45
1975	10,784	1,664,044.40	863,971.76	2,248	940,122.82	236,830.80
1976	11,284	2,089,640.12	1,180,673.86	2,048	683,568.24	211,538.25

Source: Drawn from Rokana Mine Division, Employment Returns, 1970–1976.

Note: In addition to normal pay, Total Wages include Special/bonus payments and Overtime allowances. Bonus allowances were now related to copper production and not copper price. Between 1972 and 1976, Wages for Non-Zambian Employees consisted of those for both expatriates and foreign Africans.

companies, a 5% wage increase was introduced to cover the period up to October 1973.[122] At that point, a new agreement, designed to improve pay and other conditions of service, came into effect and lasted until October 1976.[123] Under the new agreement, MUZ would cooperate in improving efficiency, safety, and discipline. Second, despite these provisions and subsequent increase in wages, workers at Nkana and the other Copperbelt mines continued to fight for better conditions of service through wildcat strikes. In 1976, there were 2 major and 12 minor stoppages, which accounted for a total of 48,363 man-hours lost.[124] Furthermore, a total of 1,440 man-hours were lost when winding engine drivers at Chingola, Konkola, and Nkana went on strike because of low salaries and grading.[125]

The companies were forced to revise conditions of service. Nkana and the other Copperbelt mines introduced improved conditions of service for both African and expatriate staff. For expatriates, "these conditions of service included, inter alia, two year contracts and new salary scales which were divorced from the Industry Basic Pay Scales introduced after the Brown Commission in 1966."[126] For expatriate senior staff, adjustments were made to their salaries as part of an exercise rationalizing wages in the mining industry. In addition to these measures, the government introduced workers' participation in industry through the effect of Part VII (Works Councils) of the Industrial Relations Act, 1971.[127] This Act empowered Works Councils to veto new management policy decisions in matters of welfare and conditions of service.

There was another strike related to conditions of service in 1980. These included inadequate remuneration, low job grading, and ill-defined jobs.[128] The dispute lasted for 18 days, and the mines lost about 15,486.5 man-hours.[129] The largest wildcat strike in the Copperbelt mines happened in 1981. It lasted for 23 days, and the mines lost over 2,299,419.9 man-hours.[130] The initial cause of the strike was the withdrawal of the credit facility for the purchase of maize meal. The government accused the leaders of the Zambia Congress of Trade Unions (ZCTU) and MUZ of not restraining workers from participating in the illegal strike and expelled 17 of them from UNIP.[131] The expulsion of the labor leaders aggravated industrial unrest on the Copperbelt mines. As a result of these strikes, wages for Africans increased by 4% in 1980, while in the last quarter of 1981, wages increased by 7.6%.[132]

As noted earlier, the government emphasized discipline and productivity on the mines. It tried to promote discipline among workers in a number of ways. In general, trade unions in Zambia, including MUZ, worked under a variety of legal restrictions and were brought under government control through ZCTU, which was founded in 1965.[133] In 1971, the Industrial Relations Act was passed, which provided for not only the registration of trade unions but also the banning of unconstitutional strikes and the establishment of an Industrial Relations Court to advise unions and deal with industrial disputes.[134] In addition to the 1971 Labour Law and the affiliation of the MUZ to ZCTU, the party's leadership ensured that trade union leaders were or became members of UNIP.

Under one-party participatory democracy, workers from individual mines were allowed to compete for elections into government. For instance, 30 mine employees from NCCM and RCM divisions were among the more than 90 candidates contesting in the primary elections in various mine-township constituencies in 1973.[135] At Nkana, 6 mine employees were among the 12 contestants in Kitwe's Nkana and Wusikili constituencies.[136] In fact, these employees contested the Nkana Constituency where the MUZ resident and incumbent member of parliament, David Mwila, was standing. Mwila retained the Nkana parliamentary seat. Nonetheless, the workers tried to resist government control through wildcat strikes.[137]

Furthermore, when the workers realized that their leaders at MUZ headquarters were compromised, they expressed resistance through their branches in the mines. For example, between 1970 and 1971, workers at Nkana, Luanshya, and Konkola staged demonstrations and strikes in solidarity with their branch leaders against Mwila, who they accused of being a sellout.[138] The workers tried to push Mwila out of the MUZ.

Capital, Labor Productivity, and Quality of Ores at Nkana

Zambianization, in particular, and labor relations, in general, coupled with capital and quality of ores treated, were all important elements of production and costs at Nkana. Table 6.4 compares productivity of underground African labor at Nkana with that of other NCCM mines.

Table 6.4 Comparative Productivity of Underground African Labor at Nkana and Other NCCM-owned Mines, 1979.

Financial Year	*1963*	*1979*	*Change from 1963 to 1979*	*Annual Change*
Rokana (Nkana):				
Labor Strength	3,498	4,169	19.2%	1.3%
Ore Hoisted per Man-shift (Tons)	4.9	3.2	34.7%	2.3%
Chingola (Nchanga):				
Labor Strength	2,314	3,062	32.3%	2.2%
Ore Hoisted per Man-shift (Tons)	4.4	2.5	43.2%	2.9%
Konkola (Bancroft):				
Labor Strength	2,775	3,074	10.8%	0.7%
Ore Hoisted per Man-shift (Tons)	2.0	1.8	10.0%	0.7%

Source: Taken from ZCCM Industrial Projects Department (ZCCM IPD), *Zambia Copper Sector Survey* (Kitwe: IPD, 1981), 37, ZCCM 11.7.9C.

Despite increased wages, productivity at Nkana and in the other NCCM-owned mines actually declined. According to table 6.4, at Nkana mine, it took 3,498 Africans to hoist 4.9 tons of copper in 1963, but in 1979, it took 4,169 Africans to hoist 3.2 tons. The reasons behind the decline in labor productivity at Nkana can be explained in four ways. First, "the decline in labour productivity reflected among other things a general apathy and lack of motivation among African mineworkers attributable in a large part to disincentives built into the dual-wage structure."[139]

Second, Nkana and the other Copperbelt mines were overstaffed at unskilled levels because of indigenization and Zambianization of labor. Overall, less productive, unskilled labor remained high. Even so, it was economic for the mines to use a "higher-labour versus capital-intensive mode of production due to the high costs of capital, shortage in foreign exchange for capital expenditure, and shortage in skilled technicians to maintain equipment."[140] In fact, capital expenditure at Nkana decreased markedly between 1970 and 1978 (see table 6.8). As discussed later, this was partly attributed to a decline in revenue due to a combination of increased production costs and low copper prices. But it was mainly the diversion of NCCM's profits into nonmining activities such as agriculture and tourism that deprived Nkana and other mines of much needed capital.[141]

Third, the decline in labor productivity was also related to changes in the manning structure in line with Zambianization. This not only reduced European workers in supervisory jobs but also weakened the discipline of African workers who became resentful of local supervisors.[142]

The fourth and most important reason for the decline in labor productivity was related to the fall in grade of ore delivered to the mill (see table 6.5). As discussed in chapters 4 and 5, this situation at Nkana mine was linked to two factors: decreasing grades of ore reserves and increasing mixture of waste rock with ore (dilution). With deep-level mining at Nkana, the quality of fully developed ore reserves declined from about 3.0% copper in 1969 to around 2.4% by 1980.[143] The grade of ore reserves remained relatively steady at Nkana (see table 6.5). By comparison, ore reserves averaged 6.5% at Chingola, 3.7% at Konkola, 3.1% at Mufulira, and 2.5% at Luanshya (Roan).[144] Nevertheless, there was a big gap between the grade of ore in reserve and mill-head grades due to dilution. Mill-head grades averaged 3.2% at Chingola, 2.9% at Konkola, 2.1% at Mufulira, 1.7% at Nkana, and 1.5% at Luanshya.[145]

In part, dilution can be explained "by geological hanging wall conditions, in particular Copperbelt mines, where the mining method [broke] waste in the footwall and ground conditions were weak."[146] The effects of geological hanging wall conditions were generally less at Nkana compared with all the other mines on the Copperbelt, with the least dilution rate of 22% in 1980.

That year, dilution rates averaged 101% at Chingola, 72% at Luanshya, 47% at Mufulira, and 27% at Konkola.[147]

Nkana had the strongest underground workings because of effectiveness of the stoping method of mining. Despite this method being expensive and slower, it was not only stronger but also safer.[148] Mining challenges were better addressed at Nkana than at any other mine on the Copperbelt. But labor productivity at Nkana was much lower than at Konkola and almost similar to that of Chingola (see table 6.4). Mufulira suffered from an underground mine disaster in September 1970, mainly due to weak hanging wall conditions.[149] The block-caving method employed at Mufulira weakened underground walls and was unsafe, although cheap and quick with a big tonnage.[150] Underground working conditions at Luanshya were also bad with 72% dilution. Compared with Nkana and the other mines, Chingola seemed to have suffered the most from weak geological wall conditions with the highest dilution rate among the Copperbelt mines. Despite this problem, Chingola remained the largest producer, because the grade of its ore reserves that contained about 6.5% copper was among the highest in the world.[151]

Table 6.5 indicates the grade of ore reserves and ore mined and milled/treated at Nkana between 1970 and 1981. Ore hoisted and milled and metal percent and content increased between 1973 and 1975 and, thereafter, fell away significantly.

Table 6.5 Comparing Ore Reserves and Ore Mined and Treated at Nkana Mine between 1970 and 1981.

	Ore Reserves		*Ore Mined and Treated*					
			Metric Tons		*Metal % of Ore Milled*		*Metal Content*	
Year	*Metric Tons*	*Copper %*	*Ore Hoisted*	*Ore Milled*	*Copper*	*Cobalt*	*Copper*	*Cobalt*
1970	129,657,000	2.62	5,857,000	5,478,000	1.93	0.11	105,725	6,026
1971	123,027,000	2.53	5,707,000	5,530.000	1.90	0.12	105,070	6,636
1972	123,246,000	2.52	5,972,000	5,746,000	1.87	0.11	107,450	6,321
1973	121,973,000	2.52	5,931.000	5,781,000	1.78	0.11	102,902	6,359
1974	119,944,000	2.44	6,528,000	6,337,000	1.88	0.11	119,136	6,971
1975	118,212,000	2.39	6,175,000	6,025,000	1.80	0.09	108,450	5,423
1976	131,336,000	2.35	5,448,000	5,426,000	1.78	0.09	96,583	4,883
1977	126,998,000	2.36	5,427,000	5,093,000	1.66	0.10	84,544	5,093
1978	121,320,000	2.35	4,818,000	4,868,000	1.54	0.11	74,967	5,300
1979	117,988,000	2.37	5,023,000	4,758,000	1.75	0.11	83,265	5,234
1980	113,402,000	2.35	4,879,000	4,794,000	1.66	0.11	77,663	4,794
1981	113,433,000	2.35	4,806,000	4,663,000	1.56	0.10	72,743	4,663

Source: Compiled from MINDECO Limited, *Mining Yearbooks*, 1970–1972, ZCCM 12.1.9C; CISB Limited, *Zambia Mining Yearbooks*, 1973–1985, ZCCM 12.1.9C.

Underground mining operations were constrained by shortages of skills and spares, as well as breakdowns of aged air compressors and ore-handling plants. Other difficulties that affected mining operations were major heat and pressure problems associated with increasing depth. The South Ore Body was the deepest on the Copperbelt at 4,190 feet.[152] The Central Ore Body was 3,560 feet deep. A major problem in 1974 was flooding, following breakdown of the main pump at the Central shaft.

In general, daily average quantities of water pumped from underground sources at Nkana averaged 72,027 m^3 during 1972 and 1973 and increased to 76,670 m^3 during 1974.[153] In order to cope with such problems, technological improvement in mining methods and equipment was required if operations were to be continued with an acceptable degree of safety and efficiency. Besides, a suitable draining system was necessary in order to make it possible "to produce 100,000,000 metric tons of relatively high grade sulphide mineralization that lay within the fold systems of the Nkana synclinorium."[154] There were also metallurgical problems in the treatment plant due to some obsolete and aged equipment making the plant expensive to maintain and operate efficiently. Between 1974 and 1976, Rokana invested K18.6 million into new machinery and technology in order to cope with such problems and improve underground safety and efficiency of processing plants.[155]

Underground mining methods were mechanized by utilizing raise borers and rubber-typed loaders, which provided flexibility in development and stoping layouts and led to more rapid extraction rates and higher recoveries.[156] There was also the introduction of the Sands Flotation Technique, which increased copper recovery concentrate by 17% and led to the treating of oxide ores for the first time in the history of Nkana.[157] Another important innovation was in the metallurgical operations involving "the successful application of tonnage oxygen to the reverberator furnaces and convertors," which increased smelter throughput and flexibility by 17%.[158] To improve the refinery process, a new system, the Periodic Current Reversal System, was introduced in the Refinery Tankhouse.[159] As a result, production shot up by about 20%.[160] Mechanization also cushioned problems associated with dilution and labor productivity. Consequently, the quantity and quality of ore hoisted and ore treated improved.

In 1971, large tonnages of additional ore were discovered near the Central, South, and Mindola orebodies, leading to the opening of two new open-pit mines in 1973, averaging 4.37% copper.[161] Thus, three open-pit mines were operated at Nkana, that is, Mindola open pit (Torco), Mindola open pit (Oxide), and Nkana Area E (Torco).[162] These were easier to mine and, therefore, low-cost sources of copper. However, the reduction in ore hoisted and treated after 1977 was mainly due to a depletion of high-grade ore in these opencast mines. Nkana's open pits were nearing the end of their economic lives and were closed in 1981. This was a big blow, as these open pits contributed about 40,000 metric tons of finished copper per year.[163] All these innovations slowed but did not arrest declining production.

Selling Price of Copper on the LME, Costs of Production, and Transport for All NCCM-operated Mines

Nkana and the other Copperbelt mines lost control of two important components of mining costs: mill-feed quality and mine operations' labor productivity. Between them, they comprised 41% to 59% of the total production costs and about 67% of the total cost of sales per metric ton of copper between 1970 and 1981.[164] Table 6.6 establishes the relationship between cost of sales and selling price of copper on the LME. After 1974, the cost of producing and transporting a ton of copper increased tremendously compared to the selling price.

The increase in cost of sales was attributed to three linked factors between 1970 and 1981.[165] As discussed earlier, the first factor was related to the fall in the metal content of ore treated, and second, the decline in productivity of African labor, which were major components of total operating costs. Third was the disruption of transport routes through Rhodesia in 1973 and Angola in 1975 due to political disturbances in the region (see Figure 6.1). This was a major blow to Nkana and the Copperbelt mines. The interruption of external railroad connections through Rhodesia closed the entire southern route to Beira and Maputo and was compounded by a suspension of operations of the Benguela railway line, which was destroyed in 1975.[166]

Table 6.6 Average Cost of Sales (K) and Selling Price of Copper (K) per Ton on the LME for All NCCM-owned Mines, Selected Years from 1971 to 1981.

Years	*1971*	*1974*	*1975*	*1976*	*1977*	*1978*	*1979*	*1980*	*1981*
Selling Price of Copper	916	1,300	1,087	768	1,072	1,002	1,159	1,690	1,629
Cost of Copper Sales	519	609.8	754.2	795.9	839.6	1,047.6	1,092.7	1,281.6	1,540.7
Cost by Expense Class:									
Mining and Labor	222.6	268	334	340	333	409	399	482	562
Mineral Processing	109.8	152	200	237	234	276	314	376	470
Inventory Charges	77.4	111	133	133	153	220	201	206	281
Transport Expenses	64.7	78.8	87.2	85.9	87.6	97.6	108.7	138.6	141.7
Other Expenses	44.5	–	–	21	32	45	71	79	86

Source: Compiled from NCCM Limited, *Annual Reports and Accounts*, 1971–1981, ZCCM 11.1.1F; ZCCM IPD, *Zambia Copper Sector Survey*, 32; MINDECO Limited, *Mining Yearbooks of Zambia*, 1970–1972; CISB Limited, *Zambia Mining Yearbooks*, 1973–1985.

Note: Mining and Labour Costs denote average cost of production at the mine. Mineral Processing Costs include total expenses on concentrating, leaching, smelting, and refining. Inventory Charges were expenses on administrative and technical services and mine general expenses. Average Transport Costs were calculated from mine station to United Kingdom and world ports. Other expenses include charges on overheads, depreciation, written down value of stocks, and abnormal expenditure. There are no figures for individual mines except for the average for all NCCM-owned mines. All figures are in kwacha.

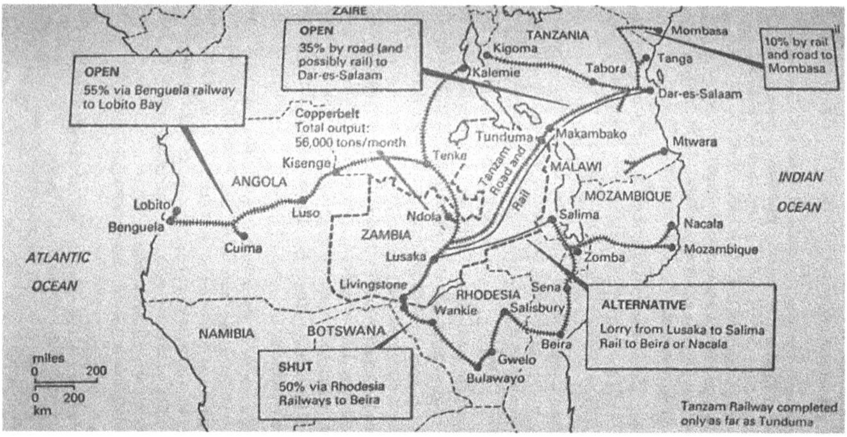

Figure 6.1 The Zambian Copperbelt and the Transport Routes. *Source:* Greg Lanning and Marti Mueller, *Africa Undermined: A History of the Mining Companies and the Underdevelopment of Africa* (Ontario: Penguin Books Limited, 1979), 221. *Note: TAZARA was completed in 1976; the road link to Mombasa was closed in 1977 due to a dispute between Kenya and Tanzania.*

This impacted Nkana and the other Copperbelt mines in three ways. First, it slowed completion of projects because of the delayed arrival of materials and equipment. Second, it blocked copper exports from reaching the coast, causing congestion. Third, it raised the cost of transport by diverting the mine traffic from rail to road and vice versa. The cost of transporting copper from Nkana mine to the port averaged K73.15 by road, K69.54 by rail to Dar-es-Salaam (Tanzania), and K114.04 to East London (South Africa).[167]

Transport problems for Rokana and the Copperbelt companies were eased following the completion of Tanzania Zambia Railways (TAZARA) to the port of Dar-es-Salaam in 1976, the opening of Rhodesia's border in 1978, and the subsequent independence of Zimbabwe in 1980. Extra carrying capacity was eased as a result of Zambia's increased self-reliance in certain fields, notably coal, fertilizers, liquid fuels, cables, and explosives.[168] Nevertheless, transport costs continued to increase because of the escalation of the civil war in Angola, the volatile political situation in Mozambique, and the subsequent transport interruptions (see table 6.6).[169]

To ease power shortages, Zambia sped up construction of her own hydroelectric stations at Kariba North Bank, Kafue Gorge, and Victoria Falls, which became operational by 1979.[170] In addition, the oil shock eased, and supplies began to increase in 1980. However, the Zambian government remained anxious about the volatile political environment in the Southern African region.

Overall Profitability of Nkana and the NCCM Mines

The overall profitability of Nkana and the other Copperbelt mines was undermined by the decline in copper prices caused by the drop in demand arising from a world recession, especially between 1975 and 1979 (see table 6.6). Because of the recession, there was a slowdown in industrial activity in the USA, Europe, and Japan, the latter being the largest buyer of Rokana and NCCM copper. The financial fall of Burmah Oil, Britain's second-largest oil company, and that of Aston Martin heightened the fears of an imminent economic depression and pushed down prices on the stocks and metal markets.[171] In addition, Japan's Nippon and Mitsubishi, companies that were major consumers of Zambian copper, were forced by the recession to close some of their smelters, contributing to the decline in copper prices.[172]

The copper price on the LME fell steadily from an average of K1,087 in 1975 to K768 in 1976 (see table 6.6). The worst result came in 1976, when the average cost of sales for Nkana and NCCM-owned mines was more than the annual average price of copper on the LME (see table 6.6). Moreover, there was an oversupply of copper following expansion programs in the main producing countries such as the USA, Soviet Union, Chile, and Peru in the late 1960s and early 1970s.

As a result, between 1975 and 1976, the copper price declined, and between 1977 and 1979, it did not increase substantially because of the increase in world stocks following excess production capacity. Copper stocks in the LME warehouses stood at 10,000 metric tons in April 1974, increased substantially to 176,000 tons by March 1975, and reached 533,000 tons by mid-1976.[173] The recession worsened, and the short-lived economic recovery in the first half of 1976, with a growth rate of approximately 6.5% throughout the Western world, fell away again in the second half of 1977, and copper prices continued to tumble.[174]

In July 1976, the Zambian government devalued the kwacha by 20%. While this temporarily improved the financial position of Zambian companies in local currency terms, increased overseas payments and loan repayments corroded gains. The overall loss arising from devaluation of the kwacha amounted to K32,021,000, leaving a profit of K2,471,000 for the 1977 financial year.[175]

In 1978, the mines faced four major problems: a lack of a reliable and efficient transport system, low shipments, inadequate foreign exchange allocations, and the low purchasing power for essential consumables.[176] Inadequate foreign exchange forced the government to seek a standby arrangement from the International Monetary Fund (IMF), totaling Special Drawing Rights (SDR) K322.6 million.[177] As part of this standby arrangement, the government devalued the kwacha by a further 10% in March 1978 and agreed to impose restrictions on local borrowings.[178]

But it became difficult for Rokana and the Copperbelt companies to operate within IMF restrictions because of problems associated with the high cost of production, transport, and foreign exchange. As indicated earlier, copper prices remained low for two major reasons: the effect of the recession and excess production capacity. The copper oversupply was reflected in the high level of world stocks at 2 million metric tons.[179] CIPEC members announced a 15% cutback on their production.[180] But there was no concerted action from other big producers such as the USA and Soviet Union. As a result, "copper prices declined 48% in real terms between 1974 and 1975, and since 1975, had risen only 2.8% per year in real terms."[181]

Mining enjoyed a brief period of profitability between 1980 and 1981, due to higher copper and cobalt prices, albeit that the benefits of the higher prices were diluted by increases in cost of sales (see tables 6.6 and 6.7). As a result, Konkola, Kansanshi, and Nkana's Mindola open-pit mines operated at a loss, although the mother company, NCCM, as a whole, produced a profit (see table 6.7).[182]

NCCM was able to make a profit by selling other metals such as cobalt, zinc, and lead. For instance, in 1979, Zambia was the world's second-largest producer of cobalt accounting for 10% (2,590 metric tons), following Zaire with 51% (148,000 tons).[183] More than two-thirds of Zambia's cobalt originated from Nkana and NCCM-owned mines.[184] The increase in the price of cobalt reduced the impact in the price of copper.[185] The USA accounted for almost half of NCCM and RCM's cobalt exports, and the United Kingdom purchased about 1,800 metric tons. The Soviet Union and Japan accounted for less than 100 metric tons, and other consumers purchased the remainder.

By comparison, in 1974, copper production accounted for 93.7% of the total value of mineral production in Zambia, followed by zinc at 3.8% and cobalt at 1.0%. In 1979, copper's share of the total value of mineral production fell to 76.8%, while cobalt's share rose tremendously to 13.1% and zinc's declined to 1.9%.[186]

Table 6.7 compares the trends in output and financial performance of all NCCM-controlled mines between 1970 and 1981. In 1980, smelter production of copper in NCCM mines was as follows: Chingola, 115,888 tons; Nkana, 87,896 tons; Konkola, 36,161 tons; and other sources, 6,721 tons.[187]

Overall, the financial performance of Nkana and other NCCM-owned mines, especially between 1976 and 1981, reflected the influence of the world industrial recession, the increase in costs of imported mining inputs, and the volatile but generally depressed copper prices. As a result, Nkana and the other Copperbelt mines recorded a loss after tax in 1976, and in the following years up to 1979, NCCM failed to pay dividends.

Table 6.7 Finished Production and Overall Profitability of NCCM-controlled Mines between 1970 and 1981.

Year	*Finished Production (Metric Tons)*		*Total Sales (Metric Tons)*	*Total Value of Sales*	*Total Cost of Sales*	*Total Tax*	*Total Net Profits*	*Total Net Dividends*
	Copper	Cobalt	Copper	Millions (K)	Millions (K)	Millions (K)	Millions (K)	Millions (K)
1970	395,511	2,073	382,719	365	–	–	–	–
1971	494,816	2,080	475,983	449	246	107	97	51
1972	401,283	2,056	420,363	348	–	18	68	36
1973	440,077	2,137	445,794	363	262	23	83	36
1974	408,753	1,870	397,385	555	276	164	113	67
1975	408,666	2,018	396,160	479	340	78	59	17
1976	385,414	1,698	386,201	327	366	54	–	–
1977	427,810	999	425,931	506	403	49	34	–
1978	377,156	1,093	384,560	422	–	40	6.5	–
1979	368,332	1,105	365,551	489	–	0.1	26	–
1980	359,816	1,258	363,815	702	–	75	56	9
1981	356,541	1,122	362,812	657	–	19	32	5

Source: Compiled from NCCM Limited, *Annual Reports and Accounts*, 1971–1981; MINDECO Limited, *Mining Yearbooks of Zambia*, 1970–1972; CISB Limited, *Zambia Mining Yearbooks*, 1973–1985.

Note: Value of Sales refers to total revenue from all the metals including lead and zinc from Broken Hill/ Kabwe mine. Net Dividends are total net paid dividends on "A" (Zambian government's) and "B" (minority shareholders') shares. In 1976, NCCM made a loss of K54 million before tax deductions; hence, the company did not declare net dividend in this year. There are no figures for individual mines except for the total for all NCCM-owned mines.

Dividends declared in 1980 and 1981 were much lower than previously. As indicated elsewhere in this chapter, total tax rates in the Zambian mining sector increased from about 74.4% in the first years of Zambian independence to above 80% after the Matero Declaration in 1969 and the 1973 reforms and were a major contributing factor in the reduction in net value of profits and dividends indicated in table 6.7. In addition, the increase in the cost of sales against low copper prices reduced revenue and capital expenditure allocations from copper proceeds at Nkana and NCCM-owned mines. This can be seen in table 6.8, which provides a breakdown of capital expenditure and revenue for NCCM mines. Total issued share capital on Preference shares, "A" (GRZ) shares, and "B" (Minority) shares of K2 each averaged K272.2 million per annum between 1973 and 1981.

Cunningham and Barton contend that nationalization restricted foreign investment in the Zambian economy. This resulted in undercapitalization, which lowered productivity levels to below consumption, triggering the country's first balance of payments in 1976.[188] In contrast to Cunningham and Barton's argument, this chapter posits that the financial performance of

Table 6.8 Breakdown of Capital and Revenue for Nkana and all NCCM Mines in Millions of Kwacha, 1971–1981.

	Issued Share Capital	*Capital Expenditure*		*Capital Employed*			
Year	*NCCM*	*NCCM*	*Nkana*	*NCCM*	*GRZ Dividends*	*Minority's Dividends*	*Retained Earnings*
1971	–	43.0	–	337	30	25	45
1972	–	42.0	–	381	20	10	35
1973	254	58.8	–	426	20	10	50
1974	254	69.0	9.0	482	30	30	40
1975	253	59.4	5.6	571	10	10	50
1976	253	39.4	4.0	841	–	–	–
1977	253	16.1	–	828	–	–	–
1978	253	23.2	–	753	–	–	–
1979	310	29.0	13.0	725	–	–	–
1980	310	63.0	22.0	692	4.6	4.4	–
1981	310	108.0	64.0	904	3	2	–

Source: Compiled from NCCM Limited, *Annual Reports and Accounts*, 1971–1981.

Note: Capital Employed includes capital expenditure, retained proceeds, and loans obtained. As indicated elsewhere in this chapter, Capital Expenditure was charged on profits during nationalization. Figures for Retained Earnings are unavailable after 1975.

Nkana and the Copperbelt mines was severely undermined by the increase in costs of production, transport, and imported mining inputs (reflecting the rise in oil prices since 1973); the impact of the global recession, which began in 1975 (reducing consumption of metals); and depressed copper prices (see table 6.6).[189] Consequently, the Zambian economy was severely hit by the reduced revenue from metal sales and the resultant economic woes, such as unbalanced payments due to expensive imports, a chronic shortage of foreign exchange and inputs, inflationary pressures, and budget deficits.[190]

Thus, Rokana and other Copperbelt companies relied on internal and external borrowing for capital projects. Owing to low internal cash generation and high levels of debt, coupled with low debt service, loans for Nkana and NCCM-owned mines reached a peak of K145.7 million in 1977.[191] In 1978, the Zambian government made an interest-free loan to NCCM of K66 million for repayment of the short-term debt held by the Bank of Zambia. But in 1979, the Zambian government realized that NCCM was struggling to repay the loan and decided to convert K57 millions of its 1978 loan to equity, thereby increasing the government's shareholding from 51% in 1970 to 60%.[192] Similarly, the government's K40 million loan to RCM was converted to equity, which increased the percentage of government ownership from 51% to 61% in this company.[193] Therefore, the government's shareholding in the mining industry was raised to approximately 60% in 1979.

CONCLUSION

Between 1970 and 1981, Nkana and the Copperbelt mines' corporate strategies and financial performance were largely driven by an augmented state participation in the industry, as well as rising cost of sales and depressed and volatile copper prices without a substantial increase. The result was a decrease in internal revenue. In turn, a decrease in internal revenue forced Nkana and the other NCCM-owned mines to rely on internal and external loans for capital, resulting in high levels of debt with low debt service.

As described earlier, the government took advantage of Rokana and the other Copperbelt companies' indebtedness and increased its equity shareholding in 1979. By mid-1981, the UNIP leadership contemplated merging the two mining firms, NCCM and RCM, into a single company, Zambia Consolidated Copper Mines Limited, which would have a significant influence on the operations of Nkana and other Copperbelt mines. Rokana under this new company is the focus of the next chapter.

Chapter 7

Rokana/Nkana during the Third Phase of Nationalization, 1982–1991

FORMATION OF ZAMBIA CONSOLIDATED COPPER MINES LIMITED

The government considered a number of factors before the formation of Zambia Consolidated Copper Mines (ZCCM) Limited. These factors ranged from corporate shareholding to mineral production and profitability. As stated in chapter 1, the merger of Nchanga Consolidated Copper Mines (NCCM) and Roan Consolidated Mines (RCM) was also "driven by increased donor [International Financial Institutions] influence on economic policy: the IMF [International Monetary Fund] provided major loans for the new ZCCM."[1]

After increasing the Zambia Industrial and Mining Corporation's (ZIMCO) issued share capital in the mining industry to about 60% in 1979, the government began to push for the amalgamation of NCCM and RCM.[2] Indeed, in May 1981, President Kaunda announced that his government had decided to merge NCCM and RCM into a single mining company.[3] He claimed that the advantages of a merger would be numerous, including "selective mining, production balanced against demand, co-ordinated planning and prospecting, firmer pressure on research and development and sharing instead of duplication of plant equipment and stores."[4] The president remarked that, since mining was the mainstay of the Zambian economy, it was important to address the industry's problems by reorganizing it in such a manner that it lived up to the challenges of the current economic situation.[5]

Yet the proposed merger was not entirely a government initiative. The minority shareholders—Zambia Copper Investments (ZCI), American Metal Climax (AMAX) International, and public investors—shared the government's concerns and felt that the effects of the world recession and the general depletion of ore reserves called for a bigger unit to face the challenges ahead.[6]

Besides, NCCM and RCM had "different problems and advantages, most of which were complimentary."[7] Therefore, the merger represented "a logical step in the development of the mining industry."[8]

Negotiations between majority and minority shareholders began soon after the president's announcement in May 1981. On December 22, 1981, representatives of the government, ZIMCO, NCCM, RCM, AMAX International, and ZCI signed the Heads of Agreement in order to facilitate the merger of NCCM and RCM.[9] The Heads of Agreement was a bill detailing terms of the merger and resolutions on matters relating to transfer of assets.[10] On March 5, 1982, parliament ratified the Amalgamation of Mining Companies (Special Provisions) Act No. 2, which effected the merger of NCCM and RCM.[11]

The Act came into operation on March 17, 1982, and enabled "the share capital of NCCM to be acquired by RCM in exchange for shares of RCM, and to enable the undertaking of NCCM to be amalgamated with that of RCM."[12] Accordingly, NCCM redeemed in full all outstanding 5.5% and 5% preference shares at the price of K2.10 and K2.20 per share, respectively.[13] NCCM paid to the holders of such shares the accruals of the preference share dividend from the date of redemption, and the share capital of RCM was reconstructed.[14] Roan purchased, while ZIMCO and ZCI transferred, their shares in NCCM to RCM.[15] Therefore, the authorized share capital of RCM increased from K190,000,000 to K900,000,000.[16] The shares in RCM were transferred into a new company, ZCCM.

The Income Tax (Special Provisions) Act No. 3 of 1982 came into operation at the same time that the negotiations for the merger took place and made provisions for the amalgamation.[17] First, this Act provided that "any transfer of assets from NCCM to RCM limited was to be treated as a transfer of assets between Companies under common control," and ZCCM incurred tax liabilities for both companies.[18]

The government also reformed the mining tax regime of the 1970s by separating income tax and export tax from mineral tax. Under the Mineral Export Tax Act, the new Mineral Export Tax (MET) was payable "on the gross amounts received from sales of minerals exported from Zambia."[19] The rate of MET, which was 4% in April 1983, was raised to 8% in August 1983 and further increased to 10% from January 1985.[20] Because of this increase in export tax, the government exempted ZCCM from paying the equity levy. Under the Equity Levy Act of 1982, the levy was introduced at a rate of 1.5% and was based on the Zambian government's interest in the Group's share capital.[21] In order to raise more revenue, the government amended the method by which it taxed imports based on the free on board (f.o.b.) value, to the value based on cost, insurance, and freight (c.i.f.).[22]

Arrangements for the merger were finalized between the government and the minority shareholders in March 1982, and on April 1, the same year

RCM was renamed ZCCM.[23] The ZCCM Board of Directors comprised representatives of majority and minority shareholders known as "A" and "B" directors, respectively. The "A" directors were appointed by ZIMCO, which held 60.3% of the issued share capital on behalf of the government.[24] The "B" directors were appointed from ZCI, AMAX International, and public investors from the United States of America (USA) and Britain. Minority shares were divided as follows: ZCI, on behalf of AAC, 27.3%; AMAX International, 6.9%; and public investors, 5.5%.[25] The AAC, Rokana/Nkana's former parent company, owned the largest minority interest in ZCCM. Although the formation of ZCCM reduced the AAC's stake in the Zambian mining industry, the former largely relied on the technical skills of the latter.[26]

Anticipated Merger Benefits for Nkana Division and the Copperbelt Mines

ZCCM comprised seven producing divisions, namely, Chingola, Nkana, Luanshya, Kalulushi, Konkola, Mufulira, and Kabwe. The two Centralised Services Divisions in Kitwe and in Ndola were merged into one centralized division.[27] ZCCM was, in effect, a mining giant, the world's second-largest copper-producing company, after Corporation Nacional del Cobre de Chile (CODELCO-Chile), with an annual capacity of over 700,000 tons of the finished metal.[28] It had the same distinction as cobalt producer, "with the 4,000 tons annually processed from ZCCM's sources accounting for a quarter" of the total world production.[29] Furthermore, ZCCM produced significant tonnages of lead and zinc, and on a minor scale, it produced gold, silver, and selenium as by-products from copper and anode slimes.[30]

To manage the divisions effectively, two head offices were created. The corporate head office was established in Lusaka to perform administrative functions, while Kalulushi in Kitwe became the operational and technical center of the ZCCM-owned mines.[31] The role of the corporate head office was confined mainly to formulating corporate policies, strategies, plans, and financial control. Divisional general managers reported to the director of operations at Kalulushi. In addition, the management and supervisory lines at Nkana and in the other divisions were streamlined through the abolition of certain management and supervisory levels to save costs. ZCCM also had 12 subsidiary companies at the time of the merger, which, by 1986, had increased to 20.[32] These provided essential supplies and services to Nkana and the other mines. Besides, and in line with the new corporate structure, MEMACO, together with ZCCM, formed MEMACO Trading Limited as a way of diversifying into specialist fields of commodity trading and supplementing the industry's marketing efforts.[33]

The merger was intended to improve coordination and direction of the capital expenditure and extraction and production of the Copperbelt mines, as well as create a larger and financially stronger unit that would be better placed to raise funds/loans in the international money market.[34] Technical and investment gains would include scaling and rationalization of benefits in areas such as marketing, purchasing, and utilization of stores and other specialist services.[35] It was also hoped that greater emphasis would be placed on research and development, prospecting and exploration, and mine development.[36]

Manpower benefits would include the better deployment of scarce technical skills. The manning structure would be streamlined or rationalized to affect savings.[37] This would be achieved by redeploying excess labor to where there was a need for additional labor, for example, to the new projects like the Roast Leach Electro-win (RLE) cobalt plant at Nkana and Tailings Leach III at Nchanga.[38] It was also envisaged that changes in technology, working methods, and various other policy and operational decisions would contribute to the effective utilization of labor at Nkana and in the other mines.[39]

The government wished to accelerate and consolidate Zambianization in the mining industry by ensuring that both foreign Africans and expatriates were phased out of the industry as soon as possible after March 1983.[40] It was also realized that the low levels of labor productivity at Nkana and in the mining sector often were a result of poor planning, work organization, and communication.[41] To redress this, it was suggested that "design and implementation of the suitable group training programs for mine captains and shift bosses would assist in the up-grading not only of technical, but also supervisory skills. This in turn would lead to the attainment of higher levels of productivity per man shift."[42] ZCCM also introduced a Staff Development Panel System in order to promote better placement and, in turn, more effective utilization of professional and skilled manpower.[43]

But the major obstacle to the accelerated phasing out of expatriates was that they were still needed to maintain machinery and other technical facilities. In fact, expatriate workers still commanded skills not available among the Zambian workforce. Yet, even as ZCCM wanted to speed up Zambianization, it needed to reduce the number of all workers by closing down some plants and shafts and declaring redundancies in order to reduce costs.[44] Rationalization of local labor was frequently stymied by pressure from the labor movement and the need to provide employment to Zambians in the mining sector.[45] In the 1980s, ZCCM employed 16% of people in formal employment, and the mining sector ranked second to government.[46] As Zambianization and maintenance of high levels of local workers in the industry were also intended to garner and entrench political support to UNIP, rationalization of labor threatened UNIP's popularity.

Nonetheless, both the government and ZCCM persisted with the objective of making savings through the rationalization of mining activities. The rationale of the merger was to minimize duplication and effect savings through better use of existing plants and equipment, processing and refining facilities.[47] Rokana was central to attaining this objective, as it possessed the largest processing and refining facilities on the Copperbelt. To effectively carry out all the aforementioned objectives, ZCCM launched a Five-Year Production and Investment Plan/Policy (FYPIP) at Nkana and in the other Copperbelt mines, aimed at increasing productivity, cutting costs, and improving overall viability.[48] A striking feature of the FYPIP was that it introduced uniform policies on all the mines, the major mines all having the same estimated mining life of 24 years.[49]

The Importance of the Rokana/Nkana Mine Division to ZCCM

At the time of the merger, the book value of ZCCM was estimated at K1,074.3 million.[50] Of this figure, an estimated K236.4 million's worth of fixed assets belonged to Rokana. This was the highest figure of all Copperbelt mines.[51] Rokana/Nkana Mine Division continued to be vital to the mining, smelting, and refining operations of the ZCCM-owned mines. As noted in the previous chapter, Rokana/Nkana Mine Division operated six orebodies: three underground operations (Nkana Central and Mindola North and South), and after 1982, the three open pits were reopened and expanded.[52] Of the total of 16 underground and open-pit operations of ZCCM, 6 were located at Nkana. Nkana's ore reserves in 1982 were estimated at 113 million tons of 2.35% copper and 0.13% cobalt, from which about 459,000 tons of ore a month were hoisted.[53] In 1982, mining by sublevel open stoping was carried out between 2,133 feet and 3,937 feet below surface, making Nkana the deepest mine on the Copperbelt.[54]

The Nkana concentrator received approximately 460,000 tons of ore a month and produced about 19,000 tons of copper concentrates at a grade of up to 30% copper and 4,000 tons of cobalt concentrates at a grade of 3% to 4% cobalt.[55] As discussed in chapter 6, the smelter was one of the largest in the world, having been upgraded from handling about 80,000 tons of concentrates annually in 1970 to treating over 235,000 tons of concentrates a year in 1982.[56] Thus, the Nkana smelter treated concentrates from three former NCCM divisions, that is, from Chingola, Konkola, and Nkana itself. The refinery was also expanded, producing about 19,000 tons of electro-refined copper a month at full capacity and casting almost 13,000 tons of wirebars.[57] The cobalt plant, which produced about 2,000 tons of cobalt a year in the 1970s, produced about 2,400 tons of cobalt metal per annum by 1982 and treated cobalt concentrates from the other divisions as well.[58] Of a total of 25 plant and metallurgical installations under ZCCM, Nkana Division alone operated 8.[59]

ZAMBIANIZATION OF LABOR AND THE NEW SINGLE-WAGE STRUCTURE

ZCCM's new Production and Investment Policy hinged on a number of issues, not least labor organization. As discussed in chapter 6, Zambianization in the 1970s increased the number of local workers at Nkana and in the other Copperbelt mines. But this was disproportionately confined to unskilled African workers. There was a shortage of local workers in technical, managerial, and supervisory positions. The government was aware of this problem. When reminded about his comment on the challenges of Zambianization in the industry during an interview with the *Times of Zambia* in 1982, Francis Kaunda, former executive chairman of ZCCM, reiterated his earlier statement:

> Some appointments, which were made into advanced positions in the 1970s, did not meet the requirements of true Zambianisation partly because there were very few technically trained Zambians, and most Zambians appointed to senior positions were not properly prepared for increased responsibilities. Another major challenge was that the mining companies were window-dressing Zambianisation of supervisory positions by not giving Zambians the responsibilities that went with the supervisory jobs formerly held by expatriates. In fact, expatriates remained entrenched in managerial and supervisory jobs. We called for an end to window-dressing Zambianisation in the ZCCM.[60]

Following the formation of the ZCCM, the government emphasized the vigorous training of Zambians to replace both expatriates and foreign or alien Africans. Zambianisation Committees were opened at all the ZCCM divisions on the Copperbelt to ensure that locals replaced expatriates. In addition, early in October 1982, the minister of state for Labour and Social Services announced that "alien [foreign African] miners must go."[61] Table 7.1 compares the impact of Zambianization on African and expatriate labor strengths at Nkana Division and in the ZCCM mines between 1982 and 1992.

Differentiations between the number of African workers at Nkana fell slightly from an average figure of 11,900 in 1982 to 11,326 in 1984, before increasing substantially to 13,860 the following year and reaching 14,622 in 1990. By comparison, the number of Africans in the mining industry increased fractionally from about 54,800 in 1982 to 55,743 in 1984, decreased substantially to an average annual strength of 50,627 in 1987, and began to increase steadily thereafter.

Table 7.1 Comparing African and Expatriate Labor Strength at Nkana Division and in All ZCCM Mines, 1982–1992.

	Rokana/Nkana Mine Division			*All ZCCM Mines*		
Year	*Africans*	*Expatriates*	*Expatriate %*	*Africans*	*Expatriates*	*Expatriate %*
1982	11,900	409	3.3	54,800	2,106	3.7
1983	11,231	287	2.5	54,197	1,790	3.2
1984	11,326	239	2.1	55,743	1,571	2.7
1985	13,860	312	2.2	51,809	1,475	2.8
1986	13,891	311	2.2	50,876	1,384	2.6
1987	13,801	315	2.2	50,627	1,160	2.2
1988	14,085	308	2.1	53,870	995	1.8
1989	14,542	307	2.1	53,828	792	1.5
1990	14,622	306	2.0	54,202	765	1.4
1991	14,421	297	2.0	54,454	723	1.3
1992	14,259	290	2.0	55,886	620	1.1

Source: Compiled from ZCCM Limited Manpower Planning and Development, Establishments: Labour Figures, November 1983–December 1988, ZCCM 1.3.1H; Parliament of Zambia, Debates, Questions and Replies, December 1991–December 1998, Order Book No. 334—Zambianisation, ZCCM 5.5.2B; ZCCM Limited, Survival-Cost Saving Measures, April 14, 1983, ZCCM 11.7.9C; ZCCM Limited, *Nkana Division Monthly Report on Operations*, July 1985, 20, ZCCM T2.1C; ZCCM Limited, Nkana Division Monthly Report on Operations, July 1986, 17, ZCCM T2.1C; ZCCM Limited, Nkana Division Report on Operations, February 1992, attachment facing 17, ZCCM T8.2A.

Note: There are no figures categorizing Africans into local and alien workers.

Fluctuations in African labor strength in this period were due to two main factors. First was the phasing out of foreign African workers. Second, the new manning structure, coupled with cost-saving measures introduced by the ZCCM after mid-1982, could have led to either a reduction or an increase in labor at different mines on the Copperbelt. The 1982 Memorandum of Agreement between the Copperbelt mines and MUZ affected the manning and salary structures. The new Memorandum of Agreement superseded the one entered into by the parties in 1970. The new Agreement provided for an 8-grade manning structure as opposed to the previous 11-grade manning structure.[62] Table 7.2 shows the new manning structure at Nkana and in the other three major mines on the Copperbelt.

As a result of the new manning structure, the ZCCM management realized that some workers were underutilized, especially in small mine divisions such as Konkola, Kalulushi, and Chibuluma. Partly to reduce the costs and wastage of manpower in small divisions, Chibuluma and Chambishi were joined with Nkana in 1985, while Konkola was merged with Chingola in 1986.[63] This restructuring affected a total of 3,000 workers, and the majority were redeployed at Nkana and Chingola.[64]

Under the ZCCM, workers could be transferred from one mine to another without difficulty, since a single firm controlled the companies. Thus, some

Table 7.2 Labor Strength in Each Grade at Nkana, Chingola, Mufulira, and Luanshya, February 29, 1988.

	Nkana		Chingola		Mufulira		Luanshya	
Grade	*Expatriate*	*Local*	*Expatriate*	*Local*	*Expatriate*	*Local*	*Expatriate*	*Local*
G1	97	412	136	545	42	303	17	262
G2	37	491	24	590	10	344	3	338
G3	1	1,360	0	1,602	0	910	0	906
G4	0	1,655	0	2,144	0	1,236	0	978
G5	0	2,000	0	2,968	0	1,379	0	1,138
G6	0	1,424	0	2,083	0	1,469	0	1,623
G7	0	4,760	0	3,762	0	1,825	0	2,546
G8	0	1,267	0	1,174	0	724	0	499
Totals	135	13,369	160	14,868	52	8,190	20	8,290

Source: Taken from Senior Manager, Manpower Development, Chingola, to ZCCM Director, Human Resources Department, Lusaka, March 7, 1988, ZCCM 1.3.1H.

workers from Luanshya and Mufulira were transferred to either Nkana or Chingola. These two divisions needed more labor because of their bigger mining and metallurgical facilities. On the other hand, as explained later in this chapter, austerity measures introduced by the ZCCM, in line with the IMF and the World Bank's (WB) borrowing conditions, reduced its overall African labor strength between 1985 and 1987.[65]

Nkana and the other Copperbelt mines also embarked on a program of early retirement and redundancies in order to save labor costs. For example, in August 1985, 95 employees were retrenched at Nkana.[66] The total number of labor losses on the Copperbelt mines in this month was 378. Nonetheless, labor gains, partly from workers redeployed from other mines and engaged under new contracts, totaled 123 in the same month at Nkana.[67] By 1988, labor losses and gains increased. For instance, in November 1985, there were 868 labor losses against 251 gains at Nkana, compared with the 4,587 job losses against 1,502 gains in all the ZCCM-owned mines in the same month.[68] The high net decrease against lower net gains in local labor strengths was due to nonreplacement of the labor wastage, except in highly specialized fields of employment and mining departments.[69]

In line with the policy of Zambianization, Nkana reduced the number of expatriate workers from 409 or 3.3% of the total labor force in 1982 to an annual average strength of 290 or 2.0% of the total number of workers in the mine in 1992.[70] Overall, the ZCCM reduced the expatriate labor force from an average of 2,106 or 3.7% of the total labor force in the mining industry in 1982 to 620 or 1.1% of the total number of workers in 1992.[71]

By comparison, there was a higher percentage of expatriates at Nkana than in the rest of the ZCCM between 1982 and 1992 (see table 7.1). This shows that ZCCM as a whole was achieving more Zambianization than Nkana Division because of the impact of the redeployment exercise explained earlier, which increased the number of expatriate workers at the mine. By one calculation, the expatriate labor force in the Zambian mining industry fell from 6,162, representing about 12.1% of the total labor force in 1966, to about 620 or 1.1% of the total number of workers in 1992, representing a Zambianization achievement of approximately 91.5%.[72] Over much the same period, the total number of foreign Africans employed in the mining industry was halved from an average figure of 8,077 or 15.9% of the total labor force in 1966 to 4,181 or almost 7.4% in 1992.[73]

Nkana and other Copperbelt mines continued to widen opportunities for Zambian women in the industry. The government also introduced a number of benefits for female workers on the mines. Through the Employment Amendment Act No. 18 of 1982, women were allowed to go on maternity leave and were provided with maternity materials, including nappies.[74] There were 569 female employees at Nkana in 1987, the majority of them Zambian.[75] The same year, there were 3,281 female African employees and only 159 female expatriates in the entire mining sector.[76] Two years later, there were 3,327 female African employees and only 74 female expatriates.[77]

While Zambianization of labor reduced expatriate workers at Nkana, in particular, and in the mining industry, in general, other factors also contributed to the reduction. As discussed in chapter 6, in the 1970s, expatriate employees had been attracted by three-year contracts, coupled with the externalization of salaries and gratuity payments of 25% after income tax in foreign exchange.[78] But this salary structure was no longer attractive. Beginning in the early 1980s, salaries in other parts of the world such as Chile, Peru, and the USA were high compared with those in Zambia where living conditions on the Copperbelt were deteriorating.[79] Taxation on salaries above K12,000 per month was also very high, at 71% from 1980 onward.[80] The lack of services, such as adequate schooling, and the increasingly fraught security problems on the Copperbelt were all major deterrents to the retention of expatriate employees.[81]

As indicated in table 7.1, a small number of expatriates still remained at Nkana and in the other Copperbelt mines, especially in skilled and managerial jobs. Table 7.3 disaggregates the Zambianization of managerial, technical, and supervisory jobs at Nkana, in particular, and the ZCCM, in general, for the years 1982, 1983, and 1988.

The table reveals that the position of general manager was not yet Zambianized at Nkana as late as 1983. Indeed, despite this position being Zambianized in most ZCCM divisions by 1985, it was first Zambianized at Nkana in 1987.[82] Peter Chileshe was the first Zambian to be appointed general manager of the Rokana Division in August 1987. However, Chileshe died in a road

Table 7.3 Zambianization of Managerial Positions at Nkana and in All ZCCM Mines in 1982, 1983, and 1988.

	Rokana/Nkana Mine Division						*ZCCM/Copperbelt: Total*					
	1982		*1983*		*1988*		*1982*		*1983*		*1988*	
Category	*E*	*L*	*E*	*L*	*E*	*L*	*E*	*L*	*E*	*L*	*E*	*L*
Management:												
General Manager	1		1		1		7		6	1	2	4
Manager—Mining	1		1		1		2		2			
Manager—Metallurgical	1		1			1	3		3			
Mining:												
Underground Manager		1	1	1	2	2	7	1	9	1	9	5
Underground Superintendent	3	2	3	2	10	4	15	7	15	6	31	16
Assistant Superintendent	7	1	5	1	41	14	35	10	31	10	140	56
Mine Captain Tech/Spec	1						18	7	6	1		
Mine Captain RBS	5	13		21			15	59	11	58		
Mine Captain Other				26			5	38	11	98		
Mine Captain Open Pit				1			1	8	1	9		
Mining Engineer (Snr/Ass.)	6	5	4	6	108	168	30	37	19	35	331	604
Senior/Planning Engineer	8		7	1			20	1	10	4		
Technical Assistant	2		1				2		1			
Senior/Rock Mech. Eng.	4		2	2			4		2	2		

Source: Compiled from *Mining Mirror*, August 28, 1987; Mining Industry Manpower Division, *Mining Industry Manpower Report*, June 1984, attached copies 1, 5, and 6, MUZ HQ; Senior Manager, Manpower Development, Chingola, to ZCCM Director, Human Resources Department, Lusaka, March 7, 1988, ZCCM 1.3.1H; ZCCM Limited, *Annual Report, 15 September 1988* (Lusaka: ZCCM Head Office, 1988), 3, ZCCM 11.1.1F.

Note: "E" stands for number of Expatriate workers, and "L" stands for number of Local workers. There are no categorized figures for Section Officers in 1988; only respective block figures are available as on February 29, 1988. The total number of section bosses at Nkana were 108 expatriates and 168 locals, and in the whole of ZCCM, there were 331 expatriate and 604 local section bosses.

accident in May 1988, and David Littleford was appointed general manager of Rokana Division.[83] Littleford held this position until 1991.

Similarly, expatriates at Nkana dominated all mining and metallurgical management positions until the late 1980s.[84] The position of underground superintendent was still filled by expatriates in 1988. The position most occupied by Zambians was that of mine captain, although there was still a substantial number of expatriate section officers. The Zambianization of managerial, supervisory, and technical positions was not very effective at Nkana, in particular, and in the Zambian mining sector, in general. A number of reasons were responsible for this state of affairs.

As noted in chapter 6, one of the main reasons the government was reluctant to Zambianize management positions at individual mines was the growing fear among UNIP politicians that complete Zambianization would create a political elite on the mines that would become a rival center of power to UNIP.[85] In line with Burawoy's observation, the government was "quite content to have expatriates control the mines. Expatriates, on three-year renewable contracts, could be easily removed if they created trouble."[86] It partly explains why the position of general manager at Nkana was not again Zambianized after the death of Mr. Chileshe.

Rokana is a unique case concerning this issue because it was one of the two divisions whose post of general manager was not yet Zambianized in 1991.[87] It should be noted, however, that the position of general manager was reserved for a technically trained person with mining experience.[88] The late Chileshe was a mining engineer, joined the then Rhokana Corporation in 1965, and, in 1985, became the second Zambian to be appointed general manager in the mining industry at Konkola Division.[89] Similarly, Littleford had a distinguished mining career and worked as general manager of the Kabwe Division before he was transferred to Rokana Division in 1988.[90] Since the position of general manager needed a highly qualified and experienced person, ZCCM could not ignore the profile of Littleford despite Zambianization.

The Zambian government and the ZCCM also continued to experience problems in the localization of positions in the mining, metallurgical, and mechanical fields. The major reason was the limited inputs of skilled personnel from the Zambian and overseas training institutions.[91] For example, out of a total requirement of 130 graduates to fill various technical fields in the mining industry in April 1985, there were only 67 graduates from the University of Zambia and overseas universities.[92] Therefore, Nkana had to either employ new expatriates or extend their contracts to accommodate the difference.

Quite apart from the low output of graduates from training institutions, there were other reasons for the inadequate number of graduates or technical workers in the industry. One major factor was the increasing number of technical workers leaving the mines. They did so for various reasons, such as poor conditions of service and the underutilization of and frustration among graduates.[93] Management at Nkana realized that graduates were frustrated partly because of underutilization. Underutilization was not due to poor manning structures or grading systems but rather "deliberate intent on the part of individual employees to slow down the progression rate of other employees."[94]

Inadequate technical workers in the mines also remained a serious problem. For example, in December 1988, of the 30 available technical positions for expatriate recruitment at Nkana, the mine only managed to recruit 7.[95] Similarly, there were 19 vacancies for locals on normal contracts in the professional and technical fields at the Nkana Division.[96] It is clear that the majority of expatriates and local graduates in technical fields chose to be employed elsewhere rather than at Nkana and the other Copperbelt mines in the late 1980s.

African workers, in general, were frustrated by the inequalities embedded in the recently introduced single-wage structure. In April 1982, the ZCCM announced far-reaching measures aimed at improving conditions of service for Zambian miners.[97] One of the proposed measures was the introduction of a single-wage structure by which expatriates would be paid salaries equal to their local counterparts.[98] The new wage structure was based on the new manning structure mentioned earlier. It affected the grade salary structure and wages, applied retrospectively from November 1, 1982, and minimum wage increases of K60 and K30 per month were guaranteed to employees in the top grades.[99] The new agreement covered a two-year period from that date. The ZCCM and the government felt that "an agreement whereby the main conditions of service, such as wages, were determined for a fixed period had proved conducive to the development and maintenance of sound industrial relations."[100]

The ZCCM also promised to maintain harmony with the Mineworkers' Union of Zambia (MUZ) by foregrounding employees' interests and providing better conditions of service such as housing. In addition, the ZCCM wished to abolish the discriminatory educational system favoring expatriates' children. Local workers were consequently given education loans for their children.[101] Table 7.4 details basic salary increases for workers in all salary grades between 1987 and 1991.

Table 7.4 demonstrates a number of insights into basic salaries in the single-wage structure at Nkana and in the Zambian copper industry. In

Table 7.4 Comparing Basic Salary Increases (K) in the Single-Wage Structure for Miners at Nkana and All ZCCM Mines, 1987–1991.

Year	*Range*	*G1*	*G2*	*G3*	*G4*	*G5*	*G6*	*G7*	*G8*
1987	Minimum	1,027	903	752	654	581	530	498	475
	Maximum	1,270	1,101	923	798	698	626	577	547
1988	Minimum	1,221	1,078	899	771	685	626	584	564
	Maximum	1,464	1,276	1,070	915	802	725	665	636
1989	Minimum	1,904	1,711	1,455	1,227	1,104	1,022	908	886
	Maximum	2,228	1,975	1,683	1,419	1,260	1,154	1,016	982
1990	Minimum	2,117	1,914	1,636	1,374	1,241	1,154	1,012	991
	Maximum	2,468	2,200	1,883	1,582	1,410	1,297	1,129	1,095
1991*	Minimum	8,171	7,345	6,512	5,467	4,915	4,550	4,000	3,880
	Maximum	8,522	7,631	6,759	5,675	5,084	4,693	4,117	3,984

Source: Compiled from Mineworkers' Union of Zambia, Memoranda of Agreements with the Association of Copper Mining Employees, April 14, 1987, April 21, 1989, and November 26, 1991, MUZ HQ.

*Note: The figures are only for basic pay scales slotted in schedule surface rates. For 1987 and 1988, pay scales for workers in underground areas in every pay grade should be the previously indicated surface pay scales increased by 10%, and for 1989, 1990, and 1991, increased by 12.5%. *The figures for 1991 are the existing basic salaries by November of that year. The increase was effected in May, June, or July of each year. The minimum was mainly the entry notch, while the maximum applied to those who served for more years or in supervisory positions.*

addition to the basic salary, workers were given new benefits such as standby, hot patching, safety, transport, high performance, water, electricity, distress, medical, and repatriation allowances.[102] Every month, Nkana and the Copperbelt mines also gave African workers subsidized mealie-meal. This was 20% of the cost of two bags of 50 kilograms of roller meal for workers with registered dependents and one bag of 50 kilograms of roller meal for those with no registered dependents.[103] As mentioned earlier, Nkana and the other Copperbelt mines were also compelled to "assist African employees with school going dependents at K150 per child per annum up to a maximum of six children."[104]

Between 1970 and 1981, basic wages had been increased every three years and at times after strikes over better conditions of service. Between 1985 and 1990, however, basic wages were increased every year. The 1982 Agreement between the MUZ and the mines stipulated that wages would be increased after two years from the previous increment. But this could not be sustained, mainly due to high levels of inflation. Therefore, after 1985, the increase rate was determined in line with the level of inflation and determined by the Association of Copper Mining Employees, representing Nkana and the other ZCCM mines, in consultation with the MUZ.[105]

Between 1982 and 1984, debt servicing consumed almost 65% of Zambia's foreign exchange earnings.[106] Reduced foreign exchange revenue, coupled with IMF pressure, forced the government to devalue the kwacha by 40% and allocate foreign exchange via an auction system, restrict wage increases to 5%, and decontrol the price of most foodstuffs.[107] These factors combined and increased inflation from about 15% in 1982 to about 25% by 1986, and "the kwacha fell to K21, one-tenth of its value before the auction. Major strikes now took place, as workers demanded pay increases to compensate for inflation."[108] In November 1986, the ZCCM awarded an out-of-time salary increase averaging 10% to all general payroll employees to cushion the effects of the escalating cost of living, following the depreciation of the kwacha.[109]

Between 1987 and 1989, the rate of annual inflation in Zambia accelerated, particularly in the lower income bracket, rising by 18%.[110] The consumer price index for the low-income earners registered an increase of 41% in 1987, went up further to 55.6% in 1988, and fluctuated between 60% and 80% throughout 1989.[111] Accordingly, the basic salary for the lowest paid miner (G8) increased from about K475 in 1987 to K886 in 1989 or by slightly above 46% (see table 7.4). Basic salaries in all categories almost quadrupled in 1991. This followed a move to increase efficiency and boost employees' morale. Consequently, the ZCCM reviewed conditions of service in late 1990 and again in early 1991, "which resulted in more benefits and better perks for employees at all levels."[112]

However, the wage increases were also a political maneuver to gain support among the workers and promote peace in the industry. Between 1983 and 1986, the UNIP government continued to pursue policies aimed at controlling the mineworkers.[113] Before 1983, the Industrial Relations Court, which was an autonomous body under the Ministry of Labour and Social Services, dealt with matters of industrial disputes in line with the Industrial Relations Act of 1971. After 1983, however, a number of clauses of the Industrial Relations Act were reviewed through various statutory instruments, which ensured that the government retained the dominant position in the final outcome.[114] Before any collective bargaining and agreement over wages could become legal and binding upon the parties, approval and ratification by the Prices and Incomes Commission had to be obtained.[115] At the same time, UNIP made sure that no local senior managers and supervisors in the mines joined unions.[116] An extension of this practice in 1985 was the removal of the so-called frontline supervisors in G1 and G2 scales from union representation.[117]

After the formation of the ZCCM and the introduction of the new single-wage structure, the government was initially successful in curbing major wildcat strikes over wages. Between 1982 and 1984, though, various work stoppages related to other conditions of service occurred. A major strike occurred in early June 1985. The strike was the result of dissatisfaction with the industry's Mukuba Pension Scheme.[118] Introduced in 1982, the Scheme was disliked by workers because they did not want to subscribe to the 5% monthly charge without a corresponding increase in basic wages.[119] Yet, membership of the scheme was a condition of employment for all local full-time and permanent employees of the ZCCM, and they were not allowed to withdraw from the scheme until they retired.[120]

The strike action, between June 1 and 7, 1985, involved more than 4,000 strikers in the Copperbelt mines, causing 510,823.5 working man-hours to be lost in 69,209 man-shifts.[121] In production terms, about 4,000 metric tons of copper and cobalt were lost, estimated at K16 million in revenue.[122] The government responded vigorously: 600 miners were fired, the check-off system was withdrawn, and employees providing essential services were not allowed to join the strike.[123] Of the 600 miners dismissed on June 11, 1985, 223 originated from Rokana's three divisions (Nkana, Chibuluma, and Chambishi).[124]

The fact that there was no major strike in the early 1980s directly linked to wages did not mean that workers were unaware of inequalities in the single-wage structure.[125] The persistent striking feature of the dual-wage structure was reflected in the disparity of basic salaries in the single-wage structure despite the government's efforts to end it. Prior to 1982, operational and general employees would receive an average of a 10.5% increase, followed by the clerical/administrative employees at 9.9%, and technical personnel at about 6.0%.[126] Further, there was a sliding scale within each employee category that lower-level staff received greater than average wage increases, while the higher-level staff received less than average increases.

The government and the ZCCM tried to correct this situation. It is clear from table 7.4 that wages increased for all workers. The new system ensured that the gap between the highest and lowest paid employee narrowed within each salary grade. Even so, the increase was not equal for all categories of workers. For example, in 1985, the lowest paid miners on G5 and G8 salary scales received the highest increment of K65 a month, while those in G3 and G4 received K54.[127] Meanwhile, miners in G1 and G2 scales received a K47 increment.[128] Nonetheless, miners in the G1 and G2 salary scales received the highest average basic salaries per month.

Similarly, operational and general employees received less than average increases, whereas technical and administrative workers received more than average increases. At the same time, disparities in earnings between expatriates and Africans at Nkana and the other mines remained very large. For example, in the late 1980s, on average, an expatriate graduate at Nkana and in the other Copperbelt mines earned over 15 times what the Zambian graduate received.[129] For instance, a Zambian graduate earned a gross of just over K2,000, while their expatriate counterpart got a handsome gross amount of K40,000 per month.[130] This was on top of other expatriate benefits, such as inducement allowances (in forex), better housing, holiday allowances, and educational allowances for children abroad.[131] Wage structures such as this, which rewarded some more than others, together with the inability of wage increases in general to keep pace with national inflation rates, were making it difficult to attract and retain qualified Zambian personnel such as technical staff. Thus, it can be observed that the inequalities of the dual-wage structure were retained and embedded into the new single-wage structure after 1982. The issue of labor was important because of its significant influence on mineral production and production costs and the overall profitability of Nkana Division.

Labor Productivity, Quality of Ores, and Finished Production at Nkana

The extent to which Zambianization and the new eight-grade manning and salary structure impacted labor productivity at Nkana needs to be considered. As demonstrated in chapters 5 and 6, management at Nkana was concerned about the deteriorating morale and productivity of most workers, mainly as a result of inequalities embedded in the wage structure such as the ones described earlier. Nonetheless, the government and the ZCCM encouraged mineworkers to be disciplined, efficient, and productive in order to promote national development. Indeed, in 1982, the ZCCM went so far as to warn that it would be counterproductive to apply improved terms of conditions for service if there was no corresponding increase in productivity from the employees.[132] On average, productivity per local employee at the Nkana mine and in the Copperbelt mines, in general, fell from about 10.1 metric tons of copper in 1981, through 9.3 tons in 1983, to 7.1 tons in 1991.[133] The relative decline in labor productivity was linked to bad discipline, substandard or poor performance, and a fall in the grade of ore reserves and ore delivered to the mill.

Bad discipline among miners in the 1980s was reflected in the frequency of cases of absenteeism, indiscipline, and substandard or poor performance.[134] For example, the frequency of cases of bad discipline per 1,000 employees at Chingola Division increased from the total average of 51.3 in January 1985 to 76.8 by June 1986.[135] In this period, the frequency of disciplinary cases increased from 43.9 to 65.5 at Luanshya, 42.3 to 64.0 at Konkola, 32.5 to 47.5 at Nkana, and 28.6 to 43.3 at Mufulira.[136]

Most of the offences that occurred at Nkana and in the other Copperbelt mines were substandard performances followed by absenteeism.[137] As mentioned in chapters 5 and 6, increases in substandard performance and absenteeism were mainly due to the relaxation of the coercive measures employed during the colonial era following independence and the introduction of Zambianization in the mines. Poor performance among local workers was also due to low morale, resulting from disincentives and disparities embedded in the new single-wage structure discussed earlier.[138]

Hand in glove with this factor was the fact that Nkana was overstaffed with unskilled workers, who were less productive in skilled labor positions, as well as operational and general workers (diggers) engaged in mineral extraction.[139] For example, in February 1988, the number of operational and general workers in the G7 and G8 grades totaled 6,027 at Nkana, 4,936 at Nchanga, 3,045 at Luanshya, and 2,549 at Mufulira.[140] As discussed elsewhere earlier, Nkana Division needed more operational and general workers because of its large mining and metallurgical facilities. At Nkana and Nchanga, this problem was exacerbated by wrong placement in the manning structure following redeployment of workers as a result of cost-saving measures.[141] As stated earlier, most of the workers from other ZCCM divisions were redeployed at Nkana and Nchanga. For political reasons, the government was reluctant to encourage the mines to reduce the excess labor. Because of Zambianization, G3 surveyors were automatically upgraded to G2 after three years, without an effective assessment of their performance, and irrespective of their skills and the normal establishment.[142] This practice was common at Nkana, Nchanga, and Mufulira Divisions.[143]

As indicated earlier, the highest frequency of offences was recorded at Nchanga and Luanshya mines. By comparison, there was a gradual increase in disciplinary cases at Nkana between January 1985 and June 1986 because of the relative success of the punitive measures applied by management at Nkana. The most effective measures included severe warnings, demotion, and dismissal.[144] While these measures could be compared to colonial-era disciplinary practices, there were notable differences in their application. As pointed out by Larmer, "Racial inequality and violent supervision . . . lay at the heart of colonial industrial relations."[145] In the colonial era, workers were arbitrarily dismissed without any lawful procedure.[146] For example, following a strike by African miners on January 3, 1955, over wages, the mining companies issued a "back to work or be sacked" ultimatum, which was ignored.[147] With the support of the "Colonial Government, the companies started evicting [workers] from their houses and employing casual labourers."[148] After independence, however, workers would not be dismissed without the Industrial Relations Court presiding over their case.[149] Workers were given an opportunity to appeal to higher courts.[150] Despite their dismissal, they were entitled to terminal benefits.[151]

Application of the measures detailed earlier acted as a deterrent to would-be offenders. While such measures seemed to have failed at Nchanga, Luanshya, and Konkola, they were apparently successful at Mufulira where there was a tremendous reduction in disciplinary cases from 84.1 to 43.3 between July 1985 and June 1986.[152] Nevertheless, the effect of bad discipline and substandard performance at Nkana and in the other Copperbelt mines was also reflected in the decline of ore hoisted per local employee from about 647 metric tons per year in 1975 to 549 tons by 1983.[153]

This relative decline in labor productivity, however, was partly related to the fall in the grade of ore delivered to the mill. In the period from 1970 to 1981, the grade of ore reserves was stable and averaged 2.43% copper, while mill-head grades averaged 1.76% copper (see chapter 6, table 6.5). Between 1982 and 1991, the decline in the grade of ore delivered to the concentrator at Nkana was partly linked to dilution. Table 7.5 compares the grades of ore reserves, ore milled or treated, and finished production at Nkana between 1982 and 1991.

Table 7.5 shows that between 1982 and 1991, the grade of ore reserves at Nkana averaged approximately 2.36% copper and 0.14% cobalt. The grade of ore hoisted, whose annual figures are not indicated in this table, averaged about 1.41% copper and 0.09% cobalt.[154] The difference between the average grade of ore reserves and ore hoisted was about 0.95% for copper and 0.05% for cobalt. This difference was a result of high levels of dilution. Dilution, in this case, refers to mixture of waste rock with ore.[155] As discussed in the previous chapters, dilution partly affected the grade of the ore sent to the mill. The metal content of ore milled or treated averaged 1.46% copper and 0.10% cobalt.

Table 7.5 Comparison of Ore Reserves, Ore Mined and Treated, and Finished Production at Nkana, 1982–1991.

	Ore Reserves			*Ore Mined and Treated*				*Finished Production*	
				Ore Hoisted	*Ore Milled and Metal (%)*			*Copper*	*Cobalt*
Year	*Metric Tons*	*Copper (%)*	*Cobalt (%)*	*Metric Tons*	*Metric Tons*	*Copper (%)*	*Cobalt (%)*	*Metric Tons*	*Metric Tons*
1982	109,986,000	2.32	0.13	4,279,000	4,597,000	1.56	0.10	149,706	1,002
1983	96,917,000	2.35	0.13	3,835,000	4,378,000	1.46	0.09	126,770	419
1984	83,848,000	2.38	0.13	3,858,000	4,247,000	1.61	0.10	141,733	1,543
1985	81,682,000	2.38	0.14	3,793,000	3,874,000	1.55	0.10	148,244	1,952
1986	79,274,000	2.40	0.15	–	3,526,000	1.40	0.10	135,888	2,555
1987	100,643,000	2.37	0.14	–	3,557,000	1.35	0.10	130,673	1,845
1988	101,135,000	2.36	0.14	–	3,454,000	1.31	0.09	142,088	2,343
1989	100,731,000	2.34	0.14	3,308,000	3,238,000	1.36	0.08	126,757	2,373
1990	98,792,000	2.33	0.14	3,203,000	3,225,000	1.43	0.09	138,272	2,228
1991	97,448,000	2.33	0.14	3,300,000	3,520,000	1.53	0.10	147,270	2,225

Source: Compiled from ZCCM Limited, *Annual Reports*, 1982–1991, ZCCM 11.1.1F; CISB Limited, *Zambia Mining Yearbook 1985* (Kitwe: Manpower Planning and Development, 1985), 21, ZCCM 12.1.9C.

Dilution was partly the result of the effects of deep-level mining at Nkana. In 1984, the Nkana Division had Zambia's deepest underground mining operation, with two shafts of more than 4,200 feet below the surface.[156] Deep-level mining at Nkana was characterized by high temperatures, inadequate ventilation, flooding, and an increased mixture of ore with rock due to weak and falling walls. All of this made mining through sublevel stoping difficult. However, sublevel stoping was important in this context because it was safe.[157] As a result, fatal accident figures recorded at Nkana declined between 1985 and 1987, and the Division recorded the lowest figure on the Copperbelt in 1988.[158] The number of fatal accidents at Nkana Division decreased from nine in 1985, through eight in 1986, to three in 1988.[159] The total number of fatal accidents in all the Copperbelt mines was 39 in 1985 and 24 in 1986.[160]

Finished copper and cobalt production fluctuated between 1983 and 1991. Several factors were behind the general fluctuation in production at Nkana other than the decline in labor productivity, high levels of dilution, and the resultant lower-than-anticipated head grades in the concentrates treated. One of the factors was related to hoisting and crushing constraints and the limited availability of diesel, air loaders, and locomotives.[161] Poor maintenance, itself the result of inadequately trained personnel, aggravated the situation.[162] Spare parts were in short supply because of inadequate allocation of foreign exchange, arising from the effects of the world recession, and supply shortages due to transportation bottlenecks.[163] The problem of shortages of consumables such as diesel, lubricants, explosives, and tires increased between 1984 and 1988.[164] Shortages of spare parts and consumables meant that the concentrator, the cobalt plant, the smelter, and the refinery operated below capacity. More than this, two of the three open-pit mines were closed in 1984, partly owing to the depletion of economic reserves, partly as a cost reduction strategy.[165] Underground development, too, was affected by compressor problems and a shortage of drilling spare parts.[166]

If this was not enough, there was another major reason for the sharp decline in copper and cobalt production in 1983. A major fire at the Nkana Division Power Station in November 1982 immobilized the smelter and other surface facilities of the Division and affected the hydrometallurgical operations such as the acid plant.[167] The resultant shortfall in acid production affected hydrometallurgical operations elsewhere on the Copperbelt, especially Nchanga Division, which relied to a large extent on acid produced by Nkana.[168] Inadequate supplies of acid from Nkana was the primary factor responsible for a 2.8% decline in the ZCCM's finished copper production in 1983.[169]

In addition, cobalt production was temporarily curtailed, partly to ease stocks due to the poor demand for the metal.[170] The closure of the old facility and the start-up of the new RLE Plant also played a role.[171] The new RLE cobalt plant was capable of handling 2,500 metric tons of metal a year and boosted production in the following years.

In 1989, copper production fell because ore deliveries from three underground sources were constrained by poor ground conditions, which caused the collapse of the stope grizzlies, as well as haulage and rock hoist breakdowns before a new 3,760-m-level crusher at the Central Shaft was commissioned.[172] The grade of ore hoisted was further diluted by overpulling from existing stopes, because of a shortage of replacement stopes.[173] Nevertheless, production at Nkana improved thereafter because, for the first time under the ZCCM, the Company invested in advanced machinery and technology, which boosted its operations.

Between 1988 and 1991, the ZCCM increased capital expenditure on the mining department at Nkana, amounting to K1,483 million compared with K167.1 million expended on capital projects between 1982 and 1987.[174] The increase in capital expenditure in all the divisions was meant to not only replace old machinery and equipment but also improve production in line with a dramatic increase in demand and metal prices.[175] Most expenditure was on the adoption of new technology and mining methods, especially at the Mindola shaft where the Vertical Crater Retreat method was implemented.[176] New machines and equipment were also bought, which included Toro loaders, drill rigs, and jackhammers.[177]

As a result of new machinery and technology, for the first time in 11 years, the quantity and quality of ore extracted and treated exceeded the forecast for the 1991 financial year. In 1991, "the grade of the ore delivered to the concentrator improved by 4.7% than the previous year while contained copper improved by 2,759 tons or by 4.8% than the previous year."[178] Finished production for the 1991 financial year also increased by 8,998 tons over the previous year (see table 7.5). Even so, between 1982 and 1991, Nkana Division and the Copperbelt mines constantly lost control of mill-feed quality and labor productivity.[179] This was compounded by poor equipment and inadequate spare parts and consumables, all important elements of production costs.[180]

Costs of Production and Transport for Nkana and the Other ZCCM Mines

By expense class, mill-feed quality and labor productivity were the major components of production costs, covering 67.4% of the total cost of sales per ton of copper between 1971 and 1981 (see chapter 6, table 6.6). By 1991, operations and labor costs at Nkana accounted for almost 91% of the total cost of sales per ton.[181] Between 1984 and 1991, the average cost of producing a ton of copper at Nkana and in the other Copperbelt mines increased markedly against high copper prices blighted with inflation.[182] Operating costs, excluding transport, mineral export tax, and other related expenses, increased from about K151.1 (US$93.2/£64.5) per ton of copper produced in 1984 to K4,026.3 (US$76.5/£44.3) in 1991 (see table 7.6).[183]

Two critical factors contributed to this high cost of production. First was the high cost of plant materials and stores. The cost of stores or consumables utilized to produce a ton of copper increased from K275.4 in 1988 to K2,000.0 in 1991.[184] This meant that the cost of stores utilized to produce a ton of copper at Nkana increased by about 86.2%. Consolidated figures indicate that, in the total operating budgets, the cost of stores accounted for 41% in 1984 and increased dramatically to 60% in 1987.[185] The second factor was the increase in labor costs. For example, labor costs for a ton of metal produced increased by about 91% from K88.5 in 1988 to K980.0 in 1991.[186] In 1991 alone, stores and labor costs contributed about 77.9% of total production costs per ton of metal produced.[187]

Labor costs increased due to the basic salary increases implemented every year since 1985. Also, the Copperbelt mines were overstaffed by local workers as a result of the need to provide employment to Zambians due to political pressure (see tables 7.1 and 7.2). Nkana, in particular, was the second-largest employer in the Copperbelt mines, partly because of its vast mining and metallurgical facilities, and as a result of the redeployment exercise implemented

Table 7.6 Average Operating Costs in All the ZCCM Mines, Selected Years from 1984 to 1991.

Financial Year	*1984*	*1985*	*1987*	*1988*	*1989*	*1990*	*1991*
By Process:	*Costs in Kwacha, Pound Sterling, and US Dollar per Ton of Copper Produced*						
Mining	K15.1	K17.1	K66.5	K217.6	K332.3	K674.4	K1,631.6
	£6.4	£5.9	£4.7	£14.6	£18.9	£16.2	£17.9
	$9.3	$7.3	$7.5	$27.2	$31.9	$26.3	$31.0
Concentrating	K11.5	K12.8	K51.0	K47.2	K80.2	K159.0	K352.6
	£4.9	£4.4	£3.6	£3.2	£4.6	£3.8	£3.9
	$7.1	$5.4	$5.8	$5.9	$7.7	$6.2	$6.7
Treatment	K93.0	K98.7	K124.8	K112.8	K187.5	K376.9	K1,000.0
	£39.7	£34.2	£8.9	£7.6	£10,7	£9.1	£11.0
	$57.4	$41.9	$14.1	$14.1	$18.0	$14.7	$19.0
Overheads	K31.5	K43.0	K125.5	K72.8	K142.7	K384.6	K1,042.1
	£13.5	£14.9	£8.9	£4.9	£8.1	£9.2	£11.5
	$19.4	$18.3	$14.2	$9.1	$13.7	$15.0	$19.8
Total	K151.1	K171.6	K367.8	K450.4	K742.7	K1,594.9	K4,026.3
	£64.5	£59.4	£26.1	£30.2	£42.3	£38.3	£44.3
	$93.2	$72.9	$41.6	$56.3	$71.3	$62.2	$76.5
Value of One	US$0.617	US$0.425	US$0.113	US$0.125	US$0.096	US$0.039	US$0.019
Kwacha:	£0.427	£0.346	£0.071	£0.067	£0.057	£0.024	£0.011

Source: Compiled from B.K. Shamutete, A paper on ZCCM Historical Background, presented at the Seminar on Investment Opportunities in Zambia, Price Water-House, Johannesburg, February 25, 1993, Appendix 2, ZCCM 1.2.5I; ZCCM Limited, *Annual Reports*, 1984–1991; ZCCM Limited, *Management Report on Operations Covering the Quarter Ended December 31, 1985*, 25–7, ZCCM 11.7.9C; ZCCM Limited, *Management Report on Operations Covering the Quarter Ended March 31, 1988*, 24–6, MUZ HQ.

Note: This table does not include transport, tax, and related costs, but these are discussed elsewhere. Mining costs refer to cost per ton of ore hoisted or mined. Treatment costs refer to expenses on low-grade material, primary processing, and refining. The figures indicated on treatment are those related to processing costs only. Overheads include expenses incurred on care, maintenance, administrative purposes, and depreciation. Figures showing production and other costs for individual mines are unavailable in the archival material consulted.

by the ZCCM. For instance, Nkana's labor force increased from 12,251 at the end of 1982 to 14,127 in 1990.[188] In fact, one of the major reasons why the cost-saving measures failed at Nkana was because labor costs were always above budget, largely due to overstaffing. Even so, it was cheaper for Nkana to utilize a higher-labor than capital-intensive mode of production due to shortages of capital expenditure (see table 7.8) and inadequate machinery and equipment.[189]

The cost of stores increased for several reasons. Stores comprised a major part of ZCCM imports, which included machinery, electricity, mineral fuels and consumables, manufactures, and chemicals.[190] Sources were mainly South Africa, the United Kingdom, and Saudi Arabia (for crude oil). Crude oil was by far the major mineral import. Mining equipment was mainly imported from the USA. For instance, US exports to Zambia's ZCCM in 1989 totaled US$49.6 million.[191] These consisted mainly of mining equipment and spare parts, while the US imports of copper and cobalt were US$24.1 million.[192] Some of the spare parts and locomotive engines were purchased from China and the Federal Republic of Germany.[193] High costs of materials and consumables utilized in mining, concentrating, and treatment activities reflected price increases due to the effects of the world recession, which began in the mid-1970s, and the depreciation of the kwacha against major currencies (see table 7.6).

Shortages of consumables worsened after 1984. Increases in fuel prices resulted in extra costs for heavy oil of K18 million per year.[194] Between July and October 1985, serious shortages of diesel were experienced following a 30% cutback in supplies of fuel from Saudi Arabia.[195] Severe oil shortages during mid-1985 also resulted from a severe shortage of foreign exchange due to the effects of the recession.[196]

The ZCCM tried to cover cash shortfalls with new loans borrowed in US dollars, which totaled the Company's total foreign debt in kwacha at over K1,500 million in 1985.[197] This debt increased dramatically as the value of the kwacha fell. Part of this amount included a US$100 million loan sourced from a consortium of foreign banks, which covered the purchase of 600,000 tons of crude oil and petroleum products.[198] However, annual interest payments of about K200 million, 75% of which was in foreign exchange, represented a severe cash drain, further weakening the financial position of Nkana and the other mines.[199]

The supply of foreign exchange available for ZCCM's mines fell well short of their requirements. For example, out of a total foreign exchange of about US$1,049 million supplied under the control of IMF to Zambia in 1982, ZCCM was awarded about US$357 million or 34%, and by 1985, the Company's share declined further to 31% of US$828 million of the total foreign exchange allocated.[200] The Company needed a minimum allocation of 40% of total foreign exchange to cover all its imports, and lacking that, its mines, including Nkana, were unable to purchase the necessary spare parts and consumables from abroad.[201]

As mentioned earlier, to increase the foreign exchange earnings, the IMF and WB advised the government to devalue the kwacha against major currencies, including the US dollar and the pound sterling.[202] This resulted in a sharp depreciation in the value of the kwacha, especially after 1985, against the US dollar and the pound sterling (see table 7.6). Accordingly, between 1984 and 1991, the value of the kwacha against the dollar depreciated by 96.8% and by 97.7% against sterling.

Depreciation of the kwacha against major currencies had two major effects for ZCCM. Devaluation made imports, especially stores, more expensive by increasing their cost in local currency.[203] But devaluation made the ZCCM's exports more remunerative, at least for a time, by increasing the amount of local currency received by the Company for every dollar or sterling it earned.[204]

In 1984, production and related costs accounted for 89.4% of total cost of sales of about K1,847 per ton.[205] The remainder was accounted for by transport costs per ton of copper delivered to a buyer in Europe, the USA, and elsewhere. About 76% of Rokana copper was, in order of importance, exported to Japan, France, Italy, Federal Republic of Germany, India, and the United Kingdom.[206] The remainder was mainly sold to the USA and China. Transportation costs for delivering copper and cobalt metals overseas were a large part of the total cost of sales for Nkana and other ZCCM mines. As a landlocked country, Zambia relied on road and rail transport through neighboring Southern and East African countries in order to export her copper and cobalt to the coast. The Copperbelt mines used the ports of Durban and East London in South Africa, Dar-es-Salaam in Tanzania, and Beira in Mozambique.[207]

Together with production costs, transport costs from the Copperbelt to buyers abroad increased between 1982 and 1991. The cost of transporting a ton of copper from Zambia to Europe and other parts of the world increased from K196 in 1984 to K953 by 1988.[208] In the early 1980s, the southern route accounted for 60% of the total traffic of copper exports, the Dar-es-Salaam route for 35%, and other minor routes for 5%.[209] The decline in usage of the Dar-es-Salaam route reflected the reduced capacity of the Tanzania–Zambia Railways (TAZARA) system because of operational problems. In the early 1980s, the TAZARA line suffered from a lack of maintenance and shortages of fuel and lubricants, even as port operations at Dar-es-Salaam were hampered by congestion and shortages of handling equipment, particularly forklifts, tractors, and trailers.[210]

All of this caused further diversions of copper through South African ports. The southern route through to South Africa was more expensive than the Dar-es-Salaam route. The problem, though, was that it cost K124 per ton to transport copper from the Copperbelt to East London in South Africa, while it only cost K68 per ton by rail and K70 per ton by road to Dar-es-Salaam.[211] The disparity was because Dar-es-Salaam is nearer to the Copperbelt than East London; the former is 1,862.5 km away from Nkana-Kitwe, and the latter, 2,866.5 km.[212]

Owing to a general rise in the price of fuel and spare parts, TAZARA increased its rates for exports and imports by 20% and 22%, respectively, effective February 1, 1985.[213] This resulted in extra transport costs for the ZCCM mines of approximately K7 million per year. Furthermore, a decision was taken by TAZARA to charge the ZCCM and other Zambian customers in foreign exchange for the Tanzanian section of the rail, amounting to an estimated K20 million a year.[214] But alternative routes to the Tanzanian one were in short supply because of the volatile Southern African political environment. The Benguela railway line, stretching 1,340 km from the Copperbelt to Lobito, had been destroyed in 1975 because of the civil war in Angola.[215] Similarly, the Beira route through Mozambique was unreliable because of the civil war.[216]

These were not the only major politically oriented transport challenges for Zambia's copper mining industry. After 1985, political relations between Zambia and South Africa were strained over the former's open support for freedom fighters opposed to the Apartheid regime.[217] The headquarters of the African National Congress (ANC) of South Africa were based in Lusaka. President Kaunda also called on the international community to impose mandatory economic sanctions against South Africa to bring down the Apartheid regime.[218] Pretoria responded by stepping up aggression against countries supporting freedom fighters in the region in what became known as the "destabilisation campaign." Between 1983 and 1986, Pieter W. Botha's government sent special forces who carried out attacks in suspected suburbs believed to be harboring insurgents against the Apartheid regime in Lusaka and Livingstone (Zambia), Harare (Zimbabwe), and Gaborone (Botswana).[219] In retaliation, suspected freedom fighters carried out bomb attacks in Johannesburg and elsewhere.[220]

As a result, in November 1986, the ZCCM stopped sending copper exports through South Africa.[221] The mines resorted to airlifting some imports and exports, further increasing transport costs. Copper exports and imports fell back on the Dar-es-Salaam route despite its many challenges, and between 1985 and 1991, this route accounted for not less than 80% of the mines' transport needs.[222] However, delays in transport of cargo such as materials, spare parts, machinery, and consumables to the Copperbelt continued the decline in production at Nkana.

In addition to all these factors, there were other transport- and sales-related charges. For instance, in January 1985, the government increased the rate of sales tax on imported goods from 12.5% to 15% and cost Nkana and the other ZCCM mines an additional K26 million per year.[223] At the same time, excise duty on petroleum fuels was increased and resulted in extra costs of about K1.8 million.[224]

Nkana and the other ZCCM mines consequently became high-cost producers in the course of the 1980s. By comparison, other major copper mines in Zaire, Chile, Canada, and the USA were still low-cost producers. In 1988, the average cost per pound of copper produced was about US$0.89 in Zambia, $0.61 in the USA, $0.54 in Canada, $0.48 in Zaire, and about $0.39 in Chile.[225] Production costs at Nkana and other Zambian producers ranked alongside Peru, where annual production costs per ton in 1988 averaged US$0.92.[226]

While the factors discussed so far were responsible for the increase in the Copperbelt mines' production costs, the increase was also attributable to the

ZCCM's low investment in advanced machinery and technology. By contrast, the government-owned CODELCO-Chile, whose ore reserves were lower than the ZCCM's, enjoyed extremely low costs.[227] CODELCO-Chile, unlike the ZCCM, reduced production costs by successfully devaluing the peso, coupled with other exchange-rate policy changes designed to deal with rising unemployment and declining output.[228] These measures lowered production costs and improved expanded investment in mining operations. CODELCO-Chile, like the ZCCM, relied on borrowed money for capital projects, but the former invested all such funds into new mines, machinery, and technology, while the latter diversified part of the borrowed money into other sectors such as agriculture, construction, and hospitality, denying its mines much needed capital.[229]

Although the average grades in 1980 of ore reserves for CODELCO-Chile at 1.68% copper were less than those of the ZCCM, averaging over 2.3% copper, CODELCO-Chile produced more copper at lower costs than the ZCCM between 1982 and 1991 because of investments in new mines and advanced equipment.[230] Similarly, the government-owned Gecamines in Zambia's neighbor, Zaire, invested in new mines, machinery, and technology in order to reduce costs.[231]

OVERALL PROFITABILITY OF NKANA DIVISION AND THE ZCCM-OWNED MINES

Between March 1981 and September 1982, Nkana, together with other ZCCM mines, experienced economic and financial challenges, not least because of depressed metal prices on the world market. The metal market on the LME in London and the Commodity Exchange (COMEX) in New York, where Zambian producers sold their copper, experienced intermittent setbacks from long recession dating back to the 1970s. The average copper price of K1,522 per ton in 1982 was lower than the average of K1,620 for 1981.[232] The decline in copper prices was caused by a slackening of industrial activity in the West against a background of rising stocks. From March 1981 to 1982, the world stock of copper increased from 1.19 million tons to 1.35 million tons, with a corresponding decrease in the copper price from K1,578 to K1,487 per ton.[233] Similarly, the West's demand for cobalt declined because of major reductions in consumption of super and magnetic alloys and tool steel industries.[234]

Between October 1982 and February 1983, the copper price increased because of heightened Western demand. This demand was partly a result of the 4% decrease to 6.24 million tons of copper output among major producing countries in 1982.[235] The decrease in copper stocks resulted from "steep production cutbacks of 400,000 to 500,000 tons in the United States of America and Canada, and to lesser output cuts in Zaire, Zambia and the Philippines. Chile and Peru recorded increases."[236]

This cutback, however, was not done by mutual agreement among these producers. After independence, it became difficult to form a big cartel like Copper Exporters Inc. of the early 1930s to control the market, for a number of reasons. In the colonial era, the copper business was dominated by the private sector.[237] After nationalization in Africa and South America, the mining companies were either private firms or government controlled.[238] New producers also emerged after independence of countries such as the Philippines, Papua New Guinea, Australia, Indonesia, Panama, Brazil, and Mexico.[239] New major consumers included Japan, China, India, and the Soviet Union.[240]

With this expansion of the copper industry, it became extremely difficult to pursue a concerted policy in the copper business. Copper producers in the USA and Canada set their own cutbacks to protect their market on the COMEX in New York.[241] CIPEC managed to woo some of the new producers but failed to fine-tune production in line with demand because the cartel only controlled 37% of world output.[242] Since its army seized power, Chile was not an active member of CIPEC, and the organization collapsed in 1988 after being unable to maintain high copper prices.[243] Craig observed that "the control of the international copper industry by the transnational companies was eroded by the establishment of . . . state mining enterprises, which undermined the transnationals' ability to stabilise the market through informal cooperation and led to greater price volatility."[244] Thus, the price of copper was largely influenced by other world output-driven demand factors.

The above decline in output coincided with increased "USA copper consumption fuelled by promising housing and car industry figures, and to speculative activity linked to firmer precious metal prices."[245] Lower US interest rates, strikes in Peruvian mines, and the decline in the value of the pound sterling against the US dollar, all contributed to the price increase.[246] These factors combined to push the monthly price of copper to a record of over K2,100 per ton in January 1983.[247] This increase in the price of copper continued between 1984 and 1985. Similarly, the cobalt market remained depressed, but its average price continued to improve primarily due to the "tightness in the supply of spot material and a renewed bullish tone on the free market."[248] In March 1984, the price of cobalt, therefore, reached a three-year peak of US$12.60 (K20.32) per pound and continued to improve thereafter.[249]

From January 1985 until 1991, the price of copper increased dramatically. This was mainly because of fresh buying interests from the Far East, particularly Japan and China.[250] This led to a drop in copper inventories. Between January and May 1986, stocks in the LME warehouses fell by about 20,900 tons, from 153,500 tons to 132,600 tons.[251] This fueled a price spiral. On the other hand, "the collapse of oil prices since 1981, which brought adverse influence on the metal markets, appeared to have waned and base metal prices including those of gold, silver, cobalt, lead and zinc were on the upswing."[252] The slump in oil, which had a dampening effect on the metal markets, "was overtaken by new events in the wake of the US bombings of Libyan bases, which precipitated a new crisis in the supply of oil from the gulf countries and increased the price of fuel."[253]

These factors combined to fuel a price spiral of the average monthly price of copper, which more than tripled from K3,125 per ton in January 1985 to K10,810 in May 1986. Subsequently, the average annual price of copper increased from record figures of K5,841 in 1986, through K11,799 in 1987, to K16,525 per ton in 1988.[254]

But the main reason for the sharp increase in the price of copper from 1989 to 1991 was supply problems among major producers, which reduced world and LME stocks.[255] Overproduction in Peru was largely counterbalanced by a strike at CODELCO-Chile's 100,000 ton a year-producing San Salvador mine, which lasted for more than 60 days.[256] At the same time, continued problems in the mines of Papua New Guinea and labor problems in the Highland Valley in British Columbia, coupled with the closure of the Cananea in Mexico, caused serious supply disruptions from these producers.[257] These gyrations in various parts of the global copper mining industry resulted in major supply disruptions and high copper price fluctuations from K28,736.84 to K32,175.44 per ton between May and September 1989.[258]

The price of cobalt improved in 1985 because of the upward consumption of the metal. It increased by 14% between 1983 and 1984 from about 15.4 million pounds to 17.9 million pounds, due to a continued demand for steel and superalloys in developed countries.[259] Between 1986 and 1991, consumption, demand, and prices of cobalt were mainly spurred by a shortage in the cobalt supply, when Zambia and Zaire, the main producers, stopped selling their metal on the open market, coupled with the latter's low supply due to constraints in production.[260] A shortage in the cobalt supply also caused a minor panic among buyers who began stockpiling, causing the average annual price of the metal to double (see table 7.7).

However, the much-anticipated metal boom, following the outbreak of the Gulf War between the USA and Iraq, did not occur. The Gulf War disrupted supplies of crude oil from the Middle East and increased the price of petroleum products.[261] As a result of low supplies of petroleum, the developed world saw a slackening of production, supply, and general industrial activity, with a significant impact on the demand and price of metals.[262] Price increases between 1984 and 1991 offset increased costs of sales. Table 7.7 shows the overall profitability of the ZCCM mines from 1982 to 1991.

Nkana Division produced 1,387,401 metric tons of copper and 18,485 tons of cobalt, representing about 28.1% and 47.8% of the ZCCM's total

Table 7.7 Profitability of Zambia Consolidated Copper Mines Limited between 1982 and 1991.

Year	*Finished Production (Metric Tons)*		*Price per Ton*		*Value of Sales*	*Cost of Sales*	*Borrowing Interest*	*Total Tax*	*Net Profit (Loss)*
	Copper	Cobalt	Copper (K)	Cobalt (K)	Millions (K)	Millions (K)	Millions (K)	Millions (K)	Millions (K)
1982	591,853	2,686	1,522	24,904	977.1	1,082.7	69.1	6.1	(173.6)
1983	575,518	2,212	1,475	14,656	973.1	1,035.8	47.1	4.5	(127.5)
1984	551,021	2,748	2,170	18,864	1,426.0	1,171.2	113.0	95.9	(1.0)
1985	525,811	3,654	2,796	45,389	1,862.0	1,484.0	146.7	144.3	0.7
1986	463,354	4,565	5,841	90,719	4,097.0	2,911.0	318.0	358.0	(56.0)
1987	470,982	4,160	11,799	80,858	6,976.0	5,628.0	793.0	773.0	(562.0)
1988	473,084	4,694	16,525	108,671	11,882.0	9,703.0	671.0	272.0	372.0
1989	415,645	4,871	25,721	130,903	18,135.0	14,114.0	758.0	891.0	1,832.0
1990	448,468	4,447	45,475	328,674	32,878.0	22,430.0	1,819.0	2,970.0	2,586.0
1991	421,590	4,674	95,723	657,210	65,559.0	47,020.0	4,544.0	6,036.0	5,189.0

Source: Compiled from ZCCM Limited, *Annual Reports,* 1982–1991.

Note: Value of Sales refers to total revenue from all the metals including lead and zinc from Broken Hill/Kabwe mine. Net Profit/(Loss) was arrived at after subtracting Cost of Sales, adding share of associated/subsidiary company profit, interest paid or charged on borrowings, exchange rate loss/gain based on the prevailing major currencies (which are not indicated in this table but in the Company's annual reports), and taxes (Total Tax). There are no figures for individual mines except for the total for all ZCCM-owned mines.

production of these two metals, respectively (see tables 7.5 and 7.7). In terms of finished copper production, Nkana Division ranked third after Nchanga and Mufulira Divisions, and Nchanga alone produced almost half of the ZCCM's total output.[263] Also, Nkana Division produced almost half of the ZCCM's cobalt output. Mainly because of the factors discussed previously, copper output from the Copperbelt mines declined between 1983 and 1991, and the ZCCM was surpassed by producers from the USA, the Soviet Union, Chile, and Canada.[264]

The financial performance of Nkana, in particular, and the ZCCM, in general, reflected the effects of various factors including price of metals, cost of sales, devaluation of the kwacha, loan payments, and tax applicable to the Company. Table 7.6 indicates that, in the 1982 and 1983 financial years, the ZCCM incurred a loss of K173.6 million and K127.5 million, respectively, mainly because of the increase in the cost of sales, which were beyond the total value of sales. The increase in production and transport costs against a background of volatile metal prices on the LME and COMEX reduced revenue from copper sales. Between 1984 and 1986, the difference between the annual value of sales and the cost of sales indicates that Nkana and the Copperbelt mines' financial results were better than in the previous years, before falling away again in 1987.

As discussed previously, the increase in copper and cobalt kwacha-denominated prices offset increased production and transport costs in this period. In general, Nkana and the other ZCCM mines made a substantial gross profit (see table 7.6 for the difference between value of sales and cost of sales per year). But the net annual losses resulted mainly from heavy borrowing interests and taxes. Equity Levy and Mineral Export Tax (MET) raised "the government's share of the profit to about 87% of the total."[265] Between 1988 and 1991, however, Nkana Division and the other ZCCM mines realized healthy net profits because they were exempted from the equity levy and MET.[266] It is clear that the fluctuation of metal prices against a background of rising costs, coupled with an increase in loan interests and tax, was responsible for the decline in ZCCM's earnings. Table 7.8 compares the distribution of capital and revenue from tax and dividends of ZCCM. The issued share capital on "A" (GRZ) shares and "B" (Minority) shares of K10 each averaged K894.4 million per year between 1982 and 1991.[267]

The decline in earnings was aggravated by the lack of adequate capital expenditure at Nkana, especially between 1984 and 1986, when the ZCCM did not initiate any capital project at the mine. In particular, Nkana and the other Copperbelt mines bore the brunt of the foreign exchange losses following the devaluation of the kwacha, heavy loan interests, and heavy MET, income tax, and equity levy, which corroded net profits, dividends, and retained earnings (see tables 7.7 and 7.8). Thus, the ZCCM failed to declare a dividend before 1989 when the taxes were relaxed.

The decline in capital expenditure was also related to the diversion of funds into other Company projects rather than mining. In the face of volatile metal prices and limited revenue from the mines, the government and the ZCCM decided in 1985 to strengthen the Company's diversification ventures in industrial enterprise, agriculture, tourism, construction, and manufacturing.[268] As a consequence, a local broad-based company named Mulungushi Investments Limited (MIL) was formed in 1986, as a holding company of the ZCCM's industrial and commercial enterprises.[269] The purpose of this diversification plan was to make the ZCCM's divisions more autonomous and save costs. However, the ZCCM only managed to accumulate a meager profit of about K273.3 million after spending over K1,891.1 million on subsidiary companies between 1982 and 1991.[270]

The ZCCM's financial problems impacted the national economy, as mining was and still is the mainstay of the Zambian economy. Throughout the 1970s, Nkana and the other Copperbelt mines accounted for 30% of real Gross Domestic Product (GDP) each year and around 96% of the foreign exchange earnings.[271] But, by 1982, the mines' contribution to annual GDP fell by

Table 7.8 Breakdown of Capital and Tax Revenue on and Dividends of ZCCM All in Millions of Kwacha, 1982–1991.

	Capital Expenditure in Millions of Kwacha					*Capital Employed*	*Taxation*			*Dividends*	
Year	*ZCCM Total*	*All Mines*	*Nkana Mine*	*Diverted*	*Losses*	*Total*	*Export Tax*	*Income Tax*	*Equity Levy*	*"A"*	*"B"*
1982	273.2	246.0	85.0	27.2	–	2,117.5	1.7		4.4	–	–
1983	252.1	243.4	55.1	8.7	82.6	2,291.2	0.8		3.7	–	–
1984	214.8	204.6	0.0	10.2	83.2	2,538.4	91.1	0.6	4.2	–	–
1985	291.0	263.0	0.0	28.0	67.4	4,960.8	140.6	3.3	0.4	–	–
1986	1,229.0	1,123.0	0.0	106.0	599.0	17,175.0	357.0	1.0	–	–	–
1987	1,097.0	789.0	27.0	308.0	219.0	25,614.0	760.0	13.0	–	–	–
1988	870.0	754.0	71.0	116.0	52.0	19,976.0	255.0	17.0	–	–	–
1989	1,191.0	940.0	187.0	251.0	103.0	23,176.0	–	891.0	–	80.8	53.2
1990	3,090.0	2,763.0	387.0	327.0	225.0	39,060.0	–	2,970.0	–	80.8	53.2
1991	6,357.0	1,979.0	838.0	709.0	385.0	122,667.0	–	2,088.0	–	80.8	53.2

Source: Compiled from ZCCM Limited, *Annual Reports*, 1982–1991; ZCCM Limited, *Report—Export Rehabilitation and Diversification Project, October 1985*, 5, ZCCM 12.3.3B.

Note: Capital Expenditure was partly charged on profits and through short-term loans between 1982 and 1991. It was also obtained from retained earnings, which averaged about 25% of total capital expenses between 1982 and 1988, and increased to 40% between 1989 and 1991. This Expenditure was mainly utilized on big or capital projects. Capital Employed includes Capital Expenditure, capital on investments, retained proceeds, loans obtained, overdrafts, subordinated borrowings, and shareholders' funds. No new Dividends were declared between 1982 and 1988 because of the Losses incurred. However, shareholders were still paid deferred dividends, which are not indicated in the Company's reports.

over half to 13.8% despite still accounting for 92.2% of foreign exchange earnings.[272] As shown by table 7.6, reduced revenue from mining between 1982 and 1986 coincided with high interest rates on foreign payments, which "created a crisis that entailed a backlog of arrears on payments abroad and substantial foreign borrowing."[273]

Zambia's economic situation continued to worsen, obliging it to seek more assistance from the IMF, the WB, and other lending institutions. A backlog of arrears meant that Zambia had to agree to tough economic measures before the IMF and WB made financial help available. The introduction of Structural Adjustment Policies included "cuts in civil service [and mine labour], relinquishing control of interest rates, elimination of price subsidies, and bolstering of agriculture prices to the producers."[274]

In mid-1986, food riots started at Nkana Division and spread to the other Copperbelt mines and compounds because of a 120% rise in the price of one of the staple foods, mealie-meal.[275] The riots were one of the many symptoms of public resentment toward the government. Repeated industrial unrest and food riots in the mine compounds and in the public sector followed in 1987.[276] In desperation, President Kaunda broke with the IMF and WB on May 6, 1987, after he described their borrowing conditions as "murderous [stifling the economy of Zambia]" and introduced a New Economic Recovery Programme (NERP) in 1988.[277] But NERP failed to improve the situation, forcing Kaunda to negotiate a new understanding with the IMF and WB. Barton claims that, in this manner, by selectively implementing monetary reform ahead of fiscal reform, Kaunda was able to maintain political exclusivity by using the popular reaction of Zambians, in general, and mineworkers, in particular, to help manage IMF/WB demands.[278]

By 1989, however, the UNIP government was extremely unpopular.[279] The leadership of the MUZ and Zambia Congress of Trade Unions (ZCTU) took advantage of UNIP's unpopularity and, in May 1990, adopted "a resolution to support and champion the return of multi-party politics."[280] Subsequently, political pressure from the donor community, International Financial Institutions (IFIs), and the public forced the UNIP government to reintroduce democracy, and elections were scheduled for 1991. The labor movement formed the Movement for Multiparty Democracy (MMD) led by ZCTU chairman, Frederick Chiluba.[281]

In Kitwe, the MMD launched vigorous campaigns at Nkana's mine compounds of Wusikili, Chamboli, and Mindola.[282] Mainly because of being central to the Copperbelt, Nkana-Kitwe and their compounds became a political base for the MMD.[283] In addition, the headquarters of MUZ, which supported the MMD, was based in Nkana-Kitwe's Wusikili mine compound. The MMD, which promised to liberalize the economy and privatize state enterprises, won the 1991 election with a landslide against UNIP, especially on the Copperbelt.[284] In line with their party manifesto, the MMD privatized the ZCCM in order to attract foreign investment in the mining sector. But even so, privatization of the mining sector was delayed until 1997, partly for political and personal reasons among the senior members of the MMD.[285] From 1997 to the present, Nkana and the Copperbelt mines remain privatized.

CONCLUSION

This chapter demonstrated that Nkana was one of the most important divisions to ZCCM. The Division's large metallurgical facilities were central to the productive capacity of ZCCM as a whole. Despite Nkana ranking in third place after Nchanga and Mufulira with regard to copper production, the former was the largest producer of cobalt. Between 1982 and 1991, Nkana cooperated in implementing most of ZCCM's policies.

This chapter partly concurs with Burawoy's suggestion that, for political reasons, Zambianization of managerial jobs in the industry was undermined by the UNIP authorities' reluctance to promote Zambians in these positions. In addition, this chapter has observed that Rokana/Nkana Mine Division could not Zambianize all supervisory and technical positions due to shortages of local workers suitable to take up these positions. Between 1983 and 1990, the number of workers at Nkana increased from 11,518 to 14,928 mainly because of labor redeployed from other divisions.[286] However, this redeployment exercise undermined the cost-saving measures under ZCCM's new FYPIP, dictated by the IMF and WB, designed to increase the Company's productivity and overall profitability, as this practice increased labor costs.

Table 7.5 shows that ore reserves and finished production at Nkana were stable. Nevertheless, production did not increase substantially due to the effect of deep-level mining and the resultant dilution, coupled with low labor productivity and poor availability of spare parts and consumables to maintain production. Similarly, ZCCM's "aim of the [FY]PIP to stabilise production at a level of 540,000 tons per annum was not achieved as production between [1986 and 1991] averaged only [448,854 tons] per annum."[287] The FYPIP "was [largely] undermined by the Government's inability to provide ZCCM with sufficient foreign exchange and by increasing the taxation of the company through a mineral export tax[, which corroded into the Company's earnings and capital]."[288]

As a consequence, the government and ZCCM resorted to excessive borrowing from IFIs to fund their operations and projects. As observed by Barton and seconded in this chapter, Kaunda's calculated relationship with the IMF frustrated the institution's efforts to invigorate the Zambian economy. The chapter also goes beyond Barton's work by positing that the Zambian economy was severely hit by high debt repayments, falling copper prices, and the resultant economic woes.

Chapter 8

Conclusion

This book has explored Rhokana/Rokana's corporate history from 1928 to 1991. The examination was centered on three major themes in the history of this company: corporate structure, labor relations, and profitability. Whereas previous studies have looked at these themes individually, this monograph combined them in a single narrative over a long period in order to offer a comprehensive understanding of the totality of mining on the Zambian Copperbelt.

The book utilized primary material from four Zambian archives, interviews, and the historiographical body of literature associated with the economic and social history of the copper mining industry in Zambia. It has to be acknowledged that the major weakness of the archival sources used is that they do not provide detailed information on the profitability of individual Copperbelt mines for the years after 1970. As mentioned in chapter 1, this is because surviving primary sources focus on the performance of the parent companies after nationalization. Nonetheless, the overall trend can still be seen from the performance of the parent companies, as demonstrated in chapters 6 and 7.

Copper King in Central Africa has sought to advance as detailed as possible an understanding of the corporate profitability of an individual mine on the Copperbelt. In this manner, it has built on Phillips's pioneering analysis of big business and the Roan Antelope mine owned by Rhodesian Selection Trust (RST).[1] In contrast to studies by Bates, Berger, Burawoy, Daniel, Mhone, Parpart, and Perrings, which emphasized the impact of labor on mining fortunes, this book has argued that national, regional, and global issues also significantly affected corporate profitability. As discussed for each period, Rhokana/Rokana's profitability between 1928 and 1991 was affected by the quantity and quality of ores, the utilization of fuel, power, machinery and technology, and modes of transport. Also critical were the changing prices of copper and successive governments' mining policies and tax regimes.

Chapter 2 examined the establishment of the Rhokana Corporation and rapid development of the Nkana mine from 1928 to 1939. The argument was raised that the formation of the Rhokana Corporation and development of its Nkana mine in 1931 were the results of the convergence of multinational interest and capital from South Africa, Britain, and the United States of America (USA). However, this coincided with the acceleration of the Great Depression, which threatened the rapid development of Nkana mine and the overall profitability of the Rhokana Corporation. Because of falling commodity prices, copper production initially fell, although, as it turned out, the Great Depression proved to be only a transitory setback for the Copperbelt mines. A range of factors from interlocking corporate strategy, through the rationalization of labor supplies, to the quality of ore milled, coupled with the booming industrial activities of the late 1930s in Europe and the USA, all enhanced the financial performance of Rhokana and the other Copperbelt companies during the Great Depression.

At the climax of the Great Depression between 1932 and 1934, the price of copper on the London Metal Exchange (LME) fell from an average of £36.4 to £33.7 per long ton (see table 2.1). As discussed in chapter 2, Copper Exporters Inc., a cartel to which Rhokana and the Copperbelt companies all belonged, encouraged its members to cut back on production in order to reduce world stocks and help improve the price. But this measure failed, as the price of copper only averaged £35.6 per ton, and the cartel collapsed in 1932. Between 1932 and 1935, production and transport costs to buyers in Europe and America per long ton of copper averaged £24.7 for Rhokana, compared with £27.7 for the mines controlled by the RST (see table 2.1), and ranged from £40 to £45 for US mines.[2]

Roberts and Parpart, following Gann, observed that Nkana and the Copperbelt mines were able to generate profit, despite the impact of the economic crash, because they utilized a higher-labor rather than capital-intensive mode of production, which was enhanced by the relative cheapness of African labor.[3] Beyond the argument by Gann, Parpart, and Roberts, chapter 2 has posited that the low production and transport costs for Rhokana were greatly enhanced by cheaper coal supplies from Wankie in Southern Rhodesia and special railway rates on the Rhodesia Railways, as well as the quality of the ore treated at Nkana. These two factors, coupled with the relative cheapness of African labor, were the main reasons behind the profitability of Rhokana and the Copperbelt companies during the Great Depression. For all these reasons, Nkana was a low-cost producer.

At the same time, the copper market improved from 1935 onward because of a boom in the automotive industry and the rearmament in Europe. Between

1935 and 1939, the value of sales totaled £20,027,696 compared with the cost of sales totalling £8,774,893 (see table 2.2). Of this figure, provision for royalty/export tax and other expenses amounted to about £6,000,154 (see table 2.2). The operating profit for the mine totaled £8,628,205 (see table 2.2). After deducting income tax from Nkana's operating surplus, and adding returns from Rhokana's investment in other mines and properties on the Copperbelt, the gross profit for the Corporation between 1935 and 1939 totaled £7,526,251. After deducting reserve amounts for depreciation and development purposes, the net profit in this period amounted to £6,152,225 (see table 2.3). Dividends paid totaled £5,184,250, leaving unappropriated profits of £967,975, which were reinvested. These figures show that Rhokana was making significant profits despite the global economic recession.

This period also witnessed the conjuncture of particular historic forces driven by the rapid development of large-scale mining, industrialization, urbanization, social transformation, and proletarianization of labor and worker consciousness. This enabled African miners on the Copperbelt to translate worker consciousness into strike action in 1935, the first of its kind in Northern Rhodesia. As demonstrated in chapter 2, European miners were worried about the increasing power and influence of African workers. Thus, two years after the historic strike by black workers, white miners formed the Northern Rhodesia European Mineworkers' Union (NRMWU). The dual labor structure gave birth to worker consciousness, collective labor action, and trade unionism, and the Nkana mine was central to both black and white labor activism on the Zambian Copperbelt. Nevertheless, Rhokana and the other Copperbelt companies were relieved that Africans were not included in the NRMWU, as they feared that a joint black and white union would be more powerful and militant in its activities.[4]

Chapter 3 has investigated the impact of financial measures introduced by the British and US governments during the Second World War and Korean Crisis on Rhokana's returns on investments in the Northern Rhodesian mining sector. Nkana and the other Copperbelt mines supplied the bulk of Britain's copper needs following the outbreak of the Second World War in 1939. Due to a high demand for minerals to sustain war efforts, there was an increased partnership between the British government and the mining companies in the colonies. The latter functioned as a direct appendage of the former's war economy between 1940 and 1945.

According to Dumett, the Second World War not only gave impetus to mineral exploitation but also, for the first time since the First World War, it extended government control over the mining sector.[5] While all the Copperbelt mines contributed greatly to the war economy, this chapter has contended that Nkana was particularly strategic for Britain's war effort because it supplied both copper and cobalt to the Ministry of Supply. Cobalt was particularly important in the making of airplane engines. Nkana, though, sometimes failed to meet the target of 9,500 short tons of copper per month requested by the Ministry of Supply. Largely, this was because of shortages of plant materials and equipment to replace worn-out ones. In turn, these shortages were caused by closed capital markets and shipping delays emanating from hostile enemy action and coupled with inadequate supplies of fuel. These problems raised the cost of producing copper and transporting it to England from about £25 per ton during the Great Depression to almost £31 between 1940 and 1945.

In line with Berger, Dumett, and Phillips, this chapter has observed that the increase in production costs can be partly ascribed to improvement in wages. African wages per man per shift increased from 1.04s in 1940 to 1.47s by 1945 (see table 3.2). The increase was, to some extent, the result of a strike by African workers in 1940, demanding, among other things, wage increments. A critical shortage of labor also increased African wages during the war. European workers took advantage of this and did not only demand a wage increase during a strike in 1940 but also secured a closed shop. Chapter 3 has noted that the shortage of labor obliged Rhokana to turn to women to do certain surface jobs. Contrary to the argument made by Chauncey, Parpart, and Dandule that women only played the reproductive role of stabilizing mine labor on the Copperbelt, this chapter found that the war effort brought women at Nkana to wage labor.[6]

Still, it was cheaper for Nkana to utilize a higher-labor as opposed to capital-intensive mode of production due to a lack of capital and inadequate machinery and spare parts throughout the war. Rhokana's African labor force increased from 7,784 in 1940 to 9,490 in 1944 (see table 3.2). By comparison, capital expenditure on major projects fell from £126,028 to £84,538. As discussed in chapter 3, Dumett, Phillips, Butler, Ronnback, and Broberg have attributed reduction in capital and profit for Rhokana and the other Copperbelt companies to financial measures introduced by the British and Northern Rhodesian governments during the war. These were the fixed price of copper in London and double taxation in the form of income tax, excess profits tax, and national defense contribution. However, Rhokana and the Copperbelt companies remained competitive vis-à-vis their established counterparts in America because the former continued to be low-cost producers.

This chapter has observed that the fixed price of copper at £62 per ton was double the cost of sales per ton, which averaged almost £31 for Nkana during the war. This was further confirmed by the value of sales totalling £33,685,643, against the total cost of sales of £20,278,366 between 1940 and 1945 (see table 3.2). But, and as noticed by the aforementioned scholars, provision for double taxation corroded the Corporation's profits and dividends. However, the total dividends paid by Rhokana throughout the war, which averaged 25%, served to keep the major shareholders, Rhodesian

Anglo American (RAA), Rio Tinto, Newmont, and Kennecott, satisfied. Britain was able to save during the war in terms of foreign exchange, as well as benefit from taxes paid (see chapter 3). For its part, Rhokana relied on loans and debentures for capital projects due to inadequate revenue from metal sales. In 1940, the value of loans and debentures for the Corporation stood at £788,294, but by the end of the war in 1945, the estimated liability in this regard almost doubled to £1,475,544.[7] Overall, the Second World War weakened the financial position of the Rhokana Corporation. But this was not the only problem.

After the war, Nkana and the other Copperbelt mines were exhausted by wear and tear. Rehabilitation and developmental work at Nkana increased capital expenditure and the demand for labor. As discussed in chapter 3, there was a corresponding increase in operating costs. However, four major factors combined and boosted Nkana and the other Copperbelt mines. These were postwar reconstruction in Europe, the boom in the electrical and automotive industry in the USA, the disruption of world production by strikes in America, and the 44% devaluation of the pound sterling against the US dollar. The devaluation of the pound was by far the most important development, since the price paid for copper from the Copperbelt by the British government was not only based on the dollar price but also increased it by the same percentage.

These combined factors almost doubled the annual average price of copper per ton in London from £62 between 1940 and 1945 to about £118.7 between 1946 and 1949. This copper price more than tripled beyond the average operating cost of £33 per ton and offset the increase in production and transport costs after the war. This chapter supports Sklar's and Phillips's argument that the price level determined the overall profitability of mining.

The increase in the copper price, coupled with double taxation relief in 1947, enhanced the profitability of the Copperbelt mines. The year 1949 marked a milestone for both the financial history of Rhokana and the other Copperbelt companies and the history of the dual labor structure. That year, the African Mineworkers Union (AMU) was formed on the Copperbelt. But this was long after the NRMWU had been founded and secured better conditions of service and a closed shop, which reserved highly skilled jobs for its members. Workers at Nkana were not only the most militant on the Copperbelt but also played a significant role in the formation of the European and African trade unions. As observed by Ferguson and noted in this chapter, Nkana-Kitwe was the "hub of the Copperbelt, a bustling industrial city" with the largest multiracial population in the country.[8] Most people were attracted by not only employment opportunities but also the city's centrality on the Copperbelt.

Initially, Rhokana and the other companies were not bothered with the monopoly status of European workers given that they relied more on cheap

African labor. But it was not to be taken for granted now that the legal basis of trade unions was built on a color-blind foundation. The formation of the AMU transformed industrial relations at Nkana and in the other Copperbelt mines. Like the NRMWU, AMU fought for better wages and other service conditions for its members. This increased labor costs, in particular, and operating expenses, in general. However, the high demand for copper and the resultant increase in the price of the red metal during the Korean War (1950–1953) offset rising labor and production costs in the industry.

As a product of Cold War tension between the Soviet Union and the USA in Asia, the Korean Crisis gave the mining companies a rationale for the pursuit of their long-ranged objectives. As observed by Navin and detailed in chapter 3, policies relating to investment, production, marketing, sales, taxation, and management in the copper industry shifted to benefit producers following the outbreak of the Korean War in 1950.[9] During the crisis, the strategic stockpiling of copper by the USA stimulated demand. Unlike the British government, who fixed the price of copper during the Second World War, the US government invested abroad in the industry and purchased copper at higher prices from producers on the Commodity Metal Exchange (COMEX) in New York. This had knock-on effects on the price of copper elsewhere on the world market. The cost of production increased to about £57 due to shortages of coal from Wankie in Southern Rhodesia, forcing Rhokana to look for alternative sources. Production costs also increased because of the dramatic increase in labor costs. As observed by Mhone and Berger, and as ascertained in chapter 3, between 1950 and 1953, the AMU staged a series of strikes against low wages. These strikes forced Nkana and the other mines to increase African wages by over 77% for surface and 63% for underground workers in this period. In addition, wages in the Copperbelt mines increased on account of significant improvements in bonus allowances and overtime expenses as the mines stepped up production during the Korean War. Accordingly, average monthly African wages per employee at Nkana and in the other Copperbelt mines increased from about £5.1 in 1950 to £10.3 by 1953 (see table 3.5).

By comparison, average monthly earnings per European worker increased substantially from £89 to £148.5 in this period. Nevertheless, the improved price of copper in London, at an average of £229 per ton throughout the Korean War, quadrupled beyond the previously stated cost of producing copper. Consequently, the Korean Crisis spawned a range of mining activities in Northern Rhodesia from investment in the sector to the marketing of copper and the record dividends distributed to shareholders.

After nearly 30 years, large-scale mining in Northern Rhodesia was beginning to pay handsomely. Rhokana Corporation, which was both an investment firm on the Copperbelt and a mining company through Nkana, benefited more from the financial incentives of the Cold War in Asia. Even more, the improved price level increased the value of sales, which almost doubled beyond the operating costs. Besides copper, Nkana sold cobalt to the USA and Europe.

Investment in other properties on the Copperbelt also began to pay off for Rhokana. Profits from Mufulira and Nchanga contributed to about one-third of the Corporation's total net profit. Annual dividends for the Corporation improved substantially from an average of £749,167 during the Second World War to almost £4,528,257 during the Korean War (see tables 3.3 and 3.9). Between 1950 and 1953, total tax paid by Rhokana to the Northern Rhodesian and British governments was over £15,783,834.[10] For the first time in the history of Nkana and the Copperbelt mines since the end of the Great Depression, there were expansion and diversification of the mining industry, mainly due to the accumulation of capital and profit. Rhokana contributed half of its profits to open new mines, Bancroft and Kansanshi. Similarly, the profits from Roan Antelope and Mufulira were partly invested in Baluba, Chambishi, and Chibuluma. The aim was to double production to maximize profits following the improved price level. Consequently, Rhokana would become the most important commercial unit in the new Federation of Rhodesia and Nyasaland.

As mentioned in chapter 4, the formation of the Federation of Rhodesia and Nyasaland in September 1953 was one of the most important political developments in British colonial Africa. The idea of amalgamating the three Central African states, however, dated back to the 1930s. Then, Rhokana and the other Copperbelt companies rejected amalgamation, citing differences in the labor policies of the states (see chapter 4). But when the idea of a federation was revived in the late 1940s and early 1950s, management at Nkana and in the other mines supported it.

Navin, Cohen, and Money attributed this shift in attitude to changes in leadership and management styles in the Copperbelt mines. Accordingly, this chapter has noticed that the new general manager of Rhokana, Oliver B. Bennett, was a liberal thinker just like Harry F. Oppenheimer, who became chairman of Anglo American Corporation (AAC) in Southern Africa. Like their counterpart, Ronald Prain of RST, these two leaders felt that their mines would benefit from the idea of partnership among races. Other compelling economic factors included the expanding influence of Southern Rhodesia as the main source of coal and the link to the southern railway network. For these reasons, Rhokana/AAC and RST funded the United Central Africa Association, an organization supporting the Federation. After the Federation was formed, Rhokana shifted its head offices from Nkana-Kitwe in Northern Rhodesia to Salisbury (Southern Rhodesia), the Federal capital, where its parent company AAC was based.

As detailed in chapter 4, Nkana and the Copperbelt mines were the major sources of Federal and territorial tax revenues between 1953 and 1963. Both an investment and a mining firm, Rhokana was a large organization in the Federation, and making additional profit indicated that it provided more tax revenue. In this period, the increase in production costs and the fluctuating price of copper on the LME influenced the overall profitability of Rhokana. Throughout the Federal period, the cost of producing and transporting a long ton of copper to buyers in Europe and the USA averaged £160. By comparison, the annual price of copper per ton averaged £264.1 between 1954 and 1959 and was reduced to £236 between 1960 and 1963 (see table 4.3).

The Rhokana Corporation was now an intermediate-cost producer for a number of reasons. In addition to an increase in labor and transport costs, production costs increased due to power and fuel shortages and technical problems associated with deeper-level mining such as dilution of ore, flooding, and the decline in the grade of ore milled. In the same period, the price of copper was affected by a combination of factors such as strikes, industrial unrest, international tension, political disturbances, and government measures (see chapter 4).

Since the copper price was unstable, Rhokana and the Copperbelt companies were kept afloat by moderating production costs. As observed by Perrings, Mhone, Berger, Parpart, and Phimister, and as advanced in chapter 4, the Copperbelt mines opted for the rationalization of labor and capital. Thus, Rhokana supported African Advancement on the Copperbelt in order to save labor costs. Through the policy of African Advancement, the Copperbelt mines also tried to promote partnership between black and white workers in the industry. The historical literature praised RST for taking center stage in pursuing the African Advancement Policy with the NRMWU. However, this chapter has posited that, behind the scenes, Rhokana Corporation and the other RAA-owned mines were preparing a workable solution and, hence, were the first to sign an agreement with the NRMWU (see figure 4.2). Consequently, the final agreement contained substantial resolutions from the RAA's scheme.

Between 1954 and 1957, labor and capital expenditure for the Corporation increased because of its investment in new projects, mines, and machinery (see table 4.2). Between 1958 and 1963, mechanization, stabilization of labor, and African Advancement gave Rhokana the rationale to reduce black labor and capital in order to save costs. Mechanization and stabilization of labor were also responsible for the generally improved production at Nkana between 1956 and 1963. However, Nkana stopped being the largest producer on the Copperbelt in the 1960s. To cushion fuel shortages, Rhokana and the other Copperbelt companies also invested in hydroelectric power. Besides, major copper producers in Africa and America voluntarily tried to adjust output to the requirements of consumers to prevent wide fluctuations in price.

Because of these factors, the total cost of sales for the Corporation was below the total value of sales throughout the Federal period. As detailed in chapter 4, Rhokana earned record profits and contributed about 20% of the total tax paid to the Northern Rhodesian and Federal governments. In addition, Rhokana contributed almost 20.2% of the total British South Africa (BSA) Company royalties between 1954 and 1963. But, as explained in chapter 4, the structure of the Federal economic policy failed to hold a proper balance between the economic interests of its territories, partly contributing to the collapse of the Federation. Since the headquarters of the Federation was based in Salisbury, Southern Rhodesia was much more developed than its partners Nyasaland and Northern Rhodesia.[11] Therefore, the African population questioned the rationale for the Federation. Furthermore, they challenged the BSA Company's title to the mineral rights, arguing that the mineral riches of the country were an inalienable possession of the people of Northern Rhodesia.[12]

What began was a renewed struggle for the mineral rights in Northern Rhodesia; however, the disputants had now changed. Before, it was the Chartered Company and the Colonial Office, on the one hand, and the Northern Rhodesian European settlers, on the other hand. Now, it was the Chartered Company and the Colonial Office, on the one hand, and the increasingly politically conscious African population, on the other.

The rise of African nationalism in Central Africa undermined the future of the Federation after 1959. The Federal government would soon cease to exist. Butler explained that RST was quick to identify with emerging nationalist politicians in the hope of safeguarding its investment on the Copperbelt.[13] As argued by Cohen, and as advanced in chapter 4, Rhokana and the AAC were more conservative, until the collapse of the Federation became a reality.[14] One indication that Rhokana and AAC did not see decolonization occurring was that, in February 1962, Bennett resigned as general manager of the former and took a political appointment as ambassador for the Federation of Rhodesia and Nyasaland in the USA.[15] Rhokana relocated its head offices to Northern Rhodesia only after the Federation was dissolved in 1963.

Chapter 5 has explained that the main economic problem at independence in 1964 was Zambia's reliance on external forces for its internal development. The mining industry depended on foreign capital, international markets, and expatriate labor. Initially, it was easier for the government to claim the mineral rights from the BSA Company. Attention was also paid to labor issues, where the government had three problems to deal with. First, the Zambianization of labor was meant to replace expatriates and foreign Africans by Zambians in managerial, supervisory, and technical positions. At Nkana, and in other mines, Zambianization was slowed down by two factors. First, this book supports Burawoy's view that Zambianization was stymied by the companies' practice whereby expatriates displaced by Zambians were employed in newly created positions within the department, earning more than their local counterparts.[16] Contrary to Sklar's argument that the mining corporations cooperated fully with the UNIP authorities in implementing new labor strategies, it would appear that the companies were merely window-dressing Zambianization.[17] Second, and beyond Burawoy's argument, chapter 5 has posited that Zambianization was often frustrated by the lack of skilled local workers to replace expatriates in managerial and technical positions. Nonetheless, Nkana and other Copperbelt mines successfully replaced foreign African workers by freezing further recruitment.

At the same time, the government failed to mobilize the mineworkers in support of national development. Zambian mineworkers were not concerned with national development but with improvement in service conditions, notably wages. As noted by Bates and seconded in this chapter, there was a discrepancy between the communication from MUZ headquarters and its local branches, with the former disseminating government policy to the latter, while the branches declined to explain policy matters to their members.[18]

The third problem was expanding mineral output while indigenizing and Zambianizing the labor force with average wage increases. African workers were angered by the fact that political independence had not brought about equal wages with their white counterparts. They continued to fight through work stoppages and strikes, forcing the government to accept a 22% increase in African wages in 1966. But when the government realized that average wages in Zambia were in 1967 85% more than wages in Tanzania and 45% more than those in Kenya, a wage freeze was introduced in 1969.[19]

Indigenization and Zambianization of labor, and the new employment conditions, had a significant effect on Rhokana's corporate profitability between 1964 and 1969. Labor productivity declined because of a breakdown in industrial discipline characterized by wildcat strikes, work stoppages, and the absenteeism of workers. The decline in the grade of ore hoisted and ore milled at Nkana was the other critical factor responsible for the relative decline in labor productivity and general production.

Cost of sales (see tables 5.4 and 5.5) increased on account of several combining factors in the local and regional political economy. Operating costs increased due to geological problems and technical difficulties associated with deep-level mining and the effect of government policies related to tax regimes, indigenization, and Zambianization of labor. In addition, Unilateral Declaration of Independence (UDI) and the volatile political environment in Southern Africa interrupted regional trade and transport networks, forcing the mining companies to look for alternative sources of consumables/stores and routes, which, in turn, raised production and transport expenses. All these factors pointed to an increasingly fraught future for the copper mining industry.

Yet, international developments were much more positive for the copper business. These followed on from the intensification of the Cold War in Asia and the prolonged strike by workers on American copper mines, which had knock-on effects on the price of the red metal. The annual price of copper per long ton almost doubled beyond the cost of sales per ton between 1964 and 1969 (see table 5.4). This allowed Rhokana to net a large profit and pay a record dividend in 1969 despite the increase in taxes and the curb on dividend remittances to shareholders abroad (see tables 5.5–5.7). The Zambian government was angered by Rhokana and the Copperbelt companies' distribution of huge dividends to shareholders abroad, even as they retained only a small proportion of their profits for investment in the industry. Moreover, the "financial structure of the companies was designed to make it easy to disengage themselves should conditions in Zambia become unfavourable."[20] This would seem to be the primary reasons for the lack of investment in expanded production rather than Barton's claim that low investment in the copper mining sector was due to government policies, which inhibited foreign investment. Dazzled by the increasing price of copper on the world market, the government nationalized an industry that was already hard hit by labor conflicts, deteriorating underground mining conditions, declining productivity, and increasing costs contingent on political instability in Southern Africa. The mines, it would seem, were nationalized on "a grand illusion" that the high price of copper would ensure that the government made substantial profits out of direct control.[21]

Nationalization of the mining sector in Zambia evolved in three stages: in 1969/70, 1973, and 1982. Accordingly, chapters 6 and 7 examined the evolving relationship between the Zambian government and the mining companies following nationalization. In essence, the relationship comprised state partnership with the mining firms. Two key considerations lay behind this partnership. On the one hand, the government argued that exploitation of the country's mineral assets should be in the national interest, without jeopardizing the smooth operations of either Rokana/Nkana or other individual mines. On the other, Nkana and the other Copperbelt mines themselves desired to align their operations with government policy, notwithstanding the changed circumstances emanating from the effects of nationalization, the Zambianization of labor, and the world recession.

In line with the new corporate structure, Rhokana lost its investments on the Copperbelt. Its name was changed to Rokana, and it became a division under Nchanga Consolidated Copper Mines (NCCM) (1970–1981) and Zambia Consolidated Copper Mines (ZCCM) (1982–1991). Its owners, AAC, became minority shareholders in the Zambian mining sector. Nonetheless, it is noted in chapters 6 and 7 that the Rokana/Nkana Mine Division remained central to the mining, refining, and smelting operations of both NCCM and

ZCCM, because it produced both copper and cobalt and owned the largest mining and metallurgical facilities in the industry. Whereas the existing scholarship suggests that there was complete cooperation between the government and the mining companies, chapters 6 and 7 observed that there was a limit to this cooperation.

To a limited extent, Rokana/Nkana Mine Division cooperated with Lusaka in implementing the new corporate structure and labor policies after 1970. Events leading to the cancellation of management contracts between Mining and Industrial Development Corporation (MINDECO), NCCM, and Roan Consolidated Mines (RCM) in 1973 added to the strained relationship between the mining companies and the government, which impacted operations at Nkana mine.

Chapter 6 goes beyond Cunningham's and Barton's argument that partial nationalization raised economic and political exclusivity in Zambia and retarded capital investment in the mining sector.[22] The chapter advanced that reactionary policies of the mining companies partly undermined government's effort to improve on operations in the industry. It demonstrated that Rokana and the Copperbelt companies held huge tracts of land in perpetuity without investing in it. Besides, NCCM and RCM's financial structure was organized to make it easier for them to syphon capital abroad. Also, Rokana and Copperbelt companies used their managerial control to slow the process of Zambianization in the sector. With few trained or skilled Zambians in managerial, supervisory, and technical positions, it became difficult for the government to monitor operations in the mines.

After 1974, the boom in the copper market ran its course as a result of the world economic recession. Consequently, the Zambian mining sector was severely hit by the resultant economic woes, such as unbalanced payments due to expensive production and transport costs, a chronic shortage of foreign exchange and inputs, budget deficits, and inflationary pressures, triggering the industry's—and, by extension, the national economy's—first balance-of-payments crisis in 1976 (see tables 6.6 and 6.7). Without much revenue from copper sales, the government and the mining companies relied heavily on borrowed money to finance their operations.

Between 1982 and 1991, Rokana/Nkana's corporate policies reflected the impact of not only nationalization and Zambianization of labor but also the fiscal measures dictated by the financial lending institutions, the International Monetary Fund (IMF) and the World Bank (WB). In the same period, production was affected by the progressive decline in the quantity and quality of ores, deeper-level mining and dilution of ore, inadequate capital, low equipment availability owing to insufficient spare parts, decline in labor productivity, unreliable transportation, and a shortage of consumables (see chapter 7).

The financial performance of Nkana and the ZCCM demonstrates the impact of cost of sales, which increased tremendously against relatively high but volatile metal prices on the LME in London and COMEX in New York. In addition, the effect of the devaluation of the kwacha against the dollar and sterling, loan interests, and high tax affected the financial position and profitability of Rokana and its parent companies. Loan interests and high taxes corroded net profits, dividends, and retained earnings. The Zambian economy was severely hit by the reduced revenue from the industry, while the resultant economic woes increased borrowing.

With all these economic problems, both the one-party state rule and nationalization proved to be politically and commercially unsustainable, and it became very difficult for the United National Independence Party (UNIP) to control the militant African mineworkers, in particular, and to govern the state, in general. Thus, in 1989, the Kaunda Regime was forced to introduce a multiparty system of government, and in the same year, mineworkers helped to create a new party, the Movement for Multiparty Democracy (MMD), under Frederick Chiluba, which removed UNIP from power in 1991. The MMD stressed its unwavering commitment to macroeconomic policy reforms and liberalization and privatization of state enterprises. As a consequence, the government stopped supporting ZCCM and privatized Nkana and the other Copperbelt mines in 1997.

This book highlights that the organization of the Northern Rhodesian/Zambian mining sector evolved in line with trends in the national, regional, and global political economy. At the time that Nkana and the other Copperbelt mines were developing, there was less government involvement. Thus, large-scale mining in Northern Rhodesia was started by private enterprise initiated by the BSA Company. During the Great Depression, the Second World War, Korean Crisis, Federation, and nationalization, there was increased government intervention in the operations of the mines. Clearly deducible from this book is that, to a limited extent, Rhokana/Rokana Corporation and its Nkana mine cooperated with stakeholders in implementing new policies, at times under difficult conditions, to safeguard their operations. This, in itself, is a reflection of the business acumen of the mining corporation.

Between 1928 and 1969, two groups of companies, Rhodesian/Zambian Anglo American (RAA/ZAMANGLO) and Rhodesian/Roan Selection Trust (RST), dominated the Northern Rhodesian/Zambian mining industry. Rhokana's relationship with these companies and their subsidiaries was mutually good. As demonstrated throughout this book, the Corporation belonged to the Anglo American group, together with Nchanga, Bancroft, Bwana Mkubwa, and Kabwe divisions. Apart from Anglo American, other shareholders in the Corporation were Rio Tinto, Kennecott, and Newmont.[23]

In this period, Rhokana performed three major functions in the two groups of companies. First, it operated the Nkana mine. Second, until the late 1950s, when Nchanga was turned into an open pit and became the second-largest open-pit mine in the world, Rhokana was the main source of income for the Anglo American group on the Copperbelt. Third, as an investment company, Rhokana was consulting engineers to the Copperbelt companies on behalf of AAC. Consequently, the Corporation owned shares in most of the other RAA and RST mines and service properties on the Copperbelt. Thus, Rhokana was the main link through which AAC corporate strategy was implemented on the Copperbelt, in particular, and in the Northern Rhodesian/Zambian mining industry, in general. RAA (1928–1964), ZAMANGLO (1964–1969), and Zambia Copper Investment (1970–1991) were shareholding companies in the Northern Rhodesian/Zambian mining sector on behalf of AAC. As a result of nationalization after 1970, Rokana lost its investments in the Zambian mining sector though remained important to the mining and processing operations of RCM (formerly RST), NCCM, and ZCCM.

In addition to trade links, Rhokana also benefited from the interlocking corporate organization of Anglo American and the BSA Company in Southern Africa and Southern Rhodesia, respectively. In fact, these companies shared some of their core directors. Rhokana also cultivated sound relations with the colonial and Federal governments between 1928 and 1963 by paying tax and identifying with the host nation. When the government requested the corporate companies to be incorporated in Northern Rhodesia in the early 1950s, Rhokana shifted its head offices from London to Kitwe. It was also a way of easing the burden of double taxation. During the Federation, Rhokana's headquarters were shifted to the capital, Salisbury in Southern Rhodesia. After Zambian independence in 1964, Rhokana relocated its head offices to Lusaka.

However, after 1968, the relationship between the mining companies and the Zambian government soured because Rhokana/Rokana and the Copperbelt companies externalized huge profits and dividends to shareholders abroad without making meaningful investments in the industry. This angered the government, and it decided to punish Rhokana and the other Copperbelt mining companies through high tax regimes, a limit on dividend remittances, and nationalization of the sector (see chapter 5). These policies were also meant to prevent a flight of capital abroad and encourage investments in the local economy. The government further accused the companies of price transferring, contractual loans, and holding vast concessions, at the expense of investment in the industry (see chapter 6). Rhokana, in particular, was guilty of these accusations since it was the largest corporate company on the Copperbelt.

The financial performance of Rhokana and the mining sector in general between 1928 and 1991 reflected the impact of operating costs and the copper price. As indicated in the chapter, operating costs kept increasing as a result of rising expenses on labor, mining, treatment and processing of ore, transport, and taxes. To maintain production costs, Nkana and the other Copperbelt mines rationalized capital, machinery, and labor. The Copperbelt mines also tried to lower costs by investing in alternative sources of fuel, power, and transport.

In general, Nkana and the Copperbelt mines were a cash cow, milked without meaningful investment in exploration, capital projects, or machinery. The only period after the Great Depression during which Rhokana invested in capital projects was in the 1950s and early 1960s. Under NCCM and ZCCM, capital expenditure declined substantially. Inadequate capital, machinery, and technology contributed to the increase in production costs. Labor costs also increased after independence because the mines could not reduce excess labor. This was due to the political role of mineworkers in Zambia.

According to Cunningham, the major economic problems after independence were clearly outside the Zambian government's control.[24] But this chapter supports McPherson's and Craig's proposition that the government and the mining companies could have done better in tackling the problems to reduce costs.[25] For example, the government should have encouraged NCCM, RCM, and ZCCM to invest more in machinery and technology to reduce excess labor in order to save costs. Following the economic downturn from the mid-1970s, the government should have stood its ground against pressure from the IMF and WB and not agreed to devalue the kwacha without meaningful investment. The government should also have reduced costs by promoting local sourcing of inputs. Furthermore, NCCM, RCM, and ZCCM should not have diverted part of the capital into nonmining activities.

The copper price depended on trends in the market. This book has discussed a number of factors in this regard. The Copperbelt mines and other major producers managed to control the copper price through concerted efforts during the Great Depression of the 1930s but failed to do so after 1970. It became extremely difficult to organize state-controlled and private-owned companies in Africa, South America, the Soviet Union, and the USA after independence. Consequently, the influence of the Intergovernmental Council of Copper Exporting Countries (CIPEC) was limited compared with that of the copper cartels of the 1930s, which were controlled by private companies.

In the Federal era, the mines paid royalties and income taxes averaging 40% of profits, which were lower than those paid by their counterparts elsewhere in the copper industry (see chapter 4). After nationalization, the new tax regimes increased government's share of profits above 80%. Chapters 5–7 detailed that Rhokana/Rokana and the other Copperbelt mining companies complained of remaining with meager profits and capital for investment because of high taxes. As indicated elsewhere earlier, the government increased taxes to punish the companies for externalizing large dividends at the expense of investment. During the 1969 and 1973 takeovers, the government wondered why the companies entered into separate agreements with their parent and associated companies abroad. These separate agreements included contractual loans, charged at a higher rate than what was obtained on the market. It was a way of evading high taxes and externalizing profits. To curb this, the government should have either encouraged local borrowing or ensured that more than half of the loan was obtained from local companies. To the present day, Zambia is still grappling with tax avoidances and evasions. Some mining companies are price transferring and underdeclaring production, sales, and profits. Even more, others repatriate and siphon profits under the guise of loan repayments to International Financial Institutions (IFIs).

While there have been, as observed in chapter 1, many studies of labor, some studies of the technology employed and some studies of the corporate organization and profits of the Copperbelt mines, all of them have been limited with regard to period or narrow focus. This book is the first, building on Phillips's work, to develop a comprehensive account of corporate structure, capital, labor, and profits of an individual mine, in a regional and global context, over a long period, namely, 1928–1991. The experiences of Rokana/Nkana in the privatization era of MMD requires a new study in its own right.

Note on Currencies and Weights Utilized in This Book

Before 1967, the currency was the pound sterling. In November that year, the Zambian government introduced a new currency, the kwacha. Between 1968 and 1991, the government devalued the kwacha against the sterling and US dollar several times in line with inflationary levels. During the colonial era and in the first years of independence, copper production was measured either in long tons or in short tons. After nationalization, the metric ton (tonne) system was introduced. In this book, these measures are utilized accordingly unless otherwise specified. The relevant annual exchange rates and conversions are provided in the table 0.1.

Table 0.1 Currencies and Weights Utilized in This Book.

Year	*Currencies and Their Exchange Rates*		
1968	K1.00	US$1.40	£0.59
1969	K1.00	US$1.40	£0.58
1970	K1.00	US$1.40	£0.58
1971	K1.00	US$1.40	£0.55
1972	K1.00	US$1.40	£0.60
1973	K1.00	US$1.55	£0.67
1974	K1.00	US$1.55	£0.66
1975	K1.00	US$1.55	£0.77
1976	K1.00	US$1.26	£0.74
1977	K1.00	US$1.32	£0.69
1978	K1.00	US$1.21	£0.65
1979	K1.00	US$1.21	£0.65
1980	K1.00	US$1.21	£0.65
1981	K1.00	US$1.19	£0.53
1982	K1.00	US$1.09	£O.61

(Continued)

Table 0.1 Continued

Year		*Currencies and Their Exchange Rates*	
1983	K1.00	US$0.84	£0.58
1984	K1.00	US$0.62	£0.43
1985	K1.00	US$0.43	£0.35
1986	K1.00	US$0.15	£0.10
1987	K1.00	US$0.11	£0.07
1988	K1.00	US$0.13	£0.07
1989	K1.00	US$0.10	£0.06
1990	K1.00	US$0.04	£0.02
1991	K1.00	US$0.02	£0.01
Measurements for Weights			
Tons (Tonnes)		**Pounds Avoirdupois**	**Kilograms**
1 Short Ton		2,000 lbs	907.2 kg
1 Long Ton		2,240 lbs	1,016.1 kg
1 Metric Ton		2,204.6 lbs	1,000 kg

Source: Compiled from ZCCM Limited, *Annual Reports*, 1982–1991, ZCCM 11.1.1F; *Mining Mirror*, March 19, 1976; Phillip Daniel, *Africanisation, Nationalisation and Inequality: Mining Labour and the Copperbelt in Zambian Development* (London: Cambridge University Press, 1979), xvii.

Abbreviations and Acronyms

AAC	Anglo American Corporation of South Africa
AMAX	American Metal Climax
AMC	American Metal Company
AMU	African Mineworkers' Union
ANC	African National Congress
ASARCO	American Smelting and Refining Company
BBCs	Boss Boys' Committees
BSA Company	British South Africa Company
CIPEC	Intergovernmental Council of Copper Exporting Countries
CODELCO-Chile	Corporation Nacional del Cobre de Chile
COMEX	Commodity Exchange
CV	Copper Ventures
EPT	Excess Profits Tax
FYPIP	Five-year Production and Investment Plan
GDP	Gross Domestic Product
GRZ	Government of the Republic of Zambia
HEP	Hydro-Electric Power
IFIs	International Financial Institutions
IMF	International Monetary Fund
IWF	Industrial Workers' Federation
LME	London Metal Exchange
MASA	Mines African Staff Association
MEMACO	Metal Marketing Company
MET	Mineral Export Tax
MINDECO	Mining Development Corporation
MMD	Movement for Multiparty Democracy

MOSSA	Mines Officials Salaried Staff Association
MUZ	Mineworkers' Union of Zambia
MUZ HQ	Mineworkers' Union of Zambia Headquarters
NAZ	National Archives of Zambia
NCCM	Nchanga Consolidated Copper Mines
NRANC	Northern Rhodesia African National Congress
NRMWU	Northern Rhodesia Mineworkers' Union
RAA/Rhoanglo	Rhodesian Anglo American
RCBC	Rhodesia Congo Border Company/Concession
RCM	Roan Consolidated Mines
RLI	Rhodes-Livingstone Institute
RST	Rhodesian/Roan Selection Trust
SAMU	South African Mineworkers' Union
ST	Selection Trust
TAZARA	Tanzania-Zambia Railways
TR	Tribal Representatives
UCAA	United Central Africa Association for Central Africa Federation
UDI	Unilateral Declaration of Independence
UMHK	Union Miniere du Haunt Katanga
UNIP	United National Independence Party
UPP	United Progressive Party
USA	United States of America
WB	World Bank
WCs	Works Committees
ZAMANGLO	Zambian Anglo American Corporation
ZCCM	Zambia Consolidated Copper Mines
ZCI	Zambia Copper Investment
ZCTU	Zambia Congress of Trade Unions
ZIMCO	Zambia Industrial and Mining Corporation
ZIT	Zambia Institute of Technology

Maps

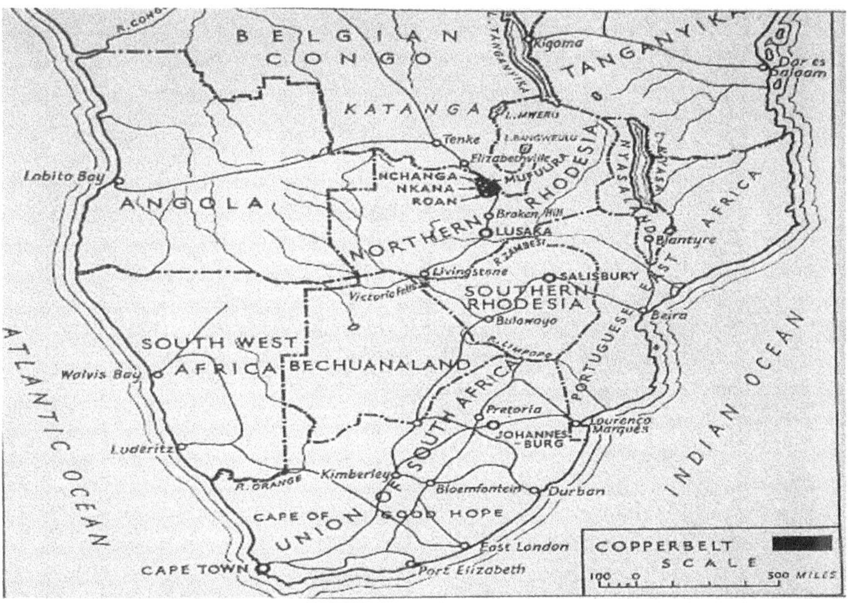

Figure 0.1 Map of Northern Rhodesia and Southern Africa showing the position of Nkana and the other Copperbelt mines before independence. *Source:* John G. Phillips, "Roan Antelope: Big Business in Central Africa, 1890–1953" (PhD thesis, University of Cambridge, Cambridge, 2000), 33.

Figure 0.2 **Map of Zambia in Southern Africa showing Nkana-Kitwe town, the Copperbelt, and other areas, after independence.** *Source:* www.pinterest.co.uk/americaikos/zambia/ (accessed March 3, 2021).

Glossary

Concentration A milling process of separating and saving valuable minerals from gangue to form a concentrate.[1] A concentrate is a product containing the valuable metal and from which most of the waste material in the ore has been eliminated.[2]

Flotation A milling process by which some mineral properties are induced to become attached to bubbles and float, and others to sink.[3] This is done in order to separate valuable minerals from worthless gangue.

Leaching A chemical process used in milling for the extraction of valuable minerals from ore.[4] This process is mainly utilized when processing oxide ores that are mixtures compared with sulfides, which are compounds. Sulfides from the Copperbelt did not require the leaching process and hence were cheaper to treat.

Metallurgical facilities Refer to concentrating or milling, smelting, and refining plants used to isolate the copper and cobalt from their associated elements.[5]

Mine development To open up ore body by sinking shafts, driving drifts, and installing requisite equipment to begin operations.[6] It also involves construction of infrastructure on the mine necessary for efficiency operations.

Mineral A naturally occurring homogenous substance having definite physical properties and chemical composition and, if formed under favorable conditions, a definite crystal form.[7]

Mineral claim A portion of mining land or concession held under the law.[8]

Mineral exploration The prospecting, diamond drilling, and other work involved in searching for ore.[9]

Mineral vein These mineral deposits occur in veins or vein-type structures in the form of fissures that extend for considerable distances.[10] Many of

Canada's deposits occurred in mineral veins, and very few of this type were found on the Katanga and Copperbelt.[11]

Mining Refers to the "science, technique, and business of mineral discovery and exploitation."[12]

Ore A rock carrying mineral values, which can be extracted and marketed at a profit.[13]

Ore grade Is normally expressed as a percentage of the metal content of "ore by weight of the ore mass."[14] The "volume of an ore mass determines the cost of mining it," while the "grade determines the relative profitability."[15] In this book, ore grade refers to the quality of ore reserves and ore milled in terms of copper and cobalt contents and how these affected labor productivity and finished production and overall profitability.

Ore reserves The ore body that has been sufficiently developed by means of either drifts and raises in it, or crosscuts through it to show the necessary grade and tonnage.[16]

Oxide ores These were mixed ores containing a binary compound of oxygen and other elements such as iron.[17]

Refining A process of removing impurities from smelted metal to the high standard required before sale.[18]

Rock A combination of minerals.[19]

Smelting The extraction of metal from its ores or concentrates by heat processes using the reverberator furnace, converter, anode furnace, and casting wheel.[20]

Stope An excavation in a mine from which ore is being or has been extracted.[21] Rhokana utilized the stoping method of mining at Nkana.

Sulfide ores These are ores containing a compound of sulfur and other elements.[22] They were found on the Copperbelt and much easier to treat than oxide ores.

Notes

CHAPTER 1

1. Richard L. Sklar, *Corporate Power in an African State: The Political Impact of Multinational Mining Companies in Zambia* (Los Angeles: University of California Press, 1975), 96.

2. John G. Phillips, "Roan Antelope: Big Business in Central Africa, 1890–1953" (PhD thesis, University of Cambridge, 2000), 27.

3. Sklar, *Corporate Power in an African State*, 97.

4. Charles A. Perrings, *Black Mineworkers in Central Africa: Industrial Strategies and the Evolution of an African Proletariat in the Copperbelt, 1911–1941* (New York: Africana Publishing Company, 1979), 207–13; Jane L. Parpart, *Labour and Capital on the African Copperbelt* (Philadelphia: Temple University Press, 1983), 34–44.

5. John S. Harington and Neil D. McGlashan, "A Century of Migrant Labour in the Gold Mines of South Africa," *Journal of the South African Institute of Mining and Metallurgy* 104, no. 2 (2004): 65.

6. Perrings, *Black Mineworkers in Central Africa*, 207–17.

7. Charles A. Perrings, "Consciousness, Conflict and Proletarianization: An Assessment of the 1935 Mineworkers' Strike on the Northern Rhodesian Copperbelt," *Journal of Southern African Studies* 4, no. 1 (1977): 31.

8. Ian R. Phimister, "Corporate Profit and Race in Central African Copper Mining, 1946–1958," *Business History Review* 85, no. 4 (2011): 767.

9. T.D.A. Etheredge, "Zambianisation on the Copperbelt," *Optima* 19, no. 4 (1969): 183.

10. Etheredge, "Zambianisation on the Copperbelt," 183..

11. Etheredge, "Zambianisation on the Copperbelt," 183.

12. See, for example: Robert H. Bates, *Unions, Parties and Political Development: A Study of Mineworkers in Zambia* (New Haven, CT, and London: Yale University Press, 1971), passim; Henry S. Meebelo, *Reaction to Colonialism: A Prelude to the Politics*

of Independence in Northern Zambia, 1893–1939 (Manchester: Manchester University Press, 1971), passim; Michael Burawoy, *The Colour of Class on the Copper Mines: From Advancement to Zambianisation* (Manchester: Manchester University Press, 1972), passim; Elena L. Berger, *Labour, Race and Colonial Rule: The Copperbelt from 1924 to Independence* (Oxford: Clarendon Press, 1974), passim; Parpart, *Labour and Capital on the African Copperbelt*, passim; Guy C.Z. Mhone, *The Political Economy of a Dual Labour Market in Africa, 1929–1969* (London and Toronto: Associated University Presses, 1982), passim; Miles Larmer, *Mineworkers in Zambia: Labour and Political Change in Zambia, 1964–1991* (London and New York: I.B. Tauris, 2007), passim.

13. Sklar, *Corporate Power in an African State*, 63–86.

14. Sklar, *Corporate Power in an African State*, 63–86.

15. Rhokana Corporation (hereafter RC) Limited, Utilisation of African Labour, Cost Trends, Policy and Programme to meet the Situation, December 6, 1956, Tables 7 and 9, Zambia Consolidated Copper Mines Archive (hereafter ZCCM) 3.8.1C; ZCCM Limited, *1990 Annual Report* (Lusaka: ZCCM Head Office, 1990), 44, ZCCM 11.1.1F.

16. Sklar, *Corporate Power in an African State*, 73.

17. Sklar, *Corporate Power in an African State*, 73.

18. For detailed information about the importance of these factors to a mining firm, see: Phillips, "Roan Antelope," 12–31.

19. Horizontal integration/growth/diversification entails the acquisition of additional shares in other mines/properties to increase company assets. Vertical integration/growth/diversification entails controlling the steps in the process of production (extraction, concentration, refining) and trade links to attain a monopoly, efficiency, and self-sufficiency in the industry. See: Phillips, "Roan Antelope," 29–30.

20. RC Limited, *Annual Reports and Accounts*, 1931–1944, ZCCM 3.8.2F; Northern Rhodesia Chamber of Mines (hereafter NRCM), *NRCM Yearbooks*, 1956–1963, ZCCM 12.1.9C; Copper Industry Service Bureau (hereafter CISB) Limited, *Copperbelt of Zambia Mining Industry Yearbooks,* 1964–1968, ZCCM 12.1.9C; CISB Limited, *Mining Industry Yearbook of Zambia 1969* (Kitwe: CISB, 1969), ZCCM 12.1.9C; RC Limited, *Annual Reports*, 1946–1969, ZCCM 12.7.2F; RC Limited, *Annual Report and Accounts for the Year Ended 30th June 1945* (London: Rhokana Head Office, 1945), ZCCM 19.2.4F.

21. RC Limited, *Annual Reports and Accounts*; NRCM, *NRCM Yearbooks*; CISB Limited, *Copperbelt of Zambia Mining Industry Yearbooks*; CISB Limited, *Mining Industry Yearbook of Zambia 1969*; RC Limited, *Annual Reports*; RC Limited, *Annual Report and Accounts for the Year Ended 30th June 1945.*

22. Andrew D. Roberts, "Notes towards a Financial History of Copper Mining in Northern Rhodesia," *Canadian Journal of African Studies* 16, no. 2 (1982): 347–59.

23. Roberts, "Notes towards a Financial History of Copper Mining in Northern Rhodesia," 347.

24. Owen Letcher, *South Central Africa* (Johannesburg: African Publications, 1932), passim; Merle J. Davis, *Modern Industry and the African: An Enquiry into the Effect of the Copper Mines of Central Africa upon Native Society and the Work of the Christian Missions* (London: Macmillan and Co., 1933), passim.

25. RLI scholars included: Godfrey Wilson, *An Essay on the Economics of Detribalization in Northern Rhodesia* (Livingstone: RLI, 1942), passim; Lynn A. Saffrey, *A Report on Some Aspects of African Living Conditions on the Copperbelt of Northern Rhodesia* (Lusaka: Mimeo, 1943), passim; Clyde J. Mitchell, *The Kalela Dance: Aspects of Social Relations among Urban Africans in Northern Rhodesia* (Manchester: Manchester University Press, 1956), passim; Arnold L. Epstein, *Politics in an Urban African Community* (Manchester: Manchester University Press, 1958), passim; Hortense Powdermaker, *Copper Town Changing Africa: The Human Situation on the Rhodesian Copperbelt* (New York: Harper and Row, 1962), passim. For further details about the RLI, see: Alfred Tembo, "The Rhodes-Livingstone Institute and Interdisciplinary Research in Northern Rhodesia (Zambia), 1937–1964," *Strategic Review of Southern Africa* 36, no. 1 (2014): 90–9.

26. Tembo, "The Rhodes-Livingstone Institute and Interdisciplinary Research in Northern Rhodesia (Zambia)," 91–2.

27. Northern Rhodesia Government (hereafter NRG), *Report of the Commission Appointed to Enquire into the Disturbances in the Copperbelt, Northern Rhodesia together with the Governor's Despatch to the Secretary of State on the Report*, Vol. I (Lusaka: Government Printers, 1935), 5, National Archives of Zambia (hereafter NAZ) 11/57/C.

28. Lewis H. Gann, *A History of Northern Rhodesia: Early Days to 1953* (London: Chatto and Windus, 1964), passim.

29. Gann, *A History of Northern Rhodesia*, 117–24.

30. Lewis H. Gann, "The Northern Rhodesian Copper Industry and the World of Copper: 1923–1952," in *Human Problems in British Central Africa: Issue no. XVIII*, eds. Clyde J. Mitchell, Elizabeth Colson, and Max Gluckman (Manchester: Manchester University Press, 1970), 1–18.

31. Tarrant D. Guernsey, "Summary of Early Prospecting in Northern Rhodesia," *Transactions of the Institution of Mining and Metallurgy* 63 (1954): 1–9.

32. Austen J. Bancroft, *Mining in Northern Rhodesia: A Chronicle of Mineral Exploration and Mining Development* (Bedford, England: The Sidney Press Limited, 1961), passim.

33. Bancroft, *Mining in Northern Rhodesia*, 5.

34. Francis L. Coleman, *The Northern Rhodesia Copperbelt, 1899–1962: Technological Development up to the End of the Central African Federation* (Manchester: Manchester University Press, 1971), 162.

35. Theodore Gregory, *Ernest Oppenheimer and the Economic Development of Southern Africa* (London: Oxford University Press, 1961), passim.

36. Gregory, *Ernest Oppenheimer and the Economic Development of Southern Africa*, 384–489.

37. Phillips, "Roan Antelope," 6.

38. Larry J. Butler, *Copper Empire: Mining and the Colonial State in Northern Rhodesia, c. 1930–1964* (New York: Palgrave Macmillan, 2007), passim; Larry J. Butler, "Business and British Decolonisation: Sir Ronald Prain, the Mining Industry and the Central African Federation," *Journal of Imperial and Commonwealth History* 35, no. 3 (2007): 459–84; Andrew Cohen, "Business and Decolonisation in Central

Africa Reconsidered," *Journal of Imperial and Commonwealth History* 36, no. 4 (2008): 641–58: This article is incorporated in a later publication: Andrew Cohen, *The Politics and Economics of Decolonization in Africa: The Failed Experiment of Central African Federation* (London and New York: I.B. Tauris, 2017), 105–92.

39. Butler, "Business and British Decolonisation," 473–4.

40. Cohen, "Business and Decolonisation in Central Africa Reconsidered," 641–2.

41. Meebelo, *Reaction to Colonialism*, passim.

42. Meebelo, *Reaction to Colonialism*, 133–85, 254–64.

43. Ian Henderson, "Labour and Politics in Northern Rhodesia, 1900–1953: A Study in the Limits of Colonial Power" (PhD thesis, University of Edinburgh, 1972), 103–68.

44. Perrings, "Consciousness, Conflict and Proletarianization," 31–51; Perrings, *Black Mineworkers in Central Africa*, passim; Charles A. Perrings, "A Moment in the Proletarianization of the New Middle Class: Race, Value and the Division of Labour in the Copperbelt, 1946–1966," *Journal of Southern African Studies* 6, no. 2 (1980): 183–213.

45. Today the term is used to describe the ever-growing size of the working class, which results from growth imperative of a capitalist economy. For further details, see: Michael P. Kelly, "Proletarianisation, the Division of Labour and the Labour Process," *International Journal of Sociology and Social Policy* 8, no. 6 (1989): 48–64.

46. Mhone, *The Political Economy of a Dual Labour Market in Africa*, passim.

47. The majority of European mineworkers in the Belgian Congo, Southern Rhodesia, and South Africa were employed in skilled jobs.

48. Berger, *Labour, Race and Colonial Rule*, passim.

49. Berger, *Labour, Race and Colonial Rule*, 46–9, 117–30.

50. Bates, *Unions, Parties and Political Development*, passim; Burawoy, *The Colour of Class on the Copper Mines*, passim; Phillip Daniel, *Africanisation, Nationalisation and Inequality: Mining Labour and the Copperbelt in Zambian Development* (London: Cambridge University Press, 1979), passim.

51. James Ferguson, *Expectations of Modernity: Myths and Meanings of Urban Life on the Zambian Copperbelt* (Berkeley: University of California Press, 1999), 6–7. For further details about the social life of workers on the Copperbelt and how Ferguson studied it, see his articles: James Ferguson, "Mobile Workers, Modernist Narratives: A Critique of the Historiography of Transition on the Zambian Copperbelt [Part One]," *Journal of Southern African Studies* 16, no. 3 (1990): 385–412; James Ferguson, "Mobile Workers, Modernist Narratives: A Critique of the Historiography of Transition on the Zambian Copperbelt [Part Two]," *Journal of Southern African Studies* 16, no. 4 (1990): 603–21.

52. George Chauncey, "The Locus of Reproduction: Women's Labour in the Zambian Copperbelt, 1927–1953," *Journal of Southern African Studies* 7, no. 2 (1981): 135–64; Parpart, *Labour and Capital on the African Copperbelt*, passim; Jane L. Parpart, "The Household and the Mine Shaft: Gender and Class Struggles on the Zambian Copperbelt, 1926–1964," *Journal of Southern African Studies* 13, no. 1 (1986): 36–56.

53. Bbole Dandule, "Women and Mineworkers' Struggles on the Zambian Copperbelt, 1926–1964" (MA dissertation, University of Zambia, Lusaka, 2012), passim; Chauncey, "The Locus of Reproduction: Women's Labour in the Zambian

Copperbelt," 135–64; Parpart, "The Household and the Mine Shaft: Gender and Class Struggles on the Zambian Copperbelt," 36–56.

54. Phimister, "Corporate Profit and Race in Central African Copper Mining, 1946–1958," 749–74.

55. Phimister, "Corporate Profit and Race in Central African Copper Mining, 1946–1958," 765.

56. Duncan Money, "No Matter How Much or How Little They Have Got, They Cannot Settle Down: A Social History of Europeans on the Zambian Copperbelt, 1926–1974" (PhD thesis, University of Oxford, 2016), 291–2; Miles Larmer, "Permanent Precarity: Capital and Labour in the Central African Copperbelt," *Labour History* 58, no. 2 (2017): 170–84.

57. Larmer, *Mineworkers in Zambia*, passim.

58. Patience N. Mususa, "There Used to Be Order: Life on the Copperbelt after the Privatisation of the Zambia Consolidated Copper Mines" (PhD thesis, University of Cape Town, 2014), passim.

59. Robert E. Baldwin, *Economic Development and Export Growth* (Berkeley and Los Angeles: University of California Press, 1966), 29–39.

60. Klas Ronnback and Oskar Broberg, *Capital and Colonialism: The Return on British Investments in Africa, 1869–1969* (London: Palgrave Macmillan, 2019), passim.

61. Ronnback and Broberg, *Capital and Colonialism*, 129.

62. Mark Bostock and Charles Harvey, eds., *Economic Independence and Zambian Copper: A Case Study of Foreign Investment* (New York: Praeger Press, 1972), passim.

63. Anthony Martin, *Minding Their Own Business: Zambia's Struggle against Western Control* (London: Penguin Books, 1975), passim.

64. Martin, *Minding Their Own Business*, 103, 107.

65. Martin, *Minding Their Own Business*, 103, 107.

66. Martin, *Minding Their Own Business*, 103; Kenneth D. Kaunda, Zambia's Guideline for the Next Decade: His Excellency the President, Addressing the National Council of United National Independence Party at Mulungushi, November 9, 1968, 9, United National Independence Party Archive (hereafter UNIP) 1–3–5.

67. Kenneth D. Kaunda, Humanism in Zambia and a Guide to Its Implementation, by His Excellency, President of the Republic of Zambia, November 1967, 27, UNIP 1–3–5.

68. Bastiaan G. Fortman, *After Mulungushi: The Economics of Zambian Humanism* (Nairobi: East African Publishing House, 1969), vi.

69. Fortman, *After Mulungushi*, vi.

70. Martin, *Minding Their Own Business*, 165, 168.

71. Martin, *Minding Their Own Business*, 165, 168.

72. Stuart J. Barton, *Policy Signals and Market Responses: A 50-Year History of Zambia's Relationship with Foreign Capital* (Basingstoke: Palgrave Macmillan, 2016), passim.

73. Barton, *Policy Signals and Market Responses*, 10–11, 66–116.

74. Sklar, *Corporate Power in an African State*, passim.

75. Simon J. Cunningham, *The Copper Industry in Zambia: Foreign Mining Companies in a Developing Country* (New York: Praeger Publishers, 1981), passim.

76. Phillips, "Roan Antelope," 7.

77. Fergus M. McPherson, *The Sequencing of Economic Reforms: Lessons from Zambia* (Amsterdam: Ministry of Foreign Affairs Development Corporation, 1995), passim.

78. McPherson, *The Sequencing of Economic Reforms*, 6.

79. McPherson, *The Sequencing of Economic Reforms*, 7–9.

80. Patricio Meller and Anthony Simpasa, "Role of Copper in the Chilean and Zambian Economies: Main Economic and Policy Issues," Global Development Network Working Paper Series No. 43, 2011, passim.

81. See, for example: Alastair Fraser and Miles Larmer, eds., *Zambia, Mining and Neoliberalism: Boom and Bust on the Globalized Copperbelt* (New York: Palgrave Macmillan, 2010), passim; Alan Whitworth, *Explaining Zambian Poverty: A History of (Non-Agriculture) Economic Policy Since Independence* (Islamabad: John Wiley and Sons Limited, 2014), passim.

82. John Lungu, "The Politics of Reforming Zambia's Mining Tax Regime," *Southern Africa Resource Watch* 8 (2009): 1–28.

83. John R. Craig, "State Enterprise and Privatisation in Zambia 1968–1998" (PhD thesis, University of Leeds, 1999), passim.

84. Craig, "State Enterprise and Privatisation in Zambia 1968–1998," iii.

85. Fraser and Larmer, eds., *Zambia, Mining and Neoliberalism*, passim.

86. Gregory, *Ernest Oppenheimer and the Economic Development of Southern Africa*, 384–489; Ferguson, *Expectations of Modernity*, passim.

87. Gann, "The Northern Rhodesian Copper Industry and the World of Copper," 1–18; Gregory, *Ernest Oppenheimer and the Economic Development of Southern Africa*, 384–489; Ronnback and Broberg, *Capital and Colonialism*, 209–34, 339–77; Roberts, "Notes towards a Financial History of Copper Mining in Northern Rhodesia," 347.

88. Bernard W.E. Alford and Charles E. Harvey, "Copperbelt Merger: The Formation of the Rhokana Corporation, 1930–1932," *Business Review* 54, no. 3 (1980): 331–58.

89. Phillips, "Roan Antelope," passim. Foster Sakala's dissertation also focused on Roan Antelope when exploring the role of women in labor stabilization on the Copperbelt during the colonial era: Foster Sakala, "The Role of Women in Labour Stabilisation at Mufulira Mine, 1930–1964" (MA Dissertation, University of Zambia, Lusaka, 2001), passim.

90. RC Limited, *Annual Reports and Accounts*, 1931–1944; RC Limited, *Annual Reports and Accounts*, 1946–1969.

91. The following are used as synonyms for Rhokana/Rokana: Rhokana/Nkana, Rokana/Nkana Mine Division, and Rokana/Nkana.

92. Nchanga Consolidated Copper Mines Limited (hereafter NCCM), *Annual Reports*, 1971–1981, ZCCM 11.1.1F; B.K. Shamutete, History of ZCCM Limited: Birth of a Giant, 1992, 18–19, ZCCM 4.10.2E.

93. Special Correspondence, "NCCM Looks Back at its Proud Record of Mining," *Mining Mirror*, March 26, 1982, 30–31.

94. The monograph benefited from interview material obtained during my PhD study. The Ethics Clearance Committee of the University of the Free State approved this study on August 1, 2017. The ethical clearance number is UFS-HSD2017/0228.

95. For a detailed account of the holdings of these archival institutions, see: Hyden Munene, "Mining the Past: A Report of Four Archival Repositories in Zambia," *History in Africa* 47 (2020): 359–73, accessed November 21, 2020, doi.org/10.1017/hia.2019.24.

96. For example, see: Barton, *Policy Signals and Market Responses*, passim; Cohen, *The Politics and Economics of Decolonization in Africa*, passim; Larmer, *Mineworkers in Zambia*, passim.

97. Another major weakness is that very few MUZ HQ files especially from the colonial period survive as a major fire destroyed most of them in the late 1970s.

98. Phillips, "Roan Antelope," 247.

99. For a detailed understanding of the official embrace of socialism through humanism, Unilateral Declaration of Independence, and the intensifying liberation struggle in Southern Africa, as well as their impact on government policy in Zambia, see the discussion on the previous historiography. Also, read variously: Fortman, *After Mulungushi*, passim; Martin, *Minding Their Own Business*, 99–120; Sklar, *Corporate Power in an African State*, 134–78; Richard L. Sklar, "Zambia's Response to the Rhodesian Unilateral Declaration of Independence," in *Politics in Zambia*, ed. William Tordoff (Berkeley and Los Angeles: University of California Press, 1974), 320–62.

100. As mentioned earlier, Zambianization, which superseded African Advancement after independence, was a policy introduced by the new government, meant to replace expatriate European and foreign (alien) African workers by Zambians or locals in technical, managerial, and supervisory positions in the mining and public sectors. The extant literature discussed in this chapter relates employment of locals and Zambianization to Africanization, the latter referring to advancing both indigenous Zambians and foreign Africans into technical, supervisory, and managerial positions in the industry. By contrast, this book distinguishes employment of locals and Zambianization from Africanization. It relates the former to indigenization of labor in the industry. For further details, see: Etheredge, "Zambianisation on the Copperbelt," 182–4; Daniel, *Africanisation, Nationalisation and Inequality*.

101. Gavin Keeton and Mike Beer, "MIASA Position on State Participation in Mining," Paper for the Mining Industries Association of Southern Africa (Johannesburg: MIASA, 2011), 1.

102. Keeton and Beer, "MIASA Position on State Participation in Mining," 22–48.

103. For further details, see: Sklar, *Corporate Power in an African State*, 96–216; Cunningham, *The Copper Industry in Zambia*, 265–82; Barton, *Policy Signals and Market Responses*, 66–116.

104. Shamutete, History of ZCCM Limited: Birth of a Giant, 2.

105. T. Moll, J. McDermott, and B. Hall, "A Message from the General Manager, Oliver B. Bennett," *Rhokana Review* 1, no. 1 (1951): 3.

106. Anglo American Corporation (hereafter AAC), "Company Histories No. 3: Rhokana Corporation," *Optima* 1, no. 3 (1951): 22.

107. RC Limited, *Directors' Report and Statement of Accounts for the Year Ended 30 June 1932* (London: Rhokana Head Office, 1932), 5, ZCCM 3.8.2F.

108. T. Howard and T. Scannell, "Cobalt: A Hard to Win Metal of the Modern Age," *Horizon* 5, no. 10 (1963): 24.

109. A. Paton, "African Advancement: A Problem of both the Copperbelt and Federation," *Optima* 5, no. 4 (1955): 105.

110. AAC, "Nkana-Kitwe: Twin Town of Copper," *Optima* 11, no. 2 (1961): 68.

111. AAC, "Nkana-Kitwe," 68. Nkana-Kitwe is the original name of the town currently called Kitwe on the Copperbelt.

112. Bancroft, *Mining in Northern Rhodesia*, 144–5; Gann, *A History of Northern Rhodesia*, 122.

113. Parpart, *Labour and Capital on the African Copperbelt*, 13.

114. Bernard W.E. Alford and Charles E. Harvey, "Copperbelt Merger: The Formation of the Rhokana Corporation, 1930–1932," *Business Review* 54, no. 3 (1980): 331.

115. Bancroft, *Mining in Northern Rhodesia*, 54–78; Coleman, *The Northern Rhodesia Copperbelt*, 6–26.

116. For a brief background of Edmund Davis and Robert Williams and their companies' relationship with the British South Africa (hereafter BSA) Company, see: Gann, *A History of Northern Rhodesia*, 120.

117. Gann, *A History of Northern Rhodesia*, 122.

118. Rhodesian Selection Trust (hereafter RST), "A Founder of the Copperbelt Looks Back," *Horizon* 4, no. 4 (1962): 33.

119. RST, "A Founder of the Copperbelt Looks Back," 33.

120. Bancroft, *Mining in Northern Rhodesia*, 145.

121. Geoffrey W. Silavwe, *Management of Human Resources in the Copper Mining Industry in Zambia* (Ndola, Zambia: Mission Press, 1995), 20.

122. AAC, "Nkana-Kitwe: Twin Town of Copper," 68.

123. Simon J. Cunningham, "Nationalization and the Zambian Copper Mining Industry" (PhD thesis, University of Edinburgh, 1985), 37–9.

124. AAC, "Nkana-Kitwe: Twin Town of Copper," 68. For detailed understanding of the trends in BSA Company mineral rights policy between 1907 and 1922, see: Alford and Harvey, "Copperbelt Merger," 332; Peter Slinn, "Commercial Concessions and Politics during the Colonial Period: The Role of the British South Africa Company in Northern Rhodesia 1890–1964," *African Affairs* 70, no. 281 (1971): 374.

125. AAC, "Nkana-Kitwe: Twin Town of Copper," 68.

126. AAC, "Nkana-Kitwe: Twin Town of Copper," 68. For further details on the formation the Bwana Mkubwa Company in 1920 by Edmund Davis; of the CV in 1921 comprising Bwana Mkubwa, Minerals Separation, and Chester Beatty's Selection Trust; the winding up of CV in 1923 and the formation of RCBC; the formation of NCCM; and the entry of AAC into the Northern Rhodesian mining industry, see variously: Gregory, *Ernest Oppenheimer and the Economic Development of Southern Africa*, xvii, 22–9, 385–406; Alford and Harvey, "Copperbelt Merger," 332–3; Roberts, "Notes towards a Financial History of Copper Mining in Northern Rhodesia," 348; Cunningham, "Nationalization and the Zambian Copper Mining Industry," 43.

127. Phillips, "Roan Antelope," 73.

128. AAC, "Nkana-Kitwe: Twin Town of Copper," 68.

129. AAC, "Company Histories No. 3: Rhokana Corporation," 22.

CHAPTER 2

1. AAC, "Nkana-Kitwe: Twin Town of Copper," *Optima* 11, no. 2 (1961): 68.

2. AAC, "Company Histories No. 3: Rhokana Corporation," *Optima* 1, no. 3 (1951): 22. In the 1930s and 1940s, the Nkana mine extracted its copper from these three shafts. The Mindola open pit was opened in the late 1950s.

3. Raymond Brooks, "How the Northern Rhodesia Coppers Were Found (III)," *Rhokana Review* 8, no. 4 (1959): 31.

4. Brooks, "How the Northern Rhodesia Coppers Were Found (III)," 31.

5. Simon J. Cunningham, "Nationalization and the Zambian Copper Mining Industry" (PhD thesis, University of Edinburgh, 1985), 74.

6. Cunningham, "Nationalization and the Zambian Copper Mining Industry," 73–7.

7. Cunningham, "Nationalization and the Zambian Copper Mining Industry," 73–4.

8. John G. Phillips, "Roan Antelope: Big Business in Central Africa, 1890–1953" (PhD thesis, University of Cambridge, 2000), 146–7.

9. Simon J. Cunningham, *The Copper Industry in Zambia: Foreign Mining Companies in a Developing Country* (New York: Praeger Publishers, 1981), 76.

10. Bernard W.E. Alford and Charles E. Harvey, "Copperbelt Merger: The Formation of the Rhokana Corporation, 1930–1932," *Business Review* 54, no. 3 (1980): 343.

11. Cunningham, *The Copper Industry in Zambia*, 77.

12. Phillips, "Roan Antelope," 148.

13. Klas Ronnback and Oskar Broberg, *Capital and Colonialism: The Return on British Investments in Africa, 1869–1969* (London: Palgrave Macmillan, 2019), 223.

14. RC Limited, *Annual Report and Accounts together with Statement by the Chairman, 30 June 1954* (Kitwe: RC Head Office, 1954), 8, ZCCM 12.7.2F; AAC, "Company Histories No. 3: Rhokana Corporation," 22.

15. Cunningham, "Nationalization and the Zambian Copper Mining Industry," 44.

16. Cunningham, "Nationalization and the Zambian Copper Mining Industry," 44.

17. Cunningham, "Nationalization and the Zambian Copper Mining Industry," 44.

18. Cunningham, "Nationalization and the Zambian Copper Mining Industry," 44.

19. Cunningham, "Nationalization and the Zambian Copper Mining Industry," 45.

20. Alford and Harvey, "Copperbelt Merger," 333–4.

21. Brooks, "How the Northern Rhodesia Coppers Were Found (III)," 31.

22. Brooks, "How the Northern Rhodesia Coppers Were Found (III)," 31.

23. RC Limited, *Directors' Report and Statement of Accounts for the Year Ended 30 June 1931* (London: Rhokana Corporation Head Office, 1931), 2, ZCCM 3.8.2F; Theodore Gregory, *Ernest Oppenheimer and the Economic Development of Southern Africa* (London: Oxford University Press, 1961), 438.

24. RC Limited, *Directors' Report and Statement of Accounts for the Year Ended 30 June 1931*; Gregory, *Ernest Oppenheimer and the Economic Development of Southern Africa*, 438.

25. RC Limited, *Directors' Report and Statement of Accounts for the Year Ended 30 June 1931*; Gregory, *Ernest Oppenheimer and the Economic Development of Southern Africa*, 438.

26. Alford and Harvey, "Copperbelt Merger," 355.

27. Gregory, *Ernest Oppenheimer and the Economic Development of Southern Africa*, 29–30.

28. Gregory, *Ernest Oppenheimer and the Economic Development of Southern Africa*, 30.

29. Roan Antelope Copper Mines (hereafter RACM), Minutes of Meetings, August 20, 1928; September 4, 1928; October 15, 1929, ZCCM 16.2.2D.

30. Cunningham, *The Copper Industry in Zambia*, 82–3.

31. Rhodesian Anglo American (hereafter RAA) Limited, *Report for the Period from Incorporation of the Company, 8 December 1928 to 31 March 1930* (London: Rhodesian Anglo American Head Office, 1930), 1, ZCCM 19.2.4F.

32. In fact, the Copperbelt companies sold their copper based on the prevailing price on the London Metal Exchange. For a detailed understanding of how the city of London connected the world, see: Ronnback and Broberg, *Capital and Colonialism*, 25–32.

33. Phillips, "Roan Antelope," 152.

34. Phillips, "Roan Antelope," 152.

35. For further details about the dual labor structure on the Copperbelt, other parts of Africa, and selected parts of the world, see: Stefano Bellucci and Andreas Eckert, eds., *General Labour History of Africa: Workers, Employers and Governments, 20th and 21st Centuries* (Suffolk, England: James Currey, 2019), passim; Thomas M. Klubock, *Contested Communities: Class, Gender, and Politics in Chile's El Teniente Copper Mine* (Durham, NC: Duke University Press, 1998), passim; Guy C.Z. Mhone, *The Political Economy of a Dual Labour Market in Africa, 1929–1969* (London and Toronto: Associated University Presses, 1982), passim; United States (hereafter US) Department of Labor, *Monthly Labor Review, Vol. 47, no. 1, July 1938* (Washington: Bureau of Labor Statistics, 1938), passim, books.google.com/books/about/Monthly_labor_Review.html?id=AH21muCPnfwc (accessed December 10, 2020); US Department of the Interior, *Bureau of Mines, Bulletin 405: Copper Mining in North America* (Washington, DC: Government Printing Office, 1938), 251–92, digital.library.unt.edu/ark:/67531/metadc12571/m1/1/ (accessed December 10, 2020).

36. Charles A. Perrings, *Black Mineworkers in Central Africa: Industrial Strategies and the Evolution of an African Proletariat in the Copperbelt, 1911–1941* (New York: Africana Publishing Company, 1979), 252.

37. AAC, "Nkana-Kitwe: Twin Town of Copper," 68.

38. Barovale District Notebook, Vol. VII, Origins of Labour Employed on Northern Rhodesia during July 1938, NAZ KDD/KTW 2/1; Secretariat Series, Vol. II, Immigration Organisation: General Control of Immigration, 1935–1948, NAZ/SEC 3/48.

39. James Ferguson, *Expectations of Modernity: Myths and Meanings of Urban Life on the Zambian Copperbelt* (Berkeley: University of California Press, 1999), 49.

40. District Commissioner, Broken Hill, to Provincial Commissioner, Ndola, January 16, 1931, NAZ, ZA1/9/19/M.

41. Elena L. Berger, *Labour, Race and Colonial Rule: The Copperbelt from 1924 to Independence* (Oxford: Clarendon Press, 1974), 12–18; Anusa Daimon,

"Ringleaders and Troublemakers: Malawian (Nyasa) Migrants and Transnational Labour Movements in Southern Africa, c. 1910–1960," *Labor History* 58, no. 5 (2017): 656–75.

42. Austen J. Bancroft, *Mining in Northern Rhodesia: A Chronicle of Mineral Exploration and Mining Development* (Bedford, England: The Sidney Press Limited, 1961), 155.

43. Bancroft, *Mining in Northern Rhodesia*, 159; RC Limited, *Annual Report Covering Period from 1 June 1931 to 30 June 1932*, 1–2, 17, ZCCM 3.8.2B.

44. RC Limited, *Annual Report Covering Period from 1 June 1931 to 30 June 1932*, 17.

45. Charles Van Onselen, *Chibaro: African Mine Labour in Southern Rhodesia, 1900–1933* (London: Pluto Press, 1976), 128–57, 227–44; Ian R. Phimister, "The Reconstruction of the Southern Rhodesian Gold Mining Industry, 1903–1910," *Economic History Review* 29, no. 3 (1976): 480; Ronnback and Broberg, *Capital and Colonialism*, 215.

46. Van Onselen, *Chibaro*, 128–57, 227–44. For further details, see: Ian R. Phimister and Charles Van Onselen, *Studies in the History of African Mine Labour in Colonial Zimbabwe* (Gwelo, Zimbabwe: Mambo Press, 1978), 1–40; Mhone, *The Political Economy of a Dual Labour Market in Africa*, 49–160; Jane L. Parpart, *Labour and Capital on the African Copperbelt* (Philadelphia: Temple University Press, 1983), 54–95; Charles A. Perrings, "Consciousness, Conflict and Proletarianization: An Assessment of the 1935 Mineworkers' Strike on the Northern Rhodesian Copperbelt," *Journal of Southern African Studies* 4, no. 1 (1977): 31–51.

47. Saso Kraner, "Causes of the Great Depression and the Great Financial Crisis" (PhD thesis, Univerza Na Primorsken, 2010), 9–10.

48. R. Palmer and J. Colton, *A History of the Modern World* (New York: Doubleday and Company, 1992), 806.

49. P. Clarke, *Hope and Glory: Britain 1900–1990* (London: Penguin, 1997), 152–58.

50. Phillips, "Roan Antelope," 194.

51. The companies were the American Smelting and Refining Company (ASARCO), American Metal Company (AMC), Kennecott, Phelps Dodge, Anaconda, and Newmont. For details, see: Thomas R. Navin, *Copper Mining and Management* (Arizona: University of Arizona Press, 1978), 128–32.

52. RC Limited, *Annual Reports and Accounts*, 1931–1939.

53. Perrings, *Black Mineworkers in Central Africa*, 101.

54. Navin, *Copper Mining and Management*, 133.

55. Phillips, "Roan Antelope," 200; Perrings, *Black Mineworkers in Central Africa*, 101.

56. Perrings, *Black Mineworkers in Central Africa*, 101.

57. As discussed later in the chapter, Europe was experiencing a resurgence in industrial developments, booming automotive and electrical industries, and rearmament, which increased demand for copper.

58. RC Limited, *Director's Report and Statement of Accounts for the Year Ended 30 June 1935* (London: Rhokana Corporation Head Office, 1935), 7, ZCCM 3.8.2F.

59. Navin, *Copper Mining and Management*, 134.

60. RC Limited, *Director's Report and Statement of Accounts for the Year Ended 30 June 1935*, 7–8; *Times*, December 11, 1934, October 31, 1935.

61. RC Limited, *Annual Reports and Accounts*, 1935–1937.

62. RC Limited, *Annual Reports and Accounts*, 1938–1939.

63. *Times*, July 9, 1931.

64. *Times*, July 9, 1931.

65. *Times*, July 9, 1931.

66. Ian R. Phimister, *Wangi Kolia: Coal, Capital and Labour in Colonial Zimbabwe* (Harare: Baobab Books, 1994), 93.

67. Phimister, *Wangi Kolia*, 93.

68. Phimister, *Wangi Kolia*, 4.

69. British South Africa (hereafter BSA) Company, *Annual Reports and Accounts*, 1929–1939, ZCCM 19.2.2B.

70. Phimister, *Wangi Kolia*, 84.

71. *Times*, July 9, 1931.

72. US Department of the Interior, *Bureau of Mines, Bulletin 405*, 9.

73. RC Limited, *Directors' Report and Statement of Accounts for the year ended 30 June 1931*, 6; RST Limited, *Report of the Directors with Balance Sheet at 30th June 1931* (RST Head Office: London, 1931), 4, ZCCM 12.6.1E; Phillips, "Roan Antelope," 367; US Department of the Interior, *Bureau of Mines, Bulletin 405*, 9.

74. RC Limited, *Annual Reports and Accounts*, 1931–1939; RST Limited, *Annual Reports and Accounts*, 1931–1939, ZCCM 12.6.1E.

75. RC Limited, *Annual Reports and Accounts*, 1931–1939.

76. AAC, "Nkana-Kitwe: Twin Town of Copper," 68.

77. US Department of the Interior, *Bureau of Mines, Bulletin 405*, 288. In the *Bureau of Mines Bulletin*, the amounts of capital investments in the mines of the USA, Canada, Chile, and Katanga are indicated in US dollars. They have been converted into British pounds for easy comparison with the figures of their counterparts in Northern Rhodesia at the exchange rate of £1 = 490 US cents = US$4.90. For further details about these exchange rates, see: New World Economics, "Foreign Exchange Rates: Just Looking at the Data," newworldeconomics.com/foreign-exchange-rates-1913-1941-just-looking-at-the-data/ (accessed May 7, 2020).

78. US Department of the Interior, *Bureau of Mines, Bulletin 405*, 288; New World Economics, "Foreign Exchange Rates."

79. RC Limited, *Directors' Report and Statement of Accounts for the Year Ended 30 June 1931*, 11; RST Limited, *Report of the Directors with Balance Sheet at 30th June 1931*, 9; Phillips, "Roan Antelope", 220.

80. US Department of the Interior, *Bureau of Mines, Bulletin 405*, 255.

81. RC Limited, *Annual Reports and Accounts*, June 1931–June 1935, ZCCM 3.8.2B; RC Limited, *Annual Reports and Accounts*, 1931–1935; RST Limited, *Reports of the Directors with Balance Sheets*, 1931–1935; Perrings, *Black Mineworkers in Central Africa*, Appendices (i) and (ii), 101, 252–3. By calculation, it can be seen that each of the 14 operating mines in the USA utilized an average of 1,584 workers per year between 1930 and 1935. By comparison, the labor force in each of the three

mines on the Copperbelt and their counterparts in the Katanga averaged 4,120 and 3,160 per year, respectively.

82. US Department of the Interior, *Bureau of Mines, Bulletin 405*, 255.

83. US Department of Labor, *Monthly Labor Review, Vol. 47, no. 1, July 1938*, 866.

84. US Department of Labor, *Monthly Labor Review, Vol. 47, no. 1, July 1938*, 866.

85. Parpart, *Labour and Capital on the African Copperbelt*, 30.

86. RC Limited, *Annual Reports and Accounts*, June 1931–June 1935.

87. RC Limited, *Annual Reports and Accounts*, 1931–1938.

88. Perrings, *Black Mineworkers in Central Africa*, 252.

89. Phillips, "Roan Antelope," 220.

90. RC Limited, *Director's Report and Statement of Accounts for the Year Ended 30 June 1934* (London: Rhokana Corporation Head Office, 1934), 19, ZCCM 3.8.2F.

91. Perrings, *Black Mineworkers in Central Africa*, 252.

92. Perrings, *Black Mineworkers in Central Africa*, 252.

93. Perrings, *Black Mineworkers in Central Africa*, 252.

94. Perrings, *Black Mineworkers in Central Africa*, 109.

95. RC Limited, *Annual Report Covering Period from 1 July 1932 to 30 June 1933*, 14, ZCCM 3.8.2B. Colored South Africans, formerly Cape Coloureds, are an ethnic group composed primarily of persons of mixed parentage between whites (English/Afrikaners) and Bantu or blacks, Asians, and Khoisan. For more details, see: R.E. Van Der Ross, "The Coloured People's Place in the Sun," *Optima* 11, no. 3 (1961): 143–7.

96. RC Limited, *Annual Report Covering Period from 1 July 1932 to 30 June 1933*, 14.

97. Mhone, *The Political Economy of a Dual Labour Market in Africa*, 104–5.

98. Perrings, *Black Mineworkers in Central Africa*, 104.

99. Ferguson, *Expectations of Modernity*, 59.

100. Ferguson, *Expectations of Modernity*, 59.

101. Michael Burawoy, "The Functions and Reproduction of Migrant Labour: Comparative Material from Southern Africa and the United States," *American Journal of Sociology* 81, no. 5 (1976): 1054.

102. D. Juif and E. Frankema, "From Coercion to Compensation: Institutional Responses to Labour Scarcity in the Central African Copperbelt," *Journal of Institutional Economics* 14, no. 2 (2018): 329.

103. Perrings, *Black Mineworkers in Central Africa*, 253.

104. Perrings, *Black Mineworkers in Central Africa*, 253.

105. Perrings, *Black Mineworkers in Central Africa*, 121–9.

106. Ian Henderson, "Labour and Politics in Northern Rhodesia, 1900–1953: A Study in the Limits of Colonial Power" (PhD thesis, University of Edinburgh, 1972), 135–8; Perrings, "Consciousness, Conflict and Proletarianization," 45–7; Butler, *Copper Empire*, 51–3; Phillips, "Roan Antelope," 231, 233.

107. Helena P. Nino, "Labour Migration," in *General Labour History of Africa: Workers, Employers and Governments, 20th and 21st Centuries*, eds. Stefano Bellucci and Andreas Eckert (Suffolk, England: James Currey, 2019), 280.

108. Butler, *Copper Empire*, 22.

109. Copper Mines Arbitration Board (hereafter CMAB), Trade Union Relations—Nkana Division: Native Strike, March 1940–June 1941, ZCCM 3.8.1A.

110. CMAB, Trade Union Relations—Nkana Division.

111. US Department of the Interior, *Bureau of Mines, Bulletin 405*, 253; US Department of Labor, *Monthly Labor Review, Vol. 47, no. 1, July 1938*, 866. Wages in these reports are indicated in US dollars. They have been converted to British pounds at an average annual rate of £1 = US 435 cents = US$4.35, between 1930 and 1935. For further information about these exchange rates, see: New World Economics, "Foreign Exchange Rates," passim.

112. RC Limited, Trade Union Relations—Nkana Division.

113. Butler, *Copper Empire*, 22.

114. Butler, *Copper Empire*, 22.

115. RC Limited, *Annual Reports and Accounts*, 1934–1935.

116. *Financial Times*, July 17, 1934.

117. For further details about rearmament in Europe, see: Philip M.H. Bell, *The Origin of the Second World War* (London: Longman Group Limited, 1986), 1–4; Mark Harrison, "Resource Mobilization for World War II: The USA, UK, USSR, and Germany, 1938–1945," *Economic History Review* 41, no. 2 (1988): 172.

118. Butler, *Copper Empire*, 21.

119. *Times*, November 23, 1937.

120. US Department of the Interior, *Bureau of Mines, Bulletin 405*, 251.

121. US Department of Labor, *Monthly Labor Review, Vol. 47, no. 1, July 1938*, 866; RC Limited, *Annual Reports and Accounts*, 1931–1935.

122. *Times*, November 23, 1937.

123. RST Limited, *Annual Reports and Accounts*, 1934–1939.

124. RST Limited, *Annual Reports and Accounts*, 1934–1939.

125. Gregory, *Ernest Oppenheimer and the Economic Development of Southern Africa*, 420, 422, 440–1; Perrings, *Black Mineworkers in Central Africa*, 245; Phillips, "Roan Antelope," 198, 206.

126. Butler, *Copper Empire*, 21–3.

127. US Department of the Interior, *Bureau of Mines, Bulletin 405*, 2, 37–49.

128. Perrings, *Black Mineworkers in Central Africa*, 245.

129. Perrings, *Black Mineworkers in Central Africa*, 245.

130. Gregory, *Ernest Oppenheimer and the Economic Development of Southern Africa*, 442.

131. Gregory, *Ernest Oppenheimer and the Economic Development of Southern Africa*, 442.

132. Phillips, "Roan Antelope," 152.

133. Gregory, *Ernest Oppenheimer and the Economic Development of Southern Africa*, 442.

134. Perrings, *Black Mineworkers in Central Africa*, 244.

135. Andrew D. Roberts, "Notes towards a Financial History of Copper Mining in Northern Rhodesia," *Canadian Journal of African Studies* 16, no. 2 (1982): 353; Butler, *Copper Empire*, 23, 34.

136. Roberts, "Notes towards a Financial History of Copper Mining in Northern Rhodesia," 353; Butler, *Copper Empire*, 23, 34.

137. RC Limited, *Annual Reports and Accounts*, 1935–1939.

138. Roberts, "Notes towards a Financial History of Copper Mining in Northern Rhodesia," 353; Butler, *Copper Empire*, 23, 34.

139. RC Limited, *Directors' Report and Statement of Accounts for the Year Ended 30 June 1934* (London: RC Head Offices, 1934), 12, ZCCM 3.8.2F; Butler, *Copper Empire*, 29–30.

140. Butler, *Copper Empire*, 29–30.

141. Roberts, "Notes towards a Financial History of Copper Mining in Northern Rhodesia," 352; Butler, *Copper Empire*, 32.

142. *Times*, May 31, 1932.

143. *Copperbelt Times*, September 28, 1934; Duncan Money, "No Matter How Much or How Little They Have Got, They Cannot Settle Down: A Social History of Europeans on the Zambian Copperbelt, 1926–1974" (PhD thesis, University of Oxford, 2016), 291–2.

144. Money, "No Matter How Much or How Little They Have Got, They Cannot Settle Down," 81.

145. T. Scannell, "A Dynamic Union with a Turbulent Career," *Horizon* 3, no. 4 (1961): 5.

146. *Copperbelt Times*, September 28, 1934.

147. *Copperbelt Times*, September 28, 1934.

148. Frank Ayer, RACM General Manager, Luanshya, to RST Limited Secretary, London, October 5, 1936, ZCCM 10.7.9A.

149. Richard Olds, "The Survival of the White Workers of Northern Rhodesia," *Copperbelt Times*, October 12, 1934 (emphasis in the original).

150. Scannell, "A Dynamic Union with a Turbulent Career," 5.

151. Olds, "The Survival of the White Workers of Northern Rhodesia."

152. RC Limited, *Annual Report and Accounts for the Year Ended 30 June 1935* (London: RC Head Office, 1935), 14, ZCCM 3.8.2B; Frank Ayer, RACM General Manager, Luanshya, to RST Limited Secretary, London, December 1, 1934, ZCCM 10.7.9A; *Northern Rhodesia Advertiser*, May 18, 1935.

153. Money, "No Matter How Much or Little They Have Got, They Cannot Settle Down," 82.

154. Money, "No Matter How Much or Little They Have Got, They Cannot Settle Down," 82.

155. Scannell, "A Dynamic Union with a Turbulent Career," 6.

156. Scannell, "A Dynamic Union with a Turbulent Career," 6.

157. Scannell, "A Dynamic Union with a Turbulent Career," 6.

158. Henderson, "Labour and Politics in Northern Rhodesia, 1900–1953," 19.

159. Ayer to RST Limited Secretary, October 5, 1936.

160. P.F. Ellis, Ellis and Company Solicitors, to Frank Ayer, RACM General Manager, October 25, 1934, ZCCM 10.7.9A.

161. Berger, *Labour, Race and Colonial Rule*, 65.

162. Henderson, "Labour and Politics in Northern Rhodesia, 1900–1953," 110.

163. Henderson, "Labour and Politics in Northern Rhodesia, 1900–1953," 112.

164. NRMWU Head Office, Luanshya, to RACM General Manager, Luanshya, April 2, 1937, ZCCM 10.7.9A.

165. Scannell, "A Dynamic Union with a Turbulent Career," 6.

166. Scannell, "A Dynamic Union with a Turbulent Career," 4, 9.

167. Henderson, "Labour and Politics in Northern Rhodesia, 1900–1953," 180.

168. ZCCM Limited, *Paper on Labour Relations on the Copperbelt*, 1930–1982, 8–9, ZCCM 11.8.3C.

169. ZCCM Limited, *Paper on Labour Relations on the Copperbelt*, 4.

170. Nsolo Mijere, "One Industry, One Union: The Rise and Governmental Control of the Mineworkers of Zambia, 1930–1982," in *Issues in Zambian Development*, eds. Kwaku Osei-Hwedie and Muna Ndulo (Nyangwe and Roxbury: Omenana, 1985), 380.

171. The Copperbelt mines became the main market for coal produced by Wankie Colliery of Southern Rhodesia and were the biggest customers of Rhodesia Railways. For more information, see: Berger, *Labour, Race and Colonial Rule*, 9; Phimister, *Wangi Kolia*, 84.

172. Butler, *Copper Empire*, 22–3.

CHAPTER 3

1. For further details about the arms race and origins of the Second World War, see: Philip M.H. Bell, *The Origin of the Second World War* (London: Longman Group Limited, 1986), 1–10; Gerhard L. Weinberg, *A World at Arms: A Global History of World War Two* (Cambridge: Cambridge University Press, 1994), 503.

2. John G. Phillips, "Roan Antelope: Big Business in Central Africa, 1890–1953" (PhD thesis, University of Cambridge, 2000), 247.

3. Raymond Dumett, "Africa's Strategic Minerals during the Second World War," *Journal of African History* 26, no. 4 (1985): 393; Ronald L. Prain, *Reflections on an Era: An Autobiography* (Letchworth, England: The Garden City Press, 1981), 64–8.

4. Prain, *Reflections on an Era*, 64.

5. Prain, *Reflections on an Era*, 63–4.

6. Prain, *Reflections on an Era*, 64.

7. Dumett, "Africa's Strategic Minerals during the Second World War," 382.

8. Dumett, "Africa's Strategic Minerals during the Second World War," 382.

9. RC Limited, *Annual Report and Accounts for the Year Ended 30 June 1945* (London: Rhokana Head Office, 1945), 11, ZCCM 19.2.4F.

10. RC Limited, *Annual Report and Accounts for the Year Ended 30 June 1945.*

11. RC Limited, *Annual Report and Accounts for the Year Ended 30 June 1945.*

12. RC Limited, *Annual Reports and Accounts*, 1931–1944.

13. Theodore Gregory, *Ernest Oppenheimer and the Economic Development of Southern Africa* (London: Oxford University Press, 1961), 394, 408, 439.

14. Gregory, *Ernest Oppenheimer and the Economic Development of Southern Africa*, 394, 408, 439.

15. Hubert W. Davis, "Nickel and Cobalt," *Minerals Yearbook: Review of 1940*, 607, images.library.wisc.edu/EcoNatRes/EFacs2/MineralsYearBk/MinYB1940/reference/econatres.minyb1940.hdavis.pdf (accessed April 6, 2020).

16. Hubert W. Davis, "Cobalt," *Minerals Yearbook: Review of 1941*, 625, images.library.wisc.edu/EcoNatRes/EFacs2/MineralsYearBk/MinYB1941/reference/econatres.Minyb1941.hdavis02.pdf (accessed April 6, 2020).

17. RC Limited, *Annual Report and Accounts for the Year Ended 30 June 1945*, 20.

18. RC Limited, *Annual Report and Accounts for the Year Ended 30 June 1945*, 20.

19. RC Limited, *Annual Report and Accounts for the Year Ended 30 June 1945*, 20.

20. Double taxation was charged on the companies for having two administrative departments, one in Britain and the other in Northern Rhodesia. During the war, EPT and national defense contribution added to the burden of double taxation. For further details, see: Phillips, "Roan Antelope," 252.

21. Victor M. Gwande, "Foreign Capital, State and the Development of Secondary Industry in Southern Rhodesia, 1939–1956" (MA thesis, University of the Free State, 2015), 22.

22. Christopher J. Schmitz, *World Non-ferrous Metal Production and Prices 1700–1976* (London: Frank Cass Publishers, 1979), 272.

23. Phillips, "Roan Antelope," 251.

24. Phillips, "Roan Antelope," 252.

25. Phillips, "Roan Antelope," 253.

26. RC Limited, *Annual Reports and Accounts*, 1940–1944; RC Limited, *Annual Report and Accounts 30 June 1945*, 11–13.

27. RC Limited, *Annual Report and Accounts 30 June 1945*, 9, 16, 19.

28. RC Limited, *Annual Reports and Accounts*, 1940–1944; RC Limited, *Annual Report and Accounts for the Year Ended 30 June 1945*, 2–6; *Daily Telegraph and Morning Post*, December 5, 1940; *Times*, December 29, 1944.

29. RC Limited, *Annual Reports and Accounts*, 1940–1944; RC Limited, *Annual Report and Accounts for the Year Ended 30 June 1945*, 2–6; *Daily Telegraph and Morning Post*, December 5, 1940; *Times*, December 29, 1944.

30. Dumett, "Africa's Strategic Minerals during the Second World War," 395; Phillips, "Roan Antelope," 251.

31. RC Limited, *Annual Reports and Accounts*, 1940–1944; RC Limited, *Annual Report and Accounts for the Year Ended 30 June 1945*, 2–6.

32. Larry J. Butler, *Copper Empire: Mining and the Colonial State in Northern Rhodesia, c. 1930–1964* (New York: Palgrave Macmillan, 2007), 64.

33. RC Limited, *Annual Reports and Accounts*, 1940–1944; RC Limited, *Annual Report and Accounts for the Year Ended 30 June 1945*, 2–6; Andrew D. Roberts, "Notes towards a Financial History of Copper Mining in Northern Rhodesia," *Canadian Journal of African Studies* 16, no. 2 (1982): 354.

34. Butler, *Copper Empire*, 64; Dumett, "Africa's Strategic Minerals during the Second World War," 395; Phillips, "Roan Antelope," 251; Klas Ronnback and Oskar Broberg, *Capital and Colonialism. The Return on British Investments in Africa, 1869–1969* (London: Palgrave Macmillan, 2019), 224.

35. RC Limited, *Annual Reports and Accounts*, 1946–1949.

36. RC Limited, *Annual Reports and Accounts*, 1946–1949.

37. RC Limited, *Utilisation of African Labour Report*, January 8, 1957, Table 7, facing 24, ZCCM 3.8.1C.

38. *Rhokana Corporation Limited Annual Reports*, 1946–1949, ZCCM 12.7.2F.
39. Phillips, "Roan Antelope," 288.
40. Butler, *Copper Empire*, 106.
41. Prain, *Reflections on an Era*, 87–8.
42. *Rhokana Corporation Limited Annual Reports*, 1946–1949, ZCCM 12.7.2F.
43. Phillips, "Roan Antelope," 252.
44. Gwande, "Foreign Capital, State and the Development of Secondary Industry in Southern Rhodesia," 22.
45. Prain, *Reflections on an Era*, 87–8.
46. Nsolo Mijere, "One Industry, One Union: The Rise and Governmental Control of the Mineworkers of Zambia, 1930–1982," in *Issues in Zambian Development*, eds. Kwaku Osei-Hwedie and Muna Ndulo (Nyangwe and Roxbury: Omenana, 1985), 381.
47. NRG, *Evidence Taken by Commission Appointed to Enquire into the Disturbances in the Copperbelt, Northern Rhodesia*, Vol. II (Lusaka: Government Printers, 1935), 548–50, NAZ 11/57/C.
48. Ian Henderson, "Labour and Politics in Northern Rhodesia, 1900–1953: A Study in the Limits of Colonial Power" (PhD thesis, University of Edinburgh, 1972), 158.
49. *Times*, April 11, 1940.
50. As cited in NRG, *Report of the Commission Appointed to Inquire into the Unrest in the Mining Industry in Northern Rhodesia in Recent Months* (Lusaka: Government Printers, 1956), 13, NAZ 11/57/H.
51. Elena L. Berger, *Labour, Race and Colonial Rule: The Copperbelt from 1924 to Independence* (Oxford: Clarendon Press, 1974), 82.
52. Berger, *Labour, Race and Colonial Rule*, 82.
53. Boss Boys or Kapitaos were underground African supervisors of gangs or groups of about 10 to 15 laborers. Therefore, BBCs were committees consisting of senior Africans who supervised and represented the interest of these gangs. The major difference between BBCs and TRs was that the former represented the economic interests of supervisors of gangs, while the latter were spokespersons for the rest of the African labor force. For further details, see: Berger, *Labour, Race and Colonial Rule*, 81–96; Henderson, "Labour and Politics in Northern Rhodesia, 1900–1953," 209–10; Mijere, "One Industry, One Union," 378; Jane L. Parpart, *Labour and Capital on the African Copperbelt* (Philadelphia: Temple University Press, 1983), 103–9.
54. Mijere, "One Industry, One Union," 380.
55. Mijere, "One Industry, One Union," 380.
56. Mijere, "One Industry, One Union," 380.
57. Berger, *Labour, Race and Colonial Rule*, 91.
58. Berger, *Labour, Race and Colonial Rule*, 92.
59. Berger, *Labour, Race and Colonial Rule*, 92.
60. As discussed in chapter 2, and elsewhere in this chapter, Nkana relied more on migrant African labor with mining experience from other mines in the Southern Africa region and on European labor mainly from South Africa. There had been a series of strikes by these white workers during and after the First World War mostly against meager wages. These workers brought ideas of labor activism and were

already exposed to strikes. For further details about labor activism in the Southern Africa region up to the early 1930s, see: Lucien van der Walt, "The First Globalisation and Transnational Labour Activism: White Labourism, the 1WW, and the ICU, 1904–1934," *African Studies* 66, no. 3 (2007): 223–51.

61. Mijere, "One Industry, One Union," 381.

62. NRG, *Report of the Commission Appointed to Inquire into the Unrest in the Mining Industry in Northern Rhodesia in Recent Months*, 14; Berger, *Labour, Race and Colonial Rule*, 92.

63. Guy C.Z. Mhone, *The Political Economy of a Dual Labour Market in Africa, 1929–1969* (London and Toronto: Associated University Presses, 1982), 139.

64. Mijere, "One Industry, One Union," 382.

65. Mijere, "One Industry, One Union," 382.

66. Berger, *Labour, Race and Colonial Rule*, 96.

67. Henderson, "Labour and Politics in Northern Rhodesia," 227.

68. NRG, *Report of the Commission Appointed to Inquire into the Unrest in the Mining Industry in Northern Rhodesia in Recent Months*, 19.

69. Mijere, "One Industry, One Union," 383.

70. For a discussion of the causes and course of the Korean Crisis, see: Christine Locher, "The Conflict with North Korea/North Korea as a Source of Conflict: An Analysis from a Peace and Conflict Resolution Studies Perspective" (PhD thesis, Fern Universitat Hagen, 2008), 12–3; O. Chang-II, "The Causes of the Korean War, 1950–1953," *International Journal of Korean Studies* 14, no. 2 (2010): 28–9.

71. Thomas R. Navin, *Copper Mining and Management* (Arizona: University of Arizona Press, 1978), 147.

72. A.G. Charles, "Prospects for Base Metal Prices and Production," *Optima* 1, no. 2 (1951): 2.

73. Charles, "Prospects for Base Metal Prices and Production," 2.

74. Charles, "Prospects for Base Metal Prices and Production," 2.

75. Charles, "Prospects for Base Metal Prices and Production," 2.

76. Leslie Tarring, "Why the Copper Price Fluctuates," *Horizon* 1, no. 2 (1959): 22; Charles, "Prospects for Base Metal Prices and Production," 3.

77. Helena M. Meyer and Gertrude N. Greenspoon, "Copper," *Bureau of Mines Minerals Yearbook 1950* (Washington, DC: US Bureau of Mines, 1950), 466, https://search.library.wisc.edu/digital/A3M2CR4ONJEVFW9A/pages/AHUCQBDBMT4JCY8T (accessed August 30, 2020).

78. Meyer and Greenspoon, "Copper," *Bureau of Mines Minerals Yearbook 1950*, 466.

79. Charles, "Prospects for Base Metal Prices and Production," 3.

80. The Editor, "The Editor's Notebook: U.S. Funds for Greater Copperbelt Power Supplies," *South African Mining and Engineering Journal* 64, no. 3150 (1953): 673; Navin, *Copper Mining and Management*, 147.

81. Navin, *Copper Mining and Management*, 146.

82. Tarring, "Why the Copper Price Fluctuates," 21–2.

83. Charles, "Prospects for Base Metal Prices and Production," 3.

84. Charles, "Prospects for Base Metal Prices and Production," 3.

85. Tarring, "Why the Copper Price Fluctuates," 22.

86. G.F.A. Burgess, "The World Centre of the Base Metal Trade," *Optima* 4, no. 3 (1954): 23.

87. Burgess, "The World Centre of the Base Metal Trade," 23.

88. Burgess, "The World Centre of the Base Metal Trade," 23.

89. The prices of the British Ministry of Supply/Materials in London were raised similarly to those on the Commodity Exchange in New York, although each increase carried the British price converted to the equivalent in cents per pound to about 1 cent above the US price. For further details, see: Meyer and Greenspoon, "Copper," *Bureau of Mines Minerals Yearbook 1950*, 484–5.

90. Navin, *Copper Mining and Management*, Table 14.1, 148.

91. The Editor, "The Editor's Notebook: U.S. Funds for Greater Copperbelt Power Supplies," 673; RC Limited, *Annual Report and Accounts together with Statement by the Chairman, 30 June 1953* (Kitwe: Rhokana Corporation Head Office, 1953), 4, ZCCM 12.7.2F.

92. Charles W. Merrill and Helena M. Meyer, "Copper," *Bureau of Mines Minerals Yearbook 1949* (Washington, DC: US Bureau of Mines, 1949), 491 Econatres.minby1949.cwmerrill.pdf (accessed August 30, 2020).

93. Helena M. Meyer and Gertrude N. Greenspoon, "Copper," *Bureau of Mines Minerals Yearbook 1951* (Washington, DC: US Bureau of Mines, 1951), 553, https://search.library.wisc.edu/digital/AJISUC7IKKA6HR9A/pages/AAWOPR543SXJKK8E (accessed August 30, 2020).

94. Meyer and Greenspoon, "Copper," *Bureau of Mines Minerals Yearbook 1951*, 554.

95. Meyer and Greenspoon, "Copper," *Bureau of Mines Minerals Yearbook 1951*, 554.

96. Meyer and Greenspoon, "Copper," *Bureau of Mines Minerals Yearbook 1950*, 498.

97. Meyer and Greenspoon, "Copper," *Bureau of Mines Minerals Yearbook 1950*, 498.

98. Meyer and Greenspoon, "Copper," *Bureau of Mines Minerals Yearbook 1951*, 553.

99. Meyer and Greenspoon, "Copper," *Bureau of Mines Minerals Yearbook 1951*, 554.

100. Meyer and Greenspoon, "Copper," *Bureau of Mines Minerals Yearbook 1951*, 554.

101. James Ferguson, *Expectations of Modernity: Myths and Meanings of Urban Life on the Zambian Copperbelt* (Berkeley: University of California Press, 1999), 53–8.

102. It is not impossible that the so-called single men who participated in migrant labor were actually married men! The difference, though, is that, in contrast to the married men in the stabilized labor regime who stayed with their families at the mines, some of these so-called single men left their wives in their villages to which they would return upon completing their contracts. For this reason, they lived in the so-called single-man quarters and in this way were regarded as single men. The available sources, however, do not make this distinction. Thus, this chapter regards both those who were not yet married in practice and those who left wives in the villages as single men, and those who stayed with their wives or families on the mines as married men.

103. Mhone, *The Political Economy of a Dual Labour Market in Africa*, 139.

104. RC Limited, *Utilisation of African Labour Report*, 4; NRCM, *Northern Rhodesia Chamber of Mines Yearbook 1956* (Kitwe: NRCM, 1957), 69, 76, ZCCM 12.1.9; Phillip Daniel, *Africanisation, Nationalisation and Inequality: Mining Labour and the Copperbelt in Zambian Development* (London: Cambridge University Press, 1979), 71.

105. Butler, *Copper Empire*, 22.

106. Ian R. Phimister, "Corporate Profit and Race in Central African Copper Mining, 1946–1958," *Business History Review* 85, no. 4 (2011): 759.

107. Butler, *Copper Empire*, 22.

108. Mhone, *The Political Economy of a Dual Labour Market in Africa*, 139.

109. Mhone, *The Political Economy of a Dual Labour Market in Africa*, 163, 174.

110. RC Limited, *Annual Reports and Accounts*, 1950–1953, ZCCM 12.7.2F.

111. Ian R. Phimister, *Wangi Kolia: Coal, Capital and Labour in Colonial Zimbabwe* (Harare: Baobab Books, 1994), 100–1, 127.

112. RAA Limited, *Report of the Directors and Statement Accounts, 30 June 1951* (Kitwe: RAA Head Office, 1951), 3, ZCCM 19.2.4F.

113. RC Limited, *Annual Report and Accounts together with Statement by the Chairman for the Year Ended 30 June 1953* (Kitwe: Rhokana Corporation Head Office, 1953), 4, ZCCM 12.7.2F.

114. NRCM, *Northern Rhodesia Chamber of Mines Yearbook 1956*, 60; Gregory, *Ernest Oppenheimer and the Economic Development of Southern Africa*, 459.

115. NRCM, *Northern Rhodesia Chamber of Mines Yearbook 1956*, 60; Gregory, *Ernest Oppenheimer and the Economic Development of Southern Africa*, 459.

116. Phimister, *Wangi Kolia*, 117.

117. RC Limited, *Annual Report and Accounts together with Statement by the Chairman for the Year Ended 30 June 1954* (Kitwe: Rhokana Corporation Head Office, 1954), 4, ZCCM 12.7.2F.

118. RST, "World's Deepest Mine Workings Reach 11,000 Feet," *Horizon* 1, no. 3 (1959): 25.

119. RST, "World's Deepest Mine Workings Reach 11,000 Feet," 25.

120. RST, "World's Deepest Mine Workings Reach 11,000 Feet," 25.

121. Rhokana Corporation Limited, *Directors' Report and Statement of Accounts for the Year Ended 30 June 1936* (London: Rhokana Head Office, 1936), 15, ZCCM 3.8.2F; Rhokana Corporation Limited, *Annual Report and Accounts together with Statement by the Chairman, 30 June 1953*, 13, ZCCM 12.7.2F.

122. RC Limited, *Utilisation of African Labour Report*, Table 7, facing 24.

123. RC Limited, *Utilisation of African Labour Report*, Table 7, facing 24. Also, see: NRCM, *Northern Rhodesia Chamber of Mines Yearbook 1956*, 60, ZCCM 12.1.9C; RST Limited, *Reports and Accounts*, 1950–53; Phillips, "Roan Antelope," Table 21, 298.

124. Charles, "Prospects for Base Metal Prices and Production," 2.

125. Charles, "Prospects for Base Metal Prices and Production," 2.

126. Charles, "Prospects for Base Metal Prices and Production," 2.

127. Charles, "Prospects for Base Metal Prices and Production," 2.

128. Charles, "Prospects for Base Metal Prices and Production," 2.

129. Burgess, "The World Centre of the Base Metal Trade," 23.

130. Meyer and Greenspoon, "Copper," *Bureau of Mines Minerals Yearbook 1950*, 485. *Glasgow Herald*, October 22, 1951.

131. Gregory, *Ernest Oppenheimer and the Economic Development of Southern Africa*, 456.

132. Burgess, "The World Centre of the Base Metal Trade," 24.
133. Charles, "Prospects for Base Metal Prices and Production," 3.
134. Charles, "Prospects for Base Metal Prices and Production," 3.
135. Northern Rhodesia Mines Department (hereafter NRMD), *Annual Reports*, 1951–1953, NAZ ML 8/4/18; RC Limited, *Annual Reports and Accounts together with Statements by the Chairman*, 1950–53; RAA Limited, *Reports of the Directors and Statements of Accounts*, 1950–1953, ZCCM 12.7.2F; RST Limited, *Reports and Accounts*, 1950–1953, ZCCM 12.6.1E, ZCCM 12.7.2F; Phillips, "Roan Antelope," Table 29, 366; Charles, "Prospects for Base Metal Prices and Production," 3.
136. Richard L. Sklar, *Corporate Power in an African State: The Political Impact of Multinational Mining Companies in Zambia* (Los Angeles: University of California Press, 1975), 31, 33.
137. NRMD, *Annual Reports*, 1951–1953.
138. *Northern News*, November 24, 1954.
139. *Daily Herald*, October 3, 1951.
140. *Times*, October 22, 1951.
141. *Birmingham Post*, October 22, 1951; *Liverpool Daily Post*, October 22, 1951; *Northern News*, October 23, 1951; *City Press*, October 24, 1952; *Northern News*, November 24, 1954.
142. *Birmingham Post*, October 22, 1951; *Liverpool Daily Post*, October 22, 1951; *Northern News*, October 23, 1951; *City Press*, October 24, 1952; *Northern News*, November 24, 1954.
143. Roberts, "Notes towards a Financial History of Copper Mining," 356.
144. NRMD, *Annual Reports*, 1951–1953.

CHAPTER 4

1. The Editor, "Rhokana Corporation, Ltd.," *South African Mining and Engineering Journal* 65, no. 3224 (1954): 507.
2. Copperbelt Companies, Submissions to the Royal (Bledisloe) Commission appointed to report whether any, and if so, what form of closer cooperation between Southern Rhodesia, Northern Rhodesia, and Nyasaland is desirable and feasible, April 5, 1938, 17, ZCCM 16.2.3C.
3. Copperbelt Companies, Submissions to the Royal (Bledisloe) Commission, April 5, 1938, 17.
4. Copperbelt Companies, Submissions to the Royal (Bledisloe) Commission, April 5, 1938, 18.
5. S.S. Taylor, Managing Director, RC Limited, London, to Secretary, Rhodesia-Nyasaland Royal (Bledisloe) Commission, Dominions Office, London, March 17, 1938, ZCCM 16.2.3C.
6. Thomas R. Navin, *Copper Mining and Management* (Arizona: University of Arizona Press, 1978), 156.
7. RC Limited, *Directors' Report and Statement of Accounts for the Year Ended 30 June 1947* (London: RC Head Office, 1947), 1, ZCCM 12.7.2F.

8. Andrew Cohen, "Business and Decolonisation in Central Africa Reconsidered," *Journal of Imperial and Commonwealth History* 36, no. 4 (2008): 643.

9. RC Limited, *Annual Report, 30 June 1962* (Salisbury: RC Head Office, 1962), 13, ZCCM 12.7.2F.

10. Duncan Money, "No Matter How Much or How Little They Have Got, They Cannot Settle Down: A Social History of Europeans on the Zambian Copperbelt, 1926–1974" (PhD thesis, University of Oxford, 2016), 162–3.

11. Cohen, "Business and Decolonisation in Central Africa Reconsidered," 644.

12. RC Limited, *Annual Report, 30 June 1962*, 13.

13. Partnership entailed that Africans and Europeans would unite and work together in harmony, promote the interests of all races, and reduce tension among races and, therefore, promote peace. Partnership in the mining and other industries was to be achieved through African Advancement. For further details about partnership in the Federation, see: Cranford Pratt, "Part Two: Why Federation Was Supported," in *A New Deal in Central Africa*, eds. Colin Leys and Cranford Pratt (New York: Frederick Praeger, 1960), 98–117; Larry W. Bowman, *Politics in Rhodesia: White Power in an African State* (Cambridge, MA: Harvard University Press, 1973), passim.

14. Larry J. Butler, "Business and British Decolonisation: Sir Ronald Prain, the Mining Industry and the Central African Federation," *Journal of Imperial and Commonwealth History* 35, no. 3 (2007): 461.

15. Butler, "Business and British Decolonisation," 461.

16. Butler, "Business and British Decolonisation," 462.

17. Butler, "Business and British Decolonisation," 462.

18. RST, *Discussion Notes*, September 7, 1951.

19. Vernon D. Johnson, "Racial Formation in Zimbabwe," in *The Changing Racial Regime, Vol. 5*, ed. Matthew Holden (New Brunswick and London: Transaction Publishers, 1995), 253.

20. Johnson, "Racial Formation in Zimbabwe," 253.

21. Johnson, "Racial Formation in Zimbabwe," 253.

22. Johnson, "Racial Formation in Zimbabwe," 253.

23. William Minter, *King Solomon's Mines Revised: Western Interests and the Burdened History of Southern Africa* (New York: Basic Books, Inc., Publishers, 1986), 112.

24. Larry J. Butler, *Copper Empire: Mining and the Colonial State in Northern Rhodesia, c. 1930–1964* (New York: Palgrave Macmillan, 2007), 206; John G. Phillips, "Roan Antelope: Big Business in Central Africa, 1890–1953" (PhD thesis, University of Cambridge, 2000), 380.

25. Marcia M. Burdette, "Industrial Development in Zambia, Zimbabwe and Malawi. The Primacy of Politics," in *Studies in the Economic History of Southern Africa, Vol. 1: The Front-line States*, eds. Zbigniew A. Konczacki, Jane L. Parpart, and Timothy M. Shaw (London: Frank Cass and Co. Ltd., 1990), 80–5.

26. Pratt, "Part Two: Why Federation Was Supported," 49.

27. Pratt, "Part Two: Why Federation Was Supported," 49.

28. Phillips, "Roan Antelope," 346.

29. Ronald L. Prain, *Reflections on an Era: An Autobiography* (Letchworth, England: The Garden City Press, 1981), 100–2; Butler, *Copper Empire*, 202–3.

30. RC Limited, *Annual Report and Accounts together with Statement by the Chairman, 30 June 1954* (Kitwe: RC Head Office, 1954), 6, ZCCM 12.7.2F.

31. RC Limited, *Annual Report, 30 June 1957* (Salisbury: Rhokana Corporation Head Office 1957), 14, ZCCM 12.7.2F.

32. Elena L. Berger, *Labour, Race and Colonial Rule: The Copperbelt from 1924 to Independence* (Oxford: Clarendon Press, 1974), 8–9.

33. While Federal income tax was charged on company profits, Northern Rhodesia territorial surcharge was deductible from declared dividends at 1.3s in the pound. For further details, see: RC Limited, *Annual Report and Accounts, 30 June 1954*, 3.

34. RC Limited, *Annual Report and Accounts, 30 June 1954*, 2.

35. Berger, *Labour, Race and Colonial Rule*, 9. As indicated in chapter 2, the Copperbelt mines were the biggest customers of Rhodesia Railways and BSA Company–owned Wankie Colliery. Therefore, the taxes paid by these two companies depended on the volume of business they would have done with Rhokana and the Copperbelt mines.

36. Federal Correspondence, "Developments in the North: Mining Maintains Lead as Major Industry in the Federation," *South African Mining and Engineering Journal* 66, no. 3251 (1955): 581.

37. United Nations, Economic Commission for Africa, and Food and Agriculture Organisation (hereafter UN/ECA/FAO), *Report on the Economic Development of Zambia* (Ndola, Zambia: Falcon Press Limited, 1964), 9, NAZ 11/57F.

38. UN/ECA/FAO, *Report on the Economic Development of Zambia*, 9.

39. Berger, *Labour, Race and Colonial Rule*, 10.

40. Berger, *Labour, Race and Colonial Rule*, 9.

41. Ronald Prain, "The Position of Copper in the Federal Economy," *South African Mining and Engineering Journal* 67, no. 3304 (1956): 881.

42. Prain, "The Position of Copper in the Federal Economy," 881.

43. Prain, "The Position of Copper in the Federal Economy," 881.

44. Prain, "The Position of Copper in the Federal Economy," 883.

45. Prain, "The Position of Copper in the Federal Economy," 883.

46. Rhokana/Nkana Division, Board of Directors: Review of Operations, 1948–1954, 6, ZCCM 3.8.2A.

47. Rhokana/Nkana Division, Board of Directors: Review of Operations, 1948–1954, 6.

48. Rhokana/Nkana Division, Board of Directors: Review of Operations, 1948–1954, 6.

49. Rhokana/Nkana Division, Board of Directors: Review of Operations, 1948–1954, 6.

50. UN/ECA/FAO, *Report on the Economic Development of Zambia*, 42.

51. RC Limited, *Utilisation of African Labour Report*, January 8, 1957, 24, ZCCM 3.8.1C.

52. RC Limited, *Utilisation of African Labour Report*, 24.

53. RC Limited, *Utilisation of African Labour Report*, 23.

54. Ernest Oppenheimer, "The Advancement of Africans in the Industry," *Optima* 3, no. 3 (1953): 1.

55. RC Limited, *Utilisation of African Labour Report*, 4.

56. UN/ECA/FAO, *Report on the Economic Development of Zambia*, 42.

57. NRCM, *NRCM Yearbook 1956* (Kitwe: NRCM, 1957), Table 17, 69, ZCCM 12.1.9C.

58. Ian R. Phimister, "Corporate Profit and Race in Central African Copper Mining, 1946–1958," *Business History Review* 85, no. 4 (2011): 759.

59. RC Limited, *Utilisation of African Labour Report*, Table 9, 25.

60. Charles A. Perrings, "A Moment in the Proletarianization of the New Middle Class: Race, Value and the Division of Labour in the Copperbelt, 1946–1966," *Journal of Southern African Studies* 6, no. 2 (1980): 183–213.

61. Perrings, "A Moment in the Proletarianization of the New Middle Class," 183–213.

62. *Northern News*, January 31, 1955.

63. *Northern News*, January 31, 1955.

64. *Northern News*, January 31, 1955.

65. Butler, "Business and British Decolonisation," 472–3.

66. *Northern News*, January 31, 1955.

67. T. Scannell, "The African Advancement Agreement," *Horizon* 3, no. 5 (1961): 6–7; *Northern News*, January 31, 1955.

68. Scannell, "The African Advancement Agreement," 6–7.

69. The Commission was appointed in consultation with the mining companies to ascertain whether there was anything to prevent African employees from advancing to the full extent of their capacities in the copper mining industry. This was after the four-party talks on the issue of advancement involving representatives of the two groups of companies, the NRMWU and the AMU, broke down, and a deadlock ensued early in May the same year. For further details, see: NRG, *Report of the Board of Inquiry into the Advancement of Africans in the Copper Mining Industry in Northern Rhodesia* (Lusaka: Government Printer, 1954), 20, NAZ 11/57F.

70. *Northern News*, January 31, 1955.

71. NRMWU and RAA, Minutes of Meeting held in Kitwe, November 3, 1954, ZCCM 10.7.9A.

72. NRMWU and RAA, Minutes of Meeting held in Kitwe, November 3, 1954.

73. NRMWU and RAA, Minutes of Meeting held in Kitwe, November 3, 1954. Other meetings were held on December 13 and 22, 1954.

74. *Northern News*, December 18, 1954.

75. *Northern News*, December 18, 1954.

76. RC Limited, *Summary of Operations*, December 1954–February 1955, 6, ZCCM 3.8.2A; RC Limited, *Summary of Operations*, August–September 1955, 5–6, ZCCM 3.8.2A.

77. NRMWU and RST, Minutes of Meeting held at the Chamber of Mines in Kitwe—Appendix A, January 25, 1955, ZCCM 10.7.9A.

78. NRMWU and RAA, Record of 4th Meeting held at the Chamber of Mines in Kitwe, December 16, 1954, ZCCM 10.7.9A.

79. RST's five categories were (i) identical or ragged-edge jobs that included certain least-skilled jobs on the European schedule, which could be given to Africans with less training; (ii) intermediate jobs that were certain other jobs within the European schedule, some of which could be simplified or subdivided and be given to Africans after some training; (iii) some identical/ragged-edge jobs, which could be valued at rates to be negotiated with the AMU; (iv) certain categories of intermediate jobs, which would require an upgrading of the then African schedule and would attract wages above the rates of the African and be fixed on the European rates and would be negotiated by both the NRMWU and AMU; and (v) certain intermediate jobs with a supervisory element to be given to MASA members whose rates would be negotiated with the MASA, as well as the NRMWU and MOSSA. For more information, see: RST, Statement Setting Out the RST Group of Companies Policy with Regard to African Advancement in Their Copper Mines and Their Proposals in Order to Effect a Solution of the African Advancement Problem, January 21, 1955, ZCCM 10.7.9A. Rhoanglo/RAA's proposed categories were (i) 13 identical/ragged-edge jobs and (ii) 11 jobs, which, although almost all done by Europeans, were generally acknowledged to be within the capacity of the Africans. For details, see: Rhokana/Nkana Division, Directors' Minutes of Meeting, July 30, 1955, ZCCM 3.8.2A; *Northern News*, August 1, 1955.

80. For further information, see: NRG, *Report of the Board of Inquiry into the Advancement of Africans in the Copper Mining Industry in Northern Rhodesia*, 1954, Appendix 3, 34–5.

81. RC Limited, Minutes of Meeting, March 4, 1955, 7, ZCCM 3.8.2A.

82. RC Limited, Minutes of Meeting, March 4, 1955, 7.

83. RC Limited, Minutes of Meeting, March 4, 1955, 8.

84. RC Limited, Minutes of Meeting, March 4, 1955, 8.

85. RC Limited, Minutes of Meeting, March 4, 1955, 9.

86. RC Limited, Minutes of Meeting, March 4, 1955, 9.

87. Scannell, "The African Advancement Agreement," 7; *Northern News*, January 31, 1955.

88. Scannell, "The African Advancement Agreement," 7; *Northern News*, January 31, 1955.

89. AAC, "Topics of the Quarter: African Advancement," *Optima* 5, no. 4 (1955): facing 105.

90. Rhokana/Nkana Division, Directors' Minutes of Meetings, August–September 1955, ZCCM 3.8.2A.

91. Phimister, "Corporate Profit and Race in Central African Copper Mining," 767.

92. AAC, "Topics of the Quarter: African Advancement," facing 105. The initial jobs considered were screwing machine operator, sampler, mechanical loading and appliance driver, overhead crane driver, tripper operator, shunter, underground store man, pump man, anode takeoff operator, holding furnace caster, weigher and loader, crane chaser, screens attendant, cathode shearing machine operator, mobile crane operator, plant environs clean-up handyman, smelter mason's handyman, trench-digging handyman, parks and gardens handyman, sand-filling operator, concrete mixture attendant, underground pipe-fitter, sublevel lasher, and tank-house inspector.

Schedule "A" jobs were those performed by members of the NRMWU at the time of signing this agreement. The importance of the agreement was that merit would be the only criterion in the future choice of a person to fill a schedule "A" vacancy. Schedule "B" jobs were those that would be filled by persons who were not members of the NRMWU and were the highest to which Africans progressed. For details, see: NRG, *Report of the Commission Appointed to Inquire into the Unrest in the Mining Industry in Northern Rhodesia in Recent Months* (Lusaka: Government Printers, 1956), Appendix 5, 74–9, NAZ 11/57H; Rhokana/Nkana Division, Directors' Minutes of Meeting, July 30, 1955, ZCCM 3.8.2A; *Northern News*, September 12, 1955; Scannell, "The African Advancement Agreement," 5.

93. RC Limited, Minutes of Meeting, March 4, 1955, 7, ZCCM 3.8.2A.

94. Berger, *Labour, Race and Colonial Rule*, 122, 124, 126–9; Butler, "Business and British Decolonisation," 460–1; Butler, *Copper Empire*, 208, 224–32; Cohen, "Business and Decolonisation in Central Africa Reconsidered," 647; Andrew Cohen, *The Politics and Economics of Decolonization in Africa: The Failed Experiment of Central African Federation* (London and New York: I.B. Tauris, 2017), 55; Phimister, "Corporate Profit and Race in Central African Copper Mining," 761–70.

95. NRG, *Report of the Commission Appointed to Inquire into the Unrest in the Mining Industry in Northern Rhodesia in Recent Months*, 19.

96. Berger, *Labour, Race and Colonial Rule*, 146; Nsolo Mijere, "One Industry, One Union: The Rise and Governmental Control of the Mineworkers of Zambia, 1930–1982," in *Issues in Zambian Development*, eds. Kwaku Osei-Hwedie and Muna Ndulo (Nyangwe and Roxbury: Omenana, 1985), 383.

97. Mijere, "One Industry, One Union," 384.

98. NRG, *Report of the Commission Appointed to Inquire into the Unrest in the Mining Industry in Northern Rhodesia in Recent Months*, 19.

99. NRCM, *Northern Rhodesia Chamber of Mines Yearbook 1956* (Kitwe: NRCM, 1957), 7, ZCCM 12.1.9C.

100. RC Limited, *Annual Report, 30 June 1956* (Kitwe: Rhokana Head Office, 1956), 7, ZCCM 12.7.2F.

101. NRCM, *Northern Rhodesia Chamber of Mines Yearbook 1956*, 11.

102. NRCM, *Northern Rhodesia Chamber of Mines Yearbook 1956*, 11.

103. RC Limited, *Annual Reports and Accounts*, 1955–1956.

104. RC Limited, *Annual Reports and Accounts*, 1955–1956.

105. *Northern News*, October 25, 1957.

106. *Northern News*, October 25, 1957.

107. RC Limited, *Annual Report, 30 June 1957*, 11.

108. RST, "Kariba and the Copperbelt," *Horizon* 1, no. 3 (1959): 13.

109. RC Limited, *Annual Reports and Accounts*, 1957–1963.

110. RST, "Kariba and the Copperbelt," 13.

111. RST, "Kariba and the Copperbelt," 13.

112. RST, "Kariba and the Copperbelt," 13.

113. Duncan L. Anderson, "Kariba Hydro-Electric Power for Central African Development," *Optima* 6, no. 2 (1956): 37; *Annual Report: Rhokana Corporation Limited, 30th June 1962* (Salisbury: Rhokana Head Office, 1962), 9, ZCCM 12.7.2F.

The construction of the Kariba HEP was the most important project undertaken during the Federation of Rhodesia and Nyasaland, a symbol of cooperation. Though the Copperbelt mines contributed most toward this project, the other funders were the BSA Company, the Colonial Development Corporation, and loans from the Commonwealth Development Finance Corporation, International Bank for Reconstruction and Development, Barclays Bank, and Standard Bank. For the politics surrounding the financing of the scheme by Rhokana and the other Copperbelt mines, see: Prain, *Reflections on an Era: An Autobiography*, 132; Butler, *Copper Empire*, 218–24; Julia Tischler, *Light and Power for a Multiracial Nation: The Kariba Dam Scheme in the Central African Federation* (Basingstoke: Palgrave Macmillan, 2013), 29–33; Cohen, *The Politics and Economics of Decolonization in Africa*, 50–3.

114. NRCM, *NRCM Yearbooks*, 1957–1963.

115. NRCM, *NRCM Yearbooks*, 1957–1963.

116. RST, "World's Deepest Mine Workings Reach 11,000 Feet," *Horizon* 1, no. 3 (1959): 25.

117. RC Limited, *Utilisation of African Labour Report*, 2.

118. RC Limited, *Utilisation of African Labour Report*, 2.

119. RC Limited, *Utilisation of African Labour Report*, 4.

120. RC Limited, *Utilisation of African Labour Report*, 4.

121. RC Limited, *Utilisation of African Labour Report*, 4.

122. Guy C.Z. Mhone, *The Political Economy of a Dual Labour Market in Africa, 1929–1969* (London and Toronto: Associated University Presses, 1982), 174.

123. Mhone, *The Political Economy of a Dual Labour Market in Africa*, 174.

124. Hubert W. Davis and Charlotte H. Buck, "Cobalt," *Minerals Yearbook Review of 1954*, 358–60, images.library.wisc.edu/EcoNatRes/EFacs2/MineralsYearBk/MinYB1954v1/reference/econatres.minyb1954v1.hdavis.pdf (accessed April 6, 2020).

125. RC Limited, *Annual Report, 30 June 1955* (Kitwe: Rhokana Head Office, 1955) 4, 25–6, ZCCM 12.7.2F.

126. RC Limited, *Annual Report, 30 June 1955*, 7.

127. UN/ECA/FAO, *Report on the Economic Development of Zambia*, 11.

128. *Northern News*, October 4, 1957.

129. RST, "The Copper Price, 1956–1959," *Horizon* 1, no. 7 (1959): 42.

130. RC, "Drop in Price of Cobalt Metal," *Rhokana Review* 6, no. 6 (1959): 23.

131. Joseph H. Bilbrey and Dorothy T. McDougal, "Cobalt," *Minerals Yearbook, 1959*, Table 5, 365, images.library.wisc.edu/EcoNatRes/EFacs2/MineralsYearBk/MinYB1959v1/reference/econatres.minyb1959v1.jbilbrey.pdf (accessed April 20, 2020).

132. Bilbrey and McDougal, "Cobalt," 366.

133. RST, "The Copper Price, 1956–1959," 42.

134. RST, "The Copper Price, 1956–1959," 42.

135. RST, "The Copper Price, 1956–1959," 43.

136. RC Limited, *Annual Report: Rhokana Corporation Limited, 30 June 1959* (Salisbury: RC Head Office, 1959), 6, ZCCM 12.7.2F.

137. RST, "The Copper Price, 1956–1959," 43.

138. RST, "The Copper Price, 1956–1959," 43.

139. RST, "The Copper Price, 1956–1959," 43.

140. RST, "The Copper Price, 1956–1959," 43.
141. RST, "The Copper Price, 1956–1959," 43.
142. NRCM, *NRCM Yearbooks*, 1961–1963.
143. Oliver B. Bennett, RC General Manager, Kitwe, to RC/RAA Board of Directors, Salisbury, October 15, 1956, ZCCM T18.6D.
144. For example, AMU vice president, A. Malitongo, was a committee member for the NRANC's Nkana Branch; N.D. Nkoloma, AMU general secretary, held the position of NRANC Nkana branch chairman; J.R. Namitengo, AMU Nkana branch president, was also a committee member for the NRANC at Nkana; and AMU Nkana branch treasurer, A. Kalumbe, was secretary general for the Nyasaland ANC. For further details, see: Bennett to RAA/RC Board of Directors, October 15, 1956.
145. Anirudha Gupta, "Trade Unionism and Politics on the Copperbelt," in *Politics in Zambia*, ed. William Tordoff (Berkeley and Los Angeles: University of California Press, 1974), 293.
146. RC Limited, *Annual Reports and Accounts*, 1960–1963.
147. NRCM, *NRCM Yearbooks*, 1956–1963; RC Limited, *Annual Reports and Accounts*, 1954–1963.
148. For further details, see: United States Bureau of Mines, *Minerals Yearbooks—Metals and Minerals—Cobalt*, 1954–1959, minerals.usgs.gov/minerals/pubs/usbm-myb.html (accessed March 30, 2020).
149. United States Bureau of Mines, *Minerals Yearbooks—Metals and Minerals—Cobalt*, 1954–1959.
150. NRCM, *Northern Rhodesia Chamber of Mines Yearbook 1963* (Salisbury: Mardon Printers, 1964), 23, ZCCM 12.1.9C.
151. NRCM, *Northern Rhodesia Chamber of Mines Yearbook 1963*, 23.
152. NRCM, *Northern Rhodesia Chamber of Mines Yearbook 1963*, 23.
153. Berger, *Labour, Race and Colonial Rule*, 11; RC Limited, *Annual Reports and Accounts*, 1954–1963.
154. RC Limited, *Annual Reports and Accounts*, 1954–1963.
155. UN/ECA/FAO, *Report on the Economic Development of Zambia*, 10.
156. UN/ECA/FAO, *Report on the Economic Development of Zambia*, 10.
157. UN/ECA/FAO, *Report on the Economic Development of Zambia*, 10.
158. UN/ECA/FAO, *Report on the Economic Development of Zambia*, 10.
159. Oliver B. Bennett, General Manager, RC Limited, Memorandum to the Monckton Commission, 12, ZCCM T1.7C.
160. Cohen, "Business and Decolonisation in Central Africa Reconsidered," 642.
161. For a detailed analysis of the copper mining companies and their reactions to the fall of the Federation between 1959 and 1962, see: Butler, "Business and British Decolonisation," passim; Cohen, "Business and Decolonisation in Central Africa Reconsidered," passim.
162. Butler, "Business and British Decolonisation," 474.
163. Butler, "Business and British Decolonisation," 473.
164. Butler, "Business and British Decolonisation," 473.
165. RC Limited, *Annual Report, 30 June 1964* (Lusaka: RC Head Office, 1964), 9, ZCCM 12.7.2F.

166. RC Limited, *Annual Report, 30 June 1964*, 9.

167. RC Limited, *Annual Report, 30 June 1963* (Salisbury: RC Head Office, 1963), 6–7, ZCCM 12.7.2F.

168. RC Limited, *Annual Report, 30 June 1963*, 6–7.

169. RC Limited, *Annual Report, 30 June 1963*, 6–7.

170. For further information, see: Butler, "Business and British Decolonisation," 459–84; and, the quotation is taken from Cohen, "Business and Decolonisation in Central Africa Reconsidered," 643.

CHAPTER 5

1. Anthony Martin, *Minding Their Own Business: Zambia's Struggle against Western Control* (London: Penguin Books, 1975), 39–41, 51, 56; Michael Burawoy, *The Colour of Class on the Copper Mines: From Advancement to Zambianisation* (Manchester: Manchester University Press, 1972), 1–2; Robert H. Bates, *Unions, Parties and Political Development: A Study of Mineworkers in Zambia* (New Haven, CT, and London: Yale University Press, 1971), 7–26; Elena L. Berger, *Labour, Race and Colonial Rule: The Copperbelt from 1924 to Independence* (Oxford: Clarendon Press, 1974), 218–26; Richard L. Sklar, *Corporate Power in an African State: The Political Impact of Multinational Mining Companies in Zambia* (Los Angeles: University of California Press, 1975), 16, 35–6; Phillip Daniel, *Africanisation, Nationalisation and Inequality: Mining Labour and the Copperbelt in Zambian Development* (London: Cambridge University Press, 1979), 8–22.

2. Martin, *Minding Their Own Business*, 39–41, 51, 56; Burawoy, *The Colour of Class on the Copper Mines*, 1–2; Bates, *Unions, Parties and Political Development*, 7–26; Berger, *Labour, Race and Colonial Rule*, 218–26; Sklar, *Corporate Power in an African State*, 16, 35–6; Daniel, *Africanisation, Nationalisation and Inequality*, 8–22.

3. Martin, *Minding Their Own Business*, 41; Burawoy, *The Colour of Class on the Copper Mines*, 2.

4. Simon M. Kapwepwe, Republic of Zambia: Budget Address by the Vice President, January 30, 1969, 3–4, United National Independence Party Archive (hereafter UNIP) 1–3–5; *Mining Mirror*, September 4, 1973. Reprint of full text of President Kenneth Kaunda's speech when he announced the changes in Zambia's mining industry.

5. Burawoy, *The Colour of Class on the Copper Mines*, 1–2; Daniel, *Africanisation, Nationalisation and Inequality*, 8–22.

6. Bates, *Unions, Parties and Political Development*, 7–26.

7. Economic liberalization involves deliberate reforms by the government aimed at reducing restrictions on the free movement of capital through the unification of the exchange rate, as well as the abolition or reduction of tariffs, taxes, subsidies, quotas, and licensing rules. For details about economic liberalization and its effects in Zambia between 1964 and 1967, see: Martin, *Minding Their Own Business*, 55–73.

8. Martin, *Minding Their Own Business*, 39–41, 51, 56.

9. Martin, *Minding Their Own Business*, 44.

10. John Lungu, "The Politics of Reforming Zambia's Mining Tax Regime," *Southern Africa Resource Watch* 8 (2009): 11; Peter Slinn, "The Legacy of the British South Africa Company: The Historical Background," in *Economic Independence and Zambian Copper: A Case Study of Foreign Investment*, eds. Mark Bostock and Charles Harvey (New York: Praeger Press, 1972), 365–85.

11. Bates, *Unions, Parties and Political Development*, 7–26; Berger, *Labour, Race and Colonial Rule*, 218–26; Burawoy, *The Colour of Class on the Copper Mines*, 1–2; Daniel, *Africanisation, Nationalisation and Inequality*, 8–22.

12. Sklar, *Corporate Power in an African State*, 34–40.

13. Sklar, *Corporate Power in an African State*, 35.

14. Ronald L. Prain, *Reflections on an Era: An Autobiography* (Letchworth, England: The Garden City Press, 1981), 158; Sklar, *Corporate Power in an African State*, 35–6.

15. Slinn, "The Legacy of the British South Africa Company: The Historical Background," 365–85.

16. Andrew Sardanis, *Zambia: The First 50 Years* (London and New York: I.B. Tauris, 2014), 62.

17. RC Limited, *Review by the Chairman, 28 October 1966* (Lusaka: RC Head Office, 1966), 2, ZCCM 12.7.2F.

18. Sardanis, *Zambia: The First 50 Years*, 62.

19. RC Limited, *43rd Annual Report 1965* (Lusaka: RC Head Office, 1965), 4, ZCCM 12.7.2F; RC Limited, *Review by the Chairman, 28 October 1966*, 1.

20. Sklar, *Corporate Power in an African State*, 53.

21. Lungu, "The Politics of Reforming Zambia's Mining Tax Regime," 11.

22. Lungu, "The Politics of Reforming Zambia's Mining Tax Regime," 11.

23. UN/ECA/FAO, *Report on the Economic Development of Zambia* (Ndola, Zambia: Falcon Press Limited, 1964), 42, NAZ 11/57F.

24. UN/ECA/FAO, *Report on the Economic Development of Zambia*, 42.

25. In 1953, there were 2,500 Africans in partly skilled jobs. By independence, however, this figure rose to 8,000. Similarly, in 1953, over 55% of the total African labor force was concentrated in the lowest grade of employment, but by 1964, this figure had declined to 30%. For more information, see: T.D.A. Etheredge, "Zambianisation on the Copperbelt," *Optima* 19, no. 4 (1969): 183.

26. RC Limited, *Annual Report: Rhokana Corporation Limited, 30 June 1959* (Salisbury: RC Head Office, 1959), 17, ZCCM 12.7.2F.

27. Etheredge, "Zambianisation on the Copperbelt," 183–5.

28. RC Limited, *43rd Annual Report 1965*, 6; Daniel, *Africanisation, Nationalisation and Inequality*, 98.

29. RC Limited, *43rd Annual Report 1965*, 6; Daniel, *Africanisation, Nationalisation and Inequality*, 98.

30. Burawoy, *The Colour of Class on the Copper Mines*, 29–30.

31. Zambianisation Committee (Mines), Minutes of Meeting of the Committee on Zambianisation in the Mining Industry held in Lusaka, April 19, 1967.

32. Zambianisation Committee (Mines), Minutes of Meeting of the Committee on Zambianisation in the Mining Industry held in Lusaka.

33. GRZ, *Manpower Report: A Report and Statistical Handbook on Manpower, Education, Training and Zambianisation, 1965–1966* (Lusaka: Government Printer, 1966), 1.

34. Etheredge, "Zambianisation on the Copperbelt," 182–7.

35. Etheredge, "Zambianisation on the Copperbelt," 182–7.

36. Etheredge, "Zambianisation on the Copperbelt," 182–7.

37. Secretary, Ministry of Labour, Lusaka, to Labour Officers, Ndola, Kitwe, Mufulira, Chingola, Luanshya, Bancroft, and Broken Hill, August 18, 1967, NAZ MLSS 1/18/3.

38. Patricio Meller and Anthony Simpasa, "Role of Copper in the Chilean and Zambian Economies: Main Economic and Policy Issues," Global Development Network Working Paper Series No. 43, 2011, 23.

39. Secretary, Ministry of Labour, to Labour Officers, August 18, 1967.

40. Mineworkers' Union of Zambia Headquarters (hereafter MUZ HQ), *A Historical Analysis of MUZ in the Harmonisation of Industrial Relations in ZCCM: An Overview of MUZ Objectives*, 1990, 13–4. At the time of this research, the records at MUZ HQ were in a poor state without reference numbers because of a major fire, which destroyed majority of the files in the 1970s. However, they are currently being cataloged and digitized following a grant secured by Duncan Money from the International Institute of Social History in Amsterdam.

41. Marcia M. Burdette, "Industrial Development in Zambia, Zimbabwe and Malawi: The Primacy of Politics," in *Studies in the Economic History of Southern Africa, Vol. 1: The Front-line States*, eds. Zbigniew A. Konczacki, Jane L. Parpart, and Timothy M. Shaw (London: Frank Cass and Co. Ltd., 1990), 85.

42. Burawoy, *The Colour of Class on the Copper Mines*, 2–3.

43. Ministry of Labour and Social Services, Strikes and Disputes—Kitwe: Report on a Labour Dispute, May 14, 1966, NAZ MLSS 1/25/137. Workers offering essential services included underground machine operators and those working in the plant, smelter, concentrator, and refinery.

44. RC Limited, *44th Annual Report 1966* (Lusaka: Rhokana Head Office, 1966), 5, ZCCM 12.7.2F.

45. RC Limited, *Review by the Chairman, 28 October 1966*, 3.

46. RC Limited, *Review by the Chairman, 28 October 1966*, 3.

47. Guy C.Z. Mhone, *The Political Economy of a Dual Labour Market in Africa, 1929–1969* (London and Toronto: Associated University Presses, 1982), 165.

48. GRZ, *Report of the Commission of Inquiry into the Mining Industry 1966* (Lusaka: The Government Printer, 1966), 163.

49. RC Limited, *Review by the Chairman, 28 October 1966*, 1.

50. RC Limited, *47th Annual Report 1969* (Lusaka: Rhokana Head Office, 1969), 6, ZCCM 12.7.2F.

51. CISB Limited, *Disciplinary Statistics in the Mines*, November 1966–May 1978, ZCCM 6.10.1A.

52. CISB Limited, *Disciplinary Report–Rhokana Corporation Limited*, November 1966, 1–2, ZCCM 6.10.1A.

53. CISB Limited, *Disciplinary Report–Rhokana Corporation Limited*, 1–2.

54. CISB Limited, *Disciplinary Report–Rhokana Corporation Limited*, 1–2.

55. Zambianisation Committee (Mines), Trainees and Trained Staff Employees of Rhokana Corporation Limited Report on their Grievances, September 29, 1969, 1, NAZ MLSS 1/18/3.

56. RC Limited, *44th Annual Report 1966*, 9.

57. RC Limited, *Annual Report, 30 June 1960*, 12; RC Limited, *Annual Report, 30 June 1964*, 12; RC Limited, *47th Annual Report 1969*, 16.

58. RC Limited, *Annual Reports and Accounts*, 1957–1969.

59. CISB Limited, *Copperbelt of Zambia Mining Industry Yearbooks*, 1965–1968.

60. RC Limited, *43rd Annual Report 1965*, 4; RC Limited, *44th Annual Report 1966*, 5.

61. RC Limited, *Review by the Chairman, 28 October 1966*, 1.

62. RC Limited, *Review by the Chairman, 28 October 1966*, 1.

63. RC Limited, *45th Annual Report 1967* (Lusaka: RC Head Office, 1967), 5, ZCCM 12.7.2F.

64. RC Limited, *46th Annual Report 1968* (Lusaka: RC Head Office, 1968), 6, ZCCM 12.7.2F.

65. RC Limited, *45th Annual Report 1967*, 5.

66. RC Limited, *Annual Reports and Accounts*, 1967–1969.

67. Simon M. Kapwepwe, Republic of Zambia: Budget Address by the Vice President, January 30, 1969, 3–4, UNIP 1–3–5. For a better appreciation of the impact of UDI on Zambia, see variously: Robert B. Sutcliffe, "Zambia and the Strains of UDI," *Royal Institute of International Affairs* 23, no. 12 (1967): 506–11; Andrew J. de Roche, "You Can't Fight Guns and Knives: National Security and Zambian Responses to UDI, 1965–1973," in *One Zambia, Many Histories: Towards a History of Post-colonial Zambia*, eds. Jan-Bart Gewald and Marja Hinfelaar (Leiden, the Netherlands: Brill, 2008), 77–97.

68. Burawoy, *The Colour of Class on the Copper Mines*, 1.

69. Burawoy, *The Colour of Class on the Copper Mines*, 1.

70. CISB Limited, *Copperbelt of Zambia Mining Industry Yearbooks*, 1965–1968; CISB Limited, *Mining Industry Yearbook of Zambia 1969* (Kitwe: CISB, 1969), 46, ZCCM 12.1.9C.

71. RC Limited, *Review by the Chairman, 28 October 1966*, 1.

72. Thomas R. Navin, *Copper Mining and Management* (Arizona: University of Arizona Press, 1978), 167.

73. RC Limited, *Review by the Chairman, 28 October 1966*, 1.

74. RC Limited, *Review by the Chairman, 28 October 1966*, 1.

75. RC Limited, *Review by the Chairman, 28 October 1966*, 1. High demand gave Rhokana the opportunity to sell previously accumulated stockpiles.

76. RC Limited, *45th Annual Report 1967*, 5.

77. RC Limited, *45th Annual Report 1967*, 5.

78. Sklar, *Corporate Power in an African State*, 80.

79. CISB Limited, *Mining Industry Yearbook of Zambia 1969*, 40.

80. Kapwepwe, Republic of Zambia: Budget Address, January 30, 1969, 3, 10; RC Limited, *Annual Reports and Accounts*, 1968–1969.

81. CISB Limited, *Copperbelt of Zambia Mining Industry Yearbooks*, 1965–1968; CISB Limited, *Mining Industry Yearbook of Zambia 1969*, 33.

82. RC Limited, *Annual Reports and Accounts*, 1964–1969.

83. Mhone, *The Political Economy of a Dual Labour Market in Africa*, Table 26, 210–1.

84. Mhone, *The Political Economy of a Dual Labour Market in Africa*, Table 26, 210–1.

85. Kapwepwe, Republic of Zambia: Budget Address, January 30, 1969, 4; *Financial Times*, April 20, 1968; *Times of Zambia*, April 20, 1968; *Times*, April 20, 1968; *Sun*, April 20, 1968; *Zambia Mail*, April 23, 1968.

86. Martin, *Minding Their Own Business*, 76.

87. *Mining Mirror*, September 4, 1973. Reprint of full text of President Kaunda's speech when he announced the changes in Zambia's mining industry.

88. RC Limited, *46th Annual Report 1968*, 1.

89. Sklar, *Corporate Power in an African State*, 55.

90. Sklar, *Corporate Power in an African State*, 55.

91. Sklar, *Corporate Power in an African State*, 55.

92. Between 1964 and 1969, unappropriated profits out of total net profits of £73,814,000 amounted to £8,218,720. For further details, see: RC Limited, *Annual Reports and Accounts*, 1964–1969.

93. *Birmingham Post*, May 3, 1968.

94. *Birmingham Post*, May 3, 1968.

95. Martin, *Minding Their Own Business*, 92.

96. Kapwepwe, Republic of Zambia: Budget Address, January 30, 1969, 4.

97. RC Limited, *46th Annual Report 1968*, 6.

98. RC Limited, *46th Annual Report 1968*, 6.

99. RC Limited, *47th Annual Report 1969*, 5.

100. Stuart J. Barton, *Policy Signals and Market Responses: A 50-Year History of Zambia's Relationship with Foreign Capital* (Basingstoke: Palgrave Macmillan, 2016), 10–1.

101. Kapwepwe, Republic of Zambia: Budget Address, January 30, 1969, 4.

102. RC Limited, *47th Annual Report 1969*, 5.

103. Martin, *Minding Their Own Business*, 165, 168.

104. RC Limited, *47th Annual Report 1969*, 6.

105. RC Limited, *47th Annual Report 1969*, 6.

106. RC Limited, *47th Annual Report 1969*, 6.

107. Kenneth D. Kaunda, Speeches by His Excellency, 1972, 4, UNIP 1–3–9.

108. Kaunda, Speeches, 1972, 3; Miles Larmer, "Zambia's Mineworkers and Political Change, 1964–1991" (PhD thesis, University of Sheffield, 2004), 84. By this point, AMAX owned 42.3% shares in RST (Zambia). For further details, see: Sklar, *Corporate Power in an African State*, 44.

CHAPTER 6

1. Greg Lanning and Marti Mueller, *Africa Undermined: A History of the Mining Companies and the Underdevelopment of Africa* (Ontario: Penguin Books Limited, 1979), 209.

2. Mining and Industrial Development Corporation (hereafter MINDECO) Limited, *Zambia's Mining Industry* (Lusaka: MINDECO, 1972), 7.

3. MINDECO, *Zambia's Mining Industry*, 7.

4. MINDECO, *Zambia's Mining Industry*, 7.

5. Lanning and Mueller, *Africa Undermined*, 209, 211.

6. Lanning and Mueller, *Africa Undermined*, 209, 211.

7. Lanning and Mueller, *Africa Undermined*, 209, 211.

8. Lanning and Mueller, *Africa Undermined*, 209, 211.

9. Lanning and Mueller, *Africa Undermined*, 212.

10. MINDECO, *Zambia's Mining Industry*, 17.

11. Richard L. Sklar, *Corporate Power in an African State: The Political Impact of Multinational Mining Companies in Zambia* (Los Angeles: University of California Press, 1975), 71.

12. Kenneth D. Kaunda, Speech by His Excellency on State Participation in the Mining Industry, March 10, 1972, 4, UNIP 1–3–9.

13. John Lungu, "The Politics of Reforming Zambia's Mining Tax Regime," *Southern Africa Resource Watch* 8 (2009): 11.

14. Oliver S. Saasa, "Determinants of Zambia's Policies towards the Mining Industry: 1964–1984," in *Issues in Zambian Development*, eds. Kwaku Osei-Hwedie and Muna Ndulo (Roxbury, MA: Library of Congress, 1985), 363.

15. Lungu, "The Politics of Reforming Zambia's Mining Tax Regime," 11.

16. Saasa, "Determinants of Zambia's Policies towards the Mining Industry," 363.

17. MINDECO, *Zambia's Mining Industry*, 7.

18. Lanning and Mueller, *Africa Undermined*, 439; Kaunda, Speech by His Excellency on State Participation in the Mining Industry, 4; *Mining Mirror*, August 21, 1973.

19. Lanning and Mueller, *Africa Undermined*, 211.

20. Lanning and Mueller, *Africa Undermined*, 211.

21. As discussed in chapter 1, Zambia partially followed the example of Chile, which introduced a 51% nationalization in the mining sector in June 1969. In addition, Zambia adopted some ideas from partial nationalization policies introduced in the mining sectors of Guinea in 1960 and Tanzania in 1967. For further details about the similarities and differences of nationalization policies in Africa, see: Lanning and Mueller, *Africa Undermined*, 439.

22. Lanning and Mueller, *Africa Undermined*, 96.

23. Lanning and Mueller, *Africa Undermined*, 211.

24. Kaunda, Speech by His Excellency on State Participation in the Mining Industry, 3.

25. *Mining Mirror*, August 21, 1973.

26. Richard L. Sklar, "Zambia's Response to the Rhodesian Unilateral Declaration of Independence," in *Politics in Zambia*, ed. William Tordoff (Berkeley and Los Angeles: University of California Press, 1974), 321.

27. Saasa, "Determinants of Zambia's Policies towards the Mining Industry," 358.

28. RC Limited, 47th Annual Report 1969, 5.

29. CISB Limited, *Mining Industry Yearbook of Zambia 1969* (Kitwe: CISB, 1969), 52, ZCCM 12.1.9C.

30. CISB Limited, *Mining Industry Yearbook of Zambia 1969*, 51.

31. MINDECO, *MINDECO Mining Yearbook of Zambia 1970* (Kitwe: CISB, 1971), 55, ZCCM 12.1.9C. In the MINDECO mining yearbooks, the figures are indicated in hectares. For easy comparison, they have been converted here into acres using the formula 1 hectare = 2.471 acres.

32. *Mining Mirror*, 26 March 1982; MINDECO, *Zambia's Mining Industry*, 8, 17.

33. Kaunda, Speech by His Excellency on State Participation in the Mining Industry, 4–5. Upon issuing new mining licenses to various companies, the government envisaged expansion in copper production from 670,000 metric tons in 1970 to about 900,000 tons by 1975.

34. MINDECO, *Zambia's Mining Industry*, 8, 17.

35. MINDECO, *Zambia's Mining Industry*, 8.

36. Manpower Planning, Training and Zambianisation (hereafter MPTZ), *Opportunities for Graduates for Zambia's Mining Industry* (Kitwe: Copper Industry Service Bureau, 1978), 17.

37. MINDECO, *Zambia's Mining Industry*, 8.

38. MPTZ, *Opportunities for Graduates for Zambia's Mining Industry*, 17.

39. MPTZ, *Opportunities for Graduates for Zambia's Mining Industry*, 17.

40. MPTZ, *Opportunities for Graduates for Zambia's Mining Industry*, 18.

41. Rokana Mine Division, Employment Returns, 1970, ZCCM T8.2A.

42. Lanning and Mueller, *Africa Undermined*, 217.

43. Lanning and Mueller, *Africa Undermined*, 218.

44. Lanning and Mueller, *Africa Undermined*, 218.

45. Lanning and Mueller, *Africa Undermined*, 218.

46. Lanning and Mueller, *Africa Undermined*, 218.

47. Sklar, *Corporate Power in an African State*, 75–6.

48. Sklar, *Corporate Power in an African State*, 75–6. In the 1969 Agreement, the government was obliged to pay around K28.7 million per year as compensation to NCCM and RCM. This amount was to be paid out of government's copper dividend earnings over a period of 12 years. The government did not envisage rising cost of sales and a slackening of industrial activity, which affected the demand and price of copper.

49. Lanning and Mueller, *Africa Undermined*, 217.

50. Nchanga Consolidated Copper Mines (hereafter NCCM) Limited, *Annual Reports*, 1971–1974, ZCCM 11.1.1F; ZCCM Industrial Projects Department (hereafter IPD), *Zambia Copper Sector Survey* (Kitwe: IPD, 1981), 32, ZCCM 11.7.9C.

51. Lanning and Mueller, *Africa Undermined*, 220.

52. Lanning and Mueller, *Africa Undermined*, 218.

53. Roan Consolidated Mines (hereafter RCM) Limited, *Annual Report 1973* (Ndola, Zambia: RCM Central Services Division, 1973), 9, ZCCM 11.1.1F.

54. NCCM Limited, *Annual Report 1971* (Lusaka: NCCM Head Office, 1971), 1, ZCCM 11.1.1F.

55. NCCM Limited, *Annual Report 1971*, 3.

56. Sklar, *Corporate Power in an African State*, 77.

57. Lanning and Mueller, *Africa Undermined*, 220.

58. Andrew Sardanis, *Zambia: The First 50 Years* (London and New York: I.B. Tauris, 2014), 82.

59. Lanning and Mueller, *Africa Undermined*, 220, 222.

60. Lanning and Mueller, *Africa Undermined*, 222.

61. Lanning and Mueller, *Africa Undermined*, 222.

62. Sardanis, *Zambia: The First 50 Years*, 82.

63. Charles B. Muchimba (director of research MUZ HQ) in discussion with the author, Kitwe, October 28, 2017.

64. Lanning and Mueller, *Africa Undermined*, 223.

65. Andrew Sardanis (former permanent secretary and INDECO chief executive) in discussion with the author, Lusaka, August 24, 2017. Sardanis held high positions in government during the first phase of nationalization in Zambia. He was INDECO chief executive from 1965 to 1968, worked as permanent secretary in the Ministry of State Participation, and at the same time, held the same position in the Ministry of Finance between 1969 and 1971. For further information about Sardanis's assessment, see: Sardanis, *Zambia: The First 50 Years*, 83–4.

66. Sardanis interviewed by author, August 24, 2017. As a wave of decolonization swept across Africa, Lonrho began to snap up investments in the continent, making the company the largest and most widely established across regions. But Tiny Rowland's dubious business transactions were frowned upon not only in Africa but also in the United Kingdom.

67. Sardanis in discussion with the author.

68. Lanning and Mueller, *Africa Undermined*, 224.

69. Sardanis, *Zambia: The First 50 Years*, 85.

70. Sardanis in discussion with the author.

71. Sardanis, *Zambia: The First 50 Years*, 85.

72. Sardanis in discussion with the author.

73. Lanning and Mueller, *Africa Undermined*, 223.

74. NCCM Limited, *Annual Report 1974* (Lusaka: NCCM Head Office, 1974), 5, ZCCM 11.1.1F.

75. NCCM Limited, *Annual Report 1974*, 5.

76. ZCCM IPD, *Zambia Copper Sector Survey*, 7.

77. Sardanis, *Zambia: The First 50 Years*, 83.

78. Sklar, *Corporate Power in an African State*, 83.

79. Sklar, *Corporate Power in an African State*, 83.

80. Francis Kaunda (former RST executive secretary, NCCM managing director, and ZCCM chief executive) in discussion with the author, Lusaka, October 25, 2017.

Like Sardanis, Francis Kaunda held high positions in the Zambian copper industry during nationalization. He worked as RST executive secretary for business and sales (1969–1972), MEMACO managing director (1973–1974), NCCM managing director (1974–1981), and ZCCM chief executive (1982–1991).

81. For a detailed understanding of the military coup and its impact on the Chilean mining industry, see: Thomas M. Klubock, "Copper Workers, Organized Labor, and Popular Protest under Military Rule in Chile, 1973–1986," *International Labor and Working-Class History* 52 (1997): 106–33; Gavin Keeton and Mike Beer, "MIASA Position on State Participation in Mining," Paper for the Mining Industries Association of Southern Africa (Johannesburg: MIASA, 2011), 31.

82. NCCM Limited, *Annual Report 1974*, 5.

83. Lanning and Mueller, *Africa Undermined*, 224.

84. Lanning and Mueller, *Africa Undermined*, 224.

85. National Council, Speeches: "Hard Work Is the Answer," Addresses to and Resolutions of the United National Independence Party at the Mulungushi Hall, Lusaka, December 14–17, 1974, UNIP 1–3–17.

86. NCCM Limited, *Annual Report 1971*, 3.

87. NCCM Limited, *Annual Report 1971*, 3.

88. NCCM Limited, *Annual Report 1971*, 3.

89. NCCM Limited, *Nkana Mining Area Annual Report on Operations*, April 1, 1979–March 31, 1980, 68, ZCCM 2.6.4A.

90. Sardanis in discussion with the author.

91. Andrew Sardanis, *Africa: Another Side of the Coin: Northern Rhodesia's Final Years and Zambia's Nationhood* (London and New York: I.B. Tauris, 2003), 233–4.

92. Sardanis in discussion with the author.

93. Sardanis in discussion with the author.

94. MPTZ, *Opportunities for Graduates for Zambia's Mining Industry*, 14.

95. Phillip Daniel, *Africanisation, Nationalisation and Inequality: Mining Labour and the Copperbelt in Zambian Development* (London: Cambridge University Press, 1979), 98.

96. NRG, *Report of the Commission Appointed to Inquire into the Unrest in the Mining Industry in Northern Rhodesia in Recent Months* (Lusaka: Government Printers, 1956), 6, NAZ 11/57/H.

97. NRG, *Report of the Commission Appointed to Inquire into the Unrest in the Mining Industry in Northern Rhodesia in Recent Months*, 6.

98. *Mining Mirror*, October 24, 1974.

99. Kankasa Chibesakunda (former member of UNIP central committee) in discussion with the author, Lusaka, September 23, 2017. Chibesakunda is one of the first female politicians in Zambia and was once High Commissioner for Kenya and member of the Central Committee of the UNIP during nationalization.

100. Chibesakunda in discussion with the author.

101. Steve Mulenga (former forklift driver) in discussion with the author, Kitwe, September 16, 2017; Cosmas Kabanda (former stick handler) in discussion with the author, Kitwe, September 17, 2017. In the past three decades, women have made significant inroads in holding technical, administrative, and supervisory jobs in the

Zambian mining sector. For further details about female workers in underground mines in Zambia, see: James Musonda, "Undermining Gender: Women Mineworkers at the Rock Face in a Zambian Underground Mine," *Anthropology Southern Africa* 43, no. 1 (2020): 32–42.

102. John Mukunka (former crane driver) in discussion with the author, Kitwe, September 18, 2017; Charles Nyerenda (former crane driver) in discussion with the author, Kitwe, September 18, 2017.

103. *Mining Mirror*, October 24, 1974.

104. *Mining Mirror*, October 24, 1974.

105. *Mining Mirror*, January 24, 1975.

106. *Mining Mirror*, January 24, 1975.

107. *Mining Mirror*, October 3, 1975.

108. *Mining Mirror*, November 28, 1975.

109. *Mining Mirror*, December 12, 1975.

110. *Mining Mirror*, December 12, 1975.

111. *Mining Mirror*, August 28, 1987.

112. Michael Burawoy, "The Colour of Class Revisited: Four Decades of Postcolonialism in Zambia," *Journal of Southern African Studies* 40, no. 5 (2014): 967.

113. Lanning and Mueller, *Africa Undermined*, 213.

114. Lanning and Mueller, *Africa Undermined*, 216.

115. Zambianisation Tour, *Report on the Progress of Zambianisation in All the Mines on the Copperbelt*, April 29, 1977, p. 30, MUZ HQ.

116. Zambianisation Tour, *Report on the Progress of Zambianisation in All the Mines on the Copperbelt*, 26.

117. Zambianisation Tour, *Report on the Progress of Zambianisation in All the Mines on the Copperbelt*, 26.

118. Zambianisation Tour, *Report on the Progress of Zambianisation in All the Mines on the Copperbelt*, 27.

119. MINDECO Limited, *Mining Yearbooks of Zambia*, 1971–1972; CISB Limited, *Zambia Mining Yearbooks*, 1973–1980; Daniel, *Africanisation, Nationalisation and Inequality*, 87–9.

120. ZCCM IPD, *Zambia Copper Sector Survey*, 10–1.

121. ZCCM IPD, *Zambia Copper Sector Survey*, 12.

122. NCCM Limited, *Annual Report 1971*, 3.

123. NCCM Limited, *Annual Report 1974*, 9.

124. NCCM Limited, *Annual Report 1976* (Lusaka: NCCM Head Office, 1976), 9, ZCCM 11.1.1F.

125. NCCM Limited, *Annual Report 1976*, 10.

126. NCCM Limited, *Annual Report 1976*, 10.

127. NCCM Limited, *Annual Report 1977* (Lusaka: NCCM Head Office, 1977), 8, ZCCM 11.1.1F.

128. ZCCM Deputy Director of Operations, Kitwe, to ZCCM Director, Human Resources, Lusaka, August 15, 1989, MUZ HQ.

129. ZCCM Deputy Director of Operations, Kitwe, to ZCCM Director, Human Resources, Lusaka.

130. ZCCM Deputy Director of Operations, Kitwe, to ZCCM Director, Human Resources, Lusaka.

131. ZCCM Deputy Director of Operations, Kitwe, to ZCCM Director, Human Resources, Lusaka.

132. ZCCM IPD, *Zambia Copper Sector Survey*, 9.

133. General Secretary, Zambia Congress of Trade Unions (ZCTU), Report presented at the 4th Annual Conference held in the Rokana Cinema in Kitwe, May 21–24, 1970, 1, MUZ HQ.

134. ZCCM Limited, *Labour Relations on the Copperbelt*, 1930–1982, 15–6, ZCCM 11.8.3C; MINDECO Limited, *MINDECO Mining Yearbook of Zambia 1971* (Kitwe: Copper Industry Service Bureau, 1972), 14, ZCCM 12.1.9C.

135. *Mining Mirror*, October 31, 1973.

136. *Mining Mirror*, October 31, 1973.

137. For a detailed analysis of mineworkers' reaction to UNIP's desire to control them between 1964 and 1981, see: Miles Larmer, "Zambia's Mineworkers and Political Change, 1964–1991" (PhD thesis, University of Sheffield, 2004), 73–213; Miles Larmer, "Zambia's Mineworkers and the Labour Movement's Resistance to the One-party State, 1973–1981," *South African Historical Journal* 56, no. 1 (2006): 154–76.

138. For further details, see: Miles Larmer, "Unrealistic Expectations? Zambia's Mineworkers from Independence to the One-party State, 1964–1972," *Journal of Historical Sociology* 18, no. 4 (2005): 338–40.

139. ZCCM IPD, *Zambia Copper Sector Survey*, 37.

140. ZCCM IPD, *Zambia Copper Sector Survey*, 37–8.

141. *Mining Mirror*, October 12, 1982.

142. Burawoy, "The Colour of Class Revisited: Four Decades of Post-colonialism in Zambia," 965.

143. NCCM Limited, *Annual Report 1980* (Lusaka: NCCM Head Office, 1980), 35, ZCCM 11.1.1F; ZCCM IPD, *Zambia Copper Sector Survey*, 35.

144. NCCM Limited, *Annual Report 1980*, 35; ZCCM IPD, *Zambia Copper Sector Survey*, 35.

145. NCCM Limited, *Annual Report 1980*, 35; ZCCM IPD, *Zambia Copper Sector Survey*, 35.

146. ZCCM IPD, *Zambia Copper Sector Survey*, 35.

147. ZCCM IPD, *Zambia Copper Sector Survey*, 35.

148. *Mining Mirror*, January 30, 1987; *Mining Mirror*, January 27, 1989; NCCM Limited, *Annual Reports*, 1971–1981.

149. For more details about the Mufulira mine disaster and its impact on the Zambian copper industry, see: Alfred Tembo, "After the Deluge: Appraising the 1970 Mufulira Mine Disaster in Zambia," *Historia* 64, no. 2 (2019): 109–31.

150. Venkata S. Vutukuri and Raghu N. Singh, "Mine Inundation: Case Histories," *Mine Water and the Environment* 14, no. 9 (1995): 120; GRZ, *The Mufulira Mine Accident: Final Report on the Causes and Circumstances of the Disaster Which Occurred on September 25, 1970* (Lusaka: Government Printer, 1971), 16, 19.

151. NCCM Limited, *Annual Report 1980*, 37.

152. NCCM Limited, *Annual Report 1974*, 22.

153. NCCM Limited, *Annual Report 1974*, 22.

154. GRZ, *A Submission to the World Bank: Rehabilitation Projects within the Zambian Copper Mining Industry* (Lusaka: Government Printer, 1982), 16, ZCCM W2.2.2G.

155. NCCM Limited, *Annual Reports*, 1974–1976.

156. NCCM Limited, *Annual Report 1971*, 2.

157. NCCM Limited, *Annual Report 1974*, 22; NCCM Limited, *Annual Report 1975* (Lusaka: NCCM Head Office, 1975), 5, ZCCM 11.1.1F.

158. NCCM Limited, *Annual Report 1971*, 2; NCCM Limited, *Annual Report 1975*, 5.

159. NCCM Limited, *Annual Report 1974*, 5.

160. *Mining Mirror*, July 9, 1974.

161. NCCM Limited, *Annual Report 1971*, 2; NCCM Limited, *Annual Report 1974*, 22.

162. NCCM Limited, *Annual Report 1974*, 22.

163. NCCM Limited, *Annual Report 1981* (Lusaka: NCCM Head Office, 1981), 5, ZCCM 11.1.1F.

164. ZCCM IPD, *Zambia Copper Sector Survey*, 33.

165. ZCCM IPD, *Zambia Copper Sector Survey*, 20.

166. ZCCM IPD, *Zambia Copper Sector Survey*, 42–3.

167. NCCM Limited, *Nkana Mining Area Annual Report on Operations*, April 1, 1979–March 31, 1980, 53.

168. NCCM Limited, *Annual Report 1971*, 3.

169. Sue Onslow and Anna-Mart van Wyk, *Southern Africa in the Cold War, Post-1974* (Washington, DC: Wilson Center, 2013), 45–73; Clarence Chongo, "Decolonising Southern Africa: A History of Zambia's Role in Zimbabwe's Liberation Struggle, 1964–1979" (PhD thesis, University of Pretoria, 2015), 111–9.

170. CISB Limited, *Zambia Mining Yearbook 1979* (Kitwe: CISB, 1980), 19, ZCCM 12.1.9C.

171. *Mining Mirror*, January 10, 1975.

172. *Mining Mirror*, January 10, 1975.

173. NCCM Limited, *Annual Report 1975*, 7; NCCM Limited, *Annual Report 1976*, 7.

174. NCCM Limited, *Annual Report 1977*, 6.

175. NCCM Limited, *Annual Report 1976*, 7.

176. NCCM Limited, *Annual Report 1978* (Lusaka: NCCM Head Office, 1978), 3, 5, ZCCM 11.1.1F.

177. NCCM Limited, *Annual Report 1978*, 5.

178. NCCM Limited, *Annual Report 1978*, 5.

179. NCCM Limited, *Annual Report 1978*, 7.

180. NCCM Limited, *Annual Report 1978*, 7.

181. ZCCM IPD, *Zambia Copper Sector Survey*, 4.

182. ZCCM IPD, *Zambia Copper Sector Survey*, 38.

183. ZCCM IPD, *Zambia Copper Sector Survey*, 8.

184. NCCM Limited, *Annual Reports*, 1971–1981.

185. The price of cobalt more than quadrupled on the international market from an average of US$3.98 per pound in 1975 to US$20 per pound in 1978. For further details about the cobalt market in the 1970s, see: United States Bureau of Mines, *Minerals Yearbooks—Metals and Minerals—Cobalt*, 1970–1980, minerals.usgs.gov/minerals/pubs/usbmmyb.html (accessed April 4, 2020).

186. ZCCM IPD, *Zambia Copper Sector Survey*, 4.

187. NCCM Limited, *Nkana Mining Area Annual Report on Operations*, April 1, 1979–March 31, 1980, 47. Note that smelter production is not the same as finished production, the latter referring to purified or refined metal.

188. Simon J. Cunningham, *The Copper Industry in Zambia: Foreign Mining Companies in a Developing Country* (New York: Praeger Publishers, 1981), 269–82; Stuart J. Barton, *Policy Signals and Market Responses: A 50-Year History of Zambia's Relationship with Foreign Capital* (Basingstoke: Palgrave Macmillan, 2016), 10–1, 66–116.

189. NCCM Limited, *Annual Reports*, 1971–1981.

190. NCCM Limited, *Annual Reports*, 1971–1981.

191. ZCCM IPD, *Zambia Copper Sector Survey*, Annex 3–2, 1.

192. ZCCM IPD, *Zambia Copper Sector Survey*, Annex 3–2, 1.

193. ZCCM IPD, *Zambia Copper Sector Survey*, Annex 3–2, 1.

CHAPTER 7

1. Miles Larmer, "Zambia's Mineworkers and Political Change, 1964–1991" (PhD thesis, University of Sheffield, 2004), 218–9.

2. CISB Limited, *Zambia Mining Yearbook 1985* (Kitwe: Manpower Planning and Development, 1985), 3, ZCCM 12.1.9C.

3. CISB Limited, *Zambia Mining Yearbook 1985*, 3.

4. B.K. Shamutete, History of ZCCM Limited: Birth of a Giant, 2, ZCCM 4.10.2E.

5. Shamutete, History of ZCCM Limited: Birth of a Giant, 2.

6. Kaunda interviewed by the author, October 25, 2017.

7. CISB Limited, *Zambia Mining Yearbook 1985*, 3.

8. Shamutete, History of ZCCM Limited: Birth of a Giant, 2.

9. Parliament of Zambia, The Amalgamation of Mining Companies (Special Provisions) Act, March 5, 1982, 1, ZCCM 11.7.8A.

10. Parliament of Zambia, Amalgamation of Mining Companies Act, 1–3.

11. CISB Limited, *Zambia Mining Yearbook 1985*, 13.

12. CISB Limited, *Zambia Mining Yearbook 1985*, 13.

13. Parliament of Zambia, Amalgamation of Mining Companies Act, 1.

14. Parliament of Zambia, Amalgamation of Mining Companies Act, 1–2.

15. Parliament of Zambia, Amalgamation of Mining Companies Act, 1–2.

16. Parliament of Zambia, Amalgamation of Mining Companies Act, 22.

17. CISB Limited, *Zambia Mining Yearbook 1985*, 13.

18. CISB Limited, *Zambia Mining Yearbook 1985*, 13.

19. ZCCM Limited, *1985 Annual Report* (Lusaka: ZCCM Head Office, 1985), 24, ZCCM 11.1.1F.
20. ZCCM Limited, *1985 Annual Report*, 24.
21. ZCCM Limited, *1982 Annual Report* (Lusaka: ZCCM Head Office, 1982), 20, ZCCM 11.1.1F.
22. Thomas O. Glover, "The Mineral Industry of Zambia," in *Bureau of Mines Minerals Yearbook Area Reports: International 1984, Vol. 3* (Washington, DC: US Bureau of Mines, 1984), 926, https://search.library.wisc.edu/digital/AQIE7W57HHYPN28W/pages/AOFLPXSNUUYO4282 (accessed October 21, 2020).
23. *Mining Mirror*, April 16, 1983.
24. Shamutete, History of ZCCM Limited: Birth of a Giant, 3.
25. ZCCM Deputy Director of Operations, Kitwe, to ZCCM Director, Human Resources Department, Lusaka, August 15, 1989, MUZ HQ.
26. John R. Craig, "State Enterprise and Privatisation in Zambia 1968–1998" (PhD thesis, University of Leeds, 1999), 48.
27. CISB Limited, *Zambia Mining Yearbook 1985*, 3–4.
28. Shamutete, History of ZCCM Limited: Birth of a Giant, 2.
29. Shamutete, History of ZCCM Limited: Birth of a Giant, 2.
30. Shamutete, History of ZCCM Limited: Birth of a Giant, 2.
31. CISB Limited, *Zambia Mining Yearbook 1985*, 3.
32. CISB Limited, *Zambia Mining Yearbook 1985*, 4.
33. CISB Limited, *Zambia Mining Yearbook 1985*, 15.
34. ZCCM Limited, *Merger Benefits Plans* (Lusaka: ZCCM Head Office, 1983), Annex 1, ZCCM 11.7.9C.
35. ZCCM Limited, *Merger Benefits Plans*, Annex 1.
36. ZCCM Limited, *Merger Benefits Plans*, Annex 1.
37. ZCCM Limited, *Merger Benefits Plans*, Annex 5, 2.
38. ZCCM Limited, *Merger Benefits Plans*, Annex 5, 2–3.
39. ZCCM Limited, *Merger Benefits Plans*, Annex 5, 2–3.
40. ZCCM Limited, *Merger Benefits Plans*, Annex 5, 2–3.
41. ZCCM Limited, *Merger Benefits Plans*, Annex 5, 3–4.
42. ZCCM Limited, *Merger Benefits Plans*, Annex 5, 4.
43. ZCCM Limited, *Merger Benefits Plans*, Annex 5, 4.
44. ZCCM Limited, *Merger Benefits Plans*, Annex 5, 3.
45. Craig, "State Enterprise and Privatisation in Zambia," 95.
46. Patricio Meller and Anthony Simpasa, "Role of Copper in the Chilean and Zambian Economies: Main Economic and Policy Issues," Global Development Network Working Paper Series No. 43, 2011, 23.
47. CISB Limited, *Zambia Mining Yearbook 1985*, 3.
48. CISB Limited, *Zambia Mining Yearbook 1985*, 3.
49. Parliament of Zambia, Amalgamation of Mining Companies Act, 55.
50. Parliament of Zambia, Amalgamation of Mining Companies Act, 52.
51. Parliament of Zambia, Amalgamation of Mining Companies Act, 55.
52. Shamutete, History of ZCCM Limited: Birth of a Giant, 18–9.
53. Shamutete, History of ZCCM Limited: Birth of a Giant, 19.

54. Shamutete, History of ZCCM Limited: Birth of a Giant, 19.
55. Shamutete, History of ZCCM Limited: Birth of a Giant, 19.
56. Shamutete, History of ZCCM Limited: Birth of a Giant, 19.
57. Shamutete, History of ZCCM Limited: Birth of a Giant, 19.
58. Shamutete, History of ZCCM Limited: Birth of a Giant, 19.
59. Shamutete, History of ZCCM Limited: Birth of a Giant, 2–3, Appendix 9.
60. Kaunda in discussion with the author; *Times of Zambia*, April 1, 1982.
61. *Times of Zambia*, October 2, 1982.
62. CISB Limited, *Zambia Mining Yearbook 1985*, 7.
63. ZCCM Limited, *1986 Annual Report* (Lusaka: ZCCM Head Office, 1986), 5–6, ZCCM 11.1.1F; CISB Limited, *Zambia Mining Yearbook 1985*, 4; *Mining Mirror*, February 2, 1985. Before this restructuring, Chibuluma and Chambishi formed Kalulushi Division. Some of the seven mining and metallurgical units of ZCCM (Kansanshi mine, Chambishi mine, Chambishi Concentrator, No. 3 Shaft at Konkola, Luanshya Smelter, Ndola Copper Refinery Tankhouse, and Nkana Oxide Concentrator) were phased out of operation, and others were placed under care and maintenance. This restructuring meant that the number of operating divisions was reduced from seven to five (Nchanga/Chingola, Mufulira, Nkana/Rokana, Luanshya, and Kabwe).
64. ZCCM Limited, *1986 Annual Report*, 6.
65. ZCCM Limited, *Annual Reports*, 1985–1987.
66. ZCCM Limited Manpower Planning and Development (hereafter ZCCM Limited MPD), Establishment, Labour Figures, August 1985, Table 2, ZCCM 1.3.1H. These separations at Nkana were distributed as follows: resignation, 18; discharged/termination, 28; medical discharge, 2; normal retirement, 17; early retirement, 16; desertion, 1; deceased, 2; and transfer out, 11.
67. ZCCM Limited MPD, Establishment, Labour Figures, August 1985, Table 2.
68. ZCCM Limited MPD, Establishment, Labour Statistics, November 30, 1988, Appendix 11, ZCCM 1.3.1H. At Nkana Division, labor losses were categorized as follows in November 1988: normal retirement, 278; early retirement, 493; medical discharge, 58; poor performance, 32; and redundancy, 7.
69. ZCCM Limited MPD, Establishment, Labour Statistics, November 30, 1988, Appendix 11.
70. ZCCM Limited MPD, Establishments, Labour Figures, November 1983–December 1985; ZCCM Limited MPD, Establishment, Labour Statistics, January–December 1988.
71. ZCCM Limited MPD, Establishments, Labour Figures, November 1983–December 1985; ZCCM Limited MPD, Establishment, Labour Statistics, January–December 1988.
72. Zambianisation Committee (Mines), attachment to Record of a Meeting Held in the Ministry of Labour's Office, Lusaka, March 1, 1967, NAZ MLSS 1/18/3; Parliament of Zambia, Debates, Questions and Replies, December 1991–December 1998, Order Book No. 334–Zambianisation, ZCCM 5.5.2B.
73. Zambianisation Committee (Mines), attachment to Record of a Meeting Held in the Ministry of Labour's Office; Parliament of Zambia, Debates, Questions and Replies, December 1991–December 1998, Order Book No. 334.

74. Parliament of Zambia, Employment Amendment Act No. 18 of 1982, August 21, 1982.

75. Parliament of Zambia, Debates, Questions and Replies, December 1991–December 1998, Order Question No. 174—ZCCM Female Employees by January 22, 1987, ZCCM 5.5.2B.

76. Parliament of Zambia, Debates, Questions and Replies, December 1991–December 1998, Order Question No. 174.

77. ZCCM Deputy Director of Operations, Kitwe, to ZCCM Director, Human Resources Department, Lusaka, August 15, 1989, MUZ HQ. The distribution of female African employees in various occupations was as follows: medical services, 1,879; secretarial services, 578; human resources (personnel), 521; supply management services (stores/buying), 101; security services, 77; education, 64; accounting and finance, 51; paramedical, 22; computers, 20; administration, 8; engineering support services, 4; and chemistry and assaying, 2. At the same time, expatriate female workers were distributed as follows: education, 53; medical services, 15; human resources personnel, 3; and paramedical, engineering support services, and assaying, 1 each.

78. ZCCM IPD, *Zambia Copper Sector Survey* (Kitwe: IPD, 1981), 12, ZCCM 11.7.9C.

79. ZCCM IPD, *Zambia Copper Sector Survey*, 12.

80. ZCCM IPD, *Zambia Copper Sector Survey*, 12.

81. ZCCM IPD, *Zambia Copper Sector Survey*, 12.

82. *Mining Mirror*, August 28, 1987, May 27, 1988, June 24, 1988; ZCCM Limited, *Annual Report: 30 September 1991* (Lusaka: ZCCM Head Office, 1991), 3, ZCCM 11.1.1F.

83. *Mining Mirror*, May 27, 1988.

84. *Mining Mirror*, August 28, 1987. Pius Maambo was the first Zambian to be appointed manager in the Metallurgical Department at Nkana Division, which was ZCCM's largest metallurgical complex.

85. Greg Lanning and Marti Mueller, *Africa Undermined: A History of the Mining Companies and the Underdevelopment of Africa* (Ontario: Penguin Books Limited, 1979), 224.

86. Michael Burawoy, "The Colour of Class Revisited: Four Decades of Post-colonialism in Zambia," *Journal of Southern African Studies* 40, no. 5 (2014): 967.

87. ZCCM Limited, *1991 Annual Report* (Lusaka: ZCCM Head Office, 1991), 3, ZCCM 11.1.1F.

88. *Mining Mirror*, June 27, 1986, May 27, 1988.

89. *Mining Mirror*, May 27, 1988.

90. *Mining Mirror*, June 24, 1988.

91. Mining Industry Manpower Division, *Mining Industry Manpower Report*, July 1984, 1, MUZ HQ.

92. ZCCM Limited MPD, attachment to Monthly Manpower Summary, July 1985, Table 1, ZCCM 1.3.1H.

93. Parliament of Zambia, Debates and Questions, February 20–25, 1985, Reply to parliamentary question about manpower utilization and Zambianization, ZCCM 5.6.3C.

94. Parliament of Zambia, Debates and Questions, February 20–25, 1985.

95. ZCCM Limited MPD, *Manpower Planning and Development Monthly Report*, December 1988, Appendix II, ZCCM 1.3.1H.

96. ZCCM Limited MPD, *Manpower Planning and Development Monthly Report*.

97. *Times of Zambia*, April 1, 1982.

98. *Times of Zambia*, April 1, 1982.

99. CISB Limited, *Zambia Mining Yearbook 1985*, 7–8.

100. CISB Limited, *Zambia Mining Yearbook 1985*, 8.

101. CISB Limited, *Zambia Mining Yearbook 1985*, 7.

102. MUZ, Memorandum of Agreement with the Association of Copper Mining Employees (hereafter ACME), April 14, 1987, MUZ HQ. For example, in 1987, workers were given a hot patching allowance of K5 per shift, a K2.50 per shift safety allowance for extremely wet working conditions, a minimum of K35 per month for transport for workers 4 km away from the workplace, and 10% of the basic pay for unhoused allowance.

103. MUZ, Memorandum of Agreement with the ACME, April 14, 1987.

104. *Mining Mirror*, April 28, 1989.

105. MUZ, Memorandum of Agreement with the ACME, November 26, 1991.

106. Larmer, "Zambia's Mineworkers and Political Change," 220.

107. Larmer, "Zambia's Mineworkers and Political Change," 220.

108. Larmer, "Zambia's Mineworkers and Political Change," 222.

109. ZCCM Limited, *1987 Annual Report* (Lusaka: ZCCM Head Office, 1987), 14, ZCCM 11.1.1F.

110. MUZ General Secretary, Report for the period from April 1988 to March 1990, presented at a conference held in Livingstone, March 15–17, 1990, 3, MUZ HQ.

111. MUZ General Secretary, Report for the period from April 1988 to March 1990, 3.

112. *Mining Mirror*, February 22, 1991.

113. For details on the reaction of mineworkers to UNIP's political control, see: Miles Larmer, "The Hour Has Come at the Pit: The Mineworkers of Zambia and the Movement for Multiparty Democracy, 1982–1991," *Journal of Southern African Studies* 32, no. 2 (2006): 293–312.

114. MUZ HQ, *A Historical Analysis of MUZ in the Harmonisation of Industrial Relations in ZCCM: An Overview of MUZ Objectives*, 1990, 11.

115. MUZ HQ, *A Historical Analysis of MUZ in the Harmonisation of Industrial Relations in ZCCM*, 11.

116. Muchimba in discussion with the author; MUZ HQ, *A Historical Analysis of MUZ in the Harmonisation of Industrial Relations in ZCCM*, 11.

117. MUZ HQ, *A Historical Analysis of MUZ in the Harmonisation of Industrial Relations in ZCCM*, 11.

118. *Times of Zambia*, July 25, 1985.

119. *Times of Zambia*, July 25, 1985; Given Sinkamba (former hoist man) in discussion with the author, Kitwe, September 12, 2017; Cosmas Kabanda (former stick handler) in discussion with the author, Kitwe, September 17, 2017.

120. *Times of Zambia*, July 25, 1985; Martin Kalunga (former section boss) in discussion with the author, Kitwe, October 12, 2017; Langford Mulundu (former machine operator) in discussion with the author, Kitwe, October 27, 2017.

121. ZCCM Deputy Director of Operations to ZCCM Director, Human Resources Department, August 15, 1989.

122. *Mining Mirror*, June 11, 1985.

123. MUZ HQ, *A Historical Analysis of MUZ in the Harmonisation of Industrial Relations in ZCCM*, 12; *Mining Mirror*, June 7, 1985.

124. ZCCM Deputy Director of Personnel, Kitwe, to General Managers of Nchanga (Chingola), Mufulira (Mufulira), Nkana (Kitwe), and Roan Antelope (Luanshya), September 2, 1985, ZCCM 1.3.1E.

125. Kalunga in discussion with the author; Mulundu in discussion with the author; Muchimba in discussion with the author; University of Zambia Graduates, Lusaka, to the Chairman and Chief Executive of ZCCM, Lusaka, June 30, 1990, MUZ HQ.

126. ZCCM IPD, *Zambia Copper Sector Survey*, 9.

127. *Mining Mirror*, June 17, 1985.

128. *Mining Mirror*, June 17, 1985.

129. University of Zambia Graduates to ZCCM Chief Executive, June 30, 1990.

130. University of Zambia Graduates to ZCCM Chief Executive, June 30, 1990.

131. University of Zambia Graduates to ZCCM Chief Executive, June 30, 1990.

132. *Times of Zambia*, April 1, 1982.

133. Mines Joint Industrial Council, Minutes of Meeting held on April 19, 1993, 4, MUZ HQ; Simon J. Cunningham, "Nationalization and the Zambian Copper Mining Industry" (PhD thesis, University of Edinburgh, 1985), Table 5.5, 77.

134. CISB Limited, Complaints, Disputes, Strikes and Disciplinary Cases, January 1985–June 1986, ZCCM 1.3.1E.

135. CISB Limited, Complaints, Disputes, Strikes and Disciplinary Cases, Table 3.2, Appendix 1.

136. CISB Limited, Complaints, Disputes, Strikes and Disciplinary Cases, Table 3.2, Appendix 1.

137. CISB Limited, Complaints, Disputes, Strikes and Disciplinary Cases, Table 3.2, Appendix 1.

138. CISB Limited, Complaints, Disputes, Strikes and Disciplinary Cases.

139. *Times of Zambia*, July 25, 1985. As discussed elsewhere in this chapter, unskilled workers were employees from other mines who were placed in departments that they were not trained for but employed for the sake of redeployment and Zambianization.

140. Senior Manager, Manpower Development, Chingola, to Director, Human Resources Department, Lusaka, March 7, 1988, ZCCM 1.3.1H.

141. ZCCM Limited, *Annual Reports*, 1985–1987; Senior Manager, Manpower Development, to Director, Human Resources Department, March 7, 1988.

142. MUZ HQ, Letter from Chief Industrial Relations Officer, Kitwe, to Deputy Director of Personnel, Manpower Services and Training, Kitwe, July 17, 1985.

143. MUZ HQ, Letter from Chief Industrial Relations Officer, Kitwe, to Deputy Director of Personnel, Manpower Services and Training, Kitwe.

144. CISB Limited, Complaints, Disputes, Strikes and Disciplinary Cases, Appendix 2.

145. Larmer, "Zambia's Mineworkers and Political Change," 145.

146. MUZ HQ, *A Historical Analysis of MUZ in the Harmonisation of Industrial Relations in ZCCM*, 5–6.

147. MUZ HQ, *A Historical Analysis of MUZ in the Harmonisation of Industrial Relations in ZCCM*, 6.

148. MUZ HQ, *A Historical Analysis of MUZ in the Harmonisation of Industrial Relations in ZCCM*, 6.

149. MUZ, Memorandum of Agreement with the ACME, April 14, 1987, 3–4, ZCCM 5.5.1S; ZCCM Limited, *Disciplinary Code and Grievance Procedure* (Kitwe: Copper Industry Service Bureau Limited, 1988), 22, ZCCM 5.6.3I; Executive Director, Personnel Services, Lusaka, to Divisional General Managers of Nchanga, Mufulira, Nkana, Luanshya, Kabwe, Central Services and Power Company, March 12, 1986, MUZ HQ.

150. ZCCM Limited, *Disciplinary Code and Grievance Procedure*, 24–5.

151. Executive Director, Personnel Services, to ZCCM Divisional General Managers, March 12, 1986; ZCCM Limited, *Disciplinary Code and Grievance Procedure*, 3.

152. CISB Limited, Complaints, Disputes, Strikes and Disciplinary Cases.

153. Cunningham, "Nationalization and the Zambian Copper Mining Industry," Table 5.5, 77.

154. ZCCM Limited, *Annual Reports*, 1989–1991.

155. ZCCM IPD, *Zambia Copper Sector Survey*, 34.

156. Glover, "The Mineral Industry of Zambia," *Minerals Yearbook—International 1984*, 928.

157. ZCCM Limited, *Annual Reports*, 1985–1991; *Mining Mirror*, January 27, 1989.

158. *Mining Mirror*, January 27, 1989.

159. *Mining Mirror*, January 27, 1989.

160. *Mining Mirror*, January 30, 1987.

161. Glover, "The Mineral Industry of Zambia," *Minerals Yearbook—International 1984*, 928.

162. Glover, "The Mineral Industry of Zambia," 928.

163. ZCCM Limited, *Annual Reports*, 1984–1988.

164. ZCCM Limited, *Annual Reports*, 1984–1988.

165. Glover, "The Mineral Industry of Zambia," *Minerals Yearbook—International 1984*, 928.

166. Glover, "The Mineral Industry of Zambia," *Minerals Yearbook—International 1984*, 928.

167. ZCCM Limited, *1983 Annual Report* (Lusaka: ZCCM Head Office, 1983), 6, ZCCM 11.1.1F.

168. ZCCM Limited, *1983 Annual Report*, 6.

169. ZCCM Limited, *1983 Annual Report*, 6.

170. ZCCM Limited, *1983 Annual Report*, 11.

171. ZCCM Limited, *1983 Annual Report*, 11.

172. ZCCM Limited, *1989 Annual Report* (Lusaka: ZCCM Head Office, 1989), 37, ZCCM 11.1.1F.

173. ZCCM Limited, *1989 Annual Report*, 37.

174. ZCCM Limited, *Annual Reports*, 1982–1991.

175. ZCCM Limited, *Annual Reports*, 1982–1991.

176. *Mining Mirror*, April 26, 1991.

177. *Mining Mirror*, April 26, 1991.

178. *Mining Mirror*, April 26, 1991.

179. ZCCM Limited, *Annual Reports*, 1982–1991.

180. ZCCM Limited, *Annual Reports*, 1982–1991.

181. ZCCM Limited, *Nkana Division: Annual Operations and Technical Report*, April 1990–March 1991, 43, ZCCM 4.1.4H.

182. B.K. Shamutete, A paper on ZCCM Historical Background, presented at the seminar on Investment Opportunities in Zambia, Price-House, Johannesburg, February 25, 1993, Appendix 2, ZCCM 1.2.5I; ZCCM Limited, *Annual Reports*, 1984–1991; ZCCM Limited, *Management Report on Operations Covering the Quarter Ended 31 December 1984*, February 6, 1985, 25–7, ZCCM 11.7.9C; ZCCM Limited, *Management Report on Operations Covering the Quarter Ended 31 March 1988*, 24–6, MUZ HQ.

183. Shamutete, ZCCM Historical Background, Appendix 2; ZCCM Limited, *Annual Reports*, 1984–1991; ZCCM Limited, *Management Report on Operations Covering the Quarter Ended 31 December 1984*, 25–7. For details on the exchange rates, see: table 7.6.

184. Shamutete, ZCCM Historical Background, Appendix 2.

185. *Mining Mirror*, March 27, 1987.

186. Shamutete, ZCCM Historical Background, Appendix 2.

187. Shamutete, ZCCM Historical Background, Appendix 2.

188. ZCCM Limited, *1990 Annual Report* (Lusaka: ZCCM Head Office, 1990), 37, ZCCM 11.1.1F.

189. ZCCM Limited, *Annual Reports*, 1982–1991.

190. Lloyd E. Antonides et al., "The Mineral Industries of Southern Africa," *Bureau of Mines Minerals Yearbook 1988, Vol. 3: Southern Africa* (Washington, DC: US Bureau of Mines, 1988), 180, https://search.library.wisc.edu/digital/AE6B6RIWCWHM6C8S/pages/A6REQ2LAUSDR3U8Q (accessed September 13, 2020).

191. Lloyd E. Antonides and George A. Morgan, "The Mineral Industry of Zambia," *Bureau of Mines: Minerals Yearbook Mineral Industries of Southern Africa 1989, Vol. 3: Zambia* (Washington, DC: US Bureau of Mines, 1989), 299, https://search.library.wisc.edu/digital/A6NHGNVWLIAG5Y8A/pages/AM666HAI6FEWI38S (accessed September 13, 2020).

192. Antonides and Morgan, "The Mineral Industry of Zambia," 299.

193. Thomas O. Glover, "The Mineral Industry of Zambia," *Bureau of Mines Minerals Yearbook Area Reports: International 1982, Vol. 3* (Washington, DC: US Bureau of Mines, 1982), 1041, https://search.library.wisc.edu/digital/A34HVS2NOHAQOH8Z/pages/A2LCULEM756DKR8A (accessed September 13, 2020).

194. ZCCM Limited, *Management Report on Operations Covering the Quarter Ended 31 December 1984*, 24.

195. ZCCM Limited, *1985 Annual Report*, 14.

196. Thomas O. Glover, "The Mineral Industry of Zambia," *Bureau of Mines Minerals Yearbook Area Reports: International 1985, Vol. 3* (Washington, DC: US Bureau of Mines, 1985), 975, https://search.library.wisc.edu/digital/AUBH5UMIZ4BID385/pages/AVLK3IDRDD3ANT8J (accessed September 13, 2020).

197. ZCCM Limited, Report—*Export Rehabilitation and Diversification Project, October 1985*, 5, ZCCM 12.3.3B.

198. Glover, "The Mineral Industry of Zambia," *Minerals Yearbook—International 1985*, 975.

199. ZCCM Limited, *Report—Export Rehabilitation and Diversification Project*, 5.

200. ZCCM Limited, *Report—Export Rehabilitation and Diversification Project*, 5.

201. ZCCM Limited, *Report—Export Rehabilitation and Diversification Project*, 5.

202. ZCCM Limited, *Annual Reports*, 1982–1991.

203. *Times of Zambia,* September 19, 1988.

204. *Times of Zambia,* September 19, 1988.

205. ZCCM Limited, *Management Report on Operations Covering the Quarter Ended 31 December 1984*, 27.

206. Glover, "The Mineral Industry of Zambia," *Minerals Yearbook—International 1982*, 1042.

207. Glover, "The Mineral Industry of Zambia," *Minerals Yearbook—International 1982*, 1042.

208. ZCCM Limited, *Management Report on Operations Covering the Quarter Ended 31 December 1984*, 27; ZCCM Limited, *Management Report on Operations Covering the Quarter Ended 31 March 1988*, 26, MUZ HQ.

209. ZCCM Limited, *Management Report on Operations Covering the Quarter Ended 31 December 1984*, 22.

210. ZCCM Limited, *Management Report on Operations Covering the Quarter Ended 31 December 1984*, 22.

211. ZCCM Limited, Paper on Proposed Measures for Increasing Metal Production and Reducing Costs, March 4, 1983, 5, ZCCM 11.7.9C.

212. ZCCM Limited, *1990 Annual Report* (Lusaka: ZCCM Head Office, 1990), 44, ZCCM 11.1.1F.

213. ZCCM Limited, *Management Report on Operations Covering the Quarter Ended 31 December 1984*, 23.

214. ZCCM Limited, *Management Report on Operations Covering the Quarter Ended 31 December 1984*, 23.

215. *Times of Zambia*, May 1, 1987, November 27, 1987.

216. Justin Pearce, "Control, Politics and Identity in the Angolan Civil War," *African Affairs* 111, no. 444 (2012): 442–3.

217. *Times of Zambia*, November 19, 1985, July 6, 1987.

218. *Times of Zambia*, November 19, 1985, July 6, 1987.

219. *Times of Zambia*, August 1, 1987.

220. *Times of Zambia*, August 1, 1987.

221. *Times of Zambia*, March 16, 1987.
222. ZCCM Limited, *Annual Reports*, 1985–1991.
223. ZCCM Limited, *Management Report on Operations Covering the Quarter Ended 31 December 1984*, 24.
224. ZCCM Limited, *Management Report on Operations Covering the Quarter Ended 31 December 1984*, 24.
225. Janice W. Jolly and Daniel L. Edelstein, "Copper," *Bureau of Mines Minerals Yearbook 1988, Vol. 1* (Washington, DC: US Bureau of Mines, 1988), Table 7, 334, https://search.library.wisc.edu/digital/AWTEBKBLELMSTD8A/pages/AT4RPVQ636C6BD8E (accessed September 25, 2020).
226. Jolly and Edelstein, "Copper," *Minerals Yearbook 1988*, Table 7, 334.
227. Janice W. Jolly and Daniel L. Edelstein, "Copper," *Bureau of Mines Minerals Yearbook—Metals and Minerals 1982, Vol. 1* (Washington, DC: US Bureau of Mines, 1982), 281, https://search.library.wisc.edu/digital/A6SPAL4ZWBVTSM8F/pages/AMT5WV3W7K7NFP83 (accessed September 25, 2020).
228. Jolly and Edelstein, "Copper," *Minerals Yearbook—Metals and Minerals 1982*, 281.
229. CISB Limited, *Zambia Mining Yearbook 1985*, 12.
230. Jolly and Edelstein, "Copper," *Minerals Yearbook—Metals and Minerals 1982*, 281.
231. Jolly and Edelstein, "Copper," *Minerals Yearbook—Metals and Minerals 1982*, 283.
232. ZCCM Limited, *1982 Annual Report*, 6.
233. ZCCM Limited, *1982 Annual Report*, 9.
234. ZCCM Limited, *1982 Annual Report*, 9.
235. *Mining Mirror*, April 29, 1983.
236. *Mining Mirror*, April 29, 1983.
237. M. Lonoff, "An Economic Overview of the World Copper Market and Computation of the Elasticity of Demand Facing Chile and Peru," paper presented to the Seminaro Sobre Politics Commeciales Optimas, June 22–24, 1981, 4.
238. Lonoff, "An Economic Overview of the World Copper Market and Computation of the Elasticity of Demand Facing Chile and Peru," 9. Private companies included Kennecott, Phelps Dodge, ASARCO, Newmont, AMAX, and Anaconda, all from the USA; Anglo American from South Africa. The major government-controlled companies included ZCCM, CODELCO-Chile, Gecamines, and Centromin (Peru).
239. Lonoff, "An Economic Overview of the World Copper Market and Computation of the Elasticity of Demand Facing Chile and Peru," 4.
240. ZCCM Limited, *Annual Reports*, 1982–1991.
241. *Mining Mirror*, April 29, 1983.
242. Felix Preston and Sian Bradley, "Cartels and Competition in Minerals Markets: Challenges for Global Governance," Research Paper (London: Royal Institute of International Affairs, 2014), 12, https://www.chathamhouse.org/sites/default/files/field/field_document/20141219CartelsCompetitionMineralsMarketsKooroshyPrestonBradleyFinal.pdf (accessed October 13, 2020). Chile, Peru, Zaire, and Zambia were

founding members of CIPEC. Yugoslavia and Indonesia joined later. Australia and Papua New Guinea became associates.

243. A. Trott et al., "Organisation of Petroleum Exporting Countries," EEP Lecture Five Notes (Berkeley: University of California, 2009), 19, are.berkeley.edu/~sberto/lecture5_OPEC_Project.pdf (accessed September 25, 2020).

244. Craig, "State Enterprise and Privatisation in Zambia 1968–1998," 52–3.

245. Trott et al., "Organisation of Petroleum Exporting Countries," 19.

246. Trott et al., "Organisation of Petroleum Exporting Countries," 19.

247. *Mining Mirror*, January 28, 1983.

248. ZCCM Limited, *1984 Annual Report* (Lusaka: ZCCM Head Office, 1984), 13, ZCCM 11.1.1F.

249. ZCCM Limited, *1984 Annual Report*, 13.

250. *Mining Mirror*, April 25, 1986.

251. *Mining Mirror*, April 25 and May 30, 1986.

252. *Mining Mirror*, April 25, 1986.

253. *Mining Mirror*, April 25, 1986.

254. ZCCM Limited, *Annual Reports*, 1986–1988.

255. ZCCM Limited, *Annual Reports*, 1989–1991.

256. *Mining Mirror*, September 29, 1989.

257. *Mining Mirror*, May 26, June 30, and September 29, 1989. In Papua New Guinea, a conflict between militant landowners and the Bougainville Copper Company forced the Company to declare a force majeure on concentrates' shipments. The mine was closed for a while in May 1989.

258. *Mining Mirror*, May 26, June 30, and September 29, 1989.

259. William S. Kirk, "Cobalt," *Bureau of Mines Minerals Yearbook Metals and Minerals 1984, Vol. 1: Cobalt* (Washington, DC: US Bureau of Mines, 1984), 271, https://search.library.wisc.edu/digital/A3BE4PHSM7DXOW84/pages/AG6YPR4JKEH7K69C (accessed September 15, 2020).

260. ZCCM Limited, *Annual Reports*, 1986–1991; Kirk, "Cobalt," *Minerals Yearbook 1984*, 271.

261. ZCCM Limited, *1991 Annual Report*, 4.

262. ZCCM Limited, *1991 Annual Report*, 13.

263. ZCCM Limited, *Annual Reports*, 1982–1991.

264. United States Bureau of Mines, *Minerals Yearbooks—Metals and Minerals—Copper*, 1982–1991, minerals.usgs.gov/minerals/pubs/usbmmyb.html (accessed September 25, 2020); CISB Limited, *Zambia Mining Yearbook 1985*, 18.

265. Sardanis, *Zambia: The First 50 Years*, 81.

266. ZCCM Limited, *Annual Reports*, 1988–1991.

267. ZCCM Limited, *Annual Reports*, 1982–1991.

268. CISB Limited, *Zambia Mining Yearbook 1985*, 4.

269. ZCCM Limited, *1986 Annual Report*, 6–7. MIL comprised the following subsidiaries: Nchanga Farms Limited, Ndola Lime Company, Mpelembe Properties Limited, Mpelembe Drilling Company, Circuit Sawmilling and Joinery Limited, Circuit Engineering and Tooling Limited, Circuit Construction Limited, and Circuit Safari Limited.

270. ZCCM Limited, *Annual Reports*, 1982–1991.
271. ZCCM IPD, *Zambia Copper Sector Survey*, 3.
272. CISB Limited, *Zambia Mining Yearbook 1985*, 20.
273. Thomas O. Glover, "The Mineral Industry of Zambia," *Bureau of Mines Minerals Yearbook Area Reports: International 1986, Vol. 3* (Washington, DC: US Bureau of Mines, 1986), 965, https://search.library.wisc.edu/digital/AHS5TDTWZOD2N59E/pages/ANEKOQ3WI7B5RL8F (accessed September 13, 2020).
274. Thomas O. Glover, "The Mineral Industry of Zambia," *Bureau of Mines Minerals Yearbook Area Reports: International 1987, Vol. 3* (Washington, DC: US Bureau of Mines, 1987), 977, https://search.library.wisc.edu/digital/A4BOGN4H5D2BMI8J/pages/AADLX6QH6TDU739C (accessed September 25, 2020).
275. Glover, "The Mineral Industry of Zambia," *Bureau of Mines Minerals Yearbook 1986*, 965.
276. John Lungu, "The Politics of Reforming Zambia's Mining Tax Regime," *Southern Africa Resource Watch* 8 (2009): 12.
277. *Times of Zambia*, May 7, 1987, and June 2, 1988.
278. Stuart J. Barton, *Policy Signals and Market Responses: A 50-Year History of Zambia's Relationship with Foreign Capital* (Basingstoke: Palgrave Macmillan, 2016), 117–35.
279. Lungu, "The Politics of Reforming Zambia's Mining Tax Regime," 12.
280. MUZ HQ, *A Historical Analysis of MUZ in the Harmonisation of Industrial Relations in ZCCM*, 11.
281. Lungu, "The Politics of Reforming Zambia's Mining Tax Regime," 12.
282. Joseph Chayinda (former supervisor production section) in discussion with the author, Kitwe, October 10, 2017; John Chiwize (former section boss) in discussion with the author, Kitwe, October 13, 2017; and Flat Mutale (former spanner man) in discussion with the author, Kitwe, October 19, 2017.
283. Edward Kamwela (former machine operator) in discussion with the author, Kitwe, September 10, 2017; Muchimba in discussion with the author.
284. Lungu, "The Politics of Reforming Zambia's Mining Tax Regime," 12.
285. Burawoy, "The Colour of Class Revisited," 976.
286. ZCCM Limited, *Annual Reports*, 1983–1990.
287. Craig, "State Enterprise and Privatisation in Zambia 1968–1998," 95.
288. Craig, "State Enterprise and Privatisation in Zambia 1968–1998," 95.

CHAPTER 8

1. John G. Phillips, "Roan Antelope: Big Business in Central Africa, 1890–1953" (PhD thesis, University of Cambridge, 2000), passim.
2. *The Times*, July 9, 1931; Jane L. Parpart, *Labour and Capital on the African Copperbelt* (Philadelphia: Temple University Press, 1983), 21; Phillips, "Roan Antelope," 201.
3. Parpart, *Labour and Capital on the African Copperbelt*, 20–1, 29–30, 46–50; Lewis H. Gann, "The Northern Rhodesian Copper Industry and the World of Copper:

1923–1952," in *Human Problems in British Central Africa: Issue no. XVIII*, eds. Clyde J. Mitchell, Elizabeth Colson, and Max Gluckman (Manchester: Manchester University Press, 1970), 7–8; Andrew Roberts, *A History of Zambia* (London: Heinemann, 1976), 49.

4. Nsolo Mijere, "One Industry, One Union: The Rise and Governmental Control of the Mineworkers of Zambia, 1930–1982," in *Issues in Zambian Development*, eds. Kwaku Osei-Hwedie and Muna Ndulo (Nyangwe and Roxbury: Omenana, 1985), 380.

5. Raymond Dumett, "Africa's Strategic Minerals during the Second World War," *Journal of African History* 26, no. 4 (1985): 381.

6. George Chauncey, "The Locus of Reproduction: Women's Labour in the Zambian Copperbelt, 1927–1953," *Journal of Southern African Studies* 7, no. 2 (1981): 135–64; Jane L. Parpart, "The Household and the Mine Shaft: Gender and Class Struggles on the Zambian Copperbelt, 1926–1964," *Journal of Southern African Studies* 13, no. 1 (1986): 36–56; Bbole Dandule, "Women and Mineworkers' Struggles on the Zambian Copperbelt, 1926–1964" (MA dissertation, University of Zambia, 2012), 22–51.

7. RC Limited, *Annual Report and Accounts, 20 November 1940* (London: Rhokana Corporation Ltd, 1940), 4, ZCCM 3.8.2F; RC Limited, *Annual Report and Accounts for the Year Ended 30 June 1945* (London: RC Head Office, 1945), 4, ZCCM 19.2.4F.

8. James Ferguson, *Expectations of Modernity: Myths and Meanings of Urban Life on the Zambian Copperbelt* (Berkeley: University of California Press, 1999), 18. See also: T. Howard, "The Copperbelt's 100 African Tribes," *Horizon* 3, no. 11 (1961): 24–9; T. Scannell, "Secondary Industry on the Copperbelt," *Horizon* 3, no. 11 (1961): 10–4; RST, "Cosmopolitan Copperbelt," *Horizon* 5, no. 3 (1963): 12–5. By 1963, Europeans from more than 40 countries and Africans of more than 100 tribes made up the Copperbelt's population, most of them staying and working in Nkana-Kitwe.

9. Thomas R. Navin, *Copper Mining and Management* (Arizona: University of Arizona Press, 1978), 147.

10. RC Limited, *Annual Reports*, 1950–1953.

11. United Nations, Economic Commission for Africa, and Food and Agriculture Organisation (hereafter UN/ECA/FAO), *Report on the Economic Development of Zambia* (Ndola, Zambia: Falcon Press Limited, 1964), 10, NAZ 11/57F.

12. Ronald L. Prain, *Reflections on an Era: An Autobiography* (Letchworth, England: The Garden City Press, 1981), 158; Richard L. Sklar, *Corporate Power in an African State: The Political Impact of Multinational Mining Companies in Zambia* (Los Angeles: University of California Press, 1975), 35–6; Peter Slinn, "The Legacy of the British South Africa Company: The Historical Background," in *Economic Independence and Zambian Copper: A Case Study of Foreign Investment*, eds. Mark Bostock and Charles Harvey (New York: Praeger Press, 1972), 365–85.

13. Larry J. Butler, "Business and British Decolonisation: Sir Ronald Prain, the Mining Industry and the Central African Federation," *Journal of Imperial and Commonwealth History* 35, no. 3 (2007): 459–84.

14. Andrew Cohen, "Business and Decolonisation in Central Africa Reconsidered," *Journal of Imperial and Commonwealth History* 36, no. 4 (2008): 643.

15. RC Limited, *Annual Report: Rhokana Corporation Limited, 30 June 1962*, 13.

16. Michael Burawoy, *The Colour of Class on the Copper Mines: From Advancement to Zambianisation* (Manchester: Manchester University Press, 1972), 29–30.

17. Sklar, *Corporate Power in an African State*, 110–6.

18. Robert H. Bates, *Unions, Parties and Political Development: A Study of Mineworkers in Zambia* (New Haven, CT, and London: Yale University Press, 1971), 98–125.

19. Elena L. Berger, *Labour, Race and Colonial Rule: The Copperbelt from 1924 to Independence* (Oxford: Clarendon Press, 1974), 226.

20. Simon M. Kapwepwe, Republic of Zambia: Budget Address by the Vice President, January 30, 1969, 4, UNIP 1–3–5.

21. The phrase comes from Ronald E. Robinson et al., *Africa and the Victorians: The Official Mind of Imperialism* (London: Macmillan & Co. Ltd, 1961), 461.

22. Simon J. Cunningham, *The Copper Industry in Zambia: Foreign Mining Companies in a Developing Country* (New York: Praeger Publishers, 1981), 269–82; Stuart J. Barton, *Policy Signals and Market Responses: A 50-Year History of Zambia's Relationship with Foreign Capital* (Basingstoke: Palgrave Macmillan, 2016), 66–116.

23. Newmont and Kennecott pulled out of the Copperbelt after 1952. It is difficult to ascertain why the two companies exited the Northern Rhodesian mining sector at a time of economic boom on the Copperbelt. Navin argued that the two firms sold out their shares in the RAA to Anglo American because they became disenchanted with slow return on their investment and, therefore, wanted to concentrate on their diversification plans. But the two firms could still have diversified into other sectors and, at the same time, maintained their investment on the Copperbelt, like the American Metal Company (AMC), which diversified into molybdenum production but kept its investment in RST. Probably, Kennecott and Newmont were frustrated by being minority shareholders in RAA and Rhokana (see chapter 2). In addition, the two companies may have been further frustrated by the change in management staff of the Copperbelt companies and the new leadership's support for a federation of the three Central African states. For further details, see: Navin, *Copper Mining and Management*, 66–7, 288–9.

24. Simon J. Cunningham, "Nationalization and the Zambian Copper Mining Industry" (PhD thesis, University of Edinburgh, 1985), 294.

25. John R. Craig, "State Enterprise and Privatisation in Zambia 1968–1998" (PhD thesis, University of Leeds, 1999), 95; Fergus M. McPherson, *The Sequencing of Economic Reforms: Lessons from Zambia* (Amsterdam: Ministry of Foreign Affairs Development Corporation, 1995), 6–9.

GLOSSARY

1. Paul W. Thrush, *A Dictionary of Mining, Mineral, and Related Terms* (Washington, DC: US Department of the Interior—Bureau of Mines, 1968), 246.
2. *Mining Mirror*, October 3, 1975.
3. *Mining Mirror*, February 20, 1976.
4. *Mining Mirror*, February 20, 1976.
5. *Mining Mirror*, October 31, 1975.
6. Thrush, *A Dictionary of Mining, Mineral, and Related Terms*, 313.
7. *Mining Mirror*, November 14, 1975.
8. *Mining Mirror*, November 14, 1975.
9. *Mining Mirror*, November 14, 1975.
10. *Mining Mirror*, October 17, 1975.
11. *Mining Mirror*, October 17, 1975.
12. Thrush, *A Dictionary of Mining, Mineral, and Related Terms*, 715.
13. *Mining Mirror*, January 9, 1976.
14. Thomas R. Navin, *Copper Mining and Management* (Arizona: University of Arizona Press, 1978), xix.
15. Navin, *Copper Mining and Management*, xix.
16. *Mining Mirror*, January 9, 1976.
17. W.G. Garlick, "How the Copperbelt Orebodies Were Formed," *Horizon* 1, no. 8 (1959): 17.
18. Navin, *Copper Mining and Management*, xx; Roan Selection Trust (hereafter RST), "Mining Has a Language All Its Own," *Horizon* 4, no. 3 (1962): 30.
19. *Mining Mirror*, September 19, 1975.
20. RST, "Mining Has a Language All Its Own," 30.
21. *Mining Mirror*, January 23, 1976.
22. *Mining Mirror*, October 31, 1975.

Bibliography

PRIMARY SOURCES

Mineworkers' Union of Zambia Headquarters (MUZ HQ) in Kitwe

General Correspondence, Memoranda and Minutes of Meetings

Chief Industrial Relations Officer to Deputy Director of Personnel-Manpower Services and Training, July 17, 1985.

Deputy Director, Zambia Consolidated Copper Mines Operations, to Director, Zambia Consolidated Copper Mines Human Resources, August 15, 1989.

Executive Director to Divisional General Managers—Nchanga, Mufulira, Nkana, Luanshya, Kabwe, Central Services, and Power Company, March 12, 1986.

Mines Joint Industrial Council. Minutes, April 19, 1993.

Mineworkers' Union of Zambia. Memoranda of Agreements, 1987–1991.

University of Zambia Graduates to the Chairman and Chief Executive—Zambia Consolidated Copper Mines, June 30, 1990.

Zambia Consolidated Copper Mines. The Employment Amendment Act No. 18 of 1982, August 21, 1982.

Reports and Notes

General Secretary, Zambia Congress of Trade Unions. Report, May 24, 1970.

Mining Industry Manpower Division. *Mining Industry Manpower Report*, July 1984.

Mineworkers' Union of Zambia. *A Historical Analysis of MUZ in the Harmonisation of Industrial Relations in ZCCM: An Overview of MUZ Objectives*, 1990.

Mineworkers' Union of Zambia. Summary Notes on Mineworkers' Union of Zambia Leadership Change since 1949.

Mineworkers Union of Zambia Secretarial. Report, March 17, 1990.

MUZ General Secretary. Report for the period from April 1988 to March 1990, presented at a conference held in Livingstone, March 15–17, 1990.
Zambian Consolidated Copper Mines Limited. *Management Report*, March 31, 1988.
Zambianisation Tour. Report, April 29, 1977.

National Archives of Zambia (NAZ) in Lusaka

Ministry of Labour and Social Services (MLSS)

Ministry of Labour and Social Services. Disputes (Mines)—General, 1940–1977. NAZ MLSS 1/25.
Nkana African Mineworkers Union. All Correspondence, 1948–1962. NAZ MLSS 1/26/18.
Zambianisation Committee (Mines). General Correspondence, 1966–1970. NAZ MLSS 1/18/3.

Secretariat Series and District Notebooks

Barovale District Notebook, Vol. VII. Origins of Labour Employed on Northern Rhodesia during July 1938. NAZ KDD/KTW 2/1.
Broken Hill District Notebook. General Correspondence, 1928–1934. NAZ ZA1/9/19/M.
Immigration Organisation. General Control of Immigration, Vol. II, 1935–1948. NAZ SEC 3/48.

Official Publications

Northern Rhodesia Government. Reports, 1935–1966. NAZ 11/57.
Northern Rhodesia Mines Department. Annual Reports, 1950–1954. NAZ ML 8/4/18.

United National Independence Party (UNIP) Archives in Lusaka

Speeches by Government Officials

National Council. Speeches, 1967–1985. UNIP 1–3.

Zambia Consolidated Copper Mines (ZCCM) Archives in Ndola

General Correspondence, Memoranda and Minutes

Bledisloe Commission. Report, March 31, 1939. ZCCM 16.2.3C.
CISB Limited. Correspondence—Complaints, Disputes, Strikes and Disciplinary Cases, January 1985–June 1986. ZCCM 1.3.1E.
Copper Industry Service Bureau (CISB) Limited. Discipline, November 1966–September 1991. ZCCM 6.10.1A.

Copper Mines Arbitration Board. Correspondence—Arbitration for European Miners, May 1940–July 1941. ZCCM 3.8.2A.
Mineworkers' Union of Zambia (MUZ). Memorandum of Agreement between the Association of Copper Mining Employees and the MUZ, April 14, 1987. ZCCM 5.5.1S.
Northern Rhodesia Mineworkers' Union (NRMWU). General Correspondence, October 1934–February 1955. ZCCM 10.7.9A.
Parliament of Zambia. The Amalgamation of Mining Companies (Special Provisions) Act, March 5, 1982. ZCCM 11.7.8A.
Rhokana Corporation (RC) Limited. Board of Directors Correspondence, December 1955–October 1956. ZCCM T18.6D.
Rhokana Corporation (RC) Limited. Correspondence—African Labour Efficiency Returns and Costs, June 1951–July 1957. ZCCM 3.7.2B.
RC Limited. Correspondence—Trade Union Relations: Nkana Division: Native Strike, March 1940–June 1941. ZCCM 3.8.1A.
RC Limited. Directors Minutes of Meetings, August 1954–December 1955. ZCCM 3.8.2A.
Roan Antelope Copper Mines (RACM) Limited. Minutes of Meetings, August 1928–October 1929. ZCCM 16.2.2D.
Rokana Mine Division. Correspondence—Employment Returns, 1970–1976. ZCCM T8.2A.
Zambia Consolidated Copper Mines (ZCCM) Limited. Minutes—Survival-Cost Saving Measures, April 14, 1983. ZCCM 11.7.9C.
ZCCM Limited Manpower Planning and Development. Establishments, Labour Figures/Statistics, November 1983–December 1988. ZCCM 1.3.1H.

Unpublished Reports, Papers, and Notes

Brown Commission. *Report on Productivity and Efficiency of African Labour from 1956 to 1966*, May 26, 1966. ZCCM 11.7.8A.
NCCM Limited. *Nkana Mining Area Annual Report on Operations*, April 1979–March 1980. ZCCM 2.6.4A.
Nchanga Consolidated Copper Mines (NCCM) Limited, *Rokana Division Quarterly Reports on Operations*, 1974–1976. ZCCM T2.1C.
RC Limited. *Annual Reports*, June 1931–June 1935. ZCCM 3.8.2B.
RC Limited. *Utilisation of African Labour Report*, January 8, 1957. ZCCM 3.8.1C.
Rhodesia Selection Trust (RST). Discussion Notes, September 7, 1951. ZCCM 16.2.6D.
Shamutete, B.K. A Paper on ZCCM Historical Background presented at the seminar on Investment Opportunities in Zambia, Price Water-House, Johannesburg, February 25, 1993. ZCCM 1.2.5I.
Shamutete, B.K. Paper—History of ZCCM Limited: Birth of a Giant, 1992.
Walden, A. *Inspection Report at Mufulira Mine*, April 14, 1970. ZCCM 10.5.5D.
Zambianisation Committee. *Report—Comparison of 1974, 1975 and 1976 Records of Actual Achievement*, April 29, 1977. ZCCM 11.7.9C.
ZCCM Board. *Quarterly Reports*, September 1984–February 1985. ZCCM 11.7.9C.

ZCCM Limited. *Management Report on Operations Covering the Quarter Ended 31 December 1984*, February 6, 1985. ZCCM 11.7.9C.

ZCCM Limited. *Nkana Division Monthly Reports on Operations*, 1985–1990. ZCCM T2.1C.

ZCCM Limited. *Nkana Division Report on Operations*, April 1990–March 1991. ZCCM 4.1.4H.

ZCCM Limited. *Paper on Labour Relations on the Copperbelt*, 1930–1982. ZCCM 11.8.3C.

ZCCM Limited. Paper on Proposed Measures for Increasing Metal Production and Reducing Costs, March 4, 1983. ZCCM 11.7.9C.

ZCCM Limited. *Report—Export Rehabilitation and Diversification Project*, October 1985. ZCCM 12.3.3B.

Official Publications

British South Africa Company. *Reports and Accounts*, 1929–1939. ZCCM 19.2.2B.

CISB Limited. *Copperbelt of Zambia Mining Industry Yearbooks*, 1964–1968. ZCCM 12.1.9C.

CISB Limited. *Mining Industry Yearbook of Zambia 1969*. Kitwe: CISB, 1969. ZCCM 12.1.9C.

CISB Limited. *Zambia Mining Yearbooks*, 1973–1985. ZCCM 12.1.9C.

Government of the Republic of Zambia (GRZ). *The Mufulira Mine Accident: Final Report on the Causes and Circumstances of the Disaster, Which Occurred on 25 September 1970*. Lusaka: Government Printer, 1971. (No reference).

GRZ. *A Submission to the World Bank: Rehabilitation Projects within the Zambian Copper Mining Industry*. Lusaka: Government Printer, 1982. ZCCM W2.2.2G.

Manpower Planning Training and Zambianisation. *Opportunities for Graduates for Zambia's Mining Industry*. Kitwe: CISB, 1978. (No reference).

MINDECO Limited. *Mining Yearbooks of Zambia*, 1970–1972. ZCCM 12.1.9C.

Mining and Industrial Development Corporation (hereafter MINDECO) Limited. *Zambia's Mining Industry*. Lusaka: MINDECO, 1972. (No reference).

NCCM Limited. *Annual Reports*, 1971–1981. ZCCM 11.1.1F.

Northern Rhodesia Chamber of Mines (NRCM). *NRCM Yearbooks*, 1956–1963. ZCCM 12.1.9C.

RACM Limited. *Summary of Operations for the Six Years ended 30th June 1945*. Luanshya: RACM, 1945. ZCCM 19.2.6D.

RC Limited. *Annual Report and Accounts for the Year ended 30th June 1945*. London: RC Head Office, 1945. ZCCM 19.2.4F.

RC Limited. *Annual Reports and Accounts*, 1946–1969. ZCCM 12.7.2F.

RC Limited. *Directors' Reports and Statement of Accounts*, 1931–1944. ZCCM 3.8.2F.

Rhodesian Anglo American (RAA) Limited. *Reports of the Directors and Statements of Accounts*, 1950–1953. ZCCM 19.2.4F.

Roan Consolidated Mines (RCM) Limited. *Annual Reports*, 1970–1981. ZCCM 11.1.1F.

RST Limited. *Annual Reports and Accounts*, 1931–1939. ZCCM 12.6.1E.

ZCCM Industrial Projects Department. *Zambia Copper Sector Survey*. Kitwe: IPD, 1981. ZCCM 11.7.9C.

ZCCM Limited. *Annual Reports*, 1982–1991. ZCCM 11.1.1F.

ZCCM Limited. *Disciplinary Code and Grievance Procedure*. Kitwe: CISB, 1988. ZCCM 5.6.3I.

ZCCM Limited. *Merger Benefits Plans*. Lusaka: ZCCM Head Office, 1983. ZCCM 11.7.9C.

Hansards

Parliament of Zambia. Debates, Questions and Replies, January 1987–December 1998. ZCCM 5.5.2B.

Parliament of Zambia. Questions and Replies, February–March 1985. ZCCM 5.6.3C.

Archival Newspapers and Periodicals

Birmingham Post, 1951, 1968.

City Press, 1952.

Copperbelt Times, 1934.

Courier, No. 85, 1984.

Daily Herald, 1951.

Daily Telegraph and Morning Post, 1940.

Financial Times, 1934, 1968.

Horizon, 1959, 1961–1963.

Liverpool Daily Post, 1951.

Mining Mirror, 1973–1976, 1982–1983, 1985–1989, 1991.

Northern News, 1951, 1954–1955, 1957.

Northern Rhodesia Advertiser, 1935.

Optima, 1951, 1953–1956, 1961, 1969.

Rhodesia Herald, 1955.

Rhokana Review, 1951, 1959.

South African Mining and Engineering Journal, 1953, 1954, 1955, 1956.

Sun, 1968.

Times, 1931–1932, 1934–1935, 1937, 1940, 1944, 1951, 1968.

Times of Zambia, 1968, 1973, 1982, 1985, 1987–1988.

Zambia Mail, 1968.

SECONDARY SOURCES

Books

Baldwin, Robert E. *Economic Development and Export Growth*. Berkeley and Los Angeles: University of California Press, 1966.

Bancroft, Austen J. *Mining in Northern Rhodesia: A Chronicle of Mineral Exploration and Mining Development*. Bedford, England: The Sidney Press Limited, 1961.

Barton, Stuart J. *Policy Signals and Market Responses: A 50-Year History of Zambia's Relationship with Foreign Capital*. Basingstoke: Palgrave Macmillan, 2016.

Bates, Robert H. *Unions, Parties and Political Development: A Study of Mineworkers in Zambia*. New Haven, CT, and London: Yale University Press, 1971.

Bell, Philip M.H. *The Origin of the Second World War*. London: Longman Group Limited, 1986.

Bellucci, Stefano, and Andreas Eckert, eds. *General Labour History of Africa: Workers, Employers and Governments, 20th and 21st Centuries*. Suffolk, England: James Currey, 2019.

Berger, Elena L. *Labour, Race and Colonial Rule: The Copperbelt from 1924 to Independence*. Oxford: Clarendon Press, 1974.

Bostock, Mark, and Charles Harvey, eds. *Economic Independence and Zambian Copper: A Case Study of Foreign Investment*. New York: Praeger Press, 1972.

Bowman, Larry W. *Politics in Rhodesia: White Power in an African State*. Cambridge, MA: Harvard University Press, 1973.

Burawoy, Michael. *The Colour of Class on the Copper Mines: From Advancement to Zambianisation*. Manchester: Manchester University Press, 1972.

Butler, Larry J. *Copper Empire: Mining and the Colonial State in Northern Rhodesia, c. 1930–1964*. New York: Palgrave Macmillan, 2007.

Clarke, Peter. *Hope and Glory: Britain 1900–1990*. London: Penguin, 1997.

Cohen, Andrew. *The Politics and Economics of Decolonization in Africa: The Failed Experiment of Central African Federation*. London and New York: I.B. Tauris, 2017.

Coleman, Francis L. *The Northern Rhodesia Copperbelt, 1899–1962: Technological Development up to the end of the Central African Federation*. Manchester: Manchester University Press, 1971.

Cunningham, Simon J. *The Copper Industry in Zambia: Foreign Mining Companies in a Developing Country*. New York: Praeger Publishers, 1981.

Daniel, Phillip. *Africanisation, Nationalisation and Inequality: Mining Labour and the Copperbelt in Zambian Development*. London: Cambridge University Press, 1979.

Davis, Merle J. *Modern Industry and the African: An Enquiry into the Effect of the Copper Mines of Central Africa upon Native Society and the Work of the Christian Missions*. London: MacMillan and Co., 1933.

Epstein, Arnold L. *Politics in an Urban African Community*. Manchester: Manchester University Press, 1958.

Ferguson, James. *Expectations of Modernity: Myths and Meanings of Urban Life on the Zambian Copperbelt*. Berkeley: University of California Press, 1999.

Fortman, Bastiaan G. *After Mulungushi: The Economics of Zambian Humanism*. Nairobi: East African Publishing House, 1969.

Fraser, Alastair, and Miles Larmer, eds. *Zambia, Mining and Neoliberalism: Boom and Bust on the Globalized Copperbelt*. New York: Palgrave Macmillan, 2010.

Gann, Lewis H. *A History of Northern Rhodesia: Early Days to 1953*. London: Chatto and Windus, 1964.

Gluckman, M., *Economy of the Central Barotse Plain* (Livingstone: RLI, 1941).
Gregory, Theodore. *Ernest Oppenheimer and the Economic Development of Southern Africa*. London: Oxford University Press, 1961.
Klubock, Thomas M. *Contested Communities: Class, Gender, and Politics in Chile's El Teniente Copper Mine*. Durham, NC: Duke University Press, 1998.
Lanning, Greg, and Marti Mueller. *Africa Undermined: A History of the Mining Companies and the Underdevelopment of Africa*. Ontario: Penguin Books Limited, 1979.
Larmer, Miles. *Mineworkers in Zambia: Labour and Political Change in Zambia, 1964–1991*. London and New York: I.B. Tauris, 2007.
Letcher, Owen. *South Central Africa*. Johannesburg: African Publications, 1932.
Martin, Anthony. *Minding Their Own Business: Zambia's Struggle against Western Control*. London: Penguin Books, 1975.
McPherson, Fergus M. *The Sequencing of Economic Reforms: Lessons from Zambia*. Amsterdam: Ministry of Foreign Affairs Development Corporation, 1995.
Meebelo, Henry S. *Reaction to Colonialism: A Prelude to the Politics of Independence in Northern Zambia, 1893–1939*. Manchester: Manchester University Press, 1971.
Mhone, Guy C.Z. *The Political Economy of a Dual Labour Market in Africa, 1929–1969*. London and Toronto: Associated University Presses, 1982.
Minter, William. *King Solomon's Mines Revised: Western Interests and the Burdened History of Southern Africa*. New York: Basic Books, Inc., Publishers, 1986.
Mitchell, Clyde J. *The Kalela Dance: Aspects of Social Relations among Urban Africans in Northern Rhodesia*. Manchester: Manchester University Press, 1956.
Navin, Thomas R. *Copper Mining and Management*. Arizona: University of Arizona Press, 1978.
Onslow, Sue, and Anna-Mart van Wyk. *Southern Africa in the Cold War, Post-1974*. Washington, DC: Wilson Center, 2013.
Palmer, Robert R., Joel G. Colton, and Lloyd S. Kramer. *A History of the Modern World*. New York: Doubleday and Company, 1992.
Parpart, Jane L. *Labour and Capital on the African Copperbelt*. Philadelphia: Temple University Press, 1983.
Perrings, Charles A. *Black Mineworkers in Central Africa: Industrial Strategies and the Evolution of an African Proletariat in the Copperbelt 1911–1941*. New York: Africana Publishing Company, 1979.
Phimister, Ian R. *Wangi Kolia: Coal, Capital and Labour in Colonial Zimbabwe*. Harare: Baobab Books, 1994.
Phimister, Ian R., and Charles Van Onselen. *Studies in the History of African Mine Labour in Colonial Zimbabwe*. Gwelo, Zimbabwe: Mambo Press, 1978.
Powdermaker, Hortense. *Copper Town Changing Africa: The Human Situation on the Rhodesian Copperbelt*. New York: Harper and Row, 1962.
Prain, Ronald L. *Reflections on an Era: An Autobiography*. Letchworth, England: The Garden City Press, 1981.
Roberts, Andrew D. *A History of Zambia*. London: Heinemann, 1976.
Robinson, Ronald E., John Gallagher, and Alice Denny, *Africa and the Victorians: The Official Mind of Imperialism*. London: Macmillan & Co. Limited, 1961.

Ronnback, Klas, and Oscar Broberg. *Capital and Colonialism: The Return on British Investments in Africa, 1869–1969*. London: Palgrave Macmillan, 2019.
Saffrey, Lynn A. *A Report on Some Aspects of African Living Conditions on the Copperbelt of Northern Rhodesia*. Lusaka: Mimeo, 1943.
Sardanis, Andrew. *Africa: Another Side of the Coin: Northern Rhodesia's Final Years and Zambia's Nationhood*. London and New York: I.B. Tauris, 2003.
Sardanis, Andrew. *Zambia: The First 50 Years*. London and New York: I.B. Tauris, 2014.
Schmitz, Christopher J. *World Non-ferrous Metal Production and Prices 1700–1976*. London: Frank Cass Publishers, 1979.
Silavwe, Geoffrey W. *Management of Human Resources in the Copper Mining Industry in Zambia*. Ndola, Zambia: Mission Press, 1995.
Sklar, Richard L. *Corporate Power in an African State: The Political Impact of Multinational Mining Companies in Zambia*. Los Angeles: University of California Press, 1975.
Thrush, Paul W. *A Dictionary of Mining, Mineral, and Related Terms*. Washington, DC: US Department of the Interior—Bureau of Mines, 1968.
Tischler, Julia. *Light and Power for a Multiracial Nation: The Kariba Dam Scheme in the Central African Federation*. Basingstoke: Palgrave Macmillan, 2013.
Van Onselen, Charles. *Chibaro: African Mine Labour in Southern Rhodesia, 1900–1933*. London: Pluto Press, 1976.
Weinberg, Gerhard L. *A World at Arms: A Global History of World War Two*. Cambridge: Cambridge University Press, 1994.
Whitworth, Alan. *Explaining Zambian Poverty: A History of (Non-Agriculture) Economic Policy since Independence*. Islamabad: John Wiley and Sons Limited, 2014.
Wilson, Godfrey. *An Essay on the Economics of Detribalization in Northern Rhodesia*. Livingstone: RLI, 1942.

Book Chapters

Burdette, Marcia M. "Industrial Development in Zambia, Zimbabwe and Malawi: The Primacy of Politics." In *Studies in the Economic History of Southern Africa, Vol. 1: The Front-line States*, edited by Zbigniew A. Konczacki, Jane L. Parpart, and Timothy M. Shaw, 75–126. London: Frank Cass and Co. Ltd., 1990.
De Roche, Andrew J. "You Can't Fight Guns and Knives: National Security and Zambian Responses to UDI, 1965–1973." In *One Zambia, Many Histories: Towards a History of Post-colonial Zambia*, edited by Jan-Bart Gewald and Marja Hinfelaar, 77–97. Leiden, the Netherlands: Brill, 2008.
Gann, Lewis H. "The Northern Rhodesian Copper Industry and the World of Copper: 1923–1952." In *Human Problems in British Central Africa: Issue no. XVIII*, edited by Clyde J. Mitchell, Elizabeth Colson, and Max Gluckman, 1–18. Manchester: Manchester University Press, 1970.
Gupta, Anirudha. "Trade Unionism and Politics on the Copperbelt." In *Politics in Zambia*, edited by William Tordoff, 288–319. Berkeley and Los Angeles: University of California Press, 1974.

Mijere, Nsolo. "One Industry, One Union: The Rise and Governmental Control of the Mineworkers of Zambia, 1930–1982." In *Issues in Zambian Development*, edited by Kwaku Osei-Hwedie and Muna Ndulo, 374–95. Nyangwe and Roxbury: Omenana, 1985.

Nino, Helena P. "Labour Migration." In *General Labour History of Africa: Workers, Employers and Governments, 20th and 21st Centuries*, edited by Stefano Bellucci and Andreas Eckert, 265–300. Suffolk, England: James Currey, 2019.

Pratt, Cranford. "Part Two: Why Federation Was Supported." In *A New Deal in Central Africa*, edited by Colin Leys and Cranford Pratt, 98–117. New York: Frederick Praeger, 1960.

Saasa, Oliver S. "Determinants of Zambia's Policies towards the Mining Industry: 1964–1984." In *Issues in Zambian Development*, edited by Kwaku Osei-Hwedie and Muna Ndulo, 355–72. Roxbury: Library of Congress, 1985.

Sklar, Richard L. "Zambia's Response to the Rhodesian Unilateral Declaration of Independence." In *Politics in Zambia*, edited by William Tordoff, 320–62. Berkeley and Los Angeles: University of California Press, 1974.

Slinn, Peter. "The Legacy of the British South Africa Company: The Historical Background." In *Economic Independence and Zambian Copper: A Case Study of Foreign Investment*, edited by Mark Bostock and Charles Harvey, 365–85. New York: Praeger Press, 1972.

Journal Articles

Alford, Bernard W.E., and Charles E. Harvey. "Copperbelt Merger: The Formation of the Rhokana Corporation, 1930–1932." *Business Review* 54, no. 3 (1980): 331–58.

Burawoy, Michael. "The Colour of Class Revisited: Four Decades of Post-colonialism in Zambia." *Journal of Southern African Studies* 40, no. 5 (2014): 961–79.

Burawoy, Michael. "The Functions and Reproduction of Migrant Labour: Comparative Material from Southern Africa and the United States." *American Journal of Sociology* 81, no. 5 (1976): 1050–87.

Butler, Larry J. "Business and British Decolonisation: Sir Ronald Prain, the Mining Industry and the Central African Federation." *Journal of Imperial and Commonwealth History* 35, no. 3 (2007): 459–84.

Chang-II, Ohn. "The Causes of the Korean War, 1950–1953." *International Journal of Korean Studies* 14, no. 2 (2010): 19–44.

Chauncey, George. "The Locus of Reproduction: Women's Labour in the Zambian Copperbelt, 1927–1953." *Journal of Southern African Studies* 7, no. 2 (1981): 135–64.

Cohen, Andrew. "Business and Decolonisation in Central Africa Reconsidered." *Journal of Imperial and Commonwealth History* 36, no. 4 (2008): 641–58.

Daimon, Anusa. "Ringleaders and Troublemakers: Malawian (Nyasa) Migrants and Transnational Labour Movements in Southern Africa, c. 1910–1960." *Labor History* 58, no. 5 (2017): 656–75.

Dumett, Raymond. "Africa's Strategic Minerals during the Second World War." *Journal of African History* 26, no. 4 (1985): 381–408.

Ferguson, James. "Mobile Workers, Modernist Narratives: A Critique of the Historiography of Transition on the Zambian Copperbelt [Part One]." *Journal of Southern African Studies* 16, no. 3 (1990): 385–412.

Ferguson, James. "Mobile Workers, Modernist Narratives: A Critique of the Historiography of Transition on the Zambian Copperbelt [Part Two]." *Journal of Southern African Studies* 16, no. 4 (1990): 603–21.

Guernsey, Tarrant D. "Summary of Early Prospecting in Northern Rhodesia." *Transactions of the Institution of Mining and Metallurgy* 63 (1954): 1–9.

Harington, John S., Neil D. McGlashan, and Elzbieta Z. Chelkowska. "A Century of Migrant Labour in the gold mines of South Africa." *Journal of the South African Institute of Mining and Metallurgy* 104, no. 2 (2004): 65–71.

Harrison, Mark. "Resource Mobilization for World War II: the USA, UK, USSR, and Germany, 1938–1945." *Economic History Review* 41, no. 2 (1988): 171–92.

Johnson, Vernon D. "Racial Formation in Zimbabwe." In *The Changing Racial Regime, Vol. 5*, edited by Matthew Holden, 241–62. New Brunswick and London: Transaction Publishers, 1995.

Juif, Dacil, and Ewout Frankema. "From Coercion to Compensation: Institutional Responses to Labour Scarcity in the Central African Copperbelt." *Journal of Institutional Economics* 14, no. 2 (2018): 313–43.

Kelly, Michael P. "Proletarianisation, the Division of Labour and the Labour Process." *International Journal of Sociology and Social Policy* 8, no. 6 (1989): 48–64.

Klubock, Thomas M. "Copper Workers, Organized Labor, and Popular Protest under Military Rule in Chile, 1973–1986." *International Labor and Working—Class History* 52 (1997): 106–33.

Larmer, Miles. "The Hour Has Come at the Pit: The Mineworkers of Zambia and the Movement for Multi-Party Democracy, 1982–1991." *Journal of Southern African Studies* 32, no. 2 (2006): 293–312.

Larmer, Miles. "Permanent Precarity: Capital and Labour in the Central African Copperbelt." *Labour History* 58, no. 2 (2017): 170–84.

Larmer, Miles. "Unrealistic Expectations? Zambia's Mineworkers from Independence to the One-party State, 1964–1972." *Journal of Historical Sociology* 18, no. 4 (2005): 318–52.

Larmer, Miles. "Zambia's Mineworkers and the Labour Movement's Resistance to the One-party State, 1973–1981." *South African Historical Journal* 56, no. 1 (2006): 154–76.

Lungu, John. "The Politics of Reforming Zambia's Mining Tax Regime." *Southern Africa Resource Watch* 8 (2009): 1–28.

Musambachime, M.C., 'The Archives of Zambia's United National Independence Party." *History in Africa* 18 (1991): 291–6.

Musonda, James. "Undermining Gender: Women Mineworkers at the Rock Face in a Zambian Underground Mine." *Anthropology Southern Africa* 43, no. 1 (2020): 32–42.

Parpart, Jane L. "The Household and the Mine Shaft: Gender and Class Struggles on the Zambian Copperbelt, 1926–1964." *Journal of Southern African Studies* 13, no. 1 (1986): 36–56.

Pearce, Justin. "Control, Politics and Identity in the Angolan Civil War." *African Affairs* 111, no. 444 (2012): 442–65.
Perrings, Charles A. "Consciousness, Conflict and Proletarianization: An Assessment of the 1935 Mineworkers' Strike on the Northern Rhodesian Copperbelt." *Journal of Southern African Studies* 4, no. 1 (1977): 31–51.
Perrings, Charles A. "A Moment in the Proletarianization of the New Middle Class: Race, Value and the Division of Labour in the Copperbelt, 1946–1966." *Journal of Southern African Studies* 6, no. 2 (1980): 183–213.
Phimister, Ian R. "Corporate Profit and Race in Central African Copper Mining, 1946–1958." *Business History Review* 85, no. 4 (2011): 749–74.
Phimister, Ian R. "The Reconstruction of the Southern Rhodesian Gold Mining Industry, 1903–1910." *Economic History Review* 29, no. 3 (1976): 465–81.
Roberts, Andrew D. "Notes towards a Financial History of Copper Mining in Northern Rhodesia." *Canadian Journal of African Studies* 16, no. 2 (1982): 347–59.
Sikamo, J., A. Mwanza, and C. Mweemba. "Copper Mining in Zambia—History and Future." *Journal of the Southern African Institute of Mining and Metallurgy*, 116 (2016): 491–6.
Slinn, Peter. "Commercial Concessions and Politics during the Colonial Period: The Role of the British South Africa Company in Northern Rhodesia 1890–1964." *African Affairs* 70, no. 281 (1971): 365–84.
Sutcliffe, R.B. "Zambia and the Strains of UDI." *Royal Institute of International Affairs* 23, no. 12 (1967): 506–11.
Tembo, Alfred. "After the Deluge: Appraising the 1970 Mufulira Mine Disaster in Zambia." *Historia* 64, no. 2 (2019): 109–31.
Tembo, Alfred. "The Rhodes-Livingstone Institute and Interdisciplinary Research in Northern Rhodesia (Zambia), 1937–1964." *Strategic Review of Southern Africa* 36, no.1 (2014): 90–9.
Van Der Walt, Lucien. "The First Globalisation and Transnational Labour Activism: White Labourism, the 1WW, and the ICU, 1904–1934." *African Studies* 66, nos. 2–3 (2007): 223–51.
Vutukuri, Venkata S., and Raghu N. Singh. "Mine Inundation: Case Histories." *Mine Water and the Environment* 14, no. 9 (1995): 120–2.

Theses/Dissertations

Chongo, Clarence. "Decolonising Southern Africa: A History of Zambia's Role in Zimbabwe's Liberation Struggle, 1964–1979." PhD Thesis, University of Pretoria, 2015.
Chongo, Clarence. "The Impact of Rhodesia's Unilateral Declaration of Independence (UDI) on Zambia's Economic and Social-political Developments, 1965–1979." MA Dissertation, University of Zambia, 2009.
Craig, John R. "State Enterprise and Privatisation in Zambia 1968–1998." PhD Thesis, University of Leeds, 1999.
Cunningham, Simon J. "Nationalization and the Zambian Copper Mining Industry." PhD Thesis, University of Edinburgh, 1985.

Dandule, Bbole. "Women and Mineworkers' Struggles on the Zambian Copperbelt, 1926–1964." MA Dissertation, University of Zambia, 2012.

Gwande, Victor M. "Foreign Capital, State and the Development of Secondary Industry in Southern Rhodesia, 1939–1956." MA Thesis, University of the Free State, 2015.

Henderson, Ian. "Labour and Politics in Northern Rhodesia, 1900–1953: A Study in the Limits of Colonial Power." PhD Thesis, University of Edinburgh, 1972.

Keeton, Gavin, and Mike Beer. "MIASA Position on State Participation in Mining." Paper for the Mining Industries Association of Southern Africa, 2011.

Kraner, Saso. "Causes of the Great Depression and the Great Financial Crisis." PhD Thesis, Univerza Na Primorsken, 2010.

Larmer, Miles. "Zambia's Mineworkers and Political Change, 1964–1991." PhD Thesis, University of Sheffield, 2004.

Locher, Christine. "The Conflict with North Korea/North Korea as a Source of Conflict: An Analysis from a Peace and Conflict Resolution Studies Perspective." PhD Thesis, Fern Universitat Hagen, 2008.

Money, Duncan. "No Matter How Much or How Little They Have Got, They Cannot Settle Down: A Social History of Europeans on the Zambian Copperbelt, 1926–1974." PhD Thesis, University of Oxford, 2016.

Mufinda, Buzandi. "A History of Mining in Broken Hill/Kabwe: 1902–1929." MA Thesis, University of the Free State, Bloemfontein, 2015.

Mususa, Patience N. "There Used to Be Order: Life on the Copperbelt after the Privatisation of the Zambia Consolidated Copper Mines." PhD Thesis, University of Cape Town, 2014.

Phillips, John G. "Roan Antelope: Big Business in Central Africa, 1890–1953." PhD Thesis, University of Cambridge, 2000.

Sakala, Foster. "The Role of Women in Labour Stabilisation at Mufulira Mine, 1930–1964." MA Dissertation, University of Zambia, 2001.

Santebe, Mbozi. "The Colonial Government and the Great Depression in Northern Rhodesia: Administrative and Legislative Changes, 1929–1939." MA Dissertation, University of Zambia, 2015.

Notes and Papers

Lonoff, M. "An Economic Overview of the World Copper Market and Computation of the Elasticity of Demand Facing Chile and Peru." Paper presented to the Seminaro Sobre Politics Commeciales Optimas, June 22–24, 1981.

Meller, Patricio, and Anthony Simpasa. "Role of Copper in the Chilean and Zambian Economies: Main Economic and Policy Issues." Global Development Network (GDN) Working Paper Series No. 43, 2011.

Simutanyi, Neo. "Copper Mining in Zambia: The Developmental Legacy of Privatisation." Institute for Security Studies (ISS) Paper Series No. 165 (Pretoria: ISS, 2008).

Internet Sources

Antonides, Lloyd E., and George A. Morgan. "The Mineral Industry of Zambia." *Bureau of Mines: Minerals Yearbook Mineral Industries of Southern Africa 1989,*

Vol. 3, 298–302. Washington, DC: US Bureau of Mines, 1989. https://search.library.wisc.edu/digital/A6NHGNVWLIAG5Y8A/pages/AM666HAI6FEWI38S (accessed September 13, 2020).

Antonides, Lloyd E., George A. Morgan, Harold R. Newman and Hendrik G. van Oss. "The Mineral Industries of Southern Africa." *Bureau of Mines Minerals Yearbook 1988*, *Vol. 3—Southern Africa* (Washington, DC: US Bureau of Mines, 1988), 159–95. https://search.library.wisc.edu/digital/AE6B6RIWCWHM6C8S/pages/AYZ5YJVECUWFZR8F (accessed September 13, 2020).

Bilbrey, Joseph H., and Dorothy T. McDougal. "Cobalt." *Minerals Yearbook, 1959*, Table 5, 363–73. images.library.wisc.edu/EcoNatRes/EFacs2/MineralsYearBk/MinYB1959v1/reference/econatres.minyb1959v1.jbilbrey.pdf (accessed January 25, 2020).

Davis, Hubert W. "Cobalt." *Minerals Yearbook: Review of 1941*, 623–6. images.library.wisc.edu/EcoNatRes/EFacs2/MineralsYearBk/MinYB1941/reference/econatres.minyb1941.hdavis02.pdf (accessed April 6, 2020).

Davis, Hubert W. "Nickel and Cobalt." *Minerals Yearbook: Review of 1940*, 597–608. images.library.wisc.edu/EcoNatRes/EFacs2/MineralsYearBk/MinYB1940/reference/econatres.minyb1940.hdavis.pdf (accessed April 6, 2020).

Davis, Hubert W., and C.H. Buck. "Cobalt." *Minerals Yearbook Review of 1954*, 349–62. images.library.wisc.edu/EcoNatRes/EFacs2/MineralsYearBk/MinYB1954v1/reference/econatres.minyb1954v1.hdavis.pdf (accessed April 6, 2020).

Glover, Thomas O. "The Mineral Industry of Zambia." *Bureau of Mines Minerals Yearbook Area Reports: International 1982, Vol. 3*, 1041–9. Washington, DC: US Bureau of Mines, 1982. https://search.library.wisc.edu/digital/A34HVS2NOHAQOH8Z/pages/A2LCULEM756DKR8A (accessed September 13, 2020).

Glover, Thomas O. "The Mineral Industry of Zambia." *Bureau of Mines Minerals Yearbook Area Reports: International 1984, Vol. 3*, 925–9. Washington, DC: US Bureau of Mines, 1984. https://search.library.wisc.edu/digital/AQIE7W57HHYPN28W/pages/AOFLPXSNUUYO4282 (accessed October 21, 2020).

Glover, Thomas O. "The Mineral Industry of Zambia." *Bureau of Mines Minerals Yearbook Area Reports: International 1985, Vol. 3*, 975–9. Washington, DC: US Bureau of Mines, 1985. https://search.library.wisc.edu/digital/AUBH5UMIZ4BID385/pages/AVLK3IDRDD3ANT8J (accessed September 13, 2020).

Glover, Thomas O. "The Mineral Industry of Zambia." *Bureau of Mines Minerals Yearbook Area Reports: International 1986, Vol. 3*, 965–70. Washington, DC: US Bureau of Mines, 1986. https://search.library.wisc.edu/digital/AHS5TDTWZOD2N59E/pages/ANEKOQ3WI7B5RL8F (accessed September 13, 2020).

Glover, Thomas O. "The Mineral Industry of Zambia." *Bureau of Mines Minerals Yearbook Area Reports: International 1987, Vol. 3*, 977–82. Washington, DC: US Bureau of Mines, 1987. https://search.library.wisc.edu/digital/A4BOGN4H5D2BMI8J/pages/AADLX6QH6TDU739C (accessed September 25, 2020).

Jolly, Janice W., and Daniel L. Edelstein. "Copper." *Bureau of Mines Minerals Yearbook 1988, Vol. 1 1988*, 309–64. Washington, DC: US Bureau of Mines, 1988. https://search.library.wisc.edu/digital/AWTEBKBLELMSTD8A/pages/AA2KCMJPTBULC68V (accessed September 25, 2020).

Jolly, Janice W., and Daniel L. Edelstein. "Copper." *Bureau of Mines Minerals Yearbook—Metals and Minerals 1982, Vol. 1*, 271–308. Washington, DC: US Bureau of Mines, 1982. https://search.library.wisc.edu/digital/A6SPAL4ZWBVTSM8F/pages/AOFFHUGHORTRP38T (accessed September 25, 2020).

Kirk, William S. "Cobalt." In *Bureau of Mines Minerals Yearbook Metals and Minerals 1984, Vol. 1*, 269–77. Washington, DC: US Bureau of Mines, 1984. https://search.library.wisc.edu/digital/A3BE4PHSM7DXOW84/pages/AAJ7WYCRLWAXXS8T (accessed September 15, 2020).

Kooroshy, Jaakko, Felix Preston, and Sian Bradley. "Cartels and Competition in Minerals Markets: Challenges for Global Governance." Research paper published for the Royal Institute of International Affairs. London: Chatham House Publishers, 2014. https://www.chathamhouse.org/sites/default/files/field/field_document/20141219CartelsCompetitionMineralsMarketsKooroshyPrestonBradleyFinal.pdf (accessed October13, 2020).

Map of Zambia in Southern Africa. www.pinterest.co.uk/americaikos/zambia/ (accessed October 26, 2020).

Merill, Charles W., and Helena M. Meyer. "Copper." *Bureau of Mines Minerals Yearbook 1949*: 459–92. https://search.library.wisc.edu/digital/ALL364NRQA5IFL8W/pages/ATOCD7JHTMZIDN8Q (accessed August 30, 2020).

Meyer, Helena M., and Gertrude N. Greenspoon. "Copper." *Bureau of Mines Minerals Yearbook 1950*, 465–502. https://search.library.wisc.edu/digital/A3M2CR4ONJEVFW9A/pages/AHUCQBDBMT4JCY8T (accessed August 30, 2020).

Meyer, Helena M., and Gertrude N. Greenspoon. "Copper." *Bureau of Mines Minerals Yearbook 1951*, 521–56. https://search.library.wisc.edu/digital/AJISUC7IKKA6HR9A/pages/AAWOPR543SXJKK8E (accessed August 30, 2020).

Munene, Hyden. "Mining the Past: A Report of Four Archival Repositories in Zambia." *History in Africa* 47 (2020): 359–73. doi.org/10.1017/hia.2019.24 (accessed November 21, 2020).

New World Economics. "Foreign Exchange Rates: Just Looking at the Data." newworldeconomics.com/foreign-exchange-rates-1913-1941-just-looking-at-the-data/ (accessed May 7, 2020).

Trott, A., S. Holmberg, and W. Wong. "Organisation of Petroleum Exporting Countries." EEP Lecture Five Notes. Berkeley: University of California, 2009. are.berkeley.edu/~sberto/lecture5_OPEC_Project.pdf (accessed September 25, 2020).

US Bureau of Mines. *Minerals Yearbooks—Metals and Minerals—Cobalt*, 1954–1959. minerals.usgs.gov/minerals/pubs/usbmmyb.html (accessed March 30, 2020).

US Bureau of Mines. *Minerals Yearbooks—Metals and Minerals—Cobalt*, 1970–1980. minerals.usgs.gov/minerals/pubs/usbmmyb.html (accessed April 4, 2020).

US Bureau of Mines. *Minerals Yearbooks—Metals and Minerals—Copper,* 1982–1991. minerals.usgs.gov/minerals/pubs/usbmmyb.html (accessed September 25, 2020).

US Department of Labor. *Monthly Labor Review, Volume 47, Number 1, July 1938*. Washington, DC: Bureau of Labor Statistics, 1938. https://books.google.co.zm/books/about.Monthly_labor_Review.html?id=z2TAD2y3k2MC (accessed December 10, 2020).

US Department of the Interior. *Bureau of Mines Bulletin 405: Copper Mining in North America*. Washington, DC: Government Printing Office, 1938. digital.library.unt.edu/ark:/67531/metadc12571/m1/1/ (accessed December 10, 2020).

Index

Note: Page references for figures, tables, and photos are italicized.

About the Author

Hyden Munene is postdoctoral fellow with the International Studies Group at the University of the Free State (UFS), Bloemfontein, South Africa. He also held another fellowship in the African Humanities Program of the American Council of Learned Societies between July 2020 and June 2021. He holds a PhD in Africa studies obtained in June 2018 from the UFS, an MA in peace and conflict studies acquired in July 2014 from the Copperbelt University in Kitwe, Zambia, and a BEd conferred in July 2007 at the University of Zambia in Lusaka. His specialization is in the political, economic, and social history of Zambia in particular and Africa in general, as well as selected parts of Europe, Asia, and America. He also specializes in issues of human rights, governance, and peacebuilding.

www.ingramcontent.com/pod-product-compliance
Ingram Content Group UK Ltd.
Pitfield, Milton Keynes, MK11 3LW, UK
UKHW021028041026
15470UKWH00013B/253

9 781538 146422